# *Biondo Flavio's Italia Illustrata*

*Text, Translation, and Commentary*

Since its inception, the Center for Medieval & Renaissance Studies of Binghamton University has earned a national and international reputation for the rigorous standards of its publications. It is, therefore, with great pride that CEMERS presents to the scholarly world Catherine Castner's *Biondo Flavio's "Italia Illustrata,"* a magnificent *opus* of critical, philological and historical analysis, with translation and commentary, of a major work by Biondo, an early humanist and one of the important founders of modern historiography and archaeology. This impressive intellectual labor will be of significant interest and value to scholars and students of humanism, history, archaeology and medieval Italy in general.

Sandro Sticca
Director, Center for Medieval
& Renaissance Studies

CEMERS wishes to express its appreciation to Lori Vandermark Fuller for her expertise in the editorial production of this manuscript.

# *Biondo Flavio's Italia Illustrata*

## *Text, Translation, and Commentary*

**Catherine J. Castner**

**VOLUME I**

**NORTHERN ITALY**

Global Academic Publishing
Binghamton University
Binghamton, New York
2005

Published by Global Academic Publishing for CEMERS



Library of Congress Cataloging-in-Publication Data

Biondo Flavio, 1392-1463.
[Italia illustrata. English & Latin]
Biondo Flavio's Italia illustrata / text, translation, and commentary Catherine J. Castner.
p. cm.
English and Latin.
Includes bibliographical references and index.
ISBN-13: 978-1-58684-255-0 (pbk. : alk. paper)
1. Italy--Description and travel--Early works to 1800. 2. Italy--History--To 1500--Early works to 1800. 3. Humanism--Italy--Early works to 1800. 4. Italy--Biography--Early works to 1800. 5. Italy--Genealogy--Early works to 1800. I. Castner, Catherine J., 1949- II. Title.
DG422.B56 2005b
911'.45--dc22

2005022178

Published by Global Academic Publishing
Binghamton University, LNG 99
Binghamton, New York 13902-6000 USA
Phone: (607) 777-4495 / Fax: (607) 777-6132
E-mail: gap@binghamton.edu
Website: http://academicpublishing.binghamton.edu/

# Contents



## Plates

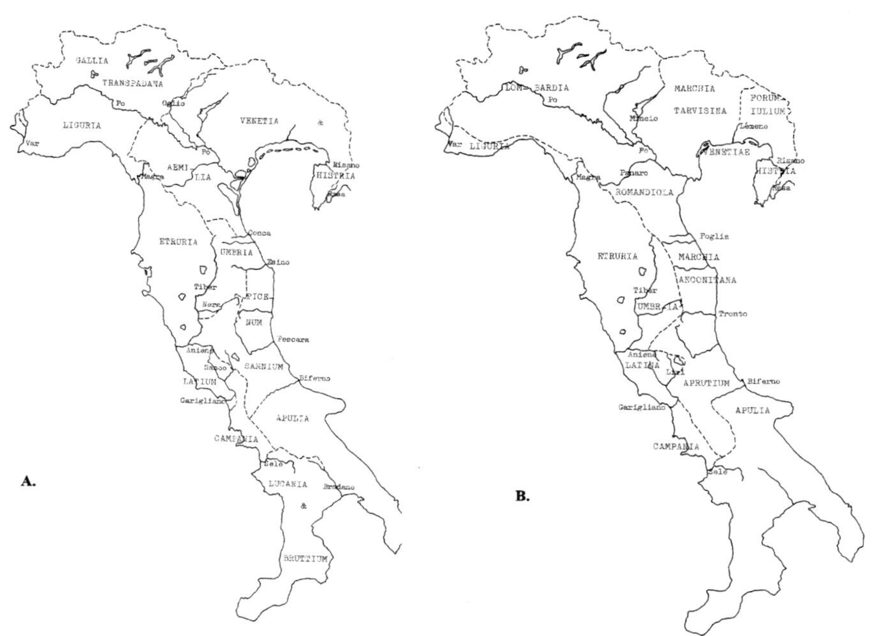


**Frontispiece**

A. The regions of Italy according to Pliny.

B. The regions of Italy according to Biondo Flavio, "Italia illustrata."

Reprinted from Ottavio Clavuot, *Biondos «Italia illustrata»: Summa oder Neuschöpfung? Über die Arbeitsmethoden eines Humanisten. Bibliotek des Deutschen historischen Instituts in Rom* 69 (Tübingen: Max Niemeyer, 1990), by permission of Max Niemeyer Verlag.

# Acknowledgments

The railroad tracks between Ancona and Ravenna lie so close to the shore that they seem to rest on the surface of the Adriatic and the train seems to skim over clear, light-blue water. Looking inland, one can see a sign "Gradara" and, high on the cliffs above, Sigismondo Pandolfo Malatesta's forbidding fortress of the same name. Here in a glimpse one can understand the rightness of Augusto Campana's comment that humanists had, in their literary attempts to flatter the warlord, softened this machine of war into a "delizia" or pleasure villa. That simple visual recognition is only one example of the advantages and benefits of conducting research in Italy.

My thanks here are scarcely sufficient to acknowledge the generous aid I received in Italy. At Cattolica, Dott.ssa Maria Lucia DeNicolò enlightened me with personal conversation on the status of that coastline in Biondo's time, and especially on the legend of the submerged city. My comments on the branch of the Po known as the "rotta di Ficarolo" owe much to conversations with archivists at the Archivio Storico Diocesano, Ferrara, in particular to the kindness of that archive's director, Dom Enrico Peverada, most generous with his time, assistance, and erudition. Maestro Adriano Franceschini spoke with me kindly and at length about the "rotta" and the area of the Po around Ferrara. Dott.ssa Claudia Giuliano, conservatore della Biblioteca Classense, Ravenna, provided invaluable help with materials and allowed me to examine ms. Casa Cavalli 203, containing the version of "Romandiola" dedicated to Malatesta Novello (Plate I). At the Archivio di Stato, Ravenna, Dott.ssa Rosalba Morticca and Dott.ssa Manuela Mantani kindly provided me answers to questions as well as access to the "Tesoro di Bernicoli," the private notes and records of Silvio Bernicoli, greatest local historian of Ravenna.

Research of this nature is, of course, time-consuming and expensive. It is a pleasure, therefore, to record here my gratitude to the University of South Carolina for repeated support. At this project's inception, I received a summer research grant from the Department of French and Classics at the University of South Carolina, an award which enabled me to begin research in the United States. Two Research and Productive Scholarship grants from the Office of Sponsored Programs and Research enabled me to conduct research in Italy in 1990 and to investigate cartographic collections in the United States in 1994. For further research in Italy in 2000, a College of Liberal Arts Scholarship Support grant subsidized travel to northern Italy, enabling me to complete the commentary to this volume. A grant from the Office of Sponsored Programs and Research at the University of South Carolina funded the publication costs of this volume.

I am grateful to Charles Mack of the Department of Art, University of South Carolina, for long ago suggesting that an English translation of *Italia illustrata* would be of practical use to art historians, a suggestion which led to my deeper interest in the treatise. The two anonymous readers for the press have improved the original manuscript in numerous and important ways: I am indebted to one for many Italian equivalents of Biondo's Latin toponyms; to the other, for valuable direction in substantial restructuring of the arrangement of the entire book. Buford Norman and Kathleen Ross of the Department of Languages, Literatures, and Cultures gave generously of their time and expertise to help with formatting of versions of the text. Finally, I feel a particular debt of gratitude to Charles Burroughs, former Director of the Center for Medieval and Renaissance Studies at Binghamton University, who encouraged me with helpful suggestions over several years of the project's development and made possible its realization. It is no exaggeration to say that without his support this book would not have seen the light of day. As this book entered the final stage of production, I found occasion to express gratitude once again to colleagues: William Rivers improved the style of the Introduction; Faust Pauluzzi prepared requests to Italian libraries and archives for permission to reproduce images; and Kristina Stefanic-Brown prepared both the general and topographical indices. The flaws which remain are mine alone and no doubt reflect the excessive ambition of Biondo's design.

My late mother, Mildred Fletcher Jones Castner, introduced me to Italy and inspired me constantly with her love of the Latin language and its literature. This book is dedicated to her memory.

Catherine J. Castner
Columbia, South Carolina, USA
May, 2004

# Credits for Illustrations

I am grateful to the Osher Map Library, University of Southern Maine, Portland, for permission to reproduce the map which illustrates the front cover of this book, Francesco Berlinghieri's *Novella Italia* of 1480. For permission to reproduce the two maps which constitute the frontispiece, the regions of Italy according to Pliny and Biondo, I am grateful to Max Niemeyer Verlag, Tübingen, Germany, the publisher of Ottavio Clavuot's *Biondos «Italia illustrata»: Summa oder Neuschöpfung? Über die Arbeitsmethoden eines Humanisten.* For permission to reproduce the dedication to Malatesta Novello of the chapter "Romandiola" in MS. Casa Cavalli 203 (Plate I), and the fifteenth-century map (Plate V) showing Ravenna between the Bedisus and Montone rivers, I thank the Biblioteca Classense, Ravenna. The map of the province of Romagna in 1699 (Plates II and III) appears thanks to the Archivio di Stato di Roma and the Ministero per i Beni e le Attività Culturali. For permission to reproduce the illustration (Plate IV) a manuscript of Luigi Ferdinand Marsili in the Biblioteca Universitaria di Bologna, I am grateful to the Ministero per i Beni e le Attività Culturali. Plate VI (*computisteria,* or bookkeeping records) is reproduced by courtesy of the Archivio di Stato, Modena. For permission to reproduce photographs of manuscript pages from MS. Vat. lat. 1960 (Plate VII), the map of the Po delta, I gratefully acknowledge the kindness of the Biblioteca Apostolica Vaticana.

# Introduction

The humanist antiquarian Biondo Flavio was a key founder, if not indeed the father of modern historiography and archaeology. During and following an ultimately unsuccessful career as papal secretary, Biondo (1392–1463) wrote four major Latin treatises between 1439 and 1460;[1] he completed the first manuscript version of *Italia illustrata* in 1453, though he went on to produce later editions with numerous additions and corrections. In early modern historiography and archaeology, Biondo was a pioneer in scientific method and critical judgment; his treatises are often the "sole authority for a wealth of information about ancient remains which have now disappeared."[2] Despite their importance for research, his works exist only as manuscripts or rare early printed books and thus must be read in special collections or rare book rooms.[3] The present work will make available the Latin text and translation of *Italia illustrata* with commentary to the reader of English with access to a standard academic library.

*Italia illustrata* is historical topography and strikingly original. Before Biondo no scholar had attemped a work that combined every characteristic of historical topography.[4] *Italia illustrata* includes a collocation of ancient

---

[1] In addition to *Italia illustrata, Roma instaurata* published 1446; *Historiarum ab inclinatione romani imperii decades* published 1453; and *Roma triumphans*, published 1459.

[2] Roberto Weiss, *The Renaissance Discovery of Classical Antiquity* (Oxford: Blackwell, 1969), 206.

[3] Bartolomeo Nogara, *Scritti Inediti e Rari di Biondo Flavio*, Studi e Testi 48 (Rome: Tipografia Poliglotta Vaticana, 1927), expressed seventy-five years ago the hope that *Italia illustrata* would receive a modern critical edition and commentary: "Farebbe opera utile per una migliore conoscenza dell'Italia e dell'umanesimo italiano nella prima metà del Quattrocento ..." (129 n. 163).

[4] Denys Hay, *The Italian Renaissance in its Historical Background* (Cambridge: Cambridge University Press, 1977), 40; Ottavio Clavuot, *Biondos «Italia illustrata»: Summa oder Neuschöpfung? Über die Arbeitsmethoden eines Humanisten.* Bibliothek des Deutschen historischen Instituts in Rom 69 (Tübingen: Niemeyer, 1990), 157.

sites with their early modern names; descriptions of Italy's towns and cities and, for many, encomia of their citizens famous in literature, politics, and the military. Roberto Weiss' definition of Biondo's general antiquarian mission is particularly accurate with regard to this treatise: "the imperious necessity of rescuing, or at any rate recording as much as possible of what was still left . . . before it should vanish for ever";[5] or as Biondo himself wrote in his Preface (**293B–C**), *vetustioribus locis eius et populis nominum novitatem, novis auctoritatem, deletis vitam memoriae dare, denique rerum Italiae obscuritatem illustrare potero.*[6]

## I. BIONDO'S BIOGRAPHY

Biondo Flavio is a pen name. Born into the Biondo family, the son of Antonio Biondi (de Blondis), the humanist was given the first name Biondo, and created his pen name by translating Biondo into Latin, resulting in Flavius, Latin for "blond"; the occurrence of the name "Blondus Flavius" in several manuscripts and in the salutation of his correspondence show his intention to be known by that name. A native of Forlì in the Romagna, his early education took place in Cremona under Giovanni Balestreri (cf. **362G**);[7] while at Cremona he came under the influence of the cultural environment around the Visconti of Milan.

After his modest beginning as a notary, Biondo's professional life falls roughly into three parts which were interwoven with his cultural development: service to various lords in the north of Italy in the 1420s and 1430s,

---

[5] Weiss, *Discovery*, 205.

[6] This and all subsequent citations from *Italia illustrata* are from the Basel, Froben 1559 edition, with its helpful reference point of marginal section numbers on each page (ABCD on odd-numbered pages; EFGH on even-numbered pages).

[7] Indispensable for biographical information are Nogara, *Scritti Inediti*; Clavuot, *Biondos «Italia illustrata»*; and Riccardo Fubini, "Biondo, Flavio," *Dizionario biografico degli italiani* 10 (Rome: Istituto dell'enciclopedia italiana, 1968), 536–559. Nogara provides a thorough account of B.'s studies, humanist contacts, and writings, reconstructing B.'s life in part from his extant correspondence with important intellectual figures like Guarino Veronese. Fubini's superb biographical article, with full references to important bibliography, relies heavily on Nogara. Dependent on both Nogara and Fubini but especially useful for biographical material is Clavuot's section on the genesis of *It. ill.* (44–55).

including a period (1420–1430) Nogara describes as stormy, from which no correspondence of Biondo's survives; his curial career, begun under Eugenius IV (r. 1431–1447), interrupted by his fall from favor under Pope Nicholas V, and resumed (although with diminished activity and importance) when he was reinstated; and the last years of his life, from the death of Nicholas in 1455 to his death in 1463, a period in which he was much occupied with the Crusade and publication of his later treatises.

After his early education at Cremona under Giovanni Balestreri, Biondo found employment as a diplomat with the Ordelaffi, lords of his native Forlì and one of many families of minor tyrants of the Romagna. In 1420 he first encountered Guarino Guarini, the founder of humanist pedagogy who had a school in Verona and who would be a lifelong mentor. This meeting marked the beginning of a period of Biondo's life which provides evidence for his studies of classical texts, and the beginning of his intellectual pursuits, in particular his intensive study of Cicero. Guarino's influence, formative for Biondo's knowledge of classical authors, reflects the crucial role that northern Italian influences would play in his intellectual formation. As Fubini notes,[8] his precise awareness of certain texts is due to his connections in northern Italy. For example, the transcription of the Ciceronian codex of Lodi (in 1442; cf. **346H–347A**) would not have been entrusted to him if he had not developed a reputation as an erudite scholar in northern humanist circles.

During the first phase of his professional life, Biondo suffered a two-year exile from Forlì, probably for political reasons,[9] after which he entered the service of Venice, specifically in its administration of its mainland possessions. In 1424–25 Biondo followed the Venetian aristocrat Francesco Barbaro to Vicenza where Barbaro was governor. Two or three years later, Biondo is found at Brescia in the service of Pietro Loredan. Between 1424 and 1427, and 1430–1431, Biondo worked as secretary to Francesco Barbaro, Pietro Loredan, and Francesco Barbarigo on the Venetian mainland. Not surprisingly, he extols all of these men's exploits and cultural attainments in the catalogue of Venice's famous men which concludes *Italia illustrata*'s eighth chapter. After this point, Biondo was able to return to Forlì, whence he engineered the beginning of his career in the Roman Curia. Dur-

---

[8] Fubini, "Biondo, Flavio," *DBI*, 538.

[9] See Fubini, "Biondo, Flavio," *DBI*, 537, for speculation as to the cause of this exile, 1423–1425, the first of two periods of exile from Forlì.

ing this second phase he published his first Latin treatise, *De Verbis Romanae locutionis ad Leonardum Aretinum*, whose addressee, Leonardo Bruni, would become Biondo's great model in historiography. In 1442, he went to Milan *publicis patriae tractandis negotiis*. At the same time, he began to copy Bruni's *De Militia*, a work which may have shaped the character of his own historical-antiquarian research. Though of Romagnol origin and persistently proud of his roots, Biondo established close connections with several northern cities: during his term at Milan as ambassador of Forlì, he took the opportunity to travel extensively in Lombardy; he served as secretary to various governors in this area between 1412 and 1432; and he held citizenship in a number of northern Italian cities both in his earlier career and throughout his lifetime.

His employment as secretary to such prominent Venetians as Francesco Barbaro and Pietro Loredan brought Biondo not only Venetian citizenship (in 1424) but also contact with Venetian humanism. By 1427, when he returned to Forlì after his first exile, the Church was in power in the Romagna, and Biondo took up service with the ecclesiastical governor of Forlì Domenico Capranica. Even his entrance into a career in the papal Curia (in 1433), to which this post was a stepping-stone, depended upon his allegiances in northern Italy, for it was under the Venetian pope Eugenius IV (Gabriele Condulmer) that he became first notary of the apostolic chamber, then papal secretary. During Eugenius's papacy Biondo intervened diplomatically in the political affairs of cities in the Romagna and Venice.

Because he was a layman, Biondo's Curial contributions were always scholarly and diplomatic. In 1432 he was summoned to Rome to begin a career in the papal Curia, probably as a result of his service to Capranica, who had left Forlì in January of 1430. His employment in the Curia may also have been prepared by a period of service as secretary to Giovanni Vitelleschi, governor of the March of Ancona. Initially notary of the apostolic chamber, he quickly rose to be papal secretary. Pope Eugenius IV further demonstrated his trust in Biondo by sending him almost immediately on a diplomatic embassy to the Romagna and the Veneto. In 1436, he became a scriptor of papal letters in the chancery, a post frequently occupied by lay humanists, one of whose functions was to write the papal bulls.[10] Pope

[10] For further explanation of these positions, see John F. D'Amico, *Renaissance Humanism in Papal Rome: Humanists and Churchmen on the Eve of the Reformation* (Baltimore and London: Johns Hopkins University Press, 1983), 26.

Eugenius entrusted Biondo not only with sensitive diplomatic missions but also with business of the Curia in Florence.

The pope's exile to Florence in the 1430s gave Biondo the opportunity to develop contacts which contributed substantially to his intellectual formation. Chief among these was Leonardo Bruni (1369–1444), whose influence and intellectual authority pervade *Italia illustrata*.[11] During Eugenius' sojourn in Florence Biondo participated as secretary in the promulgation of papal communications affecting various councils; his name appears on diplomatic missives; he was much involved in the Council of Ferrara and Florence. All in all, he accumulated considerable influence in the Curia. After 1436, however, with further advances in an ecclesiastical career shut off from him due to his lay and marital status, he devoted his professional energies to work on his historical and antiquarian writings. The massive *Historiarum ab inclinatione romani imperii decades* consumed at least fifteen years and must be understood as the background for all Biondo's intellectual activities up to the publication of the first version of *Italia illustrata*.

*Italia illustrata*, the work of Biondo's maturity, is also the work of his season in disfavor after the death of Eugenius IV in 1447. With the accession of Nicholas V (ironically, a pope most supportive of the humanist agenda), Biondo found himself unemployed, probably for no more serious offense than his devotion to Eugenius. His reinstatement to the Curia came only in 1453, two years before Nicholas's death.

In the last years of his life, Biondo was impoverished and scrambling for patronage. For example, he applied for a teaching position in the school of San Marco in Venice (ultimately awarded to Sabellico). He began working in 1459–1460 on a history of Venice, the fragmentary *Populi Veneti historiarum liber I*.[12] Hoping for remuneration for a proposed revision and

---

[11] See Eric Cochrane, *Historians and Historiography in the Italian Renaissance* (Chicago and London: University of Chicago Press, 1981), 35: "It was to Florence ... and particularly to Bruni, that Biondo owed what thereafter became his chief literary commitment, history."

[12] For correspondence on this matter, cf. Clavuot, *Biondos «Italia illustrata»,* 52 n. 98; Nogara, *Scritti Inediti*, CLXXIII–CLXXIV; M. L. King, *Venetian Humanism in an Age of Patrician Dominance* (Princeton: Princeton University Press, 1986), 47 and nn. 233 and 234. F. Gilbert, "Biondo, Sabellico, and the Beginnings of Venetian Official Historiography" (in J. G. Rowe and W. H. Stockdale, eds., *Florilegium Historiale: Essays Presented to Wallace K. Ferguson* [Toronto: University of Toronto Press, 1971], 275–293), 280–281, distinguishes the concepts of an official

completion of *Italia illustrata*, Biondo had managed by the time of his death in 1463 to finish major textual additions to his chapters on Liguria and Tuscany as well as marginal additions throughout the text. He also completed supplements to his *Decades*. In June of 1463, with negotiations for compensation from Francesco Sforza of Milan still unconsummated, Biondo died in Rome, where his tomb can be visited in the church of Sta. Maria Aracoeli. Innnovative and creative in his thought, industrious and never-tiring in his efforts to support his large family, enviably well-connected with churchmen, princes, and the elite, Biondo had nevertheless remained frustrated in his attempts to gain a comfortable livelihood, and received only from posterity the critical acclaim he deserved.

## II. BIONDO'S CULTURAL ORIENTATIONS

Biondo's involvement in the transmission of a newly discovered text of Cicero in 1422 as well as his contributions to the emendations of Livy patronized by cardinal Prospero Colonna exemplify his devotion to collecting and preserving the textual monuments of antiquity. In his historical and geographical research he moved beyond ancient sources to authors of late antiquity and the medieval period. His sense of historical perspective, philological sophistication, and consummate erudition in the treatment of classical literature place him among the foremost figures of early Quattrocento humanism. His exercise of critical judgment upon a variety of sources further distinguishes him within the humanistic movement. Biondo's ambition descends in a direct line from Petrarch's "imaginary self-transport across history";[13] however, the discovery of texts of Cicero allowed Biondo and

---

position for a historiographer and a lectureship at San Marco, and clarifies the interaction between Foscarini and Biondo in regard to such a position.

[13] See Ronald G. Witt, *"In the Footsteps of the Ancients": The Origins of Humanism from Lovato to Bruni* (Leidon, Boston, Cologne: Brill, 2000), 277, for a description of Petrarch's worship of classical antiquity which sounds strong resonances with Biondo's *Roma instaurata*, but is relevant as well to his mission in *It. ill.*: "Walks through the ruins of Rome, for example, unleashed a flood of images connecting ancient historical events with specific Roman sites." In Angelo Mazzocco's words, Petrarch's letter *De rebus familiaribus* VI.2, written in 1341, "constitutes the first antiquarian document of humanism" ("Petrarca, Poggio, and Biondo: Humanism's Foremost Interpreters of Roman Ruins," in *Francis Petrarch,*

other humanists to attain a level of Latin eloquence not possible for Petrarch (**346H–347A**).

Because Biondo's cultural and intellectual development took place in the humanist circles of Florence and only later in similar circles at Rome, his first humanist writing (*De verbis Romanae locutionis* [1435]) reveals his integral involvement in one of the most important cultural controversies of that time, the "Florentine debate" over the status of speech in classical Rome.[14] In this work he disputed the view of some scholars (including his mentor Bruni) that in ancient Rome two languages had existed, one for the erudite and a second colloquial vernacular for the masses: Biondo asserted that Latin had been one language in antiquity, but its unity had been destroyed by the barbarian invasions.

The humanist's intense interest in linguistics and classical Latin are evident in both *De verbis Romanae locutionis* and *Italia illustrata.* In *De verbis* Biondo had blamed the Germanic barbarians for the degeneration of Latin into the *volgare.* This argument persists in *Decades*, *Roma triumphans*, and *Italia illustrata.* In this latter work Biondo condemns the Lombards for changing the names of so many ancient sites, which he attempts to recover before they are lost forever. Biondo's attitude towards "barbarians" (in both *Decades* and *Italia illustrata*) is consonant with St. Jerome's description of their depredations in his native land. In fact, Biondo closes his brief treatment of Istria (**388E**) with an argument on linguistic grounds for identifying Jerome as an Italian. The following passage argues that Istria is a part of Italy, and is motivated in part by his desire to claim for Italy his patron saint.

*Italia illustrata* attests as well to Biondo's appreciation for the central role of Padua in the development of humanism. He pointed out the Paduan "protohumanists"' antiquarian interests; their recovery of Livy; and the legacy of Petrarch in the region. In his own times, the Venetian appropriation of the University of Padua had influenced the education and intellectual formation of the Venetian patrician humanists, with many of whom Biondo enjoyed close connections.

---

*Six Centuries Later*, ed. Aldo Scaglione. North Carolina Studies in the Romance Languages and Literatures, Symposia 3 [Chapel Hill and Chicago: University of North Carolina and Newberry Library, 1975]), 353–363; 355.

[14] Angelo Mazzocco, *Linguistic Theories in Dante and the Humanists* (Leiden and New York: Brill, 1993), explains thoroughly this issue and Biondo's central role in the debate.

Augusto Campana has called Biondo the greatest Romagnol humanist of the fifteenth century.[15] Biondo's regional identity is explicit in *Italia illustrata* and implicit in the posthumous authority he exerted over later geographical writers, who deferred to his authority, even when he was in error, in their identification and location of sites in the Romagna. Biondo owned a farm in San Biagio (**353C**), was attested as a citizen of Ferrara, and held property there and in Ravenna, where he boasts that his brother Matteo was abbot in the monastery of Sta. Maria Rotonda (**345D**). His tribute to his native region, the chapter "Romandiola," is the longest and most important in *Italia illustrata*. This chapter was first published separately and dedicated to Biondo's patron Malatesta Novello, lord of Cesena.[16]

The discrepancy between Biondo's local and Italian patriotism is only apparent. As Hay noted, the chapter "Romandiola" is "very unbalanced."[17] Biondo's classicism led him to a sense of the geographical unity of Italy, a sense that was corroborated by his devotion to Pliny, who acknowledged such a concept. The imbalance noted by Hay stems from the disproportionate credit Biondo gives his native region for the rebirth of Italy's eloquence and military glory.[18]

---

[15] A. Campana, "Biondo, Flavio," *Enciclopedia Dantesca* 2nd ed. (Rome: Istituto della Enciclopedia italiana, 1984), 1:634–635.

[16] The dedication appears in ms. Classense 203 (Plate I): *Viro omnem hanc regionem ex nostro instituto commendaturi*, etc. For a study of this early version, see A. Campana, "Passi inediti dell'«Italia illustrata» di Biondo Flavio," *La Rinascita* 1 (1938), 91–97. The first sentence of the dedication (*ex nostro instituto*), implying that B. had formed the plan of dedicating separately to his patrons the chapters on their native regions, supports Campana's assertion (93–4) that B. actually dedicated the chapter "Latina" to Prospero Cardinal Colonna, a dedication which no longer appears, as dedications of chapters to individuals were omitted in the first complete manuscript version which appeared dedicated to Nicholas V.

[17] Hay, "Italian View," 9, acknowledges this unbalanced treatment as "a fifteenth-century writer's best approximation of the concept of Italy."

[18] Egnazio Danti's wall maps in the Vatican Gallery from the early 1580s delineate the regions of Italy according to contemporary political boundaries and thus bear more relation to reality than do Biondo's regions. Yet it would be difficult to conceive of Danti's regions without the earlier divisions of *Italia illustrata*.

## III. *ITALIA ILLUSTRATA*'S GENESIS

Although by mid-fifteenth century the pattern of humanist historical writing for specific patrons was well established, Biondo was never as dependent as historians writing the exploits of famous patrons (e.g., Crivelli on and for the Sforza).[19] In conformity with this pattern of patronage Alfonso of Aragon, King of Naples, commissioned *Italia illustrata,* urging Biondo in 1447, through his intermediary Bishop Giacomo Antonio della Torre of Modena, to compose a catalogue of famous contemporaries of the eighteen regions of Italy. But this starting point was soon superseded by the humanist's own creative vision and the addition of a historical dimension, no doubt inspired by his having begun work on *Decades* between 1435 and 1437. Somewhat paradoxically *Italia illustrata,* the only work of Biondo initiated by a commission, is also recognized as his most personal creation, and is a freer arrangement, in a descriptive context, of the documentation of *Decades* mediated by the methodology of archaeological investigation practiced in *Roma instaurata.*[20]

Alfonso's commission was a starting point soon superseded as Biondo expanded upon it. Envisioning a work of ambitious scope, Biondo set out to describe eighteen regions of Italy, including Sicily and Sardinia, but completed only fourteen. His progress in composing the treatise was dictated in great part by the exigencies of this phase of his life (1449–1451), during which he traveled frequently to find work with princes and noblemen to support his large family.[21]

In 1449, during the composition of *Italia illustrata,* while suffering alienation from the Curia, Biondo established his family at his farm in San Biagio in the province of Ferrara (*Blasianus, in quo villam habemus locu-*

---

[19] See, for example, G. Ianziti's judgment apropos of Biondo's *Decades* (*Humanistic Historiography under the Sforzas: Politics and Propaganda in Fifteenth-century Milan* [Oxford: Clarendon Press, 1988], 46): "... Biondo is a historian *sui generis.* He does not write history under orders from any prince or pope, nor can his work be fairly described as partisan in slant."

[20] This characterization is Fubini's, "Biondo Flavio," *DBI,* 547–548.

[21] See Jeffrey A. White, "Towards a Critical Edition of Biondo Flavio's 'Italia illustrata': A Survey and an Evalution of the MSS," in Brezzi, P. and M. DePanizza Lorch, eds., *Umanesimo a Roma nel Quattrocento* (Rome and New York: Istituto di Studi Romani and Barnard College [1984]), 267–293; 274–275; Clavuot, *Biondos «Italia illustrata»,* 46–50.

*pletem e regione Zanioli sitam, in qua horum partem scripsimus*—353C). From this base he traveled both to seek patronage and to visit sites and conduct other research pertinent to *Italia illustrata*.[22] In 1450, for example, Biondo traveled from San Biagio to Milan, possibly motivated by hope of eliciting the patronage of the new Duke Francesco Sforza. In the summer of 1451 Biondo met Alfonso's ambassadors in Venice and consigned to them the part of *Italia illustrata* he had written,[23] then returned to the Romagna, but now to Ravenna.[24] He visited Naples in 1452 to give a public oration, and perhaps in hopes of finding material on the Regno for the unfinished chapters on the southern regions of Italy.[25] From Naples he returned to San Biagio. In 1453 the suspenseful, but eventually successful, negotiations for his reinstatement in the Curia brought an end to this period of composing *Italia illustrata* interspersed with seeking employment and patronage. A new phase of his career now begins, signaled by both the composition of propagandistic works advocating a Crusade and the more enduring creation of *Roma triumphans*.

Biondo explained the premature publication of *Italia illustrata* in 1453, now dedicated to Nicholas V instead of Alfonso, as an attempt to forestall the plagiarism of the treatise by an enemy in the Curia. Although the enemy's identity remains disputed, Biondo claimed that he borrowed and defaced the manuscript with the intent of publishing it under his own name.[26] Although Biondo continued to revise and augment *Italia illustrata* up to the time of his death, the final versions included only fourteen of the eighteen

---

[22] An earlier transfer of Biondo's family to a house in Ferrara in 1443 was, Samaritani believes, motivated by Biondo's developing relationship with Leonello d'Este, a patron supportive of Biondo's historical work *Decades*. See A. Samaritani, "Il 'Vicus Blasianus' tra Bessarione e Biondo Flavio," *Atti e Memorie Deputazione Provinciale Ferrarese di Storia Patria* ser. 3, v. 13 (1973): 157–172, 160–161.

[23] Nogara, *Scritti inediti*, CXX, suggests that Biondo was trying to find employment and patronage in Venice, and that this first version included regions 1–11.

[24] See Samaritani, "'Vicus Blasianus,'" 165; Nogara, *Scritti inediti*, CXX and n. 152.

[25] Alfonso never satisfied Biondo's requests for aid in completing chapters on the Regno, for written materials and information derived from the personal observation of scholars at his court familiar with these regions.

[26] See Biondo's letter to Pius II, at Nogara, *Scritti inediti*, 227: *unus, dignitate episcopus* some conjecture to be Cardinal Francesco Condulmer.

regions. He never realized descriptions of the two islands as well as the mainland regions of Calabria and Lucania.

## IV. *ITALIA ILLUSTRATA* IN THE CONTEXT OF BIONDO'S LITERARY PRODUCTION

Biondo's resurrection, systematization, and preservation of the names of the cities and towns of Italy drew on his concurrent historical enterprise, *Historiarum Decades*. The *Decades* embodies a model of historical writing recently established by Leonardo Bruni, notably in his *Florentine History*. Although Bruni was writing as official historiographer of the city of Florence, his new concept of historiography can be characterized as more objective as it involved the exercise of critical judgment upon a variety of sources. Unlike Bruni, whose history of Florence involved a highly national view but one which is Florentine, not Italian, Biondo expanded the frame of reference and took in his *Decades* a national view of Italy.[27] Whereas Bruni believed that decline started with the end of the Republic, Biondo originated the treatment of the medieval period as a historical epoch, and we still use his term.[28] He developed the concept that decline began at the end of the Roman Empire. In *Historiarum Decades* Biondo intended to continue Italian history from the point, 410 A.D., at which earlier writers had stopped. The scope of his history was the fall of empire and the ensuing disasters, as well as the origins and vicissitudes of modern peoples (particularly in Italy) down to his own time (1441). His history demonstrates as well the emerging awareness of modern Italy as distinct from its ancient past, as the Plinian sense of Italy as a geographical entity gives way to an ultimately political sense of Italian identity.

---

[27] See Cochrane, *Historians and Historiography*, 35: "… as a citizen of all Italy rather than of just one city, Biondo remained as independent of the Florentines as he had of the Curia … the scope of his interest was limited neither to Florence nor to the Papacy…. Rather, it included the whole of at least northern Italy."

[28] *Inclinatio Romani imperii* is Biondo's innovation, and the inspiration for Edward Gibbon's title; see Cochrane, *Historians and Historiography*, 36–37; and Angelo Mazzocco, "Decline and Rebirth in Bruni and Biondo," in Brezzi, P., and M. dePanizza Lorch, eds., *Umanesimo a Roma nel Quattrocento* (Rome and New York: Istituto di Studi Romani and Barnard College, 1984): 249–266.

This innovative periodicization of history, as well as the concept *illustrare*, characterize *Italia illustrata* as well, which Biondo intended to be a *non parvae partis historiarum Italiae breviarium* (295C)—a summary of a considerable part of Italian history. He drew frequently from *Decades* in composing historical summaries in the geographical work: for example, Biondo's marginal notes in a manuscript copy of Paul the Deacon's *History of the Lombards* correspond to passages in *Decades* and *Italia illustrata*, suggesting that he used Paul's material first in *Decades* and then transferred it to *Italia illustrata*.

*Italia illustrata* also contains material initially developed in *Roma instaurata* (1446), in which Biondo had attempted to reconstruct the topography of ancient Rome. In *Italia illustrata* Biondo filtered historical material taken from *Decades* through the archaeological-antiquarian method of *Roma instaurata*. An innovative departure from the tradition of medieval descriptions of cities, *Roma instaurata* inaugurates systematic historical reconstruction and can rightly be called the beginning of modern archaeology. Here, for example, Biondo "abandon[s] the medieval treatises, with their emphasis upon Christian monuments and their practical purpose in serving as guidebooks for pilgrims, and instead ... correlate[s] the relevant materials in the ancient authors with firsthand information of existing monuments."[29] Biondo was aware of how innovative his writing the history of Italy in medieval times was. He consequently drew heavily on his *Decades* in *Italia illustrata*'s description of northern Italy, emphasizing the wars and destruction of medieval times and praising the illustrious men of medieval times as well as his own time. He had this material at hand and found it convenient to use in creating a historical topography of the northern regions.

After reinstatement to the Curia under Nicholas V, and under Nicholas's successor Pius II, Biondo continued to produce orations and minor treatises supporting papal positions, especially calls to a crusade. Even *De origine et gestis Venetorum*, for example, a treatise on the government of Venice (completed in 1454), was intended as a call to arms against the Turks, whose

29 During the composition of *Roma instaurata* (dedicated in 1446 to Eugenius IV), Biondo was living in Rome just off the Via Flaminia near Montecitorio near the modern Via del Corso; see Dorothy M. Robathan, "Flavio Biondo's *Roma instaurata*," *Medievalia et Humanistica* N.S. 1 (1970): 203–216, who notes also, at 207, that in *Roma instaurata* Biondo "combines literary material with his own observation."

depredations posed a severe threat to the Venetians' overseas possessions.[30] The major occupation of his last years (1452–1459), however (in addition to the completion of *Decades*), was *Roma triumphans* (published in 1460), an antiquarian investigation of the institutions of ancient Rome: religion; magistracies and other governmental positions; the military; private life; the triumphal procession. The title does not begin to represent the exhaustive content, but expresses a vision of Rome as a timeless, transcendent and unifying cultural force.[31] In *Roma triumphans*, the culmination of the method of historical investigation developed in the three earlier major Latin treatises, Biondo continued his systematic treatment of antiquity apparent in *Decades*, *Roma instaurata*, and *Italia illustrata* and characterized by critical discernment in the valuing of sources and evidence.

## V. BIONDO FLAVIO'S METHOD IN *ITALIA ILLUSTRATA*

Although Biondo does not use the names of the Augustan regions, most of the regions of *Italia illustrata* correspond geographically to the regions of Italy according to the Augustan division as Pliny described them in the third book of his *Natural History*. The humanist's work is thus more a palimpsest than a representation of reality, describing an Italy that never existed, an Italy divided into regions that do not correspond to the political divisions of Biondo's day but are nevertheless filled with early modern toponyms. Where no ancient place-name for a site existed, the humanist created Latin toponyms through a process of back-formation from the vernacular forms of his own time. Accompanying the geographical description is a large amount of historical material, arranged spatially, not chronologically. The towns and cities are presented as they are encountered along the courses of rivers.

Much generalized, Biondo's method of procedure was to follow rivers from the coast towards the interior, describing towns and cities along their

---

[30] See Nogara, *Scritti inediti*, CXXXIV–CXXXV: the fall of Constantinople, 6 April 1453, had increased this sense of urgency; and Biondo's exhortation of a year earlier (*De expeditione in Turchos*) was addressed to Alfonso in Naples because, while the states of Genoa and Venice were threatened because of their colonial possessions and trade with the East, the Kingdom of the Two Sicilies was geographically most vulnerable to invasion.

[31] See Nogara, *Scritti inediti*, CLI and n. 185.

banks.[32] Intertwined with the geographical and historical material are biographical notices of the famous men of each city. Although his procedure was systematic, the depth and length of the chapters devoted to the regions are disproportionate. Not surprisingly, the substantial length of chapter 6, "Romandiola," on Biondo's native region, is nearly matched by the length of chapter 7 (Lombardy), reflecting Biondo's connections to Milan. Chapter 8 (Venetia) is comparatively brief and treats only the city of Venice, listing important events from its history, restricted to internal disturbances and the foundation of places.[33] As Biondo had written the definitive account of medieval Venetian history in *Decades*, he no doubt felt justified in curtailing in *Italia illustrata* the treatment of this visually and historically sensational city. But his service as secretary to Francesco Barbaro and in other capacities for the Republic had brought familiarity with many of the Venetian elite, so that he devotes much space in this chapter to their praise.

As a consequence of restricting the chapter on Venetia to the city itself, the following chapter, on the March of Treviso, is relatively long. Here we find descriptions of towns and cities within the territory ruled by Venice.

---

[32] A modern Romagnol scholar calls attention to Biondo's unconventional orientation: Augusto Campana, "Poesie Umanistiche sul Castello di Gradara," *Studi Romagnoli* 20 (1969): 502–520, 516, notes, "Biondo chiama sinistra, non so se per uso allora comune o suo personale, quella che secondo la nostra convenzione è la destra di un fiume." Biondo's orientation may be derived similarly to Dante's in *De vulgari eloquentia*, in which Dante surveys the Italian peninsula and refers to left and right in a reversal of the orientation which later became customary. Denis Hay, "The Italian View of Renaissance Italy," in Rowe, J. G. and W. H. Stockdale, eds., *Florilegium Historiale: Essays presented to Wallace K. Ferguson* (Toronto: University of Toronto Press, 1971), 3–17; 5–6 and n. 3, suggests that Dante's orientation derived from his use of a map which "displayed the peninsula as part of a circular world-map, with Jerusalem in the centre and Asia in the top half. Europe was depicted in the lower quarter on the left, separated by the Mediterranean from Africa in the lower quarter on the right. This arrangement—deriving from ancient sources and reflected in the medieval 'T & O' diagrams—meant that Italy was drawn with the Alps at the bottom left and the toe at the upper right. Dante's references to left and right are accordingly the reverse of later practice."

[33] According to Clavuot, *Biondos «Italia illustrata»*, 68 and n. 154, the chapter devoted to Venice resembles a longer and more detailed version of Biondo's standard city description. Biondo himself acknowledged the summary nature of his treatment of Venice at **369D**, . . . *eius incrementa summatim, sicut in ceteris facimus Italiae civitatibus explicando*. . . .

The result is an artificial separation in the text of Venice from its *terraferma*, unnatural given the increasing importance to Venice of its territorial possessions. Biondo's familiarity with the cities of Verona, Mantua, and Padua contributed as well to the length of the ninth chapter. Padua especially had loomed large in his personal and professional worlds.

## *A. Classical Sources*

Ancient sources to which Biondo has most frequent recourse in *Italia illustrata* include Livy, Virgil, Servius, and Pliny.[34] He inserted as authoritative into his place-descriptions many citations and paraphrases of ancient authors such as Livy and Virgil who were literary artists, not topographical authorities. Ancient geographical sources include Ptolemy's *Geography* (especially valuable to Biondo for its maps, and known to him probably through the translation into Latin by Jacopo Angeli da Scarperia in Florence in 1406); Pliny's *Natural History* (Biondo's erroneous citations indicate his possession of an inferior manuscript); and Strabo, whom Biondo may have read in the original despite his weak knowledge of Greek, since Guarino's translation was not completed until 1458, five years after the first publication of *Italia illustrata*, although Biondo may have had access to unpublished informal translations.[35] In the same way, Biondo could have acquired knowledge of the history of the first region, Liguria, through Angeli's translation into Latin of Plutarch's *Life of Marius*, an important source for Liguria's topography and history in the Roman period.[36] Biondo's citation of

[34] See Clavuot, *Biondos «Italia illustrata»*, 158–182, for exhaustive inventory of Biondo's sources and models for *It. ill.* Rather than credit each reliance on Clavuot in my commentary, I recognize and credit his work here; some elements of my work may serve chiefly to make Clavuot's analysis and judgments accessible to an American audience. I have made extensive use of Clavuot's Appendix 6 (302–322), an index of citations in *It. ill.* My translation has also benefited greatly from Clavuot's identifications of Latin toponyms with modern Italian counterparts. Clavuot has also, 163 n. 86, calculated the frequency of Biondo's citations of classical authors: 30% of Biondo's acknowledged citations from classical authors are from Livy; 20% from Pliny; and 10% from Virgil. As to Biondo's range of sources from all periods, Clavuot, 161, calculates 30% of these citations are from historiography.

[35] See N. G. Wilson, *From Byzantium to Italy: Greek Studies in the Italian Renaissance* (Baltimore: Johns Hopkins University Press, 1992), 47; 55–56.

[36] Angeli completed this translation in 1409 or 1410; see Roberto Weiss, "Iacopo Angeli da Scarperia," in *Medioevo e Rinascimento. Studi in onore di Bruno*

*Scriptores Historiae Augustae* betray his era's lack of suspicion of the dubious identities of these writers and he cites from, e.g., Julius Capitolinus, assuming his existence as an individual historian discrete from others of the *SHA*.[37]

## *B. Medieval and Humanist Sources*

For demographics, Biondo used among other sources the *Liber Cancellariae Apostolicae*, a catalogue of dioceses which provided the names and boundaries of regions recognized by the Church.[38] Several times he cites the anonymous eighth-century cosmographer of Ravenna who had summarized the work of Hyginus (c. 64 B.C.–A.D. 17) on Italian cities. Although Biondo had, in composing *Decades*, embraced a new conception of historiography that rejected the bare style of medieval chronicles, he does acknowledge his debt to a number of these documents.

Other sources are less certain. Jacopo da Varagine is a possible source for the foundation legend of Genoa.[39] Other possible medieval antecedents include the *Liber Pontificalis*, Paulus Diaconus' *Historia Langobardorum*, and chronicles of individual cities. Petrarch's *Laurea occidens* (*Bucolicum carmen* X) afforded a model of literary history within a frame of geographical description. Although Clavuot embraces a wide range of possible medieval and late-medieval models or antecedents for *Italia illustrata*, Cappelletto disagrees with the extent of these attributions as she finds Clavuot overly inclusive in listing as possible sources works that Biondo does not cite.[40] For

---

*Nardi.* 2 vols. (Florence 1955), 2: 803–817; repr. in *Medieval and Humanist Greek: Collected Essays by Roberto Weiss* (Padua: Antenore, 1977), 255–277, 273.

37 See, for this controversy, R. Syme, *Emperors and Biography: Studies in the Historia Augusta* (Oxford: Clarendon, 1971).

38 The *Liber* dates from around 1380 and lists 269 dioceses in Italy; see Clavuot, *Biondos «Italia illustrata»*, 189.

39 *Cronaca di Genova*. Vol. 85, Fonti per la storia d'Italia (Rome, 1941).

40 R. Cappelletto, "Italia illustrata di Biondo Flavio," in Alberto Asor Rosa, ed., *Letteratura italiana* (Turin: Einaudi, 1992), 1: 681–712, 704, criticizes Clavuot's assumption that Biondo used sources he does not cite outright: "Sostanzialmente inutili . . . mi sembrano gli sforzi di coloro che hanno voluto vedere 'modelli' o antecedenti dell' *Italia illustrata* nella letteratura medievale o tardo-medievale, dagli *excursus* geografico-teritoriali presenti in opere storiche quali quelle di Paolo Diacono o di Ottone da Frisinga ai vari trattati geografici (Anonimo Ravennate, Paolino Minorita), dal *De montibus, silvis, fontibus* [. . .] del Boccaccio all'*Itinerarium*

example, Petrarch's *Itinerarium Syriacum* (1358) presages the fifteenth-century interest in geographical description. It gives vital information on the state of geographical knowledge in Petrarch's time and presents a description of the Ligurian coast similar to Biondo's in "Liguria," including many of the same names of cities and towns;[41] however, because he fails to cite it we cannot be certain that Biondo used this work of Petrarch as a source for *Italia illustrata.*

Biondo consulted many humanist works, among them Ciriaco d'Ancona's *Itinerarium,* a model for a description of places connected with a catalogue of famous men; Cristoforo Buondelmonti's *Descriptio Insulae Cretae* (1417) and *Liber Insularum Archipelaghi* (1417–1422); and Giacomo Bracelli's *Descriptio orae ligusticae* (1442).

In the same way that the shift away from medieval theological explanation characterises Biondo's *Decades* as a pioneering work in the development of historiography, the new intellectual atmosphere in which people would accept a secular, demythologized geography informs *Italia illustrata.* Although Biondo composed this treatise fifty years before the great flowering of cartography that took place in Italy after 1500, the appearance of *Italia illustrata* coincided with a growing contemporary interest in geography and the production of maps of Italy in the first half of the fifteenth century.[42] In particular, this treatise's title implies a visual element, and its dependence on maps reflects the new interest. But such connections are tenuous in the first place due to the lack of a comprehensive body of cartographic evidence from the late medieval period. Moreover, a modern historian of cartography exposes the fallacy of linking the discovery of perspective, and the Florentine humanists' reception of Jacopo Angeli's translation

---

*Syriacum* del Petrarca o ad altri suoi componimenti come l'egloga *Laurea occidens.*"

[41] See now the edition of Theodore J. Cachey, Jr., *Petrarch's Guide to the Holy Land: Itinerary to the Sepulcher of Our Lord Jesus Christ* (Notre Dame, Indiana: University of Notre Dame Press, 2002).

[42] See P. D. A. Harvey, "Local and Regional Cartography in Medieval Europe" in J. B. Harley and David Woodward, eds., *Cartography in Prehistoric, Ancient, and Medieval Europe and the Mediterranean,* vol. 1 of *The History of Cartography* (Chicago and London: University of Chicago Press, 1987): 464–501, especially Appendix 20.1, 498. In *It. ill.* Biondo represented an Italy that never existed, in conformity with Harvey's assessment, at 464, of local and regional maps as "viewed from a position unattainable in reality."

of Ptolemy's *Geography*, to a fundamental change in perception and representation of space.[43] Although *Italia illustrata* is innovative as a spatialization of history, viewing it as a radical departure from late medieval geography in the development of spatial representation does not take into account, for example, that knowledge of Ptolemy's work had never completely vanished.

Instead, the treatise's connections with cartography are intensely practical and its author's cartographic concerns appear directed towards objectivity and accuracy. In composing *Italia illustrata* Biondo used maps as only one of a number of categories of sources; and he used the word *illustrare* in a non-visual meaning, in accordance not only with Ciceronian usage but also with the methods of the new historiography. *Italia illustrata* includes a number of tantalizing references to maps (*picturae*) Biondo has either used as sources, or hopes to obtain from friends or patrons. Nogara emphasises that Biondo's use of *pictura* denotes specifically a geographic map. The most notable references to maps in *Italia illustrata* and in Biondo's correspondence are his desperate pleas to Alfonso of Aragon for a map of the southern regions of Italy.[44]

Direct observation affords more concrete methodological connections. As might be expected in so personal a work, *Italia illustrata* contains numerous authorial comments on Biondo's family's residences in Italian towns and cities. Viti, comparing *Italia illustrata* with Petrarch's *Laurea occidens*, concludes that Petrarch worked entirely from written sources, while Biondo visited the places he wrote about to verify and expand upon his sources.[45] His prose suggests that he was familiar with many of the sites he describes. Furthermore, Biondo often expressly claims to have visited sites in Italy. However, he errs in their description due to his apparent neglect to observe

---

[43] Patrick Gautier Dalché, "Sur l' 'originalité' de la 'géographie' médiévale," in *Auctor et auctoritas: invention et conformisme dans l'écriture médiévale,* ed. Michel Zimmermann. Actes du colloque tenu a l'Université de Versailles-Saint-Quentin-en-Yvelines (Paris: École des Chartes, 2001), 131–143; 138–139. I owe this reference to the kindness of David Woodward.

[44] Nogara, *Scritti Inediti*, XCIII n. 114: references to *picturae*: **299C**, **353D**, **355D**, *inter alia*; at 149, Biondo's letter written to Alfonso in 1443.

[45] P. Viti, "Umanesimo letterario e primato regionale nell' «Italia illustrata» di F. Biondo," in *Studi filologici, letterari e storici in memoria di Guido Favati,* ed. G. Varanini and P. Pinagli. 2 vols. Medioevo e Umanesimo 29 (Padua, 1977), 2: 711–732; 714.

them directly. His political and patronage-hunting travels allowed him to visit or revisit sites, monuments, and libraries useful in his work. In sum, Biondo relied on direct observation when he could; but there was no consistent program of research involving travel. In White's judgment, the treatise "smacks at least equally of the study as of the open road."[46]

In whatever proportions Biondo divided his efforts between literary and documentary sources and direct observation, the most significant and extensive contribution to our understanding of his use of classical, medieval, and humanist sources is Ottavio Clavuot's thorough analysis, to which I owe my greatest debt. Clavuot traces the genesis of *Italia illustrata*, in some cases even reproducing Biondo's *marginalia* in manuscripts of earlier authors. Clavuot's major characterization of Biondo's use of classical authors helps us better understand his method and consequently the form of his work. Clavuot observes that Biondo brought citations into his text like pieces of moveable scenery brought onto a stage, without concern for their context, quarrying them for topographical identifications. Biondo's text thus often reads like a collection of thematically-organized excerpts crudely amputated from their contexts. Of course, Biondo had every reason to tear citations from their context, in order to fit them to his own agenda. And in doing so he worked in the tradition of his friend and fellow in papal service, Leon Battista Alberti, with whom he shared not only Eugenius's exile to Florence but also the patronage of Leonello d'Este of Ferrara and Sigismondo Malatesta. A year before Biondo dedicated *Italia illustrata* to Nicholas V, Alberti dedicated to the same pope his similarly-composed *De re aedificatoria*, which Biondo praises (**326E**) as *elegantissimos . . . libros*.

Yet Clavuot persuasively demonstrates that *Italia illustrata* as a whole is more than the sum of its parts, is indeed a new type of creation, as it is the prototype for early modern historical topography. Despite its stylistic shortcomings, the influence of *Italia illustrata* was both immediate and far-

[46] White, "Towards a Critical Edition," 274–275, is surely correct in his assessment of Biondo's direct observation of towns and cities *while conducting research for Italia illustrata* during the years of its composition: "We have no evidence (in the *It. ill.* or from elsewhere) of extensive peregrinations *for reasons of scholarship* for this period. Such on-the-spot investigations as Biondo did undertake in connection with the *It. ill.* must have been coincident with and subordinated to attempts to find employment—or they were reminiscences of earlier times put to a fresh application."

reaching.[47] Biondo's heirs include the Bolognese Dominican Leandro Alberti, who wrote his *Descrittione di tutta Italia*, heavily dependent upon Biondo's work, a hundred years after its publication.[48] *Italia illustrata* influenced historical topographies even outside of Italy, including the *Germania illustrata* of Konrad Celtis.[49] Later topographical writers influenced by Biondo include Schott[50] and Clüver.[51]

## VI. NOTE ON THE TRANSLATION

The entire text of *Italia illustrata* accompanied by translation and commentary demands more than one volume. In addition to satisfying the practical need to bring out the work in different volumes, I have tried to meet what I assume to be the expectations of most of my readers by dividing my treatment of Biondo's treatise in a way that deviates from the order of Biondo's chapters on fourteen regions of Italy. The humanist accepted the medieval geographical perspective of Italy as extending from west to east:[52] however, I have altered Biondo's order of treatment of the fourteen regions

---

47 "After Biondo's *Italia illustrata* investigations into the early history and topography of a town and its countryside became a frequent pursuit among humanists. Sylloges of local Roman inscriptions began to be put together, playing the roles of documentary corollaries to such dissertations . . . " Weiss, *Discovery*, 206.

48 *Descrittione di tutta Italia* (Bologna: Giaccarelli, 1550); see Fubini, "Biondo, Flavio," *DBI*, 555: a thread of Biondo's influence on the Dominicans of Bologna can be inferred from the *chronica . . . civitatis Bononiae* (1497) of G. Borselli (*RIS* 2nd ed. XXIII, A. Sorbelli, 4).

49 See G. Strauss, *Sixteenth-century Germany: Its Topography and Topographers* (Madison, Wisconsin: University of Wisconsin Press, 1959), who asserts the influence of *It. ill.* on the topographies of Hartmann Schedel (*Liber cronicarum figuris et ymaginibus ab inicio mundi usque nunc temporis* [Augsburg 1497]), Johann Stumpf, and Willibald Pirckheimer. Strauss, 17, attributes the rise of German topographical works to the influence of Aeneas Sylvius Piccolomini (Pope Pius II), and ultimately Biondo, who was Pius' model in this field.

50 *Itinerarium Italiae* (1600).

51 The geographer Philip Clüver wrote in the early seventeenth century an historical work *Italia antiqua* (Lugdunum Batavorum, 1624).

52 U. Tucci, "Credenze geographiche e cartografia," in *Storia d'Italia*, eds. Ruggiero Romano and Corrado Vivanti (Turin: Einaudi, 1973) V pt. 1 *Documenti*, 49–85.

to begin with his first chapter, "Liguria," but then continue with the sixth region, "Romandiola," and subsequent chapters on northern regions, rather than progressing down the western coast of Italy and then inland across the Apennines towards the Adriatic.[53]

The northern Italian chapters, one of which (chapter 7, "Romandiola") was initially conceived by Biondo as an independent work, bear the marks of Biondo's origins and activity in northern Italy; the longer among them testify to their author's residency, employment, and extensive travel in this area.[54] Geographically isolated by mountains and lagoons respectively, the first region, Liguria, and the eighth, Venice, were maritime empires somewhat isolated from the activities of the mainland; these anomalous topographies embrace the northern regions of the Romagna (chapter 6), Lombardy (7), and the March of Treviso (9).[55] Finally, Biondo employs a Plinian statement that he has concluded the *latitudo* of Italy to close his very brief treatments of the two very northernmost regions, Friuli (10) and Histria (11), which clearly belong logically with this northern group. Chapter 2, "Etruria" (Tuscany), has been reserved for a later volume for two reasons: first, it is a long and important chapter that would enlarge excessively this first volume; second, the close association of Florence with Biondo's career in the papal Curia argues that it should be reserved for a later volume in proximity to the related content of chapter 3, "Latina" (Latium).

After its first appearance in 1453, *Italia illustrata*, like *Historiarum Decades*, underwent various phases of editing. In his preparation of a critical edition of *Italia illustrata*, White has examined manuscripts and early printed editions and distinguishes a manuscript with the author's modifications in his own hand (Ottobonianus latinus 2369 in the Vatican Library) and a tradition descended from it; a manuscript containing modifications

[53] See the maps of Italy showing the division into Pliny's (Augustan) regions and Biondo's regions, p. vii.

[54] As Fubini, "Biondo Flavio," *DBI* 537, recognized, the fact that Biondo came from Forlì, a provincial center that was nonetheless politically inflammable and therefore open to influence from the larger states, would mark his career. In addition to the Roman Curia, Milan and Venice form the focal points both of his life and of his historical *oeuvre*. "Romandiola," "Lombardia," and "Marchia Tarvisina" are among the longest chapters in *It. ill.*, in great part because they contain minute details drawn from personal observation during Biondo's residency in these regions.

[55] See Cochrane, *Historians and Historiography*, 59, for further comments on the similarities between these two major republics of the Italian peninsula.

made later in another hand (Riccardianus 1198 in Florence); and a group which do not contain the deleted passages or the additions.[56]

Biondo's son Gaspare edited his father's writings between 1470 and 1474, and acknowledged that in doing so he attempted to improve the humanist's Latin. The *editio princeps* of *Italia illustrata* is his: Blondus Flavius Forliviensis, *Italiae illustratae libri VIII, sive descriptio XIV regionum Italiae*, ed. Gaspare Blondo (Rome: in domo nobilis viri Iohannis Philippi de Lignamine impressus, 1474). This was one of the very earliest books printed at Rome, issuing only nine years after what is considered to be the first printed book in Italy, the works of Lactantius dated in 1465 from the monastery of Subiaco. Gaspare Biondo's *editio princeps* of *Italia illustrata* is, in fact, one of the earliest books to issue from the press of De Lignamine, whose first printed book was a Quintilian of 1470, and thus one of the first to be printed by a native Italian.[57] Domenico Dominici, bishop of Brescia (whom Biondo praises at **374F**), encouraged Gaspare in this production; in return, the *editio princeps* was dedicated to him. I have, however, transcribed and translated the Latin text contained in the Basel (Froben) printed edition of 1559, the best-known, most-cited early printed edition, generally considered the most reliable.

Although Latin was the conventional vehicle for erudite treatises, Biondo's regional identity may have contributed to his choice of language.[58] Pope Pius II, who drew heavily on Biondo's work in his own writings, criticized his model's Latin as being far from the purity and eloquence of ancient writers. Cappelletto confirms this assessment, noting that Biondo fails to emulate the elegance of classical models and thereby fails to produce clarity and simplicity. She emphasizes the discontinuity of Biondo's prose, its syntactically complex periods alternating with clauses in simple and

---

[56] White, "Towards a Critical Edition," cit. n. 21, begins to disentangle the skeins of a complex tradition of additions, deletions, and revisions by Biondo himself and others, which include deletions of flattering mentions of Nicholas V and his supporters, made immediately upon this pope's death in 1455. The additions and corrections, from the Riccardianus, are printed in Nogara, *Scritti Inediti*, 219–239.

[57] See *Catalogue of Books Printed in the XV$^{TH}$ Century Now in the British Museum*, Pt. IV: Italy: Subiaco and Rome (London 1916), vii and 28. The 1474 edition of *Italia illustrata* is described at 33–34.

[58] Mazzocco, *Linguistic Theories*, 47, notes that Biondo's vernacular was "marred by infelicities peculiar to the dialect of [the Romagna]."

humble style.[59] In general, *Italia illustrata* is characterized by an incoherent and convoluted style. In particular, many of the descriptive passages devolve into mere lists of toponyms, inevitably choppy and simple. Yet in passages of historical narrative, Biondo shows the ability to compose classicizing Latin periods of complex syntax—*oratio obliqua* with infinitive verbs, ablative absolutes. However, Biondo's apparent attempt at recovery of the Ciceronian period falls short of Ciceronian rhetorical structure. Mazzocco aptly characterizes it as "… a Latin free of the straitjacket of Ciceronian rhetoric and more attuned to the needs of the new historical reality."[60] Biondo's diction reveals the influence of the "Florentine debate" in which, decades before his composition of *Italia illustrata*, he asserted that neologisms must be employed to describe new realities like modern weapons, for which classical Latin had no words. I have aimed in my translation at simple syntax and natural diction.

The work of this translation paralleled Biondo's task of correlating early modern Italian settlements with ancient Roman sites. *Italia illustrata* contains thousands of Latin toponyms. Many are back-formations from place-names Biondo would have known only in the vernacular of his time, and a number cannot be identified with modern Italian places. Towns and cities whose Latin toponyms can be securely correlated with modern Italian toponyms are denoted in the translation by their modern Italian names, in accordance with normal scholarly procedure. Where identification is less certain, I have either added a question mark or resorted to Lucio Fauno's sixteenth-century Italian translation.[61]

---

[59] "Procul Blondus ab eloquentia prisca fuit neque satis diligenter, que scripsit, examinavit: non quam vera, sed quam multa scriberet, curam habuit." A. van Heck, ed., *Pii II Commentarii rerum memorabilium quae temporibus suis contigerunt.* Studi e Testi 313 (Vatican City, 1984), 2, 711; cit. Clavuot, *Biondos «Italia illustrata»,* 6. Cappelletto, "Italia illustrata," 708.

[60] Mazzocco, *Linguistic Theories*, 4.

[61] Lucio Fauno, tr., *Biondo da Forlì, Roma restaurata et Italia Illustrata tradotte in buona lingua volgare per Lucio Fauno* (Venice: appresso Domenico Giglio, 1558). However, Fauno seems to resort to what White, "Towards a Critical Edition," 269 n. 7, terms "mere italianizing of the names of places in the text … [which] does [not] deepen understanding."

# BLONDI FORLIVIENSIS IN ITALIAM ILLUSTRATAM PRAEFATIO

Cum multi historiam variis extollant celebrentque sententiis, tum maxime [293A] Alexander Antoninus, Mammaea genitus Christiana, imperator Romanus omnium iudicio optimus, unica ratione eam amplissime videtur laudasse, qui historicos et suos appellavit et habere voluit consiliarios quorum prudentia et exemplorum copia gerendis imperii rebus quam maxime uteretur. Clarissimi etiam plerique senatores, consulares quoque viri et nonnulli gloriosissimi principes, qui bellicis actibus res gesserunt aeterna dignas memoria, delectati sunt historia usque adeo ut non solum historias libenter legerint, sed eas quoque scribendo tam praeclari muneris gloriam cum rerum scriptoribus communem habere voluerint. Nam ut ceteros taceam, Fabius patriciae gentis decus cognomento Pictor, Lucius Lucullus, Aulus Albinus, Asinius Pollio, Cornelius Nepos, et Caius Caesar eiusque nepos Octavius Augustus, ac Hadrianus scripsere historias. [293B]

Sed maximam tantum munus praeteritorum longe saeculorum malitia et infelicitate incurrit iniuriam, quod urbe Roma a variis gentibus, sicut in historiis accuratius a nobis est scriptum, oppressa, et si bonarum artium studia intermissa fuerunt, sola inprimis omnino cessavit extinctaque est historia. Factumque est ut barbaris omnia evertentibus, et nullo interim ea quae gerebantur litterarum monumentis ad posteros transmittente, nedum mille quae effluxerunt annorum gesta sciamus, sed Italiae regiones, urbes, oppida, lacus, flumina, montesque, quorum nomina a vetustis frequentantur scriptoribus, ubi sint, magna ex parte ignoremus, et quod maiorem nobis affert admirationem, multorum oppidorum et potentissimarum civitatum, quas interea in magnam amplitudinem crevisse cernimus, conditarum tempora nos lateant, et ipsi etiam conditores.

Itaque postquam propitiore nobis deo nostro, meliora habet aetas nostra, et cum ceterarum artium, tum maxime eloquentiae studia revixerunt, ac per

# Preface

## BIONDO FLAVIO OF FORLÌ
## PREFACE TO THE ITALIA ILLUSTRATA

Although many men praise and celebrate the discipline of history in various ways, [293A] the emperor Severus Alexander, son of the Christian woman Mammaea and in everyone's judgment the best Roman emperor, praised the field of history abundantly in one signal act: by making historians his confidants, and surrounding himself with historians as advisers, so that he could make full use of their wisdom and their knowledge of past examples of the management of empires. In addition, many famous senators and consulars and some renowned heads of state who have performed memorable deeds in war have been seduced by history to the point not only of reading it with pleasure, but also of writing it, so they might share in the glory enjoyed by historians. I shall omit the others, and mention as writers of histories the noble Fabius Pictor, glory of his family; Lucius Lucullus, Aulus Albinus; Asinius Pollio; Cornelius Nepos; and Gaius Caesar, his nephew Octavius Augustus, [293B] and Hadrian.

But so great an offering has met with great damage through the malice and misfortune of the centuries long past. I have written carefully in my histories about how the city of Rome has been oppressed by different peoples, and the cultivation of the liberal arts interrupted: history especially stopped completely and has been wiped out. Since the barbarians have destroyed everything, not only has there been no one to hand down these events in writing to following generations; we know still less about the events of the past thousand years. But as for the regions of Italy, her cities, towns, lakes, rivers, and mountains, whose names are much mentioned in the ancient writers, we are in large part ignorant of them. What is even more amazing, we are ignorant of the dates of the foundations, and of the founders themselves, of many towns and powerful cities which, we observe, have grown to great size.

And so our times have a better fortune (because our God is more favorable to us), in which the study of eloquence, as well as of the other arts, has

ea historiarum diligentius noscendarum amor nostros cepit homines, tentare volui, si per eam quam sum nactus Italiae **[293C]** rerum peritiam, vetustioribus locis eius et populis nominum novitatem, novis auctoritatem, deletis vitam memoriae dare, denique rerum Italiae obscuritatem illustrare potero. Nec tamen ipsam omnem nominum mutationem temeraria et inani arrogantia spoponderim indicare, sed gratias mihi potius de perductis ad litus e tanto naufragio supernatantibus, aut parum apparentibus tabulis haberi, quam de tota navi desiderata rationem exposci debere contenderim.

Italiae regiones seu provinciae XVIII

Liguria sive Genuensis
Etruria
Latina sive Campania et maritima
Umbria sive ducatus Spoletanus
Picenum sive Marchia Anconitana
Romandiola sive Flaminia et Aemilia
Gallia cisalpina sive Lombardia
Venetiae
Italia transpadana sive Marchia Tarvisina
Aquileiensis sive Foroiuliana
Istria
Samnium sive Aprutium
Terra laboris sive Campania vetus
Lucania **[293D]**
Apulia
Salentini sive terra Hydrunti
Calabria
Brutii

# BLONDI FLAVII FORLIVIENSIS ITALIAE ILLUSTRATAE LIBER PRIMUS **[294E]**

Italiam describere exorsi, provinciarum orbis primariam a laudibus suis incipere debemus, quod quidem pro ampla parataque materia, tam faciliter quam libenter fecissemus, nisi ab eximio poeta Virgilio, et post a Plinio Veronense, demum a Francisco Petrarch insigni poeta, ornatissimae illius laudationes exstarent. Itaque a suo nomine et situ duximus inchoandum.

Nomen pro temporum diversitate nacta est varium, quam Plinius et Solinus ab Italo rege quosdam, et nonnullos a bobus quos gigneret multos prisca

been reborn; because of this, men are desirous of learning history more carefully. I wish to try, through my knowledge **[293C]** of Italian affairs, to bring to light the names of Italy's older places and peoples, to give authority to the new places, and to give a record of those that have been destroyed; and, finally, to shed light upon the darkness of Italian history. Nor have I promised, through rashness and empty arrogance, to give a comprehensive assessment of all the changes in toponyms; but as from a great shipwreck the survivors swim to the shore or a few tablets appear, I have tried, from these fragments, to give an account of the entire ship. For this effort, I think that readers ought to thank me, rather than call me to account for the loss of the entire ship.

The eighteen regions or provinces of Italy

| | |
|---|---|
| Liguria or the Genoese | Aquileia or Friuli |
| Tuscany | Istria |
| Latina or Campania and the Marittima | Samnium or Abruzzo |
| Umbria or the duchy of Spoleto | Terra di Lavoro or ancient Campania |
| Picenum or the March of Ancona | Basilicata **[293D]** |
| The Romagna or Flaminia and Emilia | Apulia |
| Cisalpine Gaul or Lombardy | Salentini or Otranto |
| The Veneto | Calabria |
| Transpadane Gaul or the March of Treviso | Cantazara |

## BIONDO FLAVIO'S *ITALIA ILLUSTRATA*<br>BOOK ONE **[294E]**

I have undertaken a description of Italy, and ought to begin with the praises of this most important of countries. I would do this willingly and happily, as ample material is available, except that eloquent praise has been delivered by the outstanding poet Virgil and after him by Pliny of Verona, and finally by the remarkable poet Francis Petrarch. I think it right, therefore, to begin with the name and location of Italy.

The country has had different names in different times. Pliny and Solinus have written that some writers assert it was first called Italy after King

lingua Italiam dici voluisse scripserunt, cum tamen eam Graeci magnam interea Hesperiam appellarint, quod secutus est in septimo Virgilius Hesperia in magna. Et Servius exponit, Hesperia in magna dixisse Virgilium ad Hispaniae discretionem. Iustinus autem in Trogi epitoma scribit Italiae cultores primos fuisse Aborigenes, quorum rex Saturnus tantae fuerit iustitiae, ut neque serviret quisquam **[294F]** sub illo, neque quicquam privatae rei haberet, sed communia et indivisa fuerint omnia. Unde Italia regis nomine Saturnia fuerit appellata.

Ea vero sicut Plinius ex Octavio Augusto tradit, querno folio adsimilis, mari gemino maxima parte cingitur, quod ab oriente Adriatico sive super, et a meridie occasuque Tyrrheno sive infero abluitur, qua vero in septentrionem vergit, montes altissimi Alpes lingua Gallica a celsitudine dicti, illam a barbarorum, ut inquit Cicero, incursu naturae benignitate communiunt.

Longitudo eius ab Alpino fine Praetoriae Augustae ad Hydruntum decies centena viginti milia extenditur. Latitudo ubi est amplior, a Varo ad Arsiam quingenta, et quadraginta, et circa urbem Romam ab ostiis Aterni, nunc Piscariae in Adriaticum defluentis, ad Tiberina ostia centum et vigintisex milia. Totusque ambitus a Varo ad Arsiam tricies centena et insuper trigintaocto milia complectitur.

Habet Italia dorsum, et ceu in piscibus esse videmus a capite in infimam partem spinae formam, Apenninum, qui mons ex Alpibus qua ab infero mari recedunt oriundus, cum recto propemodum cursu Anconae urbi, ut vult Plinius appropinquavit, in mare superum ferri, **[294G]** et ibi finiri videtur. Et tamen inde rursus ab eo mari recedens per mediam Italiam in Brutios ac Siculum fretum fertur.

Situ mensuraque ostensis ad regionum divisionem locorumque descriptionem veniamus. Est vero perdifficile in tanta mutatione rerum regionumque quantam vident factam, qui Romanas historias attente legunt, modum adinvenire dividendis regionibus, recensendisque ordine civitatum, oppidorum, montium, fluminumque vocabulis. Et quidem quantum attinet ad ipsa vocabula, eximius scriptor Livius Patavinus, Romanae pater historiae, qua in parte nobis superest populorum nominibus utitur, qui nedum ad nostram, sed parva ex parte ad suam pervenerunt aetatem. Quod enim ex Strabonis Cretensis geographia ac ex Plinii Veronensis naturali historia facile est coniicere in Octavii Augusti, cuius temporibus et adiumento scripsit Livius, descriptione Italiae quam fecit accuratissimam, interierunt multa oppida plurimique populi, quorum nomina apud Livium celebrantur. In ea vero descriptione, quam Plinius ipse anno vix octogesimo post functum vita Oc-

Italus, and some think it was named after the many cattle which it produced. But the Greeks called it Magna Hesperia, and Virgil followed this tradition in his seventh book, writing "in great Hesperia." And Servius comments on this, "Virgil said 'in great Hesperia' to distinguish Italy from Spain." But Justin, in his epitome of Trogus, writes that the first inhabitants of Italy were aborigines, and Saturn **[294F]** was their king; his reign was so just that there was no slavery, no private property, but all things were held in common by all. From the name of this king, Italy has been called Saturnia.

Pliny, relying on Augustus, says Italy is shaped like an oak leaf surrounded for most of its extent by two seas, the Adriatic or upper sea on the East and the Tyrrhenian or lower sea on the south and west. But where it turns towards the north, very high mountains, called the Alps in the Gallic tongue on account of their height, as Cicero says, fortify it naturally against invasion.

The length of the country, from the border at Aosta in the Alps to Otranto, is one thousand and twenty miles. Its width, where it is wider, from the Var to the Arsia, is five hundred and forty miles and at the level of the city of Rome from the mouth of the Aternus, now the Pescara, which empties into the Adriatic, to Ostia, is one hundred twenty-six miles.

Italy has a spine, that is, the Apennine range; and we see that these mountains extend like the spine of a fish from the head to the tail. They start from the Alps, where they are set back from the Tyrrhenian Sea, extend almost in a straight line to the city of Ancona, as Pliny **[294G]** says, to the Adriatic Sea and seem to end there. But from there they turn around again from the Adriatic Sea and go through the middle of Italy to Cantazara and the straits of Sicily.

Now that I have described the location and the extent of Italy, I come to its divisions, and to the specific description of its places. It is difficult, however, to divide the regions neatly, and to set in order the cities, mountains, and rivers; because there has been a serious change in the places, as anyone can tell from reading the history of Rome. Livy, so far as we can tell from the few extant books, uses names of peoples which are unfamiliar not only in our times, but were hardly known in his own. As far as that goes, we can easily guess from Strabo's *Geography* and Pliny's *Natural History*, that in the careful description of Italy which Octavian Augustus made (in whose reign and under whose patronage Livy wrote), many towns and even more peoples are extinct and missing, whose names were often mentioned in Livy. But in that description which Pliny himself wrote with great effort

tavium diligenter fecit, maior quam pro [294H] temporum brevitate et florentium tunc Italiae rerum conditione par fuerit, mutatio est facta.

Quae autem ex Strabonis primum, post ex Plinii enumeratione, et Pomponii Melae ac Ptolemaei descriptionibus, haud quaquam multum distantibus inter se aetatibus factis, desint nobis, horrendum infinitumque fuerit referre. Quamquam licet multos interiisse populos, multa excisa oppida, multas deletas urbes non negaverim, plurimas tamen ex ipsis simul cum regionibus, montibus, et fluminibus mutasse nomina constat; quo fit, ut nec prisca legentes intellegant, neque possit novus scriptor illis uti vocabulis, magnam vel eo ipso, quod apud illustres vetustos scriptores frequentia habentur, dignitatem historiae allaturis.

Factam vero esse locorum nominumque mutationem, et simul exinanitatem esse populis et urbibus ac oppidis, quorum nomina nobis desunt, Italiam hinc tenemus, quod post habita urbis Romae populi magnitudinis, cui nihil in orbe umquam fuit estque nunc par, iactura, nulla est huius saeculi et felicium quae stante re publica fuerunt saeculorum comparatio multitudinis populorum.

Picenum enim infra ex Plinio ostendemus trecenta sexaginta milia in rei publicae deditionem dedisse, quod nunc vix decimam partem habet. Plinius etiam laudes Italiae suorum priorumque temporum narrans eam dicit diis sacram L. Aemilio Paulo C. Atilio consulibus nuntiato Gallico tumultu solam sine auxiliis externorum, atque etiam [295A] tunc sine ullis Transpadanis, equitum triginta, peditum octingenta milia armasse. Nostra vero huius temporis Italia, quantum sine Transpadanis externorumque auxiliis equitatum peditatumque armaret, non satis facile est nobis iudicare. Sed non dubitamus, quin difficile sit futurum, si tertiam quis partem conatus fuerit ita armare, ut extra fines quisque suos in bellum expeditionemque ducatur.

Quanta autem sit facta locorum mutatio, hinc etiam apparet, quod Iginius, qui de urbibus Italiae scripsit, et eum secutus Guido presbyter Ravennas, pro[d]idere septingentas fuisse Italiae civitates. Nos vero nunc Romanae ecclesiae stilum secuti, facta per singulas regiones diligenti enumeratione, sexaginta quattuor supra ducentas tantummodo invenimus; sed appellant Romanae ecclesiae instituta civitates loca, quae episcopos habent. Et Iginium videmus ac Guidonem etiam multa ex oppidis quae nostra aetate

scarcely eighty years after the death of Augustus, a greater change has happened than was in proportion to the brief time elapsed, **[294H]** and the flourishing condition of Italy at that time.

It is a dreadful and endless task to relate the names and places which have been lost to us now, but which are in the accounts, first of Strabo, and then of Pliny, and in the description of Pomponius Mela and Ptolemy, who were not many ages apart. Although I do not deny that many peoples have perished, and many towns been razed, many cities destroyed, still it is certain that very many of them, together with regions, mountains, rivers, have changed their names. The result is that neither do modern readers understand their former names, nor can a modern writer use them, if he wishes to confer prestige on his history by using the names famous and common in well-known ancient writers.

But there has been a change in the places and their names and concurrently an exhaustion of Italian populations, cities, and towns; their names are now gone. Leaving aside mention of the loss of the population of the city of Rome, a city which had no equal anywhere in the world and has none today, no comparison can be made today between the present peoples of Italy, and their numbers in the fortunate centuries of the Republic.

For the March of Ancona which, I will show later on, based on Pliny, provided three hundred and sixty thousand men for the army of Rome, now has scarcely a tenth that number in its population. Pliny also, praising the Italy of his own and former times, says that she is sacred to the gods and in the consulship of L. Aemilius Paullus and C. Atilius, upon hearing news of the Gallic invasion, marshalled thirty thousand cavalry and eighty thousand infantry without **[295A]** resorting to aid from other countries or even from the Transpadanes. But it is not easy to hypothesize how many cavalry and infantry Italy could muster in these days without Transpadane and foreign aid; nor do I doubt but that it would be difficult, if anyone tried to raise troops from a third of the country in order to mount a military expedition outside of its borders.

Furthermore, a great change has clearly taken place in the topography of Italy, from the writings of Hyginus about the cities of Italy, and his follower Guido the elder of Ravenna, who assert that Italy had seven hundred cities. But if I follow the language and usage of the Roman church and count carefully the cities in each region, I do not find more than two hundred sixty-four, although the Roman church calls cities only those places which have bishops. I note that Hyginus and Guido name as cities even the many towns

proprio carentia episcopo alterius dioeceseos censentur, pro civitatibus posuisse, et tamen omnium ab ipsis positorum pro civitatibus, quae nunc exstent, numerus vix quadraginta complectitur loca, ut aut excisas esse civitates, **[295B]** aut mutationem omnino incognitam in eis factam esse necessarium videamus. Quam aliis fortasse impossibilem visam tot locorum acceptam in Italia per sexcentos annos, qui post Guidonis tempora fluxerunt cladem, nos ideo minus mirabilem ducimus, quia scimus videmusque per saeculum nostrum, quod Dei nostri munere eorum, quae ante patrum nostrorum aetatem fuerunt, saeculorum respectu, felix appellari potest, supra triginta civitates et oppida solo aequata, ut cum eorum pars paucis nunc habitetur colonis, tum pars omnino manserit derelicta.

Cunium namque oppidum Romandiolae, a quo clarissima fluxit Comitum Cunii et Lugi familia, omnino derelictum ut nunc aretur, videmus. Pariter propinquo in loco contigit Barbiano, pariter in Latio vetustissimae urbi Praenestae, Zagarolo, et Gallicano oppidis. Pariter ad aliam urbis Romae partem Centumcellensi civitati, Morlupo castello nos accidisse conspeximus.

Par etiam affert hac in descriptione incommodum divisionis nominationisque regionum mutatio, ter quaterque in aliquibus, et in quibusdam pluries facta, adeo ut solae Etruriae vetusta cum finibus suis et integra manserit appellatio. Quam ob rem octo et decem regionibus, **[295C]** in quot Italiam sine insulis commode divisam esse iudicavimus, describendis, illa ex multis sequemur vocabula, quae cum in aetate nostra sint notiora, tum nostrae intentioni accommodatiora videbuntur. Suntque nomina: Liguria sive Genuensis, Etruria, Latina sive Campania et maritima, Umbria sive ducatus Spoletanus, Picenum sive Marchia Anconitana, Romandiola sive Flaminia et Aemilia, Gallia cisalpina sive Lombardia, Venetiae, Italia transpadana sive Marchia Tarvisina, Aquileiensis sive Foro Iuliana, Istria, Samnium sive Aprutium, Terra laboris sive Campania vetus, Lucania, Apulia, Salentini sive terra Hydrunti, Calabria, Brutii. Postquam vero omnem Italiam peragratus ero, viros praestantiores, qui singulis in urbibus et locis pridem geniti fuerunt, eosque qui sunt superstites, praesertim litterarum aut cuiuspiam virtutis gloria claros, enumerabo, atque res in singulis locis scribi dignas breviter narrabo, ut non magis haec Italiae sit descriptio quam virorum eius illustrium praestantiusque catalogus, ac non parvae partis historiarum Italiae breviarium.

which, although they lack their own bishops, are counted in our times as belonging to another bishop's diocese. And still the number comes to scarcely forty, of all the places now in existence which they adduce as cities; so that I conclude that cities have been destroyed or that such a change has taken place in them that **[295B]** they are completely unrecognizable. Perhaps others find it impossible that such a disaster has afflicted Italy in the six hundred years since Guido's time; I find it less amazing because I know and have seen in my own generation (which, through a gift of God, can be called happy in comparison with past ages) more than thirty cities and towns ruined and leveled, with the result that they are either completely abandoned, or inhabited by a few peasants.

I see that the Romagnol town of Cunio, the home of the famous counts of Cunio and the family of the Lugi, is completely deserted, to the point that it is now being tilled. The same is true of the neighboring Barbiano; and in Lazio, of the ancient city of Praeneste, and the towns of Zagarolo and Gallicano. On the other side of Rome, the city of Civitavecchia has been abandoned, and Morlupo Castello.

Another difficulty I face in this undertaking is that in the division and naming of the regions, change has taken place in their names, sometimes three and four times, or even more in certain regions, so that only Tuscany preserves the same name as it had in ancient times, and the same borders. For this reason, in describing the eighteen regions into which I have decided **[295C]** Italy is conveniently divided (excluding the islands), I shall use those names (out of the many possibilities) which are more familiar in our times and seem more appropriate to my design. And the names are: Liguria or the Genoese; Tuscany; Latina, or Campania and the Marittima; Umbria or the duchy of Spoleto; Picenum, or the March of Ancona; the Romagna, or Flaminia and Emilia; Cisalpine Gaul or Lombardy; the Veneto; Transpadane Gaul or the March of Treviso; Aquileia or Friuli; Istria; Samnium or Abruzzo; Terra di Lavoro or ancient Campania; Basilicata; Apulia; Salentini or Otranto; Calabria; Cantazara. But after I have traversed all of Italy, I shall recount the extraordinary men who were born in earlier times in the individual cities and places, especially those who are still alive, and especially those who are famous for literature or any excellence. And I shall tell briefly of events worth mentioning in the individual places, so that this will be no more a description of Italy than an enumeration of her distinguished and pre-eminent men and in no small part an epitome of Italian history.

# Regio Prima
# Liguria

Liguria autem Plinium secuti duximus inchoandum. Ea regio latissimos [295D] aliquando habuit terminos, quippe cum Pisas in Liguribus conditas Trogus scripserit, et Apuanos Ligures quos agri Pisani populos esse constat a maioribus traditum viderimus. Quin Massiliam Trogus Pompeius inter Ligures et feras Gallorum gentes positam dicit, cui opinioni concordat Livius libro XLI,

> Fulvius Flaccus primus Transalpinos Ligures domuit bello, missus in auxilium Massiliensium adversus Salvios Gallos, qui fines Massiliensium populabantur.

Et plerique Lucam Liguriae ultimam posuere. Sed haec remotiora omittentes, satis fore tenemus, si divisionem Italiae quae Romana re publica florente fuit nostris temporibus accommodare poterimus. Igitur Liguria a Varo flumine ad Macrae amnis ostia longitudinem habet, et hinc Apennino inde mari infero clauditur; qua ratione pars inferi maris adiacens a Varo ad Macram dicitur Ligusticum pelagus.

Populis eius provinciae Ligures quo tempore, quibusve ducibus Romano populo subiecti fuerint, Iordanus Constantinopolitanus monachus, qui Iustiniani imperatoris temporibus rerum a populo Romano gestarum epitoma confecit et Lucius Florus, T. Livii abbreviator, hisdem ferme verbis sic habent:

> Peracto Punico bello primo nec quantulum respirato sequitur Ligusticum. [296E] Ligures imis Alpium iugis adhaerentes, inter Varum Macramque amnes impliciti dumis silvestribus victitabant, quos paene maius fuit invenire quam vincere. Tuti siquidem locis et fuga durum atque velox genus ex occasione locorum latrocinia magis quam bella factitabant. Itaque cum diu multumque eluder-

# First Region
# Liguria

I thought that I should begin as Pliny does, with Liguria. At one time, **[295D]** this region had far-flung boundaries: Trogus has written that Pisa was founded among the Ligurians, and I have seen it handed down by our ancestors as established fact that the Apuani were Ligurians from the territory of Pisa. And furthermore, Pompeius Trogus says that Massilia (Marseilles) was located between the Ligurians and the savages of Gaul; and Livy agrees with this opinion in book 41, when he says,

> Fulvius Flaccus was the first to conquer the Transalpine Ligurians in war. He was sent to help Massilia against the Salvian Gauls who were laying waste the territory of the Massilians.

And most people identify Lucca as the last city in Liguria. But leaving aside these rather remote areas, I consider it sufficient if I can adapt to our times the division of Italy which was accepted when the Republic flourished. In that case, Liguria's length is measured from the Var river to the mouth of the Magra river. On one side it was bounded by the Apennines, on the other by the Tyrrhenian Sea. For this reason, the part of the Tyrrhenian Sea lying next to the Var at the Magra is called the Ligurian Sea.

At what time, and with what leaders, the people of this province, the Ligurians, were subjected to the Roman people, we are informed by Jordanes the monk of Constantinople, who wrote an epitome of the emperor Justinian's account of the deeds transacted by the Roman people. And Lucius Florus, the epitomator of Livy, gives nearly the same account:

> When the first Punic War was over, the Ligurian war followed after a very short pause. The Ligurians were clinging to the lowest slopes of the Alps between **[296E]** the Var and the Macra rivers, subsisting on thorn-bushes in the forests; they were almost more difficult to find than to conquer. Since this harsh and swift race of men was safe in their hiding-places and in flight, they took advantage of the location to commit robberies rather than to make war.

> rent, Salturi, Deciates, Exubii, Euburiates, Ingauni, tandem Fulvius latebras eorum igni saepsit. Baebius vero in plana deduxit, Postumius ita exarmavit, ut vix linqueret ferrum quo terra colerent.

Quod vero Iordanus summatim attigit Ligures obstinatius iugum Romanorum recusasse, et illis animose adversatos fuisse Livius ipse in libris qui exstant multis ostendit in locis. Nam libro nono,

> Dum haec geruntur consules ambo in Liguribus gerebant bellum. Is hostis velut natus ad continendam per intervalla bellorum Romanis disciplinam militarem erat, nec ulla provincia militem magis ad virtutem acuebat. In Liguribus nam erant quae militem exercerent loca montana et aspera, quae et ipsis capere labor erat, et praeoccupatis hostem deiicere. Hostis levis et velox et repentinus, qui nullum umquam tempus, nullum locum quietum aut securum Romanis sineret. **[296F]** Oppugnatio autem munitorum castellorum laboriosa simul periculosaque insidiis, regio quae si penuria astringeret militi haud multum praedae praeberet. Itaque non lixa sequebatur, non iumentorum longus ordo agmen implebat, nihil praeter arma omnem spem in armis habentibus erat. Nec deerat umquam cum his vel materia belli vel causa, quia propter domesticam inopiam vicinos agros incursabant. Numquam tamen in discrimen summae rerum pugnabant.

Hannibal post inflictam Romanis Trebiensem cladem, traiecto Apennino primum concessit in Ligures, et illi oppositus Sempronius consul Romanus se contulit Lucam. Et videmus apud Livium XXVIII, Magonem Hamilcaris filium capta Genua diu in Liguribus restitisse Romanis, ex qua regione Romanos in Gallia Cisalpina plurimum agitavit, ad quem inter Alpinos Ligures Genuamque agentem naves Carthagine venerunt.

Servius, Virgilium in undecimo exponens "Apenninicolae bellator filius," dicit quia "Liguria maiori sui parte in Apennino sita est. Ligures autem omnes fallaces sunt, sicut Cato in Origines tradit." Virgilius, "Assuetumque malo Ligurem." Et Lucanus in primo: **[296G]**

> And so when the Salturi, Deciates, Exubii, Euburiates, and Ingauni had eluded the Romans for a long time, Fulvius sealed off their hiding-places with fire. But Baebius led his army onto level ground, and Postumius disarmed them so punitively that they had scarcely iron left to till the earth.

Jordanes mentions briefly that the Ligurians rather stubbornly refused Roman domination and courageously opposed them. Livy himself in his surviving books indicates this in many passages. For in his ninth book he writes,

> While these things were going on, both consuls were waging war on the Ligurians. It was as if this enemy had been born to hold together the military discipline of the Romans in the intermissions in their wars. No other province made soldiers readier for courage. For among the Ligurians were rough mountainous places which tested the soldier, which it was troublesome to capture, from which it was troublesome to dislodge the enemy. The enemy was swift, nimble, and attacked suddenly; they left the Romans no idle time, no untroubled or safe place. Moreover, besieging **[296F]** their fortified towns was toilsome and perilous because of their ambushes: the region oppressed them with its poverty and did not offer much in the way of booty. And so an attendant would not follow, nor would a long row of pack animals fill out, the line of battle. Those whose only hope lay in arms had nothing but arms. Nor did these people ever lack the means or cause of war, since poverty at home compelled them to raid the fields of their neighbors. But they never fought to the decisive point.

After Hannibal had slaughtered the Romans at the Trebbia, he crossed the Apennines and came first to the territory of the Ligurians, and the Roman consul Sempronius came to meet him at Lucca. And we see in book 28 that Mago the son of Hamilcar resisted the Romans for a long time among the Ligurians and from that area severely harassed the Romans in Cisalpine Gaul. While he was occupied between the Alpine Ligurians and Genoa, ships came to him from Carthage.

Servius in his commentary on Virgil's eleventh book explains the phrase "the warrior son of the mountain-dweller" by the fact that "Liguria is located for the most part in the Apennines. But Cato says in his *Origines* that all Ligurians are deceitful." Virgil says, "The Ligurian, accustomed to evil." And Lucan in his first book writes, **[296G]**

Et nunc tonse Ligur, quondam per colla decora
Crinibus effusis toti praelate comatae.

Varus prisci praesentisque nominis fluvius capite Alpium et Salvii montis effusus, haud procul a Nicea mari se infundens nulla re notior est, quam quod Bracatam Galliam ab Italia disterminat. Adiacent illi ad dextera oppida, primum Rocheta, post Gilecta; et ad ortum fontemque, Busonium. Nicea inde oppidum a Massiliensibus in litore conditum Alpes dorso contingit; dehinc portus est Herculis Monoeci quondam, nunc Villa Francha. De quo Virgilius in sexto, "Aggeribus sacer Alpinis atque arce Monoeci," et Servius grammaticus exponit, "de Liguria ubi est portus Monoeci Herculis. Dictus autem Monoecus vel quod pulsis omnibus illic solus Hercules habitavit, aut quod in eius templo numquam aliquis deorum simul colitur." Caesar ex Galliis veniens illac descendit in Italiam. Et Lucanus libro primo:

Quaque sub Herculeo sacratus nomine portus,
Urget rupe cava pelagus, non Corus in illum
Ius habet, aut Zephyrus, solus sua litora turbat
Circius, et tuta prohibet statione Monoeci.

Post haec Monicus portus ut Ptolemaeo placet, nunc Monachus Genuensium **[296H]** imperii terminus. Eum sive scopulum sive collem Federicus cui Barbarosso fuit cognomen Caesar Germanicus Genuensi populo moenibus communiendum, anno nunc plus minus sexagesimo supra ducentesimum concessit. Imminet Monacho castellum nunc ignobile sola viarum asperitate notissimum, passuum prope duo milia a mari recedens, Torbia appellatum, quod Iacobus meus Bracellus vir eloquens et doctissimus Trophaea Augusti a priscis appellatum fuisse affirmat, quem quidem tenemus fuisse locum patriae Aelii Pertinacis Romani imperatoris, de quo Iulius Capitolinus sic scribit, "Natus est in Apennino in villa materna. Nam pater eius tabernam cratillariam exercuerat, sed postea quam in Liguria venit."

Sequitur Mentonum ipso in litore, et Rocha Bruna superius, sterilis soli castella; et proxime Albintimilium civitas, nunc Vintimilium, cuius latus qua in orientem vergit solem Rutuba abluit fluvius nunc Rodoria appellatus. Proximo deinceps ad mille passuum loco collis attollitur cui Appio est nomen, et inde arx est ex qua primum nascentis Apennini iugum haud procul remotum cernitur. Abest a Rutuba fluvio passuum decem milia Sancti Ro-

> And now you, shorn Ligurian, formerly your hair was spread
> Becomingly over your neck. . . .

The Var river, for that is its former as well as present name, spreads out from its source in the Alps and Monte S. Salvatore. It flows out not far from the sea of Nice, and is most famous for separating Gallia Narbonensis from Italy. Beside the river lie towns on the right, first Rocchetta, then Giglietta, and at the river's source, Busonio. Then the town of Nice, founded by the inhabitants of Marseilles and built on the shore, borders on a ridge of the Alps. From here the next place is the harbor formerly called Hercules Monoecus, now Villafranca. About this place, Virgil says in his sixth book, "The father-in-law from the ramparts of the Alps and the citadel of Monaco," and Servius explains, "This is in Liguria, where the harbor of Hercules Monoecus is. It is called Monoecus either because Hercules lived there alone after all the people had been driven out, or because in his temple no other gods were ever worshipped at the same time." It is there that Caesar, returning from Gaul, descended into Italy. And Lucan in his first book has,

> where, under the name of Hercules, the sea presses upon the hollow rock; the north-west wind does not dominate that place, nor the west wind, but only Circius disturbs those shores and keeps safe the harbor of Monoecus.

After these places comes the harbor of Monicus, as Ptolemy calls it, now Monaco, **[296H]** the boundary of the dominion of Genoa. More or less two hundred and sixty years ago the German Emperor Frederick, called Barbarossa, handed over this place, either a cliff or a hill, to the people of Genoa for fortifying with walls. About two miles distant from the sea, a fortified town called Torbia hangs over Monaco, now notorious for the lonely harshness of its roads. My friend Jacopo Bracelli, an eloquent and very learned man, asserts that it was formerly called Trophaea Augusti. Indeed, I contend that it was the birthplace of the Roman emperor Aelius Pertinax, about whom Julius Capitolinus writes, "He was born in his mother's farmhouse. For his father had worked in an inn; but afterwards he came to Liguria."

There follows Mentono, right on the shore, and higher up Rocca Bruna, a fortified town with barren soil, and next the city of Abintimilium, now called Ventimiglia, past whose eastern side the Rova river flows, now called the Roia. Next, about a mile away, rises a hill called Castel Appio, and then there is a citadel from which you can first see, not far off, the beginnings of the Apennine ridge. The fortified town of San Romulo is ten miles from the

muli castellum, cuius ager citri est palmaeque arborum in Italia rarissimarum ferax, unde Romanos pontifices vidimus palmarum ramos in dominica quadragesimalis ieiunii postrema inde appellata **[297A]** benedicendos et populo dandos habere.

Emensus inde passuum quinque milia castellum attingit exiguum duos mille passus mari propinquum, quod Tabia nomen habet a vinorum fama celeberrimum, quippe cum ea muscatum appellata, nec Cypriis, nec Creticis, nec Falernis cedere a bonis potoribus existimentur. Decem ab eo passuum milia ad Mauritium numerantur portum nomine verius, quam re; sed indicta ibi iurisdictio celebrem locum reddit. Sequitur Unelia vallis aliquot habitata vicis; mox oppidum Dianae, nunc Dianum duo prope milia a mari recedens, olea vitique undique consitum.

Post haec ipso in litore Cervum, et ipso in edito colle Andoria vitiferis collibus circumdatum. Andorianos fines parvi admodum vici excipiunt; hos Album Ingaunum urbs opibus ac vetustate nobilis nunc Albinga proculo imperatore Romano alumno et cive ornata, de quo Flavius Eutropius sic scribit, "Proculo patria Albingaunum in Alpibus maritimis, domi fuit nobilis, sed maioribus latrocinantibus." Albingae abluit latus Merula fluvius Centa appellatus quod centenis torrentibus augeatur. Hanc civitatem campestri loco vix passus quingentos a **[297B]** mari recedentem, cum validissimi exercitus Philippi Mediolanensium tertii ducis praefecto copiis omnibus Berardino Ubaldino viro fortissimo arcta obsidione cinxissent, quattuor oppugnatam mensibus omnia quae bello inferuntur mala perpeti coegerunt, et tandem constantia et fortitudine populi fatigatus hostis, re infecta obsidionem solvit.

Proximum in litore est Petra castellum, deinde ad duos mille passuum aberat Finarium oppidum ab aeris, ut vulgare sonat verbum, salubritate appellatum, quod vallis in cuius faucibus erat situm angustias claudebat. Sed Fregosi et populus Genuensis ut Charrectenses inimicos inde nobiles eiicerent, oppidum quoque proximo anno sustulerunt. Est proximo in litore Naulium civitas portu ac turribus incluta, est et vadorum Sabbatiorum portus, a quo septem milibus distat Savona urbs, multorum populorum commercio nobilis, quam Titus Livius Magonis adventum referens Savonam nominavit sicut nostra facit aetas, et tamen Plinius Sabbatium, Pompeius Mela Sabbatiam appellavit. Eam nunc possidet qui et Genuensium ducatui summa cum laude bis praefuit vir ingenti virtute, et quod aetas nostra rarum litteris ornatus Thomas Fregosus, **[297C]** multa cuius belli et pacis temporibus praeclare gesta in historiis scripsimus.

Rova river. Its land is fertile enough for citrus trees and palms, very rare in Italy. From here come the palm branches with which we see the Popes on the Sunday after Lent blessing the people [297A] and giving to them.

If you go on for five miles, you come to a small fortified town two miles from the sea, named Taggia from the great reputation of its wine, called *muscatum*, which is considered as good as or better than Cyprian, Cretan, or Falernian. Then it is ten miles to Maurizio, a harbor more in name than in actual fact, but the administration of justice there makes the place famous. There follows the Oneglia valley, which once contained villages. Soon you reach the town of Diana, now Diano, nearly two miles from the sea, and planted everywhere with olive trees and vineyards.

After these places, right on the coast is Cervo, and on a high hill is Andora, surrounded by vineyard-covered hills. The territory of Andora is still occupied by small villages. Albium Ingaunum, a city noble in wealth and history, now named Albenga, counts the Roman emperor Proculus as its child and famous citizen. Flavius Eutropius wrote about him, "Albingaunum, in the maritime Alps, was the home of Proculus. He was noble at home, but had pirates for ancestors." The Arroscia river washes Albenga's flanks; it is also called the Centa because it receives a hundred tributary streams. When the mighty armies of Filippo Maria Visconti, [297B] the third Duke of Milan, under the command of the very brave Berardino Ubaldino, had besieged and surrounded this city on a level plain scarcely five miles from the sea, it was for four months forced to suffer all the evils which war inflicts. And finally the enemy were worn down by the perseverance and courage of its people, and lifted the siege, leaving the mission incomplete.

Next, on the shore, is the fortified town of Pietra Ligure. Then, two miles away, is the town of Finale, named in the vernacular for its healthy air. The valley in whose gorge it was built surrounded a defile. But the Fregosi and the Genoans threw out the nobles from there on the grounds that they were Carrettesi and thus their enemies. In the next year they also destroyed the town. The next city on the shoreline is Noli, famed for its harbor and towers. And there is also the harbor of Vado Ligure, seven miles from the city of Savona, a renowned city busy with the trade of many peoples. Livy, narrating Mago's arrival, called this city Savona, as it is called in our times; but Pliny called it Sabbatium, and Pomponius Mela, Sabbatia. Tomaso Fregoso now rules it, who was twice the glorious doge of the Genoans, a man of enormous courage [297C] and, what is rare among princes of our age, dis-

Albissolam Cellasque vicos ignobiles in litore cernimus. Deinde Viraginem oppidum, quod quidem vicum Virginis dixere. Succedit Vultus vicus, quem Cherusa torrens interfluit. Portifera dehinc ut maior ita violentior amnis, qui valli nomen dedit, aedificiorum pulchritudine superbiaque potius solo alioquin sterili amoenissimae; portusque succedit Genuae insignis, quam mole ingenti obiecta fluctibus, ostia in Africam versa pandit. Urbs Genua quos et quo tempore habuerit conditores, incertum nobis est. Non nos satis probamus, quam de Phaethonte et eius socio Genuo Bracellius noster non improbat fabulam, nullius certioris scriptoris auctoritati nixam; et insulse fictas de Iano ineptias improbamus. Videmus vero ante belli Punici tempora, nullam alicubi eius urbis haberi mentionem, et Iordanum Florumque dum superius subactos Liguriae populos Salturios, Deciates, Euburiates, Ingaunos enumerant, Genuam si condita tunc aut nota fuisset, non omissuros fuisse crediderim.

Primam vero eius mentionem facit Livius **[297D]** libro vigesimo primo, ubi P. Scipionem dicit cum admodum exiguis copiis Genuam repetiisse eo qui circa Padum exercitu Italiam defensurum. Primum autem incrementum habuisse videtur, de quo Livius libro XXIX sic dicit, "Lucretio prorogatum imperium ut Genua oppidum a Magone Poeno destructum exaedificaret."

Post quae tempora Romani Liguribus Genuensibusque amicioribus usi fuerunt, et tamen multitudinem considerans coloniarum quas Romani per omnia paene Italiae loca deduxerunt, mirari soleo nec Genuam nec alium quempiam in Ligustinis locum pro colonia captum fuisse; quod a situs sterilitate, quam milites horruerint, crediderim processisse.

Post belli vero Punici secundi finem, Romanus populus Gallis Insubribus et Alpinis ceterisque Galliae Cisalpinae populis et inde Illyriis subigendis arma convertit, ad quae bella cum magnae copiae variaque bello usui futura mitterentur, maxime opportuna fuisse videt Genua loci natura tunc etiam portuosa, ex qua Commodus in Mediolanenses Papiensesque, sicut nunc est, transitus etiam tunc erat. Nihil autem aeque augendis opibus conducere ac frequentiam commeantium, et quibus in locis opum quaerendarum facultas adsit maxime populos coalescere constat. Nec tamen in mille annis,

tinguished in literary knowledge. I have written much in my *Decades* about his remarkable deeds in war and in peace.

We see on the shore the humble towns of Albisola and Celle Ligure; then the town of Varazze, which some have called Vicus Verginis. There follows the town of Voltri, through which the Cerusa river flows. From here you come to the Portifera river, which flows more violently the more its size increases. It gives its name to a valley, very pleasant in the beauty and magnificence of its buildings, but of otherwise sterile soil. The harbor of distinguished Genoa comes next; its mouth, blocked by a huge breakwater, faces Africa. I am not sure who the founders of Genoa were, nor when it was founded. I do not accept the story about Phaethon and his friend Genuus, although my friend Bracelli does not reject it. It is not supported by the authority of any more dependable writer. I also reject the absurd and silly fictions about Janus. But I find no mention of this city anywhere, before the Punic War; and Jordanes and Florus, while they list as people of Liguria subdued earlier the Deciates, Buriates, and Ingauni, I cannot believe would pass over Genoa, if it had been founded by then or was then known.

The first mention of Genoa is in Livy, **[297D]** book 21, where P. Scipio is said to have returned to Genoa with quite a small number of troops, intending to defend Italy with his army around the Po Valley. But it seems to have enjoyed its first growth, as Livy says in book 29, when "Lucretius' command was extended so that he might build up the town of Genoa which had been destroyed by the Carthaginian Mago."

After these times, the Romans found the Ligurians and the Genoese friendlier. But considering the large number of colonies which the Romans founded in almost every part of Italy, I always marvel that they did not capture Genoa or any other place in Liguria and make a colony of it. I should think that the veterans shrank from moving there because of the poorness of the region's soil.

After the second Punic War had ended, the Roman people directed their military might towards subduing the Insubrian Gauls, the Alpine Gauls, and the rest of the peoples of Cisalpine Gaul, and then the Illyrians. Even at that time Genoa abounded in port facilities, and so the Romans realized that, as they would be sending large armies and various war materials, Genoa would be very convenient. From there, in our times, Commodus crossed over to fight the Milanese and the Pavese. But nothing conduces to the increase of wealth as much as frequent intercourse among peoples, and it is established that populations come together especially in places where there is op-

qui bellum id secundum Punicum sunt secuti, caput multum attollere potuit Genua.

Quam anno a Lucretii instauratione plus minus septingentesimo, ad annum videlicet [298E] salutis Christianae sexcentesimum atque sexagesimum, Rotharis Longobardorum rex Romanis quorum imperio semper antea fuerat subiecta, abstulerit. Eam tamen a fera Longobardorum gente parum humane gubernatam, Carolus Magnus imperator Pipinusque filius rex Italiae et successores Franci reges per annos circiter centum, summa cum iustitia et humanitate sicut et ceteras Italiae, urbes gubernarunt, ducibus illi administrandae, qui comites appellarentur praefectis, quorum Ademarchus Corsicam a Mauris oppressam liberavit, quo ab eisdem Mauris postea interfecto, Corsica nihilominus per Genuenses recepta et naves Maurorum XIII captae ac demersae sunt. Berengario autem tertio in Italiam unde pulsus fuerat reverso, imperii nomen suis titulis foedante, et Ugone Arelatense Italiae regni nomine abutente, cum pessime apud omnes nostros ageretur, Saraceni Poenis sibi subiectis immixti, anno Christi nongentesimo et trigesimoquinto Stephani septimi pontificis Romani temporibus Genuam ceperunt spoliaruntque, et quod raro alibi est auditum, omnibus mortalibus qui caedi superfuerant populariter [298F] asportatis, muros urbis omni humano habitatore vacuos reliquerunt. Scribit tamen Andreas Dandulus Venetiarum dux Francisci Petrarchae amicitia clarus, impuberes omnes brevi Genuam fuisse reductos. Estque eius testimonium eo locupletius, quod Veneti Genuensesque magna semper aemulatione contendere soliti, per Danduli ducatus tempora gravi ac periculosissimo utrisque bello conflictati sunt.

A quadringentis vero annis maximum Genua habuit incrementum, quae vires nacta ingentes terra sed mari longe maiores Liguriae cui imperat nomen obscuravit, ut quae pars in Varum amnem exposita occidentem spectat solem Riperia occidentalis, quae ad Macram pertinens in orientem est versa dicatur Riperia Genuae orientalis. Et insuper Corsicam, Cyprum, Asiam, Thraciam, Scythiam deductis coloniis ac suis victoriis illustravit, et negotio quam otio felicior nunc illis terrori est, quorum insidiis prius et crudelitate bis concidit.

Ornata fuit Genua duobus ex gente nobili Fischa pontificibus Romanis, quarto Innocentio, et quinto Hadriano. habuitque eadem familia ad triginta Romanae ecclesiae cardinales, quorum unicus superest Georgius Praenestinus episcopus. Dux Genuae nunc [298G] est Ludovicus Fregosius ingenti

portunity for acquiring wealth. Still, in the thousand years which followed the second Punic War Genoa could not hold its head up very high.

About seven hundred years after the renewal of Lucretius' command, in A.D. 660, **[298E]** Rothari king of the Lombards took the city of Genoa away from the Romans, to whom it had always been subject. But the emperor Charlemagne and his son Pepin, king of Italy, and other kings of the Franks governed it for about one hundred years humanely and with great justice, unlike the savage Lombards. And just as they governed the other cities of Italy, they administered Genoa through the agency of leaders whom they put in charge of it and called counts. One of them was Ademarchus, who freed Corsica from the oppression of the Moors. Afterwards, he was killed by the Moors, but the Genoans took Corsica again and captured or sank fourteen Moorish ships. Moreover, when Berengar the third had returned to Italy after his expulsion, and defiled the name of empire with his bad reputation; and Hugh of Arles was abusing the name of the kingdom of Italy; when our affairs were at their lowest ebb, in the year A.D. 935, in the times of Pope Stephen VII, the Arabs along with their subjects the Moors took Genoa and laid waste to it. Something happened that is almost unheard of: all the **[298F]** people who had survived the slaughter were taken away, so that the walls of the city were left empty of any human inhabitant. But Andrea Dandolo, the doge of Venice famed for his friendship with Francis Petrarch, writes that all the youth of Genoa were brought back in a short time. His testimony is all the more credible because the Venetians and Genoans were always accustomed to compete jealously, and under Dandolo's leadership they fought a serious war dangerous to both sides.

Four hundred years ago Genoa had its greatest period of growth: it acquired enormous strength on land, but its power on the sea was far greater and it ruled Liguria and eclipsed its name. The result is that the part of Liguria which lies facing the west towards the Var river is called the Riviera of western Genoa, while the part facing the east towards the Magra river is called the Riviera of eastern Genoa. And in addition Genoa has made famous Corsica, Cyprus, Asia, Thrace, and Scythia by winning victories and planting colonies there. Genoa now enjoys more activity than leisure, as she terrorizes those through whose treachery and cruelty she fell twice before.

She has been honored as birthplace of two men of the noble family of the Fieschi: Popes Innocent IV, and Hadrian V. And the same family produced about thirty cardinals; the only one who survives is Bishop Giorgio of Praeneste. The present doge of Genoa is **[298G]** Lodovico Fregoso, a man of

praeditus humanitate, dignusque genitrice clarissima muliere Catharinae, quem ex Forliviensi Ordelaffa gente praeclara, alterum quoque genuit celebris famae Ianum Fregosium, cuius ingens spes morte nuper nobis abrepta est. Ornatur vero nunc civibus navigatione ac mercatura toto orbe notissimis, sed paucos habet egregie litteratos, quorum notiores nobis sunt Nicolaus Ceba, et noster item Iacobus Bracellus ac Gottardus principis scriba.

Genuae latus orientale Feritor amnis praeterfluit, quem nunc Bisamnem appellant. Neque tamen vetusti nominis usquequaque facta videtur oblivio, namque illum paulo supra influens minor fluvius Ferisanus dicitur. Profectus a Bisamne Nervium, Buliascum, Saulium tenues vicos, et paulopost illis maiorem Rechum inde Camulium invenit. Sunt vero quattuor et viginti milia ab amne Cherusa superius dicto ad Camulium, quae tota regio non modo mari in planitie exposita, sed quantum pertinentes ad eam valles ac colles longius extenduntur, magnifici et sumptuosi operis aedibus decoratur, ut qui alto navigantes pelago eam petunt terram, **[298H]** unam se urbem prospicere opinentur, a Camulio sinuari promontorium incipit, quod S. Fructuoso sacrum est, cuius templum in intimo recessit positum magna veneratione a vicinis populis frequentatur. Id illi promontorium Caput Montis appellant, quod arduum et saxosum in mare procurrens sinistroque latere irrumpentes aquas angustis faucibus admittens, Delphini portum efficit, quem incolae dempta prima syllaba quasi potius a bonitate quam a Delphine nominandus sit, Portum Finum appellant.

Sequitur alius a oriente sinus, quem Rapalli nominant; id convalli nomen est, quae ut inter montosas haud sterilis citrique et oleae plurimum ferax, vicum eiusdem nominis haudquaquam obscurum in litore habet. Quinque milibus abest Clavarum, novi nominis oppidum. Quippe quod ante centum et quinquaginta annos nondum moenibus cinctum erat, in eoque nunc maritimis et montanis populis fori et iurisdictionis conventus habentur. Proxime Entella fluvius mare illabitur, quem aliquando Laboniam dictum, nunc Lavaniam appellant. Habetque ad dexteram oppida: Riparosam, Mulinum, et ad fontem Rochataiam. Is Graveia, Olo, Sturla torrentibus auctus, ad dexteram orae maritimae ripam Lavanium vicum habet, a quo originem traxit Fiscorum prosapia Lavaniae comitum dicta in Italia nobilissima, quae **[299A]** pontificibus illis Romanis et cardinalibus ornata fuit. Et Sturlae Prosonasium, Graveiae vero ad sinistram adiacent Vignolum, Garibaldum, Frelium, et ad fontem Rupsa.

great humanity worthy of his very famous mother Caterina, from the renowned family of the Ordelaffi from Forlì; she also bore the famous Giano Fregoso whose great promise death recently snatched from us. But now Genoa is distinguished by her citizens who are renowned throughout the entire world for sailing and commerce. She has, however, few outstanding literary men: those best known to us are Niccolò Cebà and our friend Giacomo Bracelli and Gottardo, the duke's secretary.

The eastern side of Genoa is bounded by a river once called the Feritor, which is now called Bisagno. But the river's ancient name has not been everywhere forgotten, for a smaller river a little above it is called Ferisano. Going on from the Bisagno we find the small towns Nervi, Bogliasco, and Sori, and a little farther on the greater town of Recco, and then Camogli. It is twenty-four miles from the Cerusa river, which I mentioned previously, to Camogli. The entire region not only lies on a plain, but is graced by magnificent and opulent houses in the valleys and hills which extend beyond it; so that sailors far out to sea making for that part **[298H]** of the land think they are sighting one city. A curving promontory begins at Camogli. It is sacred to S. Fructuoso, whose temple is in a deep recess and is visited and revered by the surrounding peoples. They call that promontory Mountain's Head (Promontorio di Portofino); steep and rocky, it juts into the sea and on its left side the water rushes in through a narrow strait and forms the harbor of Delfino. The inhabitants call it Portofino, leaving off the first syllable as if it were named for its excellence rather than for the dolphin.

Another bay adjoins it on the east, called Golfo di Rapallo. This is the name of the valley which, located between mountainous regions fertile especially in lemon and olive trees, has a town of the same name on the shore. Five miles from here is the town called Chiavari, a new name; a hundred and fifty years ago, its walls were not yet built. Now, the people of the seacoast and mountains gather there for markets and the administration of justice. Nearby the river Entella flows into the sea. Formerly it was called the Labonia; now it is called the Lavagna. On its right side are the towns of Rivarola and Molino di Cichero and, at its source, Rocchetta. Into it flow the streams Graveglia, Glofa, and Sturla; and on the right bank on the side near the sea is the village of Lavagna. From there comes the noble family of the Fieschi, who **[299A]** were called the counts of Lavagna, distinguished in the past by popes and cardinals. Next to the Sturla lies Nascio (?); next to the Graveglia but on the left lie Vignolo, Garibaldo, Reghei, and, at its source, Rospo.

Ab ostio Entellae quattuor milibus abest Sigestrum vicus in litore, apud quem Sigestam Tiguliorum a Ptolemaeo et Plinio appellatam fuisse crediderim, cui obiicit se insula tenui admodum rivulo a continente divisa. Ea praeruptis montibus quasi muro cincta, incolas ab omni maritima terrestrique incursione tutos reddit, gemino portu dextra laevaque accessibilis, quamquam qui ad orientem vergit solem tutior veriorque portus est. Huic contermina sunt Monilia, quos colles duos vitiferos Moneliam nunc appellant. Superius oppida sunt Banchalesium, Matuscum, Matalana; Monilianos fines contingit Framula, quam ob saxosos asperosque colles Ferramulam accolae hinc putant dictam esse, quasi diligenter eo loci soleandas esse mulas viatores admoneantur.

Paululum inde abest Levantum nobile municipium magis quam vetustum amoenis vallibus collibusque conspicuum, ad cuius oram quinque sunt castella paribus prope intervallis inter se distantia: Mons Ruber, Vulnetia vulgo Vernatia appellata, Manarola, Rivus Maior, [299B] quae loca non in Italia magis quam in Galliis Britanniaque sive Anglia a vini odoratissimi suavissimique excellentia sunt celebria, res profecto memoratu et spectaculo digna videre montes adeo sublimes praecipitesque uti aves volando fatigent, quibus omnino saxosis et nihil umoris retinentibus, vitium palmites tam pretiosae feraces vindemiae haud secus quam hedera muris passim haereant. Eas autem vineas et alias per Liguriam aetate Plinii non fuisse hinc videmus, quod cum ille edocendis vinis optimis quae ubique habeat Italia diligens sit ac prope nimius, nullum in Liguria ponit, nisi forte haec sint vina Lunensia, quae ipse Plinius plurimum laudat.

Rivum quem Maiorem appellant inde transgressos vetustae olim et nobilissimae urbis Lunae portus excipit, a scriptoribus quidem, sed minus quam deceat, celebratus. Quantum autem ex paucis quae exstant de eo scriptis, coniicere potuimus, maximi quaestus commercium in ipso portu fuit. Unde Persius satiricus avaritiam et nimiam ad rem pecuniariam populi Romani attentionem redarguere intendens, sic ironice scribit: "Lunai portum, operae est, cognoscite [299C] cives."

Insulam, quae illum ab Austro Africoque tutum reddat, natura obiecti, secus quam vastae se pandunt fauces, multis reflexibus tortuosae, in longum amplumque sinum, qui passuum quinque milia longitudine ac latitudine protenditur, navigia admittentes. Portusque ipse omnium capacissimus navigiorum Macra augetur, quod Lucanus in secundo sic indicat,

Four miles from the mouth of the Entella, on the coast, is the village of Sestri Levante, and I believe this is called by Ptolemy and Pliny Segesta Tigulliorum. Facing it is an island separated from the mainland by a small stream. It is walled in by rugged mountains, and this keeps the inhabitants safe from any attack by sea or by land. Its double harbor makes it accessible from the right and from the left, but that to the east is the safer and true harbor. It has as a border the two vine-producing hills formerly called Monilia, now named Moneglia. Above these hills are the towns of Bancalese, Massiana, Mattarana; and bordering on the Moneglia hills is Framura. On account of its rocky and rugged hills the local people think Framura used to be called Ferramula, on the grounds that travellers were reminded to be careful to put shoes on their mules before traveling that way.

A little farther on from there is the noble town of Levanto, not very ancient, but remarkable for its pleasant valleys and hills. Five *castelli* almost equidistant from each other guard its perimeter: Monterosso, Vulnetia (commonly called Vernazza), Manarola, and **[299B]** Riomaggiore. These places are as famous in Gaul and Britain (also called England) as they are in Italy because of the excellence of their very fragrant and pleasant wines. Something indeed worthy to see and remember is the sight of the mountains, so high and steep that birds are tired out by flying over them; they are rocky, and retain no moisture, and the fruitful vine shoots stick to them here and there as ivy clings to walls. But we can tell that these vineyards and others in Liguria did not exist in Pliny's time because he is almost overly scrupulous about telling where in Italy the best wines are produced, and yet mentions none from Liguria; unless perhaps the "Lunensian" wines, which he praises highly, are from Luna.

After you pass Riomaggiore, as it is called, you come to the harbor of the ancient and formerly distinguished city of Luna, famous in literature, but less famous than it deserves. From the few extant written sources, I was able to guess that this harbor attracted very profitable commerce; for example, the satirist Persius, trying to show up as shallow and false the Romans' greed and obsession with money, wrote ironically, "It is worth your while, O citizens, to **[299C]** know the port of Luna."

The harbor is naturally protected from the south and south-west by an island. Otherwise its entrance lies open, and ships enter by a twisting inlet, five miles long and wide. The river Magra flows into the harbor, which is itself large enough for vessels of any size, as Lucan indicates in the following way in his second book:

Nullosque vado qui Macra moratur
Alvos, vicinae prorumpit in aequora Lunae.

Supremo in eius insulae fastigio Veneris olim templum, Christianis postea temporibus sancto Venerio consecratum, portui Veneris nomen dedit. Qua vero promontorium sive insula occidentem spectat solem, oppidum est Portus Veneris pariter appellatum Genuensis populi Colonia, et finium quondam terminus, et e regione Ilex est castellum vel ex hoc celebrius, quod sicut illud Genuensium, ita hoc Pisanorum agri fines terminare consuevit.

In sinuque Lunensis sive Veneris portus intimo Spedia est novum oppidum circa annos LX muro circumdatum, secus quam inspecta Italiae descriptione ac pictura a maioribus facta Tiguliam fuisse coniector. **[299D]** Idque oppidum Bartholomaeo Facio viro doctissimum est ornatum. Lunensis portus ab ea orientali parte promontorio clauditur nunc Lunensi appellato, quod praeterlabitur Macra fluvius amoenus piscosusque, et quia Liguria ab Etruria dividat notissimus. Adiacent Macrae amni ad sinistram Vetianum, Arbianum, Podentianum, Richum, Luciolum, et Mulatium. Ex quo marchionum eius cognominis familia nobilis fluxit.

Eius Ligusticae orae quam descripsimus a Varo ad Macrae ostia longitudinem olim undecim supra ducenta milia fuisse veteres prodidere, quam nostri vix centum octoginta milibus computant. Pelagusque adiacens quod Ligusticum appellari diximus tres habet insulas, scopulis tamen quam insulis similiores; unam Albingauno oppositam, quae trepidis navibus saepenumero tutelae fuit; aliam Naulo, tertiam Lunensis portus promontorio occidentali propinquam, ut continens videatur.

> The Macra delays no alder-wood ships in its shallows,
> And bursts forth into the sea at neighboring Luna.

On the heights of this island there was formerly a temple of Venus, which afterwards in Christian times became consecrated to St. Venerius, and gave the name to the harbor, Porto Venere. Looking to the west from the promontory or the island, you see the town of Porto Venere, also called Colonia by the people of Genoa. It was formerly the end point of the territory. And on the other side from this place on the Gulf, there is a fortified town, Lerici, somewhat famous because it was the customary boundary between the territory of Genoa and that of Pisa.

At the innermost point of the bay of Luna is the new town of La Spezia, whose walls were built about sixty years ago. I guess that Tigullio was near it, judging from a description and map of Italy made by our ancestors. This town **[299D]** is distinguished by Bartolomeo Facio, a most learned man. The harbor of Luna is enclosed on the east by a promontory which is now called Lunensis. Past it flows the river Magra, pleasant and full of fish. It is well-known as the dividing-line between Liguria and Etruria. Next to the Magra river, on the left, lie Vezzano, Albiano, Podenzano, Ricco, Lusuolo, and Mulazzo, home of the noble family of the Marquises of Mulazzo.

The ancient sources tell us that the length of the Ligurian coast which I have described, from the Var to the mouth of the Magra, was formerly two hundred and eleven miles; my generation measures it at scarcely one hundred and eighty miles. The Ligurian Sea which lies nearby has three islands, more like cliffs than islands. One of them is opposite Albenga and has many times protected endangered ships; the second is opposite Noli; the third island is next to the western promontory of the harbor of Luna, so close that it seems to be dry land.

# Regio Sexta
# Romandiola sive Flaminia [342E]

Sed iam finis adest Piceni seu Marchiae Anconitanae deinceps Flaminiam sive Romandiolam adeamus. Flaminiae quantum ad hanc spectat regionem vocabulum ante finitum secundum bellum Punicum nusquam reperitur. Nam Flaminium vetus oppidum iuxta Tiberim et Soracte montem fuit, de quo Virgilius in VII, "Hi Soractis habent arces Flaminiaque arva," et Flaminia dicta est via quam Octavius Augustus ab urbe Roma vel potius a circo Flaminio, sicut in Roma instaurata docuimus, Ariminum usque stravit.

Per totum vero secundum bellum Punicum, sicut et belli primi Punici temporibus factum erat, hanc regionem Livius Patavinus quantum ad Romanos spectabat solo Arimini verbo appellat. Nam libro XXIIII sic dicit, "Praetori Sempronio provincia Ariminum" obvenit, cum reliqua omnia Padum versus Apenninum et Alpes partim Boios partim Galliam diceret [342F] Cisalpinam. Pariter dicimus de Aemilia quae et ipsa in Romandiola est comprehensa. Livius autem libro XXXVIII scribit M. Aemilium cos. Liguribus subactis viam a Placentia productam Flaminiae coniunxisse, ut certum sit viam a foro Cornelii usque Placentiam inde Aemiliam appellatam. Et infra innuit Livius,

> Quintum Flaminium fratrem, qui ut meretrici Placentinae placeret, Gallum securi percussit, quando Bacchanalia Romae sublata sunt, viam stravisse quam Flaminiam appellarit.

Habuerintque fines Flaminia ab Isauro ad Vatrenum fori Cornelii nunc Imolae amnem, et Aemilia inde ad Trebiam Placentiae urbis fluvium, quam longitudinem et nunc habet Ravennatis ecclesiae exarchatus, provincia cuius tota id Romandiolae nomen olim obtinuit, quod quidem nomen ostendimus in Historiis Carolum Magnum et primum Adrianum pontificem Romanum post oppressos dominioque privatos Longobardos ea maxime ex

# Sixth Region,
# Romandiola or Flaminia [342E]

Now that we have come to the end of Picenum or the March of Ancona, let us go to Flaminia or Romandiola. As far as the name Flaminia is concerned, we do not find it anywhere before the end of the second Punic War. There was an old town Flaminium, between the Tiber and Mt. Soracte, which Virgil mentions in his seventh book: "Here are the citadels of Soracte and the fields of Flaminia." And the road is called "Flaminian" which, as I have shown in *Roma instaurata*, Octavian Augustus built to Ariminum from the city of Rome, or rather from the Circus Flaminius.

Indeed, through his entire account of the second Punic War, as also in the time of the first Punic War, Livy of Padua calls by the name Ariminum the part of this region that looks towards the Romans. For example, in book 24 he says "the province of Ariminum" fell to the lot of "the praetor Sempronius," although he calls all the remaining places in the direction of the Po river, the Apennines, and the Alps part "Boii" and part "Hither Gaul." In the same way we speak of Emilia as the land included in Romandiola [342F] itself. But Livy in book 38 writes that after he had defeated the Ligurians, the consul M. Aemilius built a road from Placentia to Flaminia; from this it is certain that the road from Forum Cornelii to Placentia was called "Aemilia" after him. And further on Livy mentions

> . . . his brother Quintus Flaminius, who in order to please his mistress who was from Placentia struck a Gaul with an axe. When the Bacchanalia were forbidden at Rome, he built a road which he called "Flaminian."

The territory of Flaminia has as its boundaries: from the Foglia river, to the Santerno river at Forum Cornelii (now called Imola), and in Emilia from there to the Trebbia river at the city of Piacenza. The exarchate of the church of Ravenna even now has this extent. All of this province formerly had the name Romandiola. I have shown in my *Decades* that, after the Lombards had been suppressed and deprived of their power, Charlemagne and before him Pope Hadrian gave this name to the area for the main reason that

causa indidisse. Quodam toto Longobardorum tempore Ravenna cum propinquis aliquot civitatibus et oppidis Romano populo fidem constantissime servavit. Sed nos consuetudini adhaerentes iam inveteratae fines Romandiolae intra Isaurum sive Foliam et Scultennam sive Panatium [342G] amnes Apenninumque montem, ac mare Adriaticum, Padusamque paludem citra Padum, et ultra illum quicquid ager Ferrariensis ad Veronensium Patavinorumque paludes et ultima usque Padi ostia Fornaces appellata mare inter Adriaticum et Padum habet, constituemus.

Ad dexteram Isauri amnis ripam primum habet Romandiola oppidum Poccium, post Montem Lurum. Inter Isaurum et proximum torrentem Crustumium, de quo Lucanus "Crustumiumque rapax," sive ut nunc appellant Concham, Focaria est promontorium quattuor habitatum oppidis: Granariolo, Castro Medio, Gabitiis, Florentiola, et vinetis et olivetis egregie consitum. Superiusque sunt oppida Tumba, Planum Montis, Mons Calvus, Pes Campi, Saxum Corbarium, et Macerata Montis Feretri. Sub Focaria Ariminum versus Catholica vicus ad quem absorptum mari oppidum Concham eminentes aquis muri turresque per aequoris tranquillitatem ostendunt.

Interius est Gradaria Sigismundi Pandulphi villa, superbis aedificiis, amoenisque consitionibus et amplissimis vinetis ornata, ad sinistram sita Conchae amnis, a quo summersum oppidum nomen habuit. Suntque superius Sanctus Ioannes in Macegnano, Mondainum, [342H] Saluditium, Mons Gridolfus, Metellum, Mons Florum, Gemanum, Tauletum, Planum castelli, Castrum Novum, Mons Tavelii. Certaldum, Petri Turci viri doctissimi patria, Planarum Ioannis Francisci nobilis et strenui a litterisque non abhorrentis viri patria, Planum Meleti, Petra Rubia, Carpegnum, a quo nomen accepit mons arduus amplissimusque pascua praebens per aestatem animalibus uberrima.

Qui quidem mons Arimino sive ut nunc dicitur Marida fluvio ab Apennino divisus, omnium Italiae Apenninum non contingentium montium est maximus. Subest item illi Castellatia, post sequitur Mons Cerognonus, monasterium Sextini, apud quod multa extant vetustatis monumenta. Ad Conchae vero dexteram Sanctus Clemens, Agellum, Corianum, Mons Scutulus, ubi haec scribimus, Albaretum, Gypsum, Tumba Gaiaeni, Mons Zardinus, Saxum, Mons Grimannus, Mons Taxorum, Mons Copiolus.

in the entire time of the Lombards Ravenna, along with some neighboring states, kept faith most reliably with the Roman people. But in keeping with my method, I shall designate the ancient boundaries of Romandiola as lying within the Isaurus or Foglia river and the Scultenna or Panaro **[342G]** and the Apennine mountains, and the Adriatic Sea, and the swamp known as Padusa on this side of the Po, and beyond that the territory of Ferrara up to the swamps of Verona and Padua, and up to the farthest mouth of the Po, called "The Ovens," between the Adriatic sea and the Po.

On the right-hand bank of the Foglia river, the first town in Emilia Romagna is Pozzo. After it comes Monte Luro, between the Foglia and the next stream lies the Conca river, about which Lucan wrote, "The Crustumium, sweeping all before it," (or, as they now call it, the Conca). The promontory, called Focara, has on it four towns (Granarola, Casteldimezzo, Gabicce Monte, and Fiorenzuola di Focara). It is well planted with vines and olives. Above it are the following towns: Tomba, Montepiano, Monte Calvo, Piede di Campo, Corvara, and Macerata Feltria. Below Focara, towards Rimini, is the village of Cattolica and near it is a town buried under water, Conca; when the sea is calm, its walls and towers are visible beneath the surface.

Towards the interior is Gradara, the villa of Sigismondo Pandolfo Malatesta, adorned with impressive buildings, pleasant orchards and abundant vineyards, located to the left of the river Conca from which the sunken town takes its name. And higher up are: San **[342H]** Giovanni in Marignano, Mondaino, Saludecio, Montegridolfo, Meldola, Montefiore, Gemmano, Tatullia, Pian di Castello, Castelnuovo, and Tavullia. There is Certaldo, the home of the very learned Pietro Turco; Piano, the home of the noble Giovanni Francesco, a man who was both energetic and enthusiastic about literature; Pian di Meleto; Pietrarubbia; and Carpegna, which gives the name to a steep and broad mountain which offers the flocks very rich summer pastures.

This mountain is divided by the river now called the Marecchia, and is the largest of all mountains in Italy which do not belong to the Apennine chain. Below it is Castellacia; after that follow Monte Cerignone, and the monastery of Sestino, where there are many documents from antiquity. On the right bank of the Conca are: San Clemente, Agello, Coriano, Montescudo, where I am writing this, Albareto, Gesso, Tomba, Gaieno, Montegiardino, Sasso, Montegrimano, Monte Tassi, and Montecopiolo.

Et mari in via Flaminia et prope mare imminet Sanctae Trinitatis ecclesia. Suntque ad eius torrentis dexteram oppida et castella, in Arimini sive Maridae amnis sinistram vergentia, Seravalle, Veruculum, Sanctus Marinus, sub arduo cuius monte torrens ipse ortum habet. Superiusque in Montis Feretri regione Mons Maius, Petra Acutula, Toranum, [343A] Sanctus Leo episcopi sedes, Scaulinum antiquum, Soane, Penna, Bilium, Maiolum, Ciconiaria, Montironum, Mercatum Ranchi.

Succedit ordine Ariminum vetusti clarique nominis colonia Romanorum simul cum Benevento sicut Livius XIIII libro scribit deducta, anno quod ex Eusebio computavimus ante Iesu Christi domini nativitatem secundo octuagesimo et ducentesimo. Ea civitas duram a Vitigite Gothorum rege pertulit obsidionem, Ioanne Vitaliani partium Iustiniani imperatoris sicut in Historiis ostendimus viriliter defensante, et nunc Sigismundo Pandulpho Malatestae clarissimo rei militaris duci vicariatus ecclesiae titulo est subiecta. Cuius latera irrigat eiusdem nominis fluvius Marida nunc dictus. Scribit Livius libro XXI,

> L. Sempronium consulem compositis Siciliae rebus decem navibus oram Italiae legentem Ariminum pervenisse, inde cum exercitu suo profectum ad Trebiam amnem.

Et libro CIX dicit belli civilis Caesaris et Pompeii initio Curionem tribunum plebis pervenisse Ariminum, quam historiam Hirtius in commentariis et Lucanus poeta diffuse narrant, ut eam prolixius a nobis scribi oportere non iudicemus.

Et beatus Hieronymus ecclesiae doctor scribit concilium aetate sua et cui ipse [343B] interfuerit Arimini celebratum fuisse, quod postea patres reprobaverint, et gesta in eo censuerint esse nulla. Eam civitatem suburbiumque coniungit pons, nunc solus integer ex veteribus quattuor, quos Octavius Augustus Flaminia via ab urbe Roma Ariminum silicibus strata praeter minorum pontium turbam maximo exstruxit opere atque impendio. Qui enim est ad Tiberim Milvius nomine a Marco Scauro sicut Ammianus Marcellinus refert constructus, multa quae ab Octavio accepit ornamenta omnino amisit. Et qui Tiberim item sub Ocriculo iungebat parte una succisus in arcis fundamenta concessit. Is vero qui sub Narnia Narem amplec-

Also overlooking the sea on the Via Flaminia, and next to the sea, is the church of Santa Trinità. And on the right bank of this river are towns and fortresses, on the left bank of the Marecchia river Vergiano, Serravalle, Verucchio, San Marino, and at the foot of a high mountain the river itself has its source. And higher up in the region of Montefeltro are Montemaggio, Pietracuta, Torriana, the seat of the bishopric of San Leo, ancient Sogliano, **[343A]** Soane, Pennabilli, Maioletto, Cicognara, Montirono, and Mercatino.

And there follows in order Rimini, along with Beneventum a Roman colony of ancient and famous name, as Livy (book 14) writes. It was founded in the year 282 B.C., as I compute it from Eusebius' chronicle. This city-state suffered a harsh siege by the king of the Visigoths, and was courageously defended by John, the nephew of Vitalian, on the side of the emperor Justinian, as I have written in my *Decades*. Now it is under the dominion of Sigismondo Pandolfo Malatesta, a very famous general, who holds the title of vicar of the church. The river of the same name which I mentioned, and is now called the Marecchia, flows past it. Livy writes in book 21,

> After settling the situation in Sicily, the consul L. Sempronius grazed the coast of Sicily with ten ships and came to Ariminum, and from there set out with his army for the Trebia river.

And in book 109 he says that at the beginning of the civil war between Caesar and Pompey, Curio, the tribune of the plebs, came to Ariminum. Hirtius in his *Commentaries* and Lucan the poet tell this story differently. For this reason I do not judge it necessary to write it more fully. The father of the church St. Jerome writes of the famous council at Ariminum in **[343B]** his time in which he himself participated, which afterwards the church fathers repudiated, and decided that its acts would be nullified.

A bridge joins that city and its suburbs; it is now the only one left whole of the four ancient bridges (in addition to a lot of lesser bridges) which Octavian Augustus built, with great labor and at great expense, on the Via Flaminia from the city of Rome to Ariminum. The Flaminia was paved with basalt. On the Tiber was built the Milvian bridge, named after Marcus Scaurus, so Ammianus Marcellinus tells us; and it was much decorated by Octavian but has lost all its decoration. And likewise the bridge on the Tiber at the site of ancient Ocriculum has had one side destroyed to make the substructure of a fortress. Indeed, the bridge which used to span the Nar river at

tebatur fluvium, multis ut videtur saeculis vel succisum vel collapsum vetustate fornicem medium amisit.

Ornata fuit Ariminensis civitas superioribus saeculis Mastino Pandulpho et Galeoto ex Malatesta gente principibus omni virtute ornatis. Ortique eodem Galeoto, Carolus Malatesta princeps fortissimus atque doctissimus, quem in historiis Marco Catoni superiori similem fuisse diximus, et Pandulphus qui Brixiae et Bergomi dominium multis obtinuit annis, inter aetatis **[343C]** nostrae principes primarii sunt habiti; cum tamen nulla ratione eis fuerit virtute inferior Malatesta tertius frater. Claram vero dulcemque sui memoriam saeculo nostro reliquit Galeotus Robertus, qui licet paternae haereditatis urbes oppidaque amplum in Italia principatum iustissime simul et prudentissime administravit, res tamen mundanas tanta elevati in aeternae salutis desideria, spiritus munditia et puritate contempsit, ut post quam adolescens in caelum unde venerat restitutus carnis sarcina est exutus, beatitudinis famam signaque in terris reliquerit. Ariminumque nunc habet Petrum ac Iacobum Perleones fratres Latinis et Graecis litteris apprime eruditos.

Ad sinistram Maridae intus est ut diximus Verruculum prima Malatestarum patria, Maiolum, Bilium, et ad fontem in Apennino Castrum Ilicis. Est etiam ut diximus in exesi montis cacumine Samarinum oppidum, olim Acer Mons dictum, perpetuae libertatis gloria clarum, ulterius via Flaminia est Sancta Iustina vicus, et supra primis in collibus Sanctus Archangelus, nobile oppidum. Et in via item Flaminia Savignanum oppidum intersecat **[343D]** Plusa vetusti nominis fluvius, qui sub Belaere castello mare influit Adriaticum. Inde habetur parvus torrens Butrius, cui supra viam Flaminiam adiacet Longianum viti oleaque in circuitu perpulchre consitum.

Sequitur magni quondam nominis torrens perexiguus Rubicon, Cisalpinae Galliae et Italiae arva disterminare solitus; Pissatellum nunc qui sub Flaminia via, Ruconem qui supra accolunt, vocant. Fuitque olim stante et integra republica Romana lege prohibitum, ne quispiam armatus illum iniussu magistratuum transgrederetur. Eaque lex loco mota in quo ab initio fuit posita, marmore litteris incisa elegantissimis etiam nunc visitur, quam libuit hic ponere:

Narni, apparently over many centuries has lost its middle arch, either destroyed or collapsed due to the ravages of time.

In the past centuries the city-state of Rimini has been distinguished by Mastino Pandolfo and Galeoto of the Malatesta family, princes endowed with every virtue. Born there also, sons of the same Galeoto, were Carlo Malatesta, a very brave and learned prince, whom I mentioned in the *Decades* as similar to Marcus Cato, and Pandolfo, who gained sovereignty over Brescia and Bergamo **[343C]** for many years; they are considered among the foremost princes of our age. In no way inferior to them in virtue is the third Malatesta brother, who left our generation a famous and sweet memory, Galeoto Roberto, who governed with wisdom and justice the towns and city inherited from his father, a substantial dominion in Italy, but was induced by his desire for eternal salvation and purity of spirit to despise the things of this world. So, departing this world in his youth for his heavenly home, he put off the trappings of the flesh and left on earth the reputation and traces of his blessed state. At present, Rimini boasts Pietro and Jacopo Perleone, brothers perfectly learned in Latin and Greek literature.

On the left side of the Marecchia, towards the interior, as I said, is Verucchio, the first home of the Malatesta;, Maioletto, Billi, and, near its source in the Apennines, Casteldelci. There is also, as I have mentioned, on the summit of a hollow mountain, the town of San Marino, formerly called Monte Titano, famous with an eternal glory. Farther along on the Via Flaminia is the village of Santa Giustina, and above it in the foothills, Santarcangelo, a noble town. And also on the Via Flaminia is the town of Savignano, through which **[343D]** the river Uso flows; a river with an ancient name, it flows at the foot of the *castello* Bellaria into the Adriatic Sea. From there comes the small stream Rigossa (?), next to which, above the Via Flaminia, lies Longiano, beautifully planted all around with vines and olives.

There follows a very small stream with a formerly great name, the Rubicon. It is the customary dividing line between Hither Gaul and the fields of Italy. It is now called the Pisciatello river by the inhabitants below the Via Flaminia and Ruco by those who live above it. In ancient times, while the Roman Republic was still strong, it was prohibited by law for anyone under arms to cross this river unless expressly ordered by a magistrate. And the inscription of this law has been moved from its original place, but can now be seen inscribed on marble in elegant letters, and I give the inscription here:

> Iussu mandatuve P.R. Cons. imperator miles tiro commilito quisquis es manipularieve centurio turmaeve legionariae hic sistito, vexillum sinito, nec citra hunc amnem Rubiconem signa ductum commeatumve traducito. Si quis huius iussionis ergo adversus ierit feceritve, adiudicatus esto hostis P. R. ac si contra patriam arma tulerit penatesque e sacris penetralibus asportaverit S.P.Q.R. SANCTIO PLEBISCITI S. VE. C.

Notiora sunt quae de huius amnis et legis transgressione C. Iulii Caesaris scripta sunt a multis, quam ut ea a nobis hic scribi oportere iudicemus, satisque fuerit et locum et legem indicasse. Incipit vero hic secundum vetustos Gallia Cisalpina de qua M. Cicero in Philippicis,

> Nec vero de virtute, constantia, gravitate Galliae taceri potest, est **[344E]** enim ille flos Italiae, illud firmamentum imperii Romani illud ornamentum dignitatis.

Et Plinius "in hoc tractu interiere Boi quorum tribus CXII fuisse auctor est Cato, item Senones qui ceperant Romam."

Qua Rubicon torrens influit Adriaticum portus est Cesena parva admittens navigia, intus supra Flaminiam sunt amoeni et feraces agri Ariminensis castella, quorum primarium est Runchfridum. Ultra Cesenatem litori propinqua est Cervia civitas rarissimo habitata colono salinas faciente, quam Malatesta Novellus Cesenae princeps praestantissimus in arctiorem restrictam orbem muro nuper valido communivit, et quinto ab inde miliario absunt Sapis fluvii ostia, adiacetque ei fluvio intus in via Flaminia civitas Cesena vetus habens nomen, quae Malatestae Novelli litteris praesertim historia ornatissimi administratione nunc gaudet, a quo ornatur biblioteca melioribus Italiae aequiparanda, cum tamen hospitale idem in urbe sumptuosissimum aedificet, ac moenibus illam novis alicubi communiat, ponte lapideo et quidem insigni Sapim fluvium ad viam Flaminiam iunxerit. Estque nunc plurisfacienda, quam innuerit M. Cicero, **[344F]** cum in ultima ad Lentulum epistola significare volens quempiam Romanum civem parvifaciendum esse,

> By order of the Roman People: consul, general, recruit, whoever you are, centurion of a company, cavalry troop, or legion, stop here, set down your standard, put down your flag. Do not lead your convoy, your standards, across this side of the Rubicon river. If anyone goes against this order, let him be judged a public enemy. And if he bear arms against his country, the Roman people will take away the household gods from their shrine in the sacred inner recesses of his house. The Senate and the Roman people: the law of the people and decree of the senate.

Some rather famous accounts of Julius Caesar's transgression of this river and the law have been written by many authors, so that I do not think it necessary for me to write them here; it will be enough to have mentioned both the place and the law.

Here, according to the ancients, begins Hither Gaul. Cicero said about this area in the *Philippics*,

> . . . cannot be silent about the virtue and reliability and importance **[344E]** of Gaul, for that region is the flower of Italy, that region is the basis of Roman power and the adornment of Rome's impressiveness.

And Pliny says "in this area the Boii, whose tribes numbered one hundred and twelve, have perished, so says Cato; and here also were the Senones, who captured Rome."

Where the stream Rubicon flows into the Adriatic, there is a small harbor at Cesena which is navigable by small craft; towards the interior beyond the Via Flaminia are the pleasant, fruitful territory of Rimini and *castelli*, of which the primary one is Roncofreddo. Beyond Cesena next to the shore is the city of Cervia, inhabited by a few colonists who labor in the saltworks; Malatesta Novello, the outstanding prince of Cesena, has fortified it recently, making it into a narrower enclosure with a strong wall. And five miles from here is the mouth of the Savio river. Lying next to this river towards the interior on the Via Flaminia is the city-state of Cesena, which bears an ancient name and now enjoys its government by Malatesta Novello, a man especially distinguished in historical literature. He has endowed a library the equivalent of the better ones in Italy; is building a most opulent hospital in the city, and fortifying Cesena with new walls; and has spanned the Savio river at the Via Flaminia with a famous bridge of stone. It is now worthy of more attention than Cicero implies when in his final letter **[344F]** to Lentulus he wishes to indicate some Roman citizen as worth-

dicit non satis dignum esse cui Cesena aut Tabernolae fuerint committendae. Plinius autem Cicerone posterior vina docens Italiae optima connumerat Cesenaticum. Ea civitas cum civilibus dissidiis tumultuaretur, ad annum salutis tricesimumoctavum supra tricentesimum et millesimum a Britonibus Romanae ecclesiae fidem servare simulantibus direpta fuit.

Superius ad Sapis fluenta intus est Emporium Saracenum vicus, et paulo supra ad Apennini radices Sassina vetustissima civitas, quae in Bois nobilissima Plautum comicum civem habuit quam Eusebius tradit propter annonae difficultatem ad molas manuarias pistori se locasse, ibique quotiens opere vacaret fabulas scribere et vendere solitum fuisse. In eiusque urbis ruinis episcopium est, cuius dioeceseos et dominii sunt castella et oppida ad viginti Boibo, pro Boio vetusto nomine appellata. Ad Sapis vero fluvii fontem vel paulo infra oppidum est Sanctae Mariae a balneis, quae intus habet lateritio opere conclusis dictum, et secundum amnis eiusdem decursum vallis est Balinea castellis vicisque plurimis frequentata. [344G]

Obtinuerunt vero Boi a principio omnem eam nunc Romandiolae regionem, quae a Sassina Bononiensem includit agrum, perhibetque Plinius Bononiam pro Boionia dictam esse, quamquam non modo Bononiensem agrum Boi, sed eos qui nunc Mutinensis Regiensisque dicuntur complexi fuisse videntur, quod indicat Livius libro XXII his verbis,

> Q. Minucius inde in agrum Boiorum legiones duxit, Boiorum exercitus haud ita multo ante traiecerant Padum, iunxerantque se Insubribus et Cenomannis, quod ita acceperant coniunctis legionibus consules rem gesturos, ut et ipsi collatas in unum vires firmarent. Postquam fama accidit alterum consulem Boiorum urere agros seditio extemplo orta est; postulare Boi ut laborantibus universi opem ferrent, Insubres negare se sua deserturos, ita divisae copiae, Bois in agrum suum Tannetum profectis.

Si itaque Tannetum fuit Boiorum, Mutina pariter et nunc Regium, ultra quam civitatem Tannetum esse ostendemus, in Bois fuere. Fuerunt tum potentissimi bellacissimique populi, quod innuit Livius libro XXI,

less, and says that he is not worthy of being entrusted with Cesena or Tabernola. More recently than Cicero, Pliny writes about the wines of Italy and numbers the wines of Cesena among the best. When this city was disturbed by civil war in the year 1338, it was torn apart by Bretons pretending to keep faith with the Roman church.

Higher up, on the Savio river towards the interior, is the village of Mercato Saraceno, and a little above it at the base of the Apennines, Sarsina, a very ancient city, among the most noble of those of the Boi. It boasts as its citizen Plautus the comic playwright, whom Eusebius tells us had to find work in a mill because of his lack of subsistence; and there, in the time he had free from his work, he would write plays and sell them. And in the ruins of this city is a bishopric, whose dioceses and dominions are about twenty fortresses and towns. It is called Boibo instead of the ancient name Boio. At the source of the Savio river, or a little below it, is the town of Bagno di Romagna, named after the baths which it has inside, enclosed by brickwork. And following the course of the same river there is a valley Balinea which has a considerable number of fortresses and villages. **[344G]**

The Boii gained possession from the beginning of all the region of Romandiola, which proceeds from Sarsina, and includes the territory of Bologna. And Pliny tells us that Bononia was given that name from Boionia, although the Boi seem to have possessed not only the territory of Bologna but those territories now said to belong to Modena and Reggio. Livy points to this conclusion in book 22:

> Q. Minucius led his legions from there into the territory of the Boii. The army of the Boii had now long before crossed the Po, and had united themselves with the Insubri and the Cenomanni, because they had heard that the consuls would act with their legions combined, in order to focus their strength. And afterwards the rumor was that one consul burned the territory of the Boii as an example against rebellion, the Boii demanded aid, the Insubri refused to desert, and so the troops were divided, and the Boii set out into their own territory, to Tannetum.

And so if Taneto was a possession of the Boii, likewise Mutina and what is now Reggio, (beyond which lies Taneto, as I will show) were also in the territory of the Boii. They were at that time a powerful and warlike people, as Livy indicates in book 21:

> Boi sollicitati ab Insubribus defecerunt, nec tam ob veteres in Romani populi iras, [344H] quam quod nuper circa Padum Placentiam Cremonamque colonias in agrum Gallium deductas aegre patiebantur, triumviri ad deducendas colonias missi Placentiae moenibus diffisi Mutinam confugerunt. Legati ad Boios missi violati sunt Mutina obsessa, et simulatum de pace agi, missique ad eam tractandam a Gallis comprehensi L. Manlius imperator effusum agmen ad Mutinam ducit, caesi sunt Romanorum octingenti, sex signa militaria adempta.

Item Livius XXXVI, "P. Cornelius Scipio Nasica cos. vir optimus a senatu iudicatus Boios Gallos victos in deditione accepit, de quibus triumphavit."

Prima post Sapis ostia in Adriatici litore loca describi digna sunt parva Candiani sive vallis sive stagni ostia, documento prudentibus rerumque peritis futura, qua in rebus humanis omnia fluxa, omnia sunt caduca. Sapis fluvius, quem octavo miliario descriptum post terga linquimus, ad annum nunc plus minus sexcentesimum ipsam illabebatur Candiani vallem, efficiebatque portum in primis Italiae celeberrimum, quam quo sicut Suetonius Tranquillus Vegetiusque et plerique vetustiores scripserunt, Octavius Augustus primus Romanus imperator classem instituit, quae sinum Adriaticum, Illyricum, Dalmatiam, Graeciam, Pontum, Armeniam, Asiam, Aegyptum, et omnem mediterranei maris oram tueretur. Scribitque Plinius in eius portus ostiis turrim fuisse phaream omnium maximam, [345A] quas Romanum ubique habuit imperium; et brevi ab instituto eo portu factum est, ut a navalibus turmis convenientibus undique mercatoribus civitas ibi sit aedificata et quidem opulentissima, de qua Aelius Spartianus in Didii Iuliani vita scribit, "Sed dum haec agit Iulianus, Severus classem Ravennatem occupat."

Ea vero civitas cum antea tum maxime beati Gregorii temporibus episcopum habuit; capta vero fuit a rege Longobardorum Luthprando atque direpta, unde et urbe sublata et quod magis crediderim fluvio Sapi in remotum averso cursum, videmus factum ut nec urbis moenium, nec turris phareae neque portus nisi minima ex parte aliquod appareat vestigium, praeter Sancti Apollinaris in ipsa Classe civitate basilicam variis ornatam marmo-

> The Boii were harassed by the Insubri, and deserted, not **[344H]** so much on account of any longstanding anger against the Roman people as because they were suffering from colonies established in Gallic land around the Po and Placentia and Cremona, and the triumvirs sent to establish the colonies didn't have confidence in the walls of Placentia, and took refuge in Modena. Legates sent to the Boi were attacked, Mutina was besieged, and they made a pretense of negotiating for peace; those sent by the Gauls to make peace were arrested. The general L. Manlius led his disordered ranks to Mutina, eight thousand of the Romans were slaughtered, six military standards were seized.

In the same vein Livy, book 36, says, "The consul P. Cornelius Scipio, judged the best man by the senate, took into captivity upon their surrender the conquered Boii, Gauls, and conducted a triumph for this."

After the mouth of the Savio, on the Adriatic coast, the first places worthy to be described are the small mouth of the Candiano, or of its valley or swamps, and they will be evidence to wise men experienced in affairs how all things in human affairs are unstable, all things are destined to perish. The river Savio, which we left behind after describing it at the eighth milestone, was flowing around the year 600 past the valley of the Candiano, and made a harbor among the most famous in Italy, written about by Suetonius, Vegetius, and very many more ancient authors. This was Classe. Octavian Augustus, the first Roman emperor, established a fleet which was to protect the Adriatic gulf, the Illyrian, Dalmatia, Greece, Pontus, Armenia, Asia, Egypt, and all the coast of the Mediterranean. And Pliny writes that in the mouth of **[345A]** this harbor was a tower, the greatest lighthouse of all those which the Roman empire possessed. Built a short time after the harbor was established, so that a city was built there as naval squadrons and merchants came together from everywhere, it was very opulent indeed; Aelius Spartianus writes about it in his *Life of Didius Iulianus*, "But while Iulianus did this, Severus took over the fleet at Ravenna."

Before Gregory the Great's times but especially during his prime, this city had a bishop. It was captured by Liutprand, king of the Lombards, and sacked. From that point the city was destroyed and (something I am more inclined to believe) the Savio river changed its course to a point farther away, and we see neither the wall of the city of Classe, nor the tower of the lighthouse nor the harbor, nor does any trace appear in the slightest degree, except the basilica of S. Apollinare in Classe. Adorned with different types

ribus, ceteris aequiparandam, quas Italia ubique habeat vetustae magnificentiae speciosiores, quae Theoderici Ostrogothorum primi regis opus fuit.

Influunt vero ipsam Candiani vallem, qui et tanti olim portus tenues conservant reliquias parvi torrentes Avela et Bevanus appellati, quorum primus latera abluit Foripompilii civitatis olim, nunc oppidi nominis vetusti. Ea civitas in via Flaminia unum fuit ex quattuor **[345B]** foris, quem Plinius illa in regione simul enumerat, quam civitatem ad annum salutis septingentesimum Vitaliani pontificis Romani natione Signiensis temporibus Grimoaldus Longobardorum tyrannus, dum sabbato sancto conficeretur crisma furto occupatam diripuit, solo aequavit. Et eandem postmodum a Foroliviensibus instauratam iterum destruxit, ararique fecit ad annum salutis tredecies centenum atque sexagesimum Egidius Sabinensis Romanae cardinalis ecclesiae celeberrimus.

Supra eminenti in colle est Bretenorium civitas, in quam destructi Foripompilii episcopalis dignitas est translata. Fuitque id oppidum quod Plinius vetustiora repetens [Butrium] appellat, Umbriae apud Ravennam ultimum. Et postea inter quattuor fora enumeratum dicit esse Forum Brintanorum. Sub Bretanorii colle imminet torrenti Avexae Polenta oppidum paucis habitatum colonis, ad quem locum ostendimus in Historiis proelium illud Romae et Italiae infelicissimum fuisse commissum, in quo lacessiti magis quam clade aliqua confecti Visigothi omissa ad Gallias quam intendebant profectione arma in urbem Romanam victricia converterunt; **[345C]** et ea capta direptaque ac alicubi incensa Romani imperii inclinatio nostrae Historiae titulus initiumque inchoavit.

Post Classensem Candiani portum prima sunt Hedesi amnis ostia, Ravennae portum efficientia. Distatque inde secundo miliario Ravenna urbs vetusta, quam diximus fuisse oppidum Sabinorum, unde Livius libro XXI

> Cornelius consul cum audiisset a Bois ante suum adventum incursiones in agrum sociorum factas, duabus legionibus subitariis tumultus eius causa scriptis additisque ad eas quattuor cohortibus de exercitu suo Gaium Appium praefectum suum hac tumultuaria manu per Umbriam, quam tribum Sabinianam vocant, agrum Boiorum invadere iussit.

of marble, comparable to any other beautiful ones of ancient splendor anywhere in Italy, it is the work of Theoderic, the first king of the Ostrogoths.

The rivers which flow into the valley of the Candiano and preserve the slender remains of the formerly great harbor are small streams: the Avellana and the Bevano river. The first of these flows past Forlimpópoli, a city-state in former times, now a town with an ancient name. This city on the Via Flaminia was one of the four Fora which **[345B]** Pliny lists in that region. This city was sacked by Grimoald the tyrant of the Lombards in the 700th year A.D. in the time of Pope Vitalianus (from Segni); while the crisma (anointing) was being performed on holy Saturday, Grimoald took it by stealth and leveled it to the ground. Afterwards, the city was re-established by the people of Forlì; but he destroyed it a second time and in the year A.D. 1360 the famous Sabine cardinal Gil Albornoz caused it to be ploughed under.

Towering above on a high hill is Bertinoro, a city to which was transferred the episcopate of the destroyed Forlimpópoli. And it was this town which Pliny, repeating material from older sources, calls Brintum [Butrium], the last town in Umbria around Ravenna; and afterwards among the four Fora he lists, he names Forum Brintanorum. At the foot of the hill of Bertinoro the town Polenta projects over the river Avessa. Inhabited by a few colonies, it is the place where I showed in my *Decades* that battle took place which was most unfortunate for Rome and Italy, in which the Visigoths, more wounded than done in by slaughter, turned their victorious weapons upon the city of Rome; **[345C]** and captured, sacked, and burned it; thus began the decline of the Roman empire, which is the title of my history.

After the harbor at Classe made by the Candiano, the first mouth of the Edeso river makes a harbor at Ravenna. Two miles distant is the ancient city of Ravenna, which I said was a town of the Sabines. Livy writes about it (book 21):

> The consul Cornelius, when he had heard that before his arrival the Boii had made depredations into the territory of the allies, because of this disturbance enrolled an emergency force of two legions, and adding to them four cohorts from his own army, he ordered C. Appius, the commander of the allied forces, to take this improvised force and with it to invade the territory of the Boi, marching by way of Umbria, through the district known as the tribe of the Sabines.

Fuit itaque ager Ravennas haec tribus Sabiniana. Et infra addit Livius, "Deinde ad castrum Mutillum," ubi nunc dicitur Mutilina.

Cinxit Ravennam muris nunc exstantibus Tiberius imperator, quod litterae docent cubitales ad portam eius clausam, quem Aurea dicitur, quadrato lapide speciosam. Auxit vero ipsam Ostrogotha gens, cuius rex Theodoricus Italiae omnis Dalmatiae, Ungariae, Germaniae, et partis non parvae Galliarum dominus, annis duodequadraginta eandem incoluit civitatem, et quod constat superbas in ea aedes basilicasque construxit, **[345D]** visit eius regis monumentum ab Amalasuntha filia positum extra Ravennae moenia, in quo Sanctae Mariae monasterium est aedificatum in rotundo ea ratione appellatum, quod altare maius ecclesiae chorusque XX capax monachorum, ordine ut est moris in stallo psallentium, unico atque integro rotundo lapide conteguntur. Praeestque illi monasterio abbas Matthaeus Blondus nobis frater germanus.

Populo nunc Ravenna est infrequens, quae viros olim habuit cum sanctos tum etiam doctos, Apollinarem, Vitalem, et eius filios Gervasium et Prothasium, Urcinumque medicum, omnes martyrio coronatos; Ioannem nominis ordine decimumseptimum pontificem Romanum; Petrum Ravennatem Foricornelii episcopum, qui multas sacri eloquii scripturas eloquentissime dilucidavit; et Cassiodorum urbis Romae senatorem regumque Ostrogothorum epistolarum scriptorem, et post monachum, qui praeter scripta saecularibus litteris haud quamquam contemnenda libros de anima gravissime ac eruditissime scriptos reliquit.

Videtur etiam genuisse Faustinum, ad quem Martialis poeta multa scripsit,

> Quos Faustine dies qualem tibi Roma Ravennam abstulit.

Genuitque superiori saeculo Ravenna Guilielmum physicum, quem Petruspaulus Vergerius notissimum amicissimumque sibi hominem magis effert laudibus. Genuit etiam **[346E]** eodem tempore Ioannem grammaticum rhetoremque doctissimum, quem solitus dicere fuit Leonardus Aretinus omni in re sed potissime in hac una gravissimus locupletissimusque testis, fuisse primum a quo eloquentiae studia tantopere nunc florentia longo postliminio in Italiam fuerint reducta, digna certe cognitio, quae a nobis nunc illustranda Italia in medium adducatur.

Vident intelleguntque qui Latinas litteras vero et suo cum sapore degustant, paucos ac prope nullos post doctorum ecclesiae Ambrosii Hieronymi et Augustini, quae et eadem inclinantis Romanorum imperii tempora fuerunt,

And so this territory of Ravenna was of the Sabine tribe. And further on Livy adds, ". . . then to Castrum Mutillum," which is now called Modigliana.

The emperor Tiberius surrounded Ravenna with walls which are still standing, as is shown by the cubit-high letters at the gate, now closed, which is called Porta Aurea, beautiful in square stone. The Ostrogoths added to it. Their king Theoderic, lord of all Italy, Dalmatia, Hungary, Germany, and not a small part of Gaul, lived in this city for 38 years. He built a magnificent basilica and palaces in it. A monument to this king can be seen, **[345D]** put there by his daughter Amalasuntha, outside the walls of Ravenna, in which the monastery of St. Mary in the Round was built, called that for this reason, that the greater altar of the church and the chorus can hold twenty monks, praying as is the custom in the stall, covered by a single and whole round stone, and the head of that monastery is the abbot Matteo Biondo, my brother.

The population of Ravenna is now sparse; it formerly had men not only holy but also learned, Apollinaris, Vitalis, and his sons Gervasius and Prothasius, the doctor Urcinus, all crowned in martyrdom; Pope John XVII; Peter the bishop of Ravenna and Imola, who eloquently commented on many of the scriptures of sacred eloquence; and Cassiodorus, a senator of the city of Rome and writer of epistles of the Ostrogoth kings, and afterwards a monk who, in addition to writings in secular literature, left behind estimable books about the soul, written in serious and learned fashion.

Ravenna also seems to have been the birthplace of Faustinus, to whom the poet Martial wrote many lines:

> Faustinus, how many days of Ravenna Rome has taken away. . . .

Born at Ravenna also, in the previous century, was the physician Guglielmo da Ravenna whom Pier Paolo Vergerio praised highly as a very famous friend. Also born there in **[346E]** the same period was Giovanni the grammarian and teacher of rhetoric, a very learned man; who, Leonardo Bruni (a very authoritative and trustworthy observer in every matter but especially in this one) used to say, was the first to restore the study of eloquence to Italy, a pursuit which has been flourishing in a long return to its rightful home, worthy of recognition which I bring now into the open through my illumination of Italy.

Those who taste the flavor of Latin literature see and understand that there were few men, almost none, after the fathers of the church Ambrose, Jerome, and Augustine, in the time of the decline of the Roman empire who

aliquali cum elegantia scripsisse, nisi illis propinqui temporibus Beatus Gregorius ac venerabilis Beda, et qui longo post tempore fuit beatus Bernardus, in praedictorum numero sint ponendi. Primus vero omnium Franciscus Petrarcha magno vir ingenio maioreque diligentia, et poesim et eloquentiam excitare coepit, nec tamen is attigit Ciceronianae eloquentiae florem, quo multos in hoc saeculo videmus ornatos, in quo quidem nos librorum magis quam ingenii carentiam defectumque culpamus. Ipse enim et si epistolas Ciceronis Lentulo inscriptas Vercellis reperisse gloriatus est, tres Ciceronis de **[346F]** Oratore et Institutionum Oratoriarum Quintiliani libros non nisi laceros mutilatosque vidit, ad cuius notitiam Oratoris Maioris et Bruti de Oratoribus Claris, item Ciceronis libri nullatenus pervenerunt.

Ioannes autem Ravennas Petrarcham senem puer novit, nec dictos aliter quam Petrarcha vidit libros, neque aliquid, quod sciamus a se scriptum, reliquit, et tamen suopte ingenio et quodam Dei munere, sicut fuit solitus dicere Leonardus, eum Petrum Paulumque Vergerium, Omnebonum Schola Patavinum, Robertum Rossum et Iacobum Angeli filium Florentinos, Poggiumque, Guarinum Veronensem, Victorinum Feltrensem, ac alios, qui minus profecerunt auditores suos, si non satis, quod plene nesciebat, docere potuit, in bonarum, ut dicebat, litterarum amorem Ciceronisque imitationem inflammabat.

Interea Emanuel Chrysoloras Constantinopolitanus vir doctrina et omni virtute excellentissimus cum se in Italiam contulisset partim Venetiis, partim Florentiae, partim in curia, quam secutus est, Romana praedictos paene omnes Ioannis Ravennatis auditores litteras docuit Graecas, effecitque eius doctrina paucis tamen continuata annis, ut, qui Graecas nescirent litteras, Latinis viderentur indoctiores. Et cum magnus bene discendi ardor **[346G]** multos in Italia apprehendisset, conciliumque apud Constantiam Germaniae ab universo populo Christiano haberent, quaerere ibi et investigare coeperunt ex nostratibus multi, si quos Germaniae loca Constantiae proxima, ex deperditis Romanorum et Italia olim libris in monasteriorum latebris occultarent. Quintilianusque integer repertus a Poggio primum transcriptus in Italiam venit, secutaeque sunt incerto nobis datae libertatis patrono Ciceronis ad Atticum epistolae, cumque hic in Quintiliani Institutionibus et ad Atticum epistolis nostrorum Italiae adolescentium ingenia desudarent, Gasparinus Bergomensis grammaticus rhetorque celeberrimus Venetiis meliori solito doctrina nonnullos erudivit, plurimos ad ea imitanda studia incitavit.

wrote with any elegance unless they were close to those times. St. Gregory, the Venerable Bede, and a long time after them St. Bernard, have to be categorized as preachers. Francis Petrarch was truly the first of all; a man of great talent and greater diligence, he began to arouse poetry and eloquence, and although he did not attain the peak of Ciceronian eloquence which we see adorning many men in this century, I find fault more in his lack of books than in a lack of genius. This man exulted that he had found the letters of Cicero to Lentulus at Vercelli, he saw the three books of Cicero *de Oratore* and the **[346F]** *Institutiones Oratoriae* of Quintilian, although torn and damaged; and he had news of the *Orator Maior* and *Brutus de Oratoribus Claris*, likewise works of Cicero.

As a boy, Giovanni da Ravenna knew Petrarch when the latter was an old man. He did not see the books I mentioned in any other way than Petrarch did; nor did he leave any writings of his own which we know about. And nevertheless, by his talent and a certain gift of God, as we are accustomed to say, he inspired with a love of good literature and of imitating Cicero (even if he was not able to teach sufficiently what he did not fully know) Leonardo Bruni, Pierpaolo Vergerio, Ognibene Scola of Padua, the Florentines Roberto Rossi and Iacopo Angeli, Poggio, Guarino of Verona, Vittorino da Feltre, and others of his students who were less successful.

Meanwhile Manuel Chrysoloras of Constantinople arrived in Italy, a man who excelled in learning and every virtue, and taught Greek literature, partly in Venice, partly in Florence, partly in the Roman curia to nearly all the students of Giovanni I mentioned. His influence was such that in a few years those who were ignorant of Greek seemed incompetent **[346G]** in Latin. And when a great passion for learning well had seized many men in Italy, and the Council of Constance was held in Germany by the entire Christian population, many of our countrymen began to search there and investigate, whether places in Germany near to Constance were hiding in the recesses of a monastery formerly lost books of the Romans and Italy. An entire manuscript of Quintilian was found by Poggio and first transcribed and arrived in Italy, and the letters of Cicero to Atticus followed, given to me by an unknown patron of freedom. Here the young men of Italy exerted their talents on the *Institutions* of Quintilian and the *Letters to Atticus*; and Gasparino of Bergamo the grammarian and famous teacher of rhetoric taught some at Venice with learning better than they were accustomed to in a teacher, and inspired very many to imitate those pursuits.

Florebantque iam et fama celebrabantur Petruspaulus Vergerius, Omnebonum Schola natu maiores; Leonardus Aretinus, Robertus Rossus, Iacobus Angeli, et Poggius, ac Nicola Mediceus, quem praeceptor domi assiduus erudierat Aretinus, Guarinusque Venetiis et Victorinus Mantuae multos coeperant erudire, cum Philippus Mediolanensis dux tertius **[346H]** Gasparinum a Bergomo subditum hominem invitum Mediolanensibus edocendis Padua et Venetia evocavit. Ubi id maxime adiumenti studiis eloquentiae attulit, quod repertus Laudae a summo viro Gerardo Landriano tunc ibi episcopo, multis maximisque in ruderibus codex Ciceronis pervetustus et cuius litteras vetustiores paucissimi scirent legere, ad eius perveniens manus interitum evasit. Continebat is codex praeter rhetoricorum novos et veteres qui habebantur, tres quoque de Oratore integerrimos, Brutum de Oratoribus claris et Oratorem ad Brutum M. Tullii Ciceronis, unde liberatus est bonus ipse vir Gasparinus ingenti, quem assumpserat labore supplendi quoad poterat librorum de Oratore defectus, sicut diu antea in Quintiliani Institutionibus multo labore suppleverat. Et cum nullus Mediolani esset repertus, qui eius vetusti codicis litteram sciret legere, Cosmus quidam egregii ingenii Cremonensis tres de Oratore libros primus transcripsit, multiplicataque inde exempla omnem Italiam desideratissimo codice repleverunt.

Nos vero cum publicis patriae tractandis negotiis adolescentes Mediolanum adiissemus, Brutum de Claris Oratoribus primi omnium mirabili ardore ac celeritate transcripsimus, ex quo primum Veronam Guarino post Leonardo Iustiniano Venetias misso, omnia **[347A]** Italia exemplis pariter est repleta. Quo ex tot librorum ipsius eloquentiae fomitum allato nostris hominibus adiumento, factum videmus ut maior meliorque ea quam Petrarcha habuit dicendi copia in nostram pervenerit aetatem. Nec parvum fuit cum adiumentum ad discendum eloquentiam, tum etiam incitamentum Graecarum accessio litterarum, quod qui eas didicere praeter doctrinam et ingentem historiarum exemplorumque copiam inde comparatam, conati sunt multa ex Graecis in Latinitatem vertere, in quo usu aut assiduitate scribendi reddiderunt quam habebant eloquentiam meliorem, aut qui nullam prius habebant, inde aliquam effecerunt.

Hinc ferbuerunt diu magisque nunc ac magis fervent per Italiam gymnasia, plerique sunt civitatibus ludi, in quibus pulcherrimum iucundumque est videre discipulos, nedum postquam sunt dimissi, sed quousque etiam sub ipsa ferula declamant et scribunt, praeceptores dicendi scribendive elegantia superare. Ex his autem quos Ioanni nostro Ravennati diximus fuisse discipulos duo aetate priores, Guarinus et Victorinus hic Mantuae **[347B]** ille Vene-

And older men, Pier Paolo Vergerio and Ognibene Scola, were flourishing and enjoying fame. Leonardo Bruni, Roberto Rossi, Jacopo Angeli, and Poggio, and Niccolò Medici, who was diligently taught at home by Bruni, Guarino in Venice and Vittorino in Mantua, began to teach many, when Filippo Maria Visconti, **[346H]** the third Duke of Milan, summoned Gasparino da Bergamo from Padua and Venetia, and stole him away against his will to teach at Milan. He brought a very great aid to the study of eloquence, because the great Gerardo Landriani, then a bishop, found at Lodi a very old codex of Cicero, in damaged condition, whose ancient hand could be read by very few men, and this came into Gasparino's hands and thereby survived. This codex contained, in addition to the old and new works on rhetoric, which were already available, three undamaged books *de oratore*, *Brutus*, and the *Orator ad Brutum* of M. Tullius Cicero. The good Gasparino was freed from the enormous toil which he had undertaken of supplying the deficiencies to the extent he was able of the books *de oratore*, as he had a long time before supplemented, with much labor, those in Quintilian's *Institutions*. When no one was found in Milan who could read the hand of this ancient codex, Cosmo of Cremona, a man of outstanding talent, first transcribed the three books *de oratore*, and multiple copies filled all of Italy with this longed-for manuscript.

And when I was a young man in Milan on state business, I was the first to transcribe, with remarkable passion and speed, the *Brutus*. From this, which I sent first to Verona to **[347A]** Guarino, then to Leonardo Giustinian at Venice, all Italy has also been filled with copies. A greater and better degree of eloquence than Petrarch had has reached our age because of the help we have received from all these books, inspirations to eloquence. Nor has it been a negligible help that we have been inspired by the availability of Greek literature. Those who have learned it, in addition to the learning and its great abundance of history and examples, have tried to translate much from Greek into Latin, and their eloquence has improved through this process, and those who had no eloquence before then gained some.

From this source, for a long time before this and now, schools have risen up through Italy, most of them in states where it is a beautiful sight to see the students before they have been dismissed, while still under the teacher's rod, declaiming and writing, surpassing their teachers in eloquence in the written and spoken word. Of those who I said were the students of our Giovanni da Ravenna, the two elder, Guarino and Vittorino (the latter from Mantua; the **[347B]** former from Venice, Verona, Florence,

tiss, Veronae, Florentiae et demum Ferrariae infinitam paene turbam et in his Ferrarienses Mantuanosque principes erudierunt. Georgius Trapezuntius publico Romae gymnasio Hispanos, Gallos, Germanosque multos, ut qui nonnulli aliquando sunt magni praestantesque viri, simul cum Italicis oratoriae ac poeticae auditores habet. Franciscus vero Philelphus ab ipsa gente Chrysolora Constantinopoli eruditus Venetiis Florentiae, Senis, Bononiae et demum Mediolani Graecas plurimos litteras docuit, et Latinas. Quid quod Valla Laurentius non modo suis elegantiis quosdam Neapoli implevit, sed eas quoque per omnem Italiam disseminari obtinuit, Petrusque Perleo Ariminensis Mediolani primum, post Genuae, Iacobus frater suus Bononiae, Porcellius Romae et Neapoli et Thomas Pontanus Perusiae, variisque civitatibus Seneca Camertinus, Italia bonis litteris implenda pro viribus enituntur.

Auctor est Plinius olim nebulas nutrire uvas, disputat Ravennae vina praesertim vermicula haberi optima. Sed Martialis contra sentit his versibus:

Sit cisterna mihi quam vinea malo Ravennae.
Nam possum multo vendere pluris aquam.

Et alibi dicit nullo in solo gratiorem gigni asparagum iis, [347C] quos vidit in hortis Ravennatium, quod Martialis confirmat his versibus,

Mollis et aequorea quae crevit spina Ravenna;
Non erit incultis gratior asparagis.

Et alio item loco scribit Plinius in Ravennatium mari rombum esse optimum. Martialis vero indicat Ravennae semper alias sicut nunc est, ranas fuisse multas:

Cum comparata rictibus tuis ora,
Niliacus habeat crocodillus angusta,
meliusque ranae garriant Ravennates.

Cingunt Ravennam amnes duo Bedisum facientes, quorum qui ad dexteram Montonus, qui ad sinistram olim Vitis nunc Aquaeductus dicitur, ortum in Apennini iugis propinquo Tiberis fonti loco habens. Adiacetque illi intus Meldula oppidum, et superius Galeata, post Sancta Sophia. Ad Montoni fluminis sinistram in Via Flaminia est Forumlivii civitas vetusti nominis, tertium obtinens locum inter quattuor fora quae innominata Plinium ea in regione diximus posuisse. Videmus autem Eusebium de temporibus dicere Gallum poetam cuius saepe Virgilius et Horatius meminerunt

and finally Ferrara), taught an almost innumerable crowd, among them Ferrarese and Mantuan princes. George of Trebizond has, in the Studio Romano, Spanish, French, and many German students of rhetoric and poetry, along with Italians; some of them are great and important men elsewhere. Francesco Filelfo was taught by the family of Chrysoloras of Constantinople at Venice and Florence; he taught many men Greek and Latin literature at Siena, Bologna, and finally at Milan. Lorenzo Valla not only filled certain men at Naples with his *Elegantiae*, but also sent this work through all of Italy; Pietro Perleone of Rimini at Milan, afterwards at Genoa, his brother Jacopo at Bologna, Porcellio at Rome and Naples and Tommaso Pontano at Perugia, and in different city-states Seneca Camertino, all went to great effort to fill Italy with good literature.

Pliny once said that grapes are fed by clouds, and contends that the wines of Ravenna are considered the best, especially the type called "vermicula." Martial, on the other hand, gives his opinion in these verses:

> I prefer a vat at Ravenna rather than a vineyard.
> For I can sell water for a higher price than wine will bring.

And elsewhere Pliny says that asparagus grows in no soil better than in the gardens of [347C] Ravenna, an opinion Martial confirms in these verses:

> The soft stalks of asparagus grown in the wetlands at Ravenna will
> not be more pleasing than wild asparagus.

And in the same vein, elsewhere, Pliny writes that in the ocean at Ravenna the turbot is the best. But Martial indicates that at Ravenna, there were in ancient times many frogs, just as there are now:

> Although compared to your gaping jaws
> the crocodile of the Nile has a narrower mouth,
> the frogs of Ravenna croak better.

Two rivers encircle Ravenna, making the Bedente. On the right is the Montone; the one on the left was formerly called the Vitis, but is now called Aquaeductus. It has its source in the ridges of the Apennines in a place near the source of the Tiber. Next to it, towards the interior, lies the town of Meldola, and above it Galeata, and after that Santa Sofia. On the left bank of the Montone river on the Via Flaminia is Forlì, a city with an ancient name, in third place of the four Fora which I mentioned Pliny located in this region. We see that Eusebius (in *de temporibus*) also says that the poet Gallus was from Forum Livii, according to Virgil and Horace. And Pliny in-

fuisse Foroliviensem, et Plinius in vinis Italiae optimis Livienses enumerat. Fuit vero ea civitas, quod procul a vanitate mendacii de patria nostra **[347D]** sit dictum, viris praestantissimis praesertim litteratis fecunda, quae praeter Gallum poetam Guidonem Bonactum astrologorum principem habuit, quae Rainerium Arsendum iureconsultum celebrem Bartoli Saxoferratensis praeceptorem, et per eadem ferme tempora Checho Rubeo et Nereo Morando viris doctissimis et Francisco Petrarchae sicut ipse in epistolis saepe memorat amicis ornata fuit.

Excelluit vero per aetatem nostram Iacobus de Turre Forliviensis cunctos philosophiam medicinamque professos; et Iacobi Alegreti Forliviensis bucolicum carmen exstare videmus ceteris post Virgilianum eo in genere scriptis carminibus facile ut periti iudicant praeponendum. Quid quod Ugolinus cognomine Urbevetanus Forlivii genitus et nutritus omnes aetatis nostrae musicos sine contradictione superat, editusque ab eo de musica liber haud secus omnium qui ante se scripserunt labores obscurabit, quod Bonacti opera vetustissimorum scripta astrologorum seponi faciunt? Obiitque nuper Ludovicus Forliviensi et episcopus et civis philosophorum aetatis nostrae theologorumque facile princeps. Rei autem bellicae gnaros et in eo munere claros habuit patria nostra Ioannem Ordelaffum, Brandolinum et Tibertum Brandulos ac Mostardam, quae etiam nunc ornata est Nicolao Hasteo Recanetensi ac Maceratensi episcopo litteris moribus et bonitate conspicuo, pariterque eius pro nepote Stephano **[348E]** Nardino camerae apostolicae clerico, doctrina virtutibusque decorato. Magnam item spem dei munere constitutam videmus in quinque Blondis natis nostris, qui litteris omnes pro aetate sunt pleni.

Feracissimi etiam et in multis naturae benignitate praecipui est patria nostra soli, quae praeter communes ceteris Italiae urbibus fruges, vini, olei, frumenti, seminibus quoque abundat aromaticis, nulli in Italia alteri solo quam Apulo concessis, aniso, cardamomo, fenograeco, cumino, coriandro. Eam civitatem quartus Martinus pontifex Romanus murorum munitione spoliatam, in vici rurisve formam redegit, quam ignominiam honestissima populo et male a pontifice existimata praecessit causa. Cum enim Galli ecclesiae soliti militare Guidone [sic] Appiensi ductore urbem durissima ac diutina pressissent obsidione, cuius meminit vulgaris poeta Dantes, populus Forliviensis hortante Bona<c>to Guidone armis correptis facta eruptione magnam in illis edidit occidionem. Sed qui armis resistendo fortes fuerant cives suasionibus postea mollissimis se decipi permiserunt, in quos pontifex immerito iratus in moenium urbis excidio desaeviit. **[348F]**

cludes the wine of Forlì among the best wines of Italy. Indeed, this was **[347D]** a city—and I do not mean to indulge in false boasting about my own city—especially abundant in outstanding men of letters. In addition to the poet Gallus, it claims Guido Bonatti, foremost among astrologers, and Raniero Arsendi, famous legal scholar and teacher of Bartolo of Sassoferrato; and at almost the same time, Cecco Rossi and Nereo Morando, most learned men in the law, and friends of Francis Petrarch, as he himself often says in his letters.

Iacopo da Torre of Forlì stood out above all the professors of philosophy and medicine. And we see the Bucolic poem of Iacopo Alegreti of Forlì surpassing all others after Virgil which were written in that genre, in the judgment of experts. And what about Ugolino da Orvieto, born and raised at Forlì, who without argument surpasses all the musicians of our age, and whose book about music puts in the shadows the work of all who wrote before him, as the works of Bonatti put to rest the writings of the very ancient astrologers? Lodovico of Forlì recently died: as bishop and as citizen he was easily the king of the theologians and of the philosophers of our age. Our city also has men brilliant in warfare and famous in that gift, Giovanni Ordelaffi, Brandolino and Tiberto Brandulo and Mostarda, and even now is adorned by Nicolò dall'Aste of Recanati, the bishop of Macerata, outstanding in literary knowledge, character, and **[348E]** goodness, and also his great-nephew Stefano Nardino, a cleric of the apostolic chamber, accomplished in learning and in virtues. In the same way, I see great hope, by the gift of God, in my five Biondo sons, who are all for their age accomplished in literature.

My native region is also blessed with very fertile soil, and extraordinary beyond other Italian cities in crops, wine, oil, grain, and aromatic seeds, in which it abounds. No other place in Italy except Apulia is so rich in anise, cardamom, fenugreek, cumin, and coriander. Pope Martin IV fortified the city's walls and restored the beauty of its village and countryside after it suffered the devastation of its walls. This disgrace was caused by the people's sincere action followed by a pope's unjust reaction. For when French mercenaries under the command of Jean d'Eppes had besieged the city (the poet Dante wrote about this in the vernacular), Guido Bonatti encouraged the people of Forlì to take up arms and burst out of the city and slaughter them. But those citizens who bravely resisted weapons later weakly allowed themselves to be deceived by persuasions. The pope, unjustly enraged against them, retaliated by tearing down the city walls. **[348F]**

Ad Montoni dexteram Castrum Carum est oppidum prius Salsubium a scatente ibi salso fonte dictum; inde Donadula, post Cassianum; deinceps arduo in colle est Porticus, eloquentissimo et Graece Latineque doctissimo Ambrosio Camaldulensi principe monacho quem genuit clarum, ut non immerito nos aliquando gloriari soleamus, quod vetusti patriae nostrae agri, ius a Forliviensi praetore patrum nostrorum memoria petere soliti, oppida, Plautum Sassina, Ambrosium Porticus genuerunt.

Ravennae moenia secus Montonum amnem fossa attingit, a vetustissimis ut inquit Plinius Messanicum appellata, duodecim milibus navigia in Padum perferens. Padusa ad eam fossam incipit palus vetusti nominis, et quam geographi unicam in Italia paludem esse volunt, de qua in Georgicis Virgilius, "piscosove amne Padusa." Complectitur vero quicquid lacunae aut stagnorum aut palustris soli, ab ea Ravennate fossa quinquagesimo ferme miliario Padum inter et Flaminiae aut Aemiliae agros intercedere videmus.

Annomoque fluvius nec Adriaticum mare nec Padum attingens in eam primus delabitur paludem; cui fluvio primus in sicco adiacet Traversaria Ravennatum vicus, et pari spatio ad **[348G]** dexteram Bagnacavallum novi nominis oppidum prius Tiberiacum et aliquando Ad Caballos appellatum. Dividit autem interius Annomo Faventiam vetusti nominis civitatem, cuius tamen factam primo mentionem invenimus apud Livium libro LXXXIX, "Sulla Carbonem cum exercitu ad Clusium, ad Faventiam, Fidentiolamque caeso Italia expulit." Et Aelius Spartianus in vita Hadriani, "Interfecti insidiatores Hadriani consulares, Palma Terracinae, Nigrinus Faventiae." Idemque Spartianus, "Ceionius Commodus qui et Aelius Verus natus est maioribus Faventinis." Et Iulius Capitolinus Lucii Veri Aelii imperatoris vitam scribens sic habet, "Origo eius paterna ex Etruria fuit, materna ex Faventia."

Eamque urbem Gothi sustulerunt, et postea reaedificatam Federicus cognomine Barbarossus male habitam reddidit immunitam. Et anno abinde vix dum ducentesimo Brittones in Italia tunc militantes diripuerunt. Nuper vero Guidatius Manfredus primo, post Astorgius frater, praestantes rei militaris duces eandem vicariatus ecclesiae titulo gubernantes, muro cingere praevalido inceperunt. Ornata fuit Faventia nuper Martino praestanti rei militaris ductore. **[348H]**

On the left bank of the Montone river is Castrocaro, in antiquity the town of Salsubium, named for the fountain of salt water which gushes forth there. Then comes Dovadula, and after that San Cassiano; then, on a steep hill, Portico, birthplace of Ambrogio Traversari, the head of the Camaldolensian order, a monk very eloquent and learned in both Greek and Latin. In fact, I am accustomed sometimes to boast, not unjustly, because men were accustomed to seek the law from the praetor of Forlì in the memory of our fathers' generation, and of the towns of the ancient territory of my homeland, Sarsina gave birth to Plautus and Portico to Ambrogio.

There is a ditch which lies adjacent to the walls of Ravenna along the Montone river. The very ancient sources called it the Messanicus, as Pliny tells us, and for twelve miles it carries ships into the Po. The swamp called Padusa begins at this ditch; this is an ancient name, and the only swamp which the geographers acknowledge to exist in Italy. Virgil in the *Georgics* says about it: "The Padusa, full of fish." Indeed, it encloses whatever pond or pools or marshy soil there is from this ditch at Ravenna; we see it cover about fifty miles between the Po and the territory of Flaminia or Aemilia.

The river Lamone does not touch either the Adriatic Sea nor the Po, but runs down first into that swamp. Next to this river, the first town on dry land is Traversaria, a **[348G]** parish of Ravenna, and equidistant on the right bank is Bagnacavallo, a town with a new name formerly called Tiberiacum and sometimes Ai Cavalli. The Lamone river sets off the city of Faenza, whose name is ancient. Nevertheless we find it first mentioned in Livy, book 89: "Sulla drove Carbo with his army out of Italy to Clusium, Faventia, and Fidentiola." And Aelius Spartianus in the *Life of Hadrian*: "The traitors were killed, the consulars, Palma at Terracina, Nigrinus at Faventia." And the same author says, "Ceionius Commodus and Aelius Verus were born from ancestors from Faventia." And Julius Capitolinus, in his *Life* of the emperor Lucius Verus Aelius, says, "His father came from Etruscan origins, his mother from Faventia."

The Goths destroyed this city, and afterwards it was rebuilt. Frederick Barbarossa made it exempt, as it was not well inhabited. Scarcely two hundred years later, the Bretons, making war in Italy, destroyed it. But recently, Guidaccio Manfredi first, and later his brother Astorre, both outstanding commanders, governed it with the title of vicar of the church, and began to surround it with a strong wall. Faenza has been recently distinguished by Martino, the outstanding military commander. **[348H]**

Tradi videmus a multis Octavium Augustum M. Lepidum, et M. Antonium de scelestissimo triumviratu suo apud Confluentia prope Bononiam convenisse. Abesse autem non potest, quin aut Faventia aut proxime apud Bagnacavallum Cutignolam et Lugum ubi flumina Annomo, Sennius, et Vatrenus ac Padus in mare unis ostiis confluunt ea fuerint Confluentia, de quo nefario scelere in hanc sententiam scribit Livius libro CXIX,

> In triumviratu proscriptio facta est in qua plurimi equites, senatores CXXX vicissim concessi. Lepidus enim L. Paulum fratrem, Antonius L. Caesarem avunculum, et Octavius M. Ciceronem, qui a Popilio legionario milite, cum haberet annos LXIIII occisus est, caputque cum dextra manu in rostris posita, ubi multos defenderat.

Plinius de lino Italiae tractans Faventinum in Aemilia via miris effert laudibus. Et alio loco eos numerans, quos Vespasianus imperator facta Italiae descriptione excellenter inveteratos reperit, unam dicit mulierem Faventiae inventam fuisse, quae annos XXV supra centesimum nata erat.

Interius quarto supra Faventiam miliario Aureolum est oppidum, ecclesiae Ravennatis amoenissimo in colle situm, sub quo in Annomonem defluit Martianus torrens, qui latera abluit Mutilanae vetustissimi oppidi, cuius Mutili tunc appellati Livius in principio belli [349A] Macedonici, sicut in Ravenna ostendimus meminit.

Fuitque ante quingentos annos nobilis familiae comitum, qui Guido cognomine per Flaminiam et Etruriam floruerunt. Supra Faventiam ad Annomonis fluenta Convallis est fluvii nomen retinens populis frequentata, in qua Brasgella, Rontana, Grattaria, Castilionum, Castella, Marrate, et Bifurcus vici, et sub Apennino Crispinus. Post Annomonem Padusam paludem influit Sennius amnis, cui ipsa in palude et in silva quam Lugi dicunt adiacet Fusignanum oppidum. Et ad dexteram Sennii ripam Cutignola est oppidum, unde Attendula gens Sfortiorum familia fluxit in Italis nunc clarissima.

Adiacet Lugo Zagonaria castellum acceptae a Florentino populo cladis in Philippensi bello, et capti in eo proelio Caroli Malatestae, quod in historiis diffuse ostendimus memoria celebratum. Et infra secundum inde miliarium ad Sennii ripam excisum est oppidum Cunium, ex quo operis huius principio diximus familiam nobilem Cunii comitum originem duxisse, quae

Many authorities have stated that Octavius Augustus, Marcus Lepidus, and Marcus Antonius had a meeting concerning their criminal triumvirate near Bologna at an island in the river Reno; this spot cannot be far from Faenza, or very near it, at Bagnacavallo, and Cotignola, and Lugo, where the Lamone, the Senio, and the Santerno and the Po rivers flow with one mouth into the sea. About this crime Livy writes in book 119:

> In the triumvirate, a proscription took place in which very many knights and 130 senators were given up. Indeed, Lepidus gave up his brother L. Paulus; Antonius his uncle L. Caesar; and Octavius, M. Cicero, who in his sixty-fourth year was killed and his head with his right hand displayed on the rostra, where he had defended many clients.

Pliny in his discussion of the linen of Italy lavishly praises that of Faventia on the Via Aemilia. In another place, listing those the emperor Vespasian found who had lived to an advanced age, he says one woman was found at Faventia who was one hundred and twenty-five years old.

Towards the interior, four miles above Faenza, is the town of Riolo Terme, belonging to the church of Ravenna, located on a very pleasant hill. Beneath it the Marzeno stream flows down into the Lamone River and flows alongside the very ancient town of Modigliana, whose inhabitants are now called Mutilli. In his treatment of the beginning of the **[349A]** Macedonian war, Livy records this fact—as I showed in my discussion of Ravenna.

Five hundred years ago there was a noble family with the surname Guido which flourished in Flaminia and Etruria. Above Faenza at the Lamone river is a thickly-inhabited valley which keeps the name of the river. In it are the villages of Brisighella, Rontana, Gattara, Castiglione, Castellina, Marradi, and Biforco. Beneath the Apennines is Crespino; after the Lamone the Senio river flows into the swamp Padusa; near this, in the swamp itself, and in the forest which they call Lugo, lies the town of Fusignano. And on the right bank of the Senio is the town of Cotignola, which brought forth the family of the Attendolo Sforza, now famous among the Italians.

Next to Lugo lies the *castello* of Zagonara, which was taken by the Florentines in the war with Duke Filippo Maria of Milan. Carlo Malatesta was captured in that battle, a famous event which I recorded in my *Decades*. And below the second milestone from there, on the bank of the Senio, is the destroyed town of Cunio. At the beginning of this work I noted that from this town originated the noble family of the Counts of Cunio, which sup-

multos habuit belli duces. Non itaque duximus omittendum, quod maxime ad praesentem facit intentionem, Albricum Cunii comitem, qui primus hoc nomine in [349B] ea familia fuit, fato quodam illum fuisse, qui maximam in re militari Italica fecit mutationem.

Ut enim remotiora omittamus tempora rei publicae et imperatorum, qui ad inclinationem usque imperium Romae et in Italia integrum tenuerunt, ut etiam illa omittamus quae per annos ferme quadringentos malo suo Italia per Visigothorum, Erulorum, Ostrogothorum et Longobardorum tempora vidit accurate nostris in historiis narrata, magnam quietem Italia sub Carolo Magno et suis filiis ac nepotibus Romae imperantibus, per annos circiter centum habuit.

Sed mox ad pristinos paene labores sub Italicis tribus tyrannis Berengariis redacta, brevi post Germanorum regum imperii titulo ornatorum temporibus varia uti fortuna coepit. Quae aliquot ex ipsis tyrannos, aliquot inertes malignos passa nihil minus mali vidit, quam cum inter seipsam divisa est. Et parte oppressa pars astu, dolis aut fortitudine usa calamitatem ad tempus potuit declinare.

Unicum vero tantis malis remedium aliquando excogitatum est, cum implorata Romanorum pontificum auxilia aliquos a mali regis, sive imperatoris Germani saevitia tutabantur. Quamquam tempora saepe fuerunt, in quibus magis ipsa pontificum [349C] dissidia cum malis principibus nocuere. Cum itaque ad Romanorum pontificum aliquando inefficax remedium esset visum, coepere urbes in Italia potentiores, praesertim Lombardiae et Marchiae Tarvisinae, sese in libertatem erigere, et societatibus initis invicem se tueri.

Irruerunt vero aliquotiens Germani reges, Otto tertius, tres Henrici, tertius et quartus, et postea septimus. Deinde primus Federicus, et secundus, et demum Ludovicus Bavarus, et hinc pontificibus sociisque bello populis inde regibus, vel impugnantibus, vel iniuriam propulsantibus strages ubique, caedes, direptiones, incendia in Italis sunt commissa, ut ausim affirmare plus aliquando calamitatis ab hac gente acceptum, quam raro alias a barbaris omnino Christianae fidei hostibus perpessum erat. In tantis malis ultimo paene Bavari tempore coeperunt Romani pontifices atque etiam aliquae bellorum sociae civitates adversus Germanicam tyrannorum rabiem externos milites, Francos, Hispanos, Anglicos, Brittonesque mercede conductos in Italiam vocare. Quin etiam quotiens orta inter electores imperii, quod saepe contingit, aut aliter inter Romanos principes discordia, visum est tutum esse Germanorum electo imperatori inimicorum praesidia pretio sunt accepta. [349D]

plied many leaders in war. I must mention here a point relevant to my purpose in this work: Alberico, Count of Cunio, who was the first of this name in this family, was also fated to be the instrument **[349B]** of great change in Italian military history.

I pass over ancient history, the times of the Republic and Empire, when things were held together in Italy until the decline of the Roman Empire. And I pass over also the nearly four hundred years of misery in Italy which saw the rule of Visigoths, Eruli, Ostrogoths, and Lombards. (I have narrated all this accurately in my *Decades*.) Italy then enjoyed approximately one hundred years of quiet under Charlemagne and his descendants.

But soon the three Italian tyrants, the Berengars, brought us back to nearly the original state of trouble; and a short while after that, we began to suffer varying fortunes under the rule of the German kings who were crowned emperors. Some of these rulers conducted themselves at times in Italy as tyrants, and at times were simply passive and malevolent, but no less evil for that. Italy was divided, part oppressed, part subject to treachery or bravery, each part sank according to the disaster of the time.

But the only remedy for these evils was the occasional intervention of the Roman popes, when they were begged to preserve us from the savagery of either an evil king or a German emperor. There were, however, times when more harm was done by the schisms together with the secular rulers. **[349C]** And so, when it seemed useless to resort to the popes for aid, the more powerful Italian cities, especially those in Lombardy and the March of Treviso, began to claim their freedom, and form common bonds for self-preservation.

But from time to time there were invasions by German kings: Otto III, the three Henrys, the third and fourth and after them the seventh; then Frederick I, and Frederick II, and finally Ludwig of Bavaria. On this side the popes and peoples allied in war, on that side the kings, brought fires, plundering, slaughter everywhere among the Italians, by their conflicts or damage. I venture to say that such disaster at times afflicted the Italians as seldom at other times had been suffered from utter infidels. In the midst of such evils, at the time of the last Bavarian king, the popes and the cities allied with them began to summon foreign mercenaries against the insanity of German tyranny: Franks, Spanish, Angles, and Bretons. But often dissension arose among the imperial electors, or among the Roman leaders, so that purchased protection seemed safe to an emperor elected to rule over hostile Germans. **[349D]**

Unde factum est, ut per annos circiter centum a Martini quarti pontificatu usque ad Gregorii XI tempora diversis in regionibus Italia, aut Theotonicos, aut Brittones, aut Anglicos habuerit mercede conductos. Nulla enim erat Italiae civitas, quae Italico homini stipendia penderet; sed singuli populi inter se centuriati suae rei publicae munera gratis obibant. Et vexilla curru vecta, quod appellarunt Charrotium in expeditiones ac proelia ducebantur, acciditque dimissos aliquando aut alias cum praedandi libido incessit, huiusmodi conductos mercenarios milites plura maioraque damna nostratibus, quam eos a quibus timebatur intulisse. Dicunt hoc maximo experti damno Perusini clade ingenti XII milium, vel ferro caesorum, vel Tiberi enectorum a Brittonibus Anglicisque afflicti. Testantur Cesena Faventiaque crudeliter direptae, et omnis regio affirmat urbi Romae adiacens, in qua ferunt, qui interfuerunt supra LX oppida, et castella partim funditus, ut nunc manent excisa. Partim habitatoribus pulsis spoliata fuisse, ut felices habiti sint ex ipsis, quod nihil rerum amissione durius ab Anglicis Brittonibusque fuerunt passi.

Crescebat interim Vicecomitum in Lombardis potentia Benedicti XI pontificis Romani auctoritate in Bavari damnum dedecusque Luchino Vicecomiti et Ioanni eius fratri Mediolanensi archiepiscopo attributa. **[350E]** Et varie per aliquot tempora inter Lombardos, quod diffuse in historiis diximus, est certatum. Quibus in bellis cum Brittones, Anglicique contraria Bernabovi Vicecomiti sentirent, armavit ille cum alios in Italia tum in primis Albricum, de quo dicere coepimus Cunii comitem, qui externo militi saepe congressus superior victorque evasit. Et tamen variante ut fit fortuna exercitu Bernabovis fracto fugatoque Albricus est captus, quem ut militari aetatis nostrae more dimitterent, cum illi precibus rationibusque aliis adduci non possent, Bernabos argento ad trutinam quanti ponderaret impenso redemit.

Isque praestantissimus ductor eam gentem externam brevi expulit Lombardia, quae Vicecomiti erat subdita. Bernabove postmodum a nepote in carcerem coniecto, Albricus stipendio dimissis Italis omnibus, qui arma ferre coeperant, sese ducem ea ratione exhibuit, ut coacti eam in militiam praestantiores quique inito foedere, quod sacramento firmatum est, una essent societas Sancti Georgii appellata. Qua cum societate adeo ardenti celsoque animo externos Albricus est insectatus, ut nullus qui paterna avitaque origine in Italia genitus non esset, arma per eum circumferre sit ausus. Fuisse autem ad quadraginta equitum milia **[350F]** externos Italia tunc pulsos

For this reason, for about one hundred years, from the reign of Martin IV to that of Gregory XI, mercenaries, either Germans, Bretons, or English, were active in the various areas of Italy. Indeed there was not an Italian city-state which hired Italian mercenaries; but the individual populations discharged without pay the duty of soldiering for their own states. They had standards carried in a cart, which they called *carroccio* and brought along on their expeditions and into battle. When the mercenaries were demobilized, they were often seized by a desire to plunder, and these soldiers brought more losses on our ancestors than did those people they feared as enemies. It is said that the citizens of Perugia suffered a very great slaughter of this kind when twelve thousand of them were either cut down by the sword or killed in the Tiber by the Bretons and English. The destructions of Cesena and Faenza also bear witness to this cruelty. The entire region near Rome also declares it, where of over sixty towns and *castelli* part were totally destroyed, as they now remain, and part had their citizens driven out, and these people are considered fortunate that they suffered nothing worse than loss of their possessions at the hands of the English and Bretons.

Meanwhile, the power of the Visconti in Lombardy was growing, and Pope Benedict XI gave to Lucchino Visconti and his brother Giovanni authority over the see of Milan, to the **[350E]** disadvantage of the Bavarian emperor. I have narrated in different places in my *Decades* how the Lombards fought amongst themselves for some time. In these wars, the Bretons and Angles came to disagreement with Bernabò Visconti, and he called to arms other Italians, most notably Alberico, who I mentioned was Count of Cunio, and who had often fought successfully against foreign mercenaries. But still, as fortune would have it, the army of Bernabò was defeated and routed, and Alberico was captured. When his captors could not be prevailed upon to release him in accordance with the military custom of our age, Bernabò ransomed him for his weight in silver.

Alberico was an outstanding general, who quickly drove that foreign race out of Lombardy, and made it subject to the Visconti. Bernabò's nephew subsequently threw him into jail, and Alberico paid and let go from service all the Italians who had begun to bear arms. He presented himself as leader with the following procedure: the superior men were forced into military service by entering into a compact confirmed by an oath, called the Company of St. George. At the head of this group Alberico with his burning spirit pursued the foreigners, to the extent that no one who was not born of Italian father or grandfather dared to serve under **[350F]** him. I have heard

audivimus, cum Albricus sua societate repentino tumultu congregatos, vix duodecim milia habuerit.

Fomesque id et origo quaedam fuit omnium rei militaris ducum, quos audivimus et ipsi vidimus administrandorum bellorum gloria excelluisse. Nam Braccius Montonensis domesticus Albrico familiarisque fuit. Sfortia cum Laurentio Attendulo consanguineo prima ductu Brandolini Foroliviensis in Albrici exercitu tirocinia fecit. Pariter Paulus Ursinus Mostarda Foroliviensis, Tartaliaque Lavellensis, et Thomasinus Cribellus Mediolanensis, Albrici ductu, auspiciis, et disciplina, militiam sunt secuti. Institutae autem in Italia militiae Albricus novum addidit ornamentum, quod ubi thoraces, ocreas, brachialiaque ex corio, quod nos vidimus, vel externi, vel cives in tumultibus patriae militantes induebantur, ferro ipse et chalibe totum armari hominem primus edocuit, et in sua societate curavit.

Externis Italia pulsis Albricus in Neapolitanum se conferens regnum Ladislao regi, a quo magni commestabilis dignitate ornatus fuit, talem praestiti operam, ut nedum regno a multis potentissimisque invasoribus occupato sit potitus, **[350G]** sed talia per Italiam iecerit fundamenta, ex quibus apparuit eum nisi morte post Albricum praeventus fuisset regni Italici atque imperii dignitates in Italiam reducturum fuisse. Sentiant vero quicquid alii volunt, nostra fert opinio, tanti fuisse externos milites, Anglos, Brittones, Germanos Italia pulsos esse, ut et opibus magis abundaverit, et maiorem certe tutiorem quietem postea semper habuerit. Nam etsi in bellis, quae post eam externorum eiectionem sunt gesta urbium oppidorumque direptiones committuntur, ab excidio tamen incendio et sanguine nostri saepius temperant, et quod uni in expilatione damno est, opes alteri Italico accumulat, quas externus barbarusque asportasset.

Quin etiam econtra factum videmus, ut cum multi ex Italicis magna conducti mercede Francis et Anglicis coeperint militare, spolia inde et pecuniae in Italiam deferantur. Nullusque mihi ostenderet aedificandi, vestiendi, ornandi, et ceteram omnem vitae nostrae, quam hoc saeculo vivimus luxuriem, lautitiam, ceterosque magnificos apparatus certe superioribus saeculis fieri solitis maiores aliunde, quam ab hac securitate et tutela originem habuisse. **[350H]** Quae omnia Albrico nostro Cunii alumno, quod excisum nunc aratur, non immerito laudem gloriamque perpetuam accumulant.

that forty thousand foreign cavalry were at that time driven out of Italy; after this sudden upheaval, scarcely twelve thousand remained to join Alberico.

This was the beginning of the *condottieri*, whom I have heard about, and seen, excelling in the skills of war. For Braccio da Montone was a member of Alberico's household; Sforza, along with his kinsman Lorenzo Attendolo served their apprenticeship in Alberico's army, under the command of Brandolino of Forlì. Paolo Orsino (Mostarda) of Forlì as well, and Tartaglia Lavellensis, and Tommaso Crivelli of Milan, all served in the military under Alberico's generalship, guidance, and training. Alberico added, too, a new equipment to the Italian military profession: breastplates, greaves, and armlets of leather, which I myself have seen. Either foreigners, or citizens fighting for their cities against other cities, put these on; he himself first showed men, with iron or with steel, how to use full body armor, and took care to arm this way the men in his company.

When he had driven the foreign mercenaries out of Italy, Alberico went to the Neapolitan kingdom of King Ladislas, who honored him with the title of Great Count. Alberico rendered such outstanding service that not only did he take possession of the kingdom, which had been seized by many powerful invaders, **[350G]** but laid the groundwork throughout Italy so that, except for the intervention of his death, Alberico would have restored the greatness of the Italian kingdom and empire. Let others think what they may; in my opinion, his expulsion of the foreign mercenaries (English, Bretons, and Germans) from Italy was so valuable that it brought about an abundance of wealth and a more secure peace forever afterwards. For even in wars which were joined after the expulsion of these foreigners, there was plundering of cities and towns; but the combatants usually held off from destruction by fire, and from spilling Italian blood. And when pillaging did occur, the wealth plundered (which had previously been carried off by barbarians and foreigners) now enriched other Italians.

Indeed, I have seen the opposite happen: when many Italians, lured by good pay, began to fight for the French and English, they brought back to Italy from those lands spoils and money. I am persuaded that the buildings, clothing, accessories, and all the other luxuries of our present lifestyle, splendor, and the rest of the magnificence greater than in past ages, have their roots in this security and protection. All of these improvements redound to the perpetual glory **[350H]** of our countryman, Alberico of Cunio (a town laid waste and now ploughed under).

Nec tamen negamus Romanae curiae in Italiam ab Avinione reversionem opulentiam Italiae plurimum adauxisse. Nam cum per annos LXX Avionione Romani pontifices curiam tenuissent, Gregorius XI natione Lemovicensis eandem ad annum salutis LXXX supra millesimum et trecentesimum, in Italiam traduxit. At postquam dei munere et eloquentia per viri Romandioli Ravennae geniti virtutem reviviscere coepit, et nova tutiorque rei militaris forma in Italia externis eiectis per Albricum item Romandiolum est reddita, eandem quoque Romandiolam per nostras manus tertiam in rebus maximis gloriam Italiae speramus, qui latentem supra mille annos historiam tanta attigimus diligentia, ut omnem nedum Italiae, sed totius olim Romani imperii provinciarum, regionumque statum, ad quorum vel regum, vel principum, vel nationum manus pervenerit, clare magis et quam fieri posse videretur, diffuse ostenderimus, cum Roma interim instaurata, Italiam quoque abstersa errorum obscuritatumque multa rubigine, noverimus illustrare.

Interius Via Flaminia Sennium iungit pons Proculeius, et ad dexteram in eadem via Bolognesium est novi nominis oppidum, quod patrum nostrorum memoria Bononiensis populus a fundamentis aedificavit. Supra sunt Sosenana et in Apennino **[351A]** Palatiolum castella olim rei militaris gloria clarissimae genti Ubaldinae subdita, quae superiori saeculo simul cum longissimi tractus Apennini vicis, castellis, et oppidis ab eadem gente possessis populus Florentinus per arma cepit.

In Padusa item Vatrenus sequitur amnis, quem Plinius scribit solitum fuisse ostia Padi, nunc Primaria ubi Spineticum appellabatur adaugere. Sed nunc averso paene viginti milibus cursu novi nominis ostia in Padusam et Padum habet Zaniolum appellata, ubi clarae memoriae Nicolaus Estensis Marchio magnifici operis arcem, et postea Leonellus successor, ac filius viam, quae duodecimo miliario perducit Lugum fecerunt.

Intus ad Vatreni dexteram in via Flaminia est Imola, Forum Cornelii priscis appellata, ad quod erat Aemiliae regionis initium. Martialisque poeta hanc urbem inhabitasse videtur, sicut his in versibus innuit,

Si quibus in terris qua simus in urbe rogabit,
Cornelii referas me licet esse foro.

Now I agree that the return of the papal Curia from Avignon to Italy has increased our country's wealth. After the popes had held court at Avignon for seventy years, Gregory XI transferred it to Italy in the year 1380. But after that, by a gift of God and through the virtue of a man of the Romagna, born at Ravenna, eloquence too began to be reborn. And in the same way, after the expulsion of the barbarians, a new, safer form of military activity was invented by another man of the Romagna, Alberico. The same Romagna has, I hope, given a third source of glory to Italy: by my careful work, our history, which has lain hidden for a thousand years, has again been brought to light. I have displayed abundantly, clearly, and to the best of my ability the position, not only of Italy, but of all the former provinces of the Roman Empire, and of its regions; have told which kings, or princes, or nations, have possessed it. As I restored Rome a while ago with my *Roma instaurata*, I have brought to light Italy too, cleansed of errors, darkness, and blight.

Towards the interior, on the Via Flaminia, the Proculeian bridge spans the Senio River. On the right bank on the same road is the town of Castel Bolognese, a modern name; its foundation by the people of Bologna lies within the memory of our fathers' generation. **[351A]** Above it are Susinana and, in the Apennines, Palazzuolo. Both are *castelli* once subject to the Ubaldini, a family very glorious in military affairs, but in the last century the Florentines captured them, along with a great area of the Apennines containing the villages, *castelli*, and towns belonging to the Ubaldini.

Next, in the Padusa, comes the Santerno river, which Pliny says was the mouth of the Po, but now the Santerno flows into the Po di Primaro, where it was called Spinetoli. But now it turns aside from its course for nearly twenty miles and has a mouth with a new name into the Po and its marshes, called the Zeno, where the famous Marquis Niccolò d'Este, and his son and successor Leonello, have built a magnificent citadel and a road which goes twelve miles to Lugo.

Towards the interior, on the right bank of the Santerno, is Imola, the ancient Forum Cornelii and the beginning of the region of Aemilia. The poet Martial seems to have lived here, or so he implies in the following verses,

> If he asks in what lands, in what city I am living,
> you may answer that I am at Forum Cornelii.

Ea civitas a Narsetis militibus sicut in historiis diximus diruta, et brevi post a Clephi immanissimo Longobardorum rege sub novo hoc Imolae nomine, ut Ravennatibus fidem pontificum Romanorum servantibus opponeretur aedificata est. [351B] Habuitque paulo supra aetatem nostram Benevenutum, qui grammaticus et ludi magister tunc in Italia primarius, cum historias nosset aliqua scripsit. Claruitque diebus nostris Ioannes Imolensis pontificii et civilis iurium peritissimus.

Est interius ad Vatreni sinistram septimo ab Imola miliario Taxignanum oppidum, quod decimum Ioannem Romanum pontificem genuit ingentis certe virtutis et famae virum, a quo Saraceni mediam ferme Italiam obtinentes in fugam primo conversi, post ad Lirim fluvium magna occisione profligati Italiam reliquerunt. Fuit quoque Taxignanum superiori saeculo ornatum Petro excellenti medico. Et nuper ex vico Codregnano, qui Taxignano mille quingentis passibus abest, originem habuit Ioannes Ferrariensis episcopus vir cum doctus, tum omnimoda vitae sanctimonia redundans.

Supra ad Vatreni dexteram Coderonchum, et superius sub ipsis Apennini radicibus est Florentiola novum oppidum a populo Florentino, cui subest aedificatum. Proximo item in Padusae loco oppidum est Caput Silicis appellatum, per quod transmissa lintribus septimo miliario Padusa per Zaniolum navigatur in Padum. Via quae ab eo oppido Imolam [351C] XII dicit miliario Silicis nomen retinet, inde olim inditum quod silicibus Roma avectis strata fuit. Cum enim Romano imperio florente, aliqua belli aut pacis usibus necessaria in Aemiliam deferri esset opus, ea mari advecta per Padi ostia, et inde per Padusam huc loci comportabantur, unde viam natura soli et paludis propinquitate caenosam, et raro tunc sicut et nunc etiam aestate plaustra perferentem sterni necessitas adegit. Silices autem Roma avectos, ut dicamus facit Plinius, qui genus id lapidis nullo alio quam circa urbem et mare Etruscum loco reperiri dicit. Dispersos vero per Ferrariam Imolam ac circumstantia loca silices, ab hac nunc spoliata via acceptos videmus esse ex his, qui nunc in stratis circa urbem Romam viis passim conspiciuntur.

Sequitur torrens in Padusam labens Siler, cui intus apposita sunt agri Bononiensis oppida S. Petri ad dexteram, et Ducia ad sinistram. Superius

As I have noted in my histories, this city was destroyed by the soldiers of Narses. A little while after that, the cruel Lombard king Cleph rebuilt it (with its new name of Imola) to stand as an opponent to the Ravennates, who were faithful to the pope. **[351B]** This city, in times a little before ours, boasted Benvenuto, who was then the foremost teacher in Italy, as well as a historian. And in our times there was the famous Giovanni da Imola, expert in canon and civil law.

Towards the interior, on the left bank of the Santerno and seven miles from Imola, is the town of Tossignano, birthplace of Pope John X, a man of great virtue and glory; he was first to rout the Saracens when they had taken possession of central Italy. Then, after they were overwhelmed in a bloody battle at the Garigliano river, they left Italy. Tossignano in the last century was also proud of her son Pietro, an outstanding physician. Recently Giovanni, bishop of Ferrara, came from the village of Codrignano, 1500 yards from Tossignano; a learned man, he was not only a bishop, but also full of holiness in every way.

Higher up, on the right bank of the Santerno, is Poggio Roncaccio, and above that, right at the foothills of the Apennines, is Firenzuola, a new town built by the Florentines and subject to them. And the next place in the southern Po delta is a town called Conselice, and seven miles from it you can cross the swamp in a small boat and pass through the Zeno river into **[351C]** the Po. The road which goes from this town twelve miles to Imola has the name "Selice" which it was given in ancient times, because it was paved with stones brought from Rome. For when the Empire was at its height, some things for war- or peace-time use were needed in Emilia; and these things were transported by sea through the mouth of the Po, and from there they were carried through the Padusa to this place. It was necessary to lay a road which could bear wagons, but the road was muddy due to the nature of the soil and its proximity to the swamp and used rarely, just as is now the case even in summer. But I think hard paving-stones were brought from Rome, because they are a type of stone which Pliny says can be found nowhere but around the city and the Tyrrhenian Sea. We can see these stones were scattered through Ferrara and Imola and the surrounding places, and I know they were taken from this road because now they can be seen scattered on the paved roads around the city of Rome.

There follows the stream Sillaro, which drains into the swamps of the Po; and opposite it, towards the interior on the right bank, is a town of the Bolognese territory, Castel S. Pietro; and on the left bank, Dozza. Higher up

vero in montibus est Flagnanum oppidum, II Honorio pontifice Romano ibi genito decoratum. Torrens inde habetur Claterna Padusam iuxta vicum Ad Caballos petens, ad cuius nominis pontem viam Flaminiam iungentem oppidum **[351D]** fuit Claterna, cuius modica apparent fundamenta, de quo Cicero ad Lentulum, "Erat Claternae noster Hirtius, ad Forum Cornelii Caesar."

Parvo inde spatio a Padusa absunt oppida: hinc Medicina, inde Butrium populo et quidem divite frequentissimum. Supra est in collibus Varagnana. Idex inde habetur fluvius apud Mulinellam vicum Padusam attingens, unde vigesimo stadio ad Padi ripas lintribus navigatur. Ad sinistramque Idicis primo in colle castellum est Brittonum sub Apennino, ad sinistram Visanum, ad dexteram Caburatium.

Amni Savenae Padusam illabenti Bononia adiacet. Suntque intus ad eius amnis sinistram via Florentina vici Planorium primo, post in montibus Loianum, inde Scarcalasinum, et in Apennino Caprenum. Deinceps est Rheni Bononiensis pars fossa manufacta per urbem ducta, quae Avesam torrentulum urbem dividentem ad pomerium augens, lintres per Padusam dimittit in Padum. Secundum huius navigationis sinistram Padusae adiacet Ocelinum turris in Ferrariensi via ad limitis agri Bononiensis custodiam communita. Apud Ocelini turrem Padusae finem olim fuisse, et Rhenum Bononiensem eo in loco aut propinquo Padum influxisse, indicant pervetusti utriusque amnis alvei. Indicantque pariter Ptolemaei ac aliorum geographorum descriptio ac pictura, cum vero Padus quattuor fere milia passuum retrocesserit, quicquid praesentem **[352E]** Padi ripam et Ocelinum intercedit, Padusae accessit. Nec ut ante consueverant, Padum illabuntur Rhenus et Scultenna, sed Lavinio et Samogia auctus Rhenus et Scultennae et Formigini torrentulo iungitur, coactaque huiusmodi aquarum moles per ultima Padusae ostia ad Bondenum illabitur Padum.

Id vero Bononiensis agri, quod Rhenum Padusam et ipsam intercedit urbem, plurimis vicis, oppidis, et castellis frequentatur: Podio Lambertinorum, Prosperio Platesiorum, Venantio, Galleria, Peretulo, Centio et Plebeio. Bononiam urbem vetustam scribit Plinius, urbium quas Etrusci ultra Apenninum habuere primariam Boiorum postea caput fuisse, ut pro Felsina

in the mountains is the town Fagnano, distinguished as the birthplace of Pope Honorius II. From there, the Quaderna stream flows towards the Padusa next to the village Bagnocavallo. The town of Claterna was located at a bridge of the same name spanning the Via Flaminia **[351D]**; all that remains of it are a few foundations. Cicero wrote to Lentulus about Claterna, "Our friend Hirtius was at Claterna, and Caesar at Forum Cornelii."

A little farther on from the marshes of the Po lies the town of Medicina, then Budrio, the latter densely inhabited by a wealthy population. Above them in the hills is Varignana. Then comes the Idice river, which skirts the marshes at the village of Molinella. Twenty stades from there, one can navigate in small boats to the banks of the Po. On the left bank of the Idice, on the first hill next to the Apennines, is Castel dei Britti, on the left bank is Bisano, on the right Caburaccio.

And beside the Savena river, which flows into the Padusa, lies Bologna. On the left bank of this river, towards the interior on the Via Flaminia, are these villages: first Pianoro, then in the mountains Loiano, then Scaricalasino, and, in the Apennines, Caprenno. Then comes a man-made canal, called the Reno of Bologna, part of which goes through the city, joins the stream Avesa which divides the city at its outer boundary, and on which ships go through the Padusa into the Po. Following the left bank of this waterway, the military tower Oggioli lies next to the Padusa on the road to Ferrara, fortified in order to protect the boundary of Bolognese territory. The ancient beds of these rivers show that the boundary of the Padusa formerly lay at this tower, and the Bolognese Reno flows into the Po at this point or very near it. The maps and descriptions of Ptolemy and other geographers corroborate this finding. But when the Po receded nearly four miles, whatever was between the present bank of the Po and **[352E]** Oggioli was added to the Padusa; and the Reno and the Scultenna do not, as they had before, flow into the Po; but the Reno receives the Lavino and Samoggia streams, and is joined with the Scultenna and the small stream Formigine. The mass of water combined in this way flows through the farthest mouths of the Padusa into the Po at Bondeno.

This part of Bolognese territory lying between the Reno, Padusa, and the city itself, is densely inhabited with villages, towns, and *castelli*. They include Poggio Renatico, San Prospero, Venenta, Galliera, Porretta, Cento, and Pieve di Cento. Pliny writes that the city of Bologna is ancient, and was the chief city among those beyond the Apennines held by the Etruscans, and afterwards was the capital of the Boii. It is commonly believed that it was

credatur primum Boionia post Bononia esse dicta. Eam Livius XXXVII dicit coloniam a Romanis deductam, agrumque eum fuisse captum de Bois Gallis, qui ager primus fuerat Etruscorum, quam per Augusti et aliquot imperatorum tempora trium opulentissimarum Italiae civitatum supero mari adiacentium unam fuisse, cum alii dicunt scriptores, tum affirmat Plinius. Suetonius autem dicit Octavianum Bononiensibus, quod in Antoniorum clientela antiquitus fuerant **[352F]** gratiam fecisse coniurandi cum tota Italia pro partibus suis. Idemque Suetonius scribit Neronem imperatorem orasse Latine pro Bononiensibus ad consulem et ad senatum. Iulius Capitolinus in XXX tyrannorum gestis rebus de Censorio dicit, "Erat eius sepulcrum grandibus litteris circa Bononiam, incisi sunt eius honores; tamen ascriptum est 'Felix per omnia infelicissimus.' "

Ad annum salutis XXXX supra DCCC, Sergii pontificis Romani Os Porci prius appellati temporibus, cum Lotharius tunc imperator Ludovicum filium Romam cum copiis mitteret, Bononienses illum multis incommodis damnisque affecerunt. Quam ob rem ille converso, qui iam praeterierat exercitu ultionis modum excessit, quod post agri vastationem, factamque in insontibus per vicos villasque repertis, caedem, obsessam urbem captamque reddidit immunitam. Et tamen illam ad annum salutis LXXI supra ducentesimum et millesimum tam scimus fuisse potentem, ut adversus Venetos liberam mari Adriatico navigationem prohibentes, tribus annis bello contenderint, in quo Bononiae praetor castra habens apud Padi ostia, ubi castellum Bononienses aedificaverant, **[352G]** quadraginta milia equitum peditumque in exercitu tenuerit Repulsique Veneti amissis aliquot copiis, cum ducis Venetiarum Laurentii Teupoli ductu paratiores rediissent, inter Bononienses Venetosque pax firmata est, in qua actum est, ut Padi ostiorum custodia Venetis relicta, possent Bononienses per ea sal et frumenta absque vectigali ad libitum deportare.

Sequenti anno orta civili dissensione Bononienses factionem civium, ut dicebant, imperialem, patria eiecerunt, Lambertatios et eorum partes secutos: Asinellos, de Andalo, Comites Panici, Carbonesios, Storletos, Albaros, de Villanova, de Principibus, de Abbate, comites Butrii, Fuscardos, de Alberto, de Fratta, de La Mola, de Rusticanis. Exinde cum pars quae in civitate victrix manserat, extorres animosius insecuta Forumlivium, in quam illi se receperant, civitatem obsedisset, Bononiensis exercitus fractus est et fugatus, quo in proelio legi in Venetorum monumentis octo milia Bononien-

first called Boionia, instead of Felsina, and then Bononia. Livy says in book 37 that the Romans established a colony there on land captured from the Boii, who were Gauls, and that its land had first belonged to the Etruscans. Not only other writers, but also Pliny, agree that it was, during the Imperial times, one of the wealthiest city-states of Italy near the Adriatic Sea. Moreover, Suetonius says that Octavian excused the people of Bononia from swearing the common oath with all Italy to support him, because they had been from ancient times part **[352F]** of Antony's clientele. In the same vein, Suetonius writes that the emperor Nero delivered a Latin oration on behalf of the Bolognese to the consul and the Senate. Julius Capitolinus, in book 30 of *Deeds of the Tyrants*, says of Censorinus, "His tomb near Bologna bore an inscription in large letters, describing his offices; but at the end was inscribed 'Fortunate, but through all his experiences most unhappy.'"

In the year 840, in the reign of Pope Sergius (whose surname had been Pig's mouth), Lothar was emperor and sent his son Louis to Rome with troops. He was received by the Bolognese with harassment and loss. Lothair had gone ahead of the army, but he turned it around and went beyond the normal level of revenge in not only devastating the territory, but slaughtering innocent people he came upon in the villages and farms. He besieged Bologna, captured it, and then left it undefended. But we know that in 1271 Bologna was powerful, as the Bolognese prevented the Venetians from free use of the Adriatic Sea. They fought a war of three years with them, during which the praetor of Bologna had his camp at the mouth of the Po, where the Bolognese had built a fort; **[352G]** here he kept forty thousand cavalry and infantry. The Venetians were driven back and lost some of their forces, but returned in better form under the leadership of Lorenzo Tiepolo, and peace was concluded between the Bolognese and Venetians, on the condition that the Venetians would have custodial rights over the mouth of the Po, but the Bolognese could export through it as much salt and grain as they pleased without paying tax.

In the following year a civil war arose in Bologna and its citizens threw out the Ghibelline faction, the Lambertazzi and their followers the Asinelli, degli Andalò, the counts of Panico, Carbonesi, Storleti, Alboresi, de Villanova, Principi, degli Abati, the counts of Budrio, the Foscardi, degli Alberti, della Fratta, Lamola, and Rustignani. The faction which had remained in the city was victorious, and boldly pursued the exiles to Forlì, where they had taken refuge, and besieged the city. The Bolognese army was defeated and routed, and in this battle, as I have read in the record of the Venetians, eight

sium cecidisse. Quoquo autem modo res postea se habuerint, Bononiam anno XC vix dum elapso fuisse a Romanae ecclesiae magistratibus hoc novo, quem nunc habet, circumdatam muro scimus. Constatque eam non muro magis per id temporis, ac diu postea quam opibus amplificatam fuisse. **[352H]**

Habuit Bononia, sicut tradit Eusebius, L. Pomponium Bononiensem Atellanarum scriptorem, et paulo post per M. Tullii Ciceronis tempora, sicut ipse in Bruto dicit, C. Rusticellum oratorem haudquaquam contemnendum. Et secundo Lucio pontifice Romano Alberti filio cive ornata fuit. Martialis vero eam urbem Rufo ornatam fuisse dicit his versibus,

> Funde tuo lacrimas orbata Bononia Rufo,
> Et resonet tota planctus in Aemilia.

Pliniusque refert cum Vespasiani imperatoris edicto Italiae census haberetur, L. Termicium Marci filium Bononiensem XXV et centum annos fuisse natum. Idemque Plinius dicit nullos calamos aptiores esse sagittis, quam Bononienses, et speculares lapides breves, maculososque complexus silicis in Bononiensi agro reperiri. Habuit autem paulo supra aetatem nostram Bononia Ioannem Andreae Calderinum iureconsultorum aetatis suae celeberrimum. Gaudemusque aetatem nostram tulisse Nicolaum Albergatum, qui primo Cartusiae monachus, post Bononiae episcopus, demum Romanae eccesiae cardinalis, vir fuit cum celebris sanctimoniae, tum etiam sapientiae singularis. Nuper quoque Antonius claruit Bentivolius, vir nobilium aetatis suae in Bononia potentissimus; et potentium sui saeculi, bonarum artium, ceterarumque virtutum, praesertim liberalitatis gloria celeberrimus. **[353A]**

Obiitque proximis temporibus philosophorum sui saeculi praestantissimus Nicolaus Faba Bononiensis. Supersunt autem Gaspar nunc episcopus Imolensis et philosophus insignis, et multi iurium civilis et pontificii et philosophiae ac medicinae studiis ornatissimi, Ludovicus de gente *Ludovisia* facti palatii Apostolici auditor, Baptista Floriani iureconsultissimi filius, Gaspar Arrengherius et noster Bornius Salensis. Matrem vero studiorum Bononiam tam paucis nunc ornari eleganter doctis nullus mirabitur, qui meminerit (quod cum horrore dicimus) civiles discordias plures ferro per aetatem nostram Bononiae abstulisse praestantes cives, his quos nunc ipsa et duae similes in Italia habeant civitates.

thousand men of Bologna were killed. But however the situation stood afterwards, scarcely yet ninety years after its administration by the church, we know that Bologna was surrounded by this new wall which it has now; and it is established that the city was enlarged less by a wall at that time, than by wealth for a long time afterwards. **[352H]**

Eusebius tells us that L. Pomponius, the writer of Atellan farces, was from Bononia and a little later in the time of Cicero, as he himself says in the *Brutus*, the esteemed orator C. Rusticellus; and Pope Lucius II son of Albertus have brought distinction to Bologna. Martial says that Bononia was honored by producing Rufus:

> Pour out your tears, Bononia, since you have lost Rufus,
> And let this lament resound through all of Aemilia.

And Pliny relates that when the emperor Vespasian ordered a census to be held, a man born at Bononia, L. Termicius, son of Marcus, was found to be one hundred and twenty-five years old. Pliny also says that no reeds furnish better arrows than those from Bononia; and that short stones speckled with a mixture of flint good for mirrors, are found in the fields around Bononia.

In times a little before ours, Bologna has produced Giovanni Andrea Calderini, the most famous expert in law of his generation. We rejoice too that our generation has produced Nicolò Albergati, who was first a Carthusian monk, and then bishop of Bologna, and finally a cardinal at Rome, a man famous not only for his purity, but also for his extraordinary wisdom. Recently Antonio Bentivoglio has become famous, the most famous man of our generation among the nobility, and most renowned among the powerful men of his century for knowledge of the liberal arts, and the other virtues, and especially for his generosity. **[353A]**

Very recently Niccolò Fava of Bologna has died, the outstanding philosopher of his age. But Gaspare, bishop of Imola, now survives, an eminent philosopher. And many men of Bologna are still living who excel in the knowledge of civil and canon law, philosophy, and medicine: Lodovico Lodovisi, judge of the Holy See; Battista, son of Fiorano the legal expert; Gaspare Arrengherio, and my friend Bornio da Sala. Truly Bologna is the mother of the liberal arts, and no one is amazed that she is now distinguished by so few learned men, if he remembers the many civil wars (I shudder to recall them) in which the sword has snatched away her foremost citizens, from those whom she, and two similar city-states in Italy, now possess.

Ad Rheni sinistram interius Olivetum, ubi Convallis Rheni incipit vicus. Ad dexteram sub Apennino Casium, in Apennino Granariolum arx altissima. Inter Samogiam torrentem et Scultennam amnem sunt oppida et castella: Crevalcorium, Persicetum, Francum, ubi olim fuit Forum Gallorum, apud quod oppidum M. Antonium Hirtius et Pansa consules proelio superarunt, de quo proelio sic habet Livius, libro CXIX:

> Cum Pansa consul male adversus Antonium pugnasset, M. Hirtius consul cum exercitu superveniens fusis Marci Antonii **[353B]** copiis fortunam utriusque partis aequavit. Victus deinde ab Hirtio et Caesare Antonius in Galliam confugit. At Hirtius, qui post victoriam in ipsis hostium castris ex vulnere ceciderat, et L. Pansa ex vulnere defunctus in campo Martio sepulti sunt.

Deinceps intus sunt Pluinatium, Bazanum, Mons Velius, agri Bononiensis castella. Est etiam in Bononiensi agro in paludem Padusam vergenti Novantula oppidum monasterio insigni ornatum, quod gloriosae Matildis comitissae opera impensaque aedificatum est.

Sed iam Scultennae ripa ad quam pervenimus, Cispadanae Romandiolae regionis finis, ad Transpadanam eiusdem partem transeundum esse admonet. Ad prima Padi ostia Spinam urbem Diomedicis opibus fuisse conditam scribit Plinius, sed eius nunc parva exstant vestigia partim Vallis, partim Dorsum Spinae appellata, unde propinquum Padum veteres Spineticum appellant, de quo in Spinetico tradit Suetonius Claudium imperatorem de Britannis triumphaturum navem aedificasse omnium maximam, quae potius magna domus potuerit appellari.

Primum ea dextera Padi ripa vicum habet Sanctalbertum, ubi **[353C]** nunc anno LXXIX atque centesimo Veneti castellum aedificarunt Marcomama appellatum, ut Bononiensibus resisteret hostibus, qui aliud castellum in adversa Padi ripa, sed inferius iuxta mare magnis sumptibus communiverant. Estque is Sancti Alberti locus, unde per fossam Padusae Messanicum XII miliario Ravennam itur. Ea in Padi ripa frequentes et prope contigui intra viginti milia sunt vici, Humana, Fossa, Putula, Longastrinus, Filus, a Padi rectitudine milia passuum sex continuata dictus, Rupta, Blasianus in

On the left bank of the Reno, towards the interior, is Oliveto, where the valley of the Reno begins. On the right bank, at the foot of the Apennines, is Cassio, and in the mountains themselves the lofty citadel Granaglione. Between the stream Samoggia and the Panaro river are the following towns and *castelli*: Crespellano, S. Giovanni in Persiceto, and Castelfranco, which in ancient times was Forum Galli; here M. Antonius was defeated by the consuls Hirtius and Pansa. Livy writes about this battle in book 119,

> When the consul Pansa had contended unsuccessfully with Antony, the other consul, Hirtius, arrived with his army and put Antony's troops to flight; the luck **[353B]** of each side was then evenly matched. From there, after his defeat at the hands of Hirtius and Caesar, Antony fled to Gaul. But Hirtius had fallen dead from a wound in the enemy camp after the victory. Pansa, too, died from his wounds; both were buried in the Campus Martius.

Next, towards the interior, come Ponzano, Bazzano, and Monteveglio, all *castelli* of the Bolognese territory. There is also, in Bolognese territory where it borders on the Padusa, the town of Nonantola, distinguished by a famous monastery, which was built through the generosity of the glorious Countess Matilda.

But now that we have arrived at the banks of the Panaro, which is the border of the part of Romandiola called Cispadane Gaul, we must cross over to the part called Transpadane Gaul. At the first of the Po's mouths, Pliny writes, the city of Spina was built by the wealth of Diomedes; but now meager remains are left, referred to as the valley of Spina and the hill of Spina. From this name the ancients gave to the nearby part of the Po the name Spinetico. Suetonius says that in the Po Spinetico the emperor Claudius, after his triumph over the Britons, built the largest of all of his ships, of such a size that it could rather be called a large house.

This right-hand bank of the Po contains first the village of Sant'Alberto, **[353C]** where the Venetians one hundred and seventy-nine years ago built a *castello* called Marcamò which they intended as a defense against their enemies the Bolognese. The latter had fortified at great expense another *castello* on the opposite bank of the Po, but this one was lower on the river, next to the sea. Sant'Alberto is the point of departure for Ravenna, twelve miles on the canal through the Padusa called Mezzano. The villages along this bank of the Po are densely concentrated and nearly continuous for twenty miles: Humana, Fossa, Putula, Longastrino, Filo (named from the continuous straight six-mile stretch of the Po), Rupta, and San Biagio,

quo villam habemus locupletem e regione Zanioli sitam, in qua horum partem scripsimus.

Et post Argenta oppidum simul cum Ferraria a Smaragdo exarcho, sicut in historiis diximus primo moenibus communitum, duodeviginti milia passuum distans a Ferraria civitate, quo in spatio secundum Padi ripam distat ab Argenta tribus passuum milibus Cosandala villa Marchionum Estensium magnifici operis aedibus ornatissima. Ad eamque villam rectus et primarius Padi cursus, qui praeterlabitur anno nunc centesimo tortuosiore veniebat alveo, quem nunc a vico Coderea corrupte pro capite Eridani dicto, secus villam Belreguardam desiccatum videmus. **[353D]** Nam pictura Italiae, quam in primis sequimur, Roberti regis Siciliae et Francisci Petrarchae eius amici opus, Vicuentiam Viceriamque et Conam vicos profluenti Pado appositos habet. Quare partes ipsas Padi a Ferraria Cosandalam, et a Coderea in mare nunc defluentes a centesimo anno initium habuisse non dubito.

Supra Cosandalam alia est villa, Monasteriolum appellata. At secundum maris litus distant a primariis Padi ostiis passus quindecim mille stagni, quod prisci Capresiam dixere, ostia nunc Magna Vaca vulgo appellata. Ad quod stagnum passuum supra duodecim milia in circuitu patens Comaclensis sita est vetusta civitas, quam per Gothorum Longobardorumque tempora classem armare solitam Veneti ab Alberto Berengarii regis filio Comaclensium auxilio iniuria lacessiti, ad annum salutis nongentesimum tricesimumsecundum destruxerunt, ut semper postea, sicut et nunc a paucis fuerit incolis habitata.

Mirum vero est cernere quantam id stagnum praestet piscium copiam, quod anguillarum cephalorumque sale conditorum vis maxima inde habita, magnum Estensibus Marchionibus vectigal omni propemodum Italiae satisfaciat. Scimus vero, vidimusque hac in piscatione contingere, quod Plinius de Baenaco Mintioque scripsit his verbis,

> In Benaco Octobri **[354E]** mense glomeratae anguillae volvuntur mirabili multitudine, ut in excipulis eius fluminis Mintii, ob hoc ipsum fabricatis singulorum milium globi capiantur.

Volana sequuntur vetusti praesentisque nominis ostia, quae ramus auget a Pado veteri apud Codeream, sive caput Eridani scissus. Suntque ea in insula, quam bifurcatus hac scissura Padus mare Adriaticum, ac palus Capre-

where I have a substantial farm in the area of the Zeno, and where I wrote part of this chapter.

After these villages is the town of Argenta, which was first fortified at the same time as Ferrara by the exarch Smaragdus (I have related this in my *Histories*). It is eighteen miles from the city of Ferrara, and if you follow the bank of the Po, in this same area, three miles from Argenta, is the villa Consandolo, magnificently furnished with buildings through the effort of the marquises of the Este family. At this villa the original course of the Po ran straight; now, a hundred years later, it glides past twisting and turning. We see it dried up from the village of Codrea (a corruption of the name "Head of the Po"), beside the villa of Belriguardo. **[353D]** For the map of Italy on which I am principally relying, the work of king Robert of Sicily and his friend Francis Petrarch, locates opposite the running water of the Po the villages of Voghenza, Voghiera, and Cona. For this reason, I believe that the parts of the Po which now flow from Ferrara to Consandolo, and from Codrea into the sea, originated only a hundred years ago.

Above Consandolo is another villa, called Monestirolo. But fifteen miles from the chief mouth of the Po, going along the seacoast, are swamps which the ancients called Caprasia, but which are now a river-mouth called in the vernacular Magnavacca (Porto Garibaldi). At this swamp, which extends more than twelve miles in a circle, is located the ancient city of Comacchio. It had been a naval center through the Gothic and Lombard periods. Then the Venetians destroyed it in 932, in revenge for its peoples' aid to Adalbert, son of King Berengar, when he was injuring them. After that time it has remained sparsely inhabited.

It is quite remarkable to see the quantity of fish produced in this swamp. It is a great source of eels and fish, which are then cured in salt; from this trade, the marquises of Este receive a great duty from nearly all of Italy. I know from personal observation that what Pliny describes in Lago di Garda and the Mincio actually happens:

> In Lake Benacus, in October, **[354E]** eels gather together in a round mass, in such great number that thousands of them are caught in a ball in the special basins made for this purpose in the Mincio.

There follows the harbor today called Volania, which was also its ancient name; the branch split off from the ancient Po flows into it at Codrea (or "head of the Eridanus"). And in this harbor is an island created by this splitting in two of the Po, the Adriatic, and the swamp called Magnavacca.

sia efficiunt vici populis frequentissimi, et villis civium, ac omnimodo agresti cultu amoenissimi, in quibus eminent inferius Massa et Fossadalbarum, Miliare et Milliarinumque et Medelana, et supra Portus ac Belreguardum, ingentia cuius villae magnificentissimi operis palatia a praeclaro praestantissimoque principe Nicolao marchione Estensi in veteri vico Vicoeria aedificata, ceteris aequiparari possunt omnibus, quae in civitatibus alios Italiae principes aedificasse viderimus. Hicque Volanae ramus vigesimo supra mare miliario dextrorsum se in alterum scindit ramum, cuius ostia appellant Ghorum.

Sunt quoque in insula inde facta Codeghorium, et Massentia vici populis refertissimi. Inest quoque clarissimum, aedificiisque superbissimum Pomposiae monasterium. Quartus dehinc habetur ramus Padi, quem contra Ficarolum diximus primum ab eo scindi; **[354F]** diciturque in ostio Ad Fornaces sic a vico, vel potius ab hospitatoria taberna denominatus. Idque ultimum Padi ostium limitem efficit, quo Romandiola secundum mare dividitur a Venetiis.

In ea vero insula, quam duo hi rami a veteri Pado quintodecimo secundum ripam superiorem distantes miliario efficiunt, Ferraria est ad secundum veteri Pado apposita, quam civitatem in historiis primum fuisse moenibus circumdatam a Smaragdo patricio et Italiae exarcho ostendimus. Nominis causam hanc afferunt vetusta Ravennatium ecclesiae monumenta, quae urbis illius archiepiscopi tria iurium ecclesiae suae loca a tribus metallorum nominibus appellaverint. Aureolum Forliviensis agri in amoeno colle situm ab auro, et Argentam Pado Primario appositam ab argento; Ferrariamque a ferro.

Ob eam autem quae in Padi ramorum scissura et alveorum mutatione facta est locorum confusionem non satis indicare possumus, utrumne in hoc Ferrariae loco, an supra ubi ramus est Ficaroli, incoluerunt Assarigi, quos populos Etruria oriundos vult Plinius Assagiam fossam in Adrianorum paludes derivasse, et inde urbis Adriae summersionem inchoasse. Sed vetera haec, ut sunt dubia, relinquentes ad nostrum redeamus institutum. **[354G]** Cum Ferraria urbs ab ipso condicionis initio in partibus Ravennatium Romanorumque simul adversus Longobardos durasset, illis a Carolo victis post donationem de exarchatu Ravennate factam Romanae ecclesiae, in eius

It contains densely populated villages and farms, and is thoroughly pleasant, with rustic cultivation. Here the principal towns are, downstream, Massa Fiscaglia and Fossadalbero, Migliaro and Migliarino and Medelana; and upstream, Portomaggiore and Belriguardo, the latter an enormous and splendid estate whose palatial buildings were built in the ancient village of Voghiera by the illustrious prince Niccolò d'Este. They compare favorably with any I have seen built by princes in other city-states in Italy. Here this branch of the Volano splits into another branch, twenty miles inland from the coast, on the right-hand side. The mouth of this branch is called Goro.

There is also an island made by this branching, and on it are located the densely populated villages of Codegoro and Massenzatico. Here too is the very famous monastery of Pomposa, with its splendid buildings. There is a fourth branch of the Po which arises here, although this one is opposite the branch at Ficarolo, as I mentioned, and **[354F]** is intersected by it. They call the mouth of this one At the Ovens after the name of the village, or rather that of the inn for travelers. And this farthest mouth of the Po makes a boundary, dividing the Romagna at the sea from the territory of the Venetians.

On this island, created by these two branches fifteen miles from the ancient Po as you follow the upper bank, is Ferrara. This city lies opposite the ancient Po beside the second branch. As I noted in my *Decades*, it was first fortified by the patrician Smaragdus, exarch of Italy. The old records of the Ravennate church give the origin of the name Ferrara. It seems the archbishop of Ravenna named the three places under his church's jurisdiction after the names of three metals. Loreo, in the territory of Forlì, was named after gold because it was situated on a pleasant hill. Argenta, the town opposite the Po di Primaro, was named after silver; and Ferrara from iron.

On account of the topographical confusion which has arisen as a result of the splitting of the Po into different branches and the changes in the riverbeds, I cannot say for sure whether the Assarigi lived on the site of Ferrara, or higher up where the branch called Ficarolo is. The Assarigi were, according to Pliny, a people who originated in Etruria and diverted the canal Assagia into the Adriatic marshes; and this is the source of the submersion of the city of Adria. But I need to leave these ancient matters and return to my established order. **[354G]**

The city of Ferrara held out against the Lombards from the beginning of the creation of factions of Ravennates and Romans, and when they were conquered by Charlemagne, and after the donation to the church had been

oboedientia perseveravit. Tandem quo tempore Germani imperatores ecclesiae adversari coeperunt, ipsa quoque civitas sub alterutris vacillavit. Sed ad annum salutis undecies centenum Matildis comitissa Venetorum Ravennatiumque auxilio eandem urbem ab Henrico III ecclesiae hoste occupatam sibi subegit. Et anno ab inde centesimo et XXI cum marchiones Estenses amicitiis divitiisque potentissimi in Ferraria essent, Salinguerra quidam Ferrariensis per eorum et Ecelini de Romano amicitiae occasionem praesidio usus, Federici Barbarossi instigationibus, auxilioque Ferrariae dominium occupavit, quem Innocentius IIII pontifex Romanus Venetorum auxilio ad annum salutis duodecies centenum atque quadragesimum expulit. Et marchiones Estenses Ferrariam sibi paulo post subigere inceperunt. Sed anno abinde LXVIII Veneti ipsis marchionibus per arma pulsis Ferraria **[354H]** sunt potiti, eamque ut dimitterent adduci non potuerunt, licet Clemens quintus pontifex Romanus civitatem Venetiarum ecclesiastico supposuerit interdicto, unde omnia eorum bona per Gallias Britanniamque direpta fuerunt.

Nec paruissent iussionibus papae Veneti, nisi legatus ecclesiae in Italiam Avinione veniens, marchionum Estensium et Ferrariensium extorrum auxilio fretus Venetos vi et armis Ferraria primum, post castello Thedaldo, quod ad pontem retinebant, magnis utrimque commissis caedibus deturbasset. Fuitque postea semper Ferraria sub Estensis familiae gubernatione pontificibus oboedientissima, et adeo tali domino felix, ut cum opibus et potentia creverit per singulos annos. Tum maxime proximis XX annis mirabile habuerit incrementum, quod tum multiplicare fecit concilium a quarto Eugenio pontifice Romano ibi celebratum. Cui interfuerunt Ioannes Palaeologus imperator Constantinopolitanus, et quicquid praesentis temporis Graecia Christianis subdita virorum habuit excellentissimum. Inchoata namque est Ferrariae quam Florentiae conclusam fuisse diximus orientalis unio cum ecclesia occidentali.

Habuit etiam Ferraria per aetatem nostram praestantissimum principem Nicolaum Estensem, cui ad summam gloriam nihil praeter litterarum ornamenta defuit, quam **[355A]** felicitatis partem additam vidimus principi Leonello, quem nuper amisimus. Et novus marchio Borsius, et si litterarum ornamento caret, humanitate tamen, liberalitate, et prudentia genitorem Nicolaum nobis redolet. Quod vero praeteritis temporibus novae, sed splendidissimae civitati defuit, praesens supplevit saeculum, in quo viros habemus nobiles, litteris humanitatis ornatos: Nicolaum, Laurentium, Robertum,

made of cities in the exarchate of Ravenna, Ferrara stayed obedient to it. Finally in the time of the German emperors' opposition to the church the city of Ferrara wavered between the rules of these two powers. But then in 1100 the Countess Matilda, aided by the Venetians and the Ravennates, took away from the emperor Henry III this city which had been occupied by the papal army. For one hundred and twenty years after that, the princes of the d'Este family, with their wealth and connections, have held the power in Ferrara. The Ferrarese Salinguerra took advantage of their friendship and that of Ezzelino da Romano to use it as a garrison, and occupied it, pushed and aided by Frederick Barbarossa; but in 1240 he was driven out by Pope Innocent IV, aided by the Venetians. A little after that the Estense princes began to bring Ferrara under their rule. But sixty-eight years after that, the **[354H]** Venetians drove them out and took possession of the city, and could not be persuaded to release them, although Pope Clement V put the city-state of Venice under a papal interdiction. As a result, all their goods were plundered by the French and English.

But the Venetians did not obey the pope's command. And a papal envoy traveled from Avignon to Italy, allied with the Estense princes and other Ferrarese exiles, and dislodged the Venetians from Ferrara by force of arms. After that they perpetrated a great slaughter on both sides at Castel Tedaldo, which they kept at the bridge. And ever since, Ferrara has been governed by the Este family and subject to the popes. To the present time, this rule has been a happy one, and the city has grown year by year in wealth and power. Its most marvelous growth has taken place in the last twenty years, due to Pope Eugenius IV's holding the council there. Among the participants was John Palaeologus, the emperor of Constantinople; also attending were the most outstanding contemporary Greek churchmen. For the negotiations for the union of the Eastern and Western churches, which I mentioned was concluded at Florence, began at Ferrara.

In our own age Ferrara also had the eminent prince Niccolò III d'Este, whose glory lacks nothing except the embellishment of literary expertise. I have seen this **[355A]** fortunate element added to the attainments of prince Leonello, whose loss we have recently mourned. And the new marquis, Borso, may lack the distinction of literary knowledge; but in his humanity, generosity, and wisdom he reminds us of his father Niccolò. What this new but magnificent city lacked in times past, it enjoys in this century. We are now blessed with noblemen who are also distinguished in their knowledge of the liberal arts: Niccolò, Roberto, and Tito, the Strozzi brothers; Lippo

et Titum fratres Strozzas; Lippum Platesium, et qui peritissimus etiam est medicus et philosophus Hieronymum Castellum.

Difficilis nunc nobis restat limitum huius regionis designatio, praesertim Adriam exarchatui Ravennae subiectam simul cum Ferraria in Romandiola claudere cupientibus. Pado quem Ficaroli diximus appellari, decimo supra mare miliario ad dexteram ubi primum tellus habetur solida, et aratri patiens, adiacent Corbulae vici duo, aliquot passuum milibus inter se distantes. Dehinc Crispinum, post est fossa Pelosella; cui intus adiacet Orchanum speciosa villa praedictorum, Nicolai, Laurentii, Roberti et Titi Strozzarum doctrina aeque ac nobilitate gentis ornatorum.

Multas ab ostio fossae Pelosellae Padus alienas accipit aquas. Nam parvo **[355B]** ducta tractu ipsa fossa paludes exonerat amplissimas, utpote quas magna pars Athesis fluvii Veronensium, et totus Tartarus, totusque Menacus torrentes adeo late longeque augent, ut maris sinum amplitudine, ac sublatis quandoque fluctibus ostentent. Insuntque quam plura castella et vici, quorum ad dexteram primum est Fratta oppidum, in quo ad annum salutis duodeciescentenum atque vigesimum quartum magna ac prope universalis populi utriusque sexus caedes facta est ab Azzone Novello, marchione Estense, partes Salinguerrae Ferrariensis tyranni acrius insequente.

Ad sinistramque paludum Pelosella ingredientibus est silvestris domus, unde Patavina via in Arquatam vicum peninsulae Rodiensis est passuum duorum milium traiectus. Mediaque in valle sunt Tresienta, et oppidulum Guilielmum, ac ipsius vetustae Adriae fundamenta, inter quae vicus est ecclesia una, et aliquot domibus, sed casis ut plurimum piscatoriis frequentatus. Ea urbs olim praeclarissima, quam mari Adriatico nomen dedisse ostendimus, a Graecis, Lydis, sicut vult Iustinus, et ab Etruscis, sicut Livius Pliniusque scribunt, originem habuit, quae etiam nunc civitatis titulum ac dioecesim retinet. **[355C]**

Oritur Menachus torrens ad Magnanum agri Veronensis vicum Ceretamque et Praetellas vicos praeterlabitur. Tartarus item in agro Veronensi ad Graecianum oriundus, Micarolum insulam Porcariam ad sinistram, et Gagium ad dexteram vicos habet. Athesis autem pars, quae dictas illabitur paludes, sub Liniaco et villa Bartholomacha primam ad Castagnarium scis-

Platesio; and the most learned of all in medicine and philosophy, Girolamo Castelli.

I should like to bring to an end my treatment of this region, but find difficulty in defining its boundary, especially as regards Adria, which was, like Ferrara, subject to the exarchate of Ravenna. Next to the branch of the Po which I called Ficarolo, ten miles above the sea on the right-hand bank, where the first solid and arable ground is found, lie the two villages of Corbola, a few miles from each other. From here, you come to Crespino, and after that the canal Pelesella, next to which, towards the interior, lies Orcano, the beautiful villa of the aforementioned Strozzi brothers who are equally distinguished in their learning and their noble birth.

The Po receives many tributaries from the mouth of the Pelesella canal; indeed, **[355B]** this same canal extends for a small distance and then discharges abundantly, far and wide, because its waters are increased by a great part of the Adige river from Verona, and the entire stream of the Tartaro river, and of the Menago river. As a result, even when one accounts for the fact that it has no waves, it rivals a marine bay in width. There are very many *castelli* and villages here. The first one on the right is the town of Fratta, in 1224 the site of the great slaughter of a population, both men and women, on an almost global scale, when Azzo Novello, the Marquis d'Este pursued without mercy the faction of Salinguerra the tyrant of Ferrara.

On the left side of the swamp as you enter by way of the Pelesella canal, there is a woodland dwelling. From here, a road leads for 12 miles to the village of Arquà Polesino, on the peninsula of Rovigo. And in the middle of the valley are Tresienta, the small town of Castel Guglielmo, and the ruins of the ancient city of Adria itself. Among these ruins is a village, and a church; it is inhabited by some houses, but mainly by fishing huts. This was once a famous city which, as I have noted, took its name from the Adriatic Sea. Justin thinks it was settled by the Greeks and Lydians; Livy and Pliny say by the Etruscans. Even now it has the title of city-state and diocese. **[355C]**

The Menago stream has its source at Magnano in Veronese territory, and flows past the villages of Cerea and Predelle. The stream Tartaro, in the same way, has its origin at Grezzano in Veronese territory, and leaves on its left the island of Micarolum and the village of Procaria, on its right the village of Gabbia. But part of the Adige river, which flows into the swamps I mentioned, splits off first at Castagnaro, at the foot of Legnago and Villa Bartolomea. The three rivers made in this way flow down through the adja-

suram facit. Trium vero huiusmodi fluviorum per contiguam regionem Marchiam Tarvisinam delabentium, ideo in hac cursum descripsimus, ut peninsulam Rodigiensem Hatriensium dioeceseos ac regionis, quam claudunt, sicut par est in partibus Romandiolae colligamus.

Estque ea in peninsula Rodigium nobile oppidum Bartholomaeo ornatum Roverella archiepiscopo Ravennate studiis eloquentiae ac humanitate plurimum decorato. Est et Venetium castellum antiquae Venetiae nomen servans. Sunt quoque oppida Lendenaria et Abbatia populis frequentata. Supra fossae Pelosellae ostium sunt ad sinistram Francolinus, ad quem via Paduana profecti Ferraria Padum transmittunt. Et ad dexteram pontis Lacus Obscuri vicus. Supraque pervenitur **[355D]** ad Padi integri ripam, unde ramus scinditur Ficaroli, deincepsque integer est Padus. Hunc vero Ficaroli ramum intra centum proximos annos inchoasse, ideo non dubitamus, quia Roberti regis Neapolitani, et Francisci Petrarchae pictura Italiae, quam nos sequi supra diximus, ipsum non habet ramum.

Praeterea monasterium Sancti Salvatoris, in quo arx Ficaroli aedificata fuit, et eius vices obtinens Sancti Laurentii de Casellis ecclesia, monasterio Sancti Marci Ferrariensis annexa, vetusta habet annorum quadringentorum iurium suorum monumenta, in quibus facile intelligitur, ubi Padus ipse nunc est Ficaroli dictus fuisse agros. Confirmatque nos in hac novitatis huius rami opinione appositi singulis praediis, singulisque iuribus monasterii ultra citraque Padum hunc existentibus fines, quibus designandis nulla umquam ipsius rami mentio facta est.

Sunt ea in Padi integri ripa Serravallae et Castrum Novum arces. Massa, Brigantinus et Melaria vici tum opulentissimi, tum etiam populis frequentissimi. Deinceps terra, et per Padi ripam Lombardiae, et ad contiguas Melariae ac Brigantini agro paludes Tarvisinae Marchiae limites habentur.

cent region of the March of Treviso. In my description of that region, I have told of the course of these rivers, It makes sense for me to treat in the chapter on Romandiola the peninsula of Rovigo which they create.

And on this peninsula is the noble town of Rovigo, distinguished by Bartolomeo Roverella, the archbishop of Ravenna, a man very eminent in the study of rhetoric and liberal arts. There is also a *castello*, Venetium, which retains the name of ancient Venice. There are also the densely inhabited towns of Lendinara and Badia Polesine. Above the mouth of the Pelesella Canal is, on the left-hand bank, Francolino, where travelers from Ferrara on the road to Padua cross the Po. And on the right-hand side of the bridge is a village called Pontelagoscuro. And higher up one comes to the bank of the Po river before it splits, the point from **[355D]** which the branch called Ficarolo splits off. And after this, the Po flows undivided. I am certain that this branch, the Ficarolo, developed only within the last hundred years, because the map of Italy of King Robert of Naples and Francis Petrarch, which, as I mentioned before, I am following, does not show this branch.

Besides, the monastery of S. Salvatore, where the citadel of Ficarolo was built, and the church of San Lorenzo delle Caselle which was annexed to the monastery of San Marco at Ferrara, and obtained its functions, have records of its rights going back four hundred years, so that one can easily see that where the branch of the Po itself now called Ficarolo is, used to be fields. And my judgment about the recent origin of this branch of the Po is confirmed by the placement of the boundaries of the estates, the individual lands opposite it over which the monastery has rights, beyond and on this side of this branch of the Po: in the designation of their boundaries, no mention is ever made of this branch.

On that bank of the undivided Po lie the citadels of Seravalle and Castel Nuovo. Then come the towns of Massa, Bergantino, and Melara, in the past wealthy and densely populated. Finally, the land on the bank of the Po begins to form the border of the Romagna with Lombardy; and the land of the swamps adjacent to the territory of Melara and Bergantino forms the border of the Romagna with the March of Treviso.

# Regio Septima
# Lombardia

[356E]

Perducta est superiori libro Romandiola hinc ad sinistram Scultennae amnis ripam, inde ad Melariam agri Ferrariensis vicum, certos ultra citraque Padum limites suos, Lombardiae nunc opera est impendenda. Id nomen a Lombardis tractum esse constat. Quando enim Carolus Magnus, et Hadrianus primus pontifex Roman nomen, ut diximus, Romandiolae indiderunt, hanc quoque partem Italiae aliquando dictam prius Galliam Cisalpinam, voluerunt censeri nomine Lombardiae, quod a Longobardis ad X et VIII supra ducentos annos fuerat occupata. Sicque eam Romana ecclesia ab ipso tempore citra suis in monumentis per annos sexcentos quinquaginta fecit appellari. Et quamquam Verona, Vincentia, Padua et Tarvisium civitas, ac omnis regio Aquileiensis ecclesiae ab eisdem quoque Longobardis semper fuerint possessae, certa tamen nobis ratione, quam ipsas descripturi regiones afferemus, quattuor illae civitates cum aliquot aliis Marchia Tarvisina, et reliqua pars Italiae illi adiacens. Tum Aquileiensis, tum [356F] Foroiulii regio ab eo tempore fuerunt nominatae.

Sunt Lombardiae fines Scultenna et Padus amnes, Apenninus et Alpes citra Padum, et ultra eum quicquid intra Alpes Benacumque lacum et amnem ipso clauditur Pado. Igitur ad Scultennae dexteram qua influit Formigo torrens fossae immixtus a Mutina defluenti Bomportus est vicus. Infra est Finale oppidum, ad quod ea quam diximus aquarum moles Rheno, Scultenna, Formigine, et plerisque torrentibus coeuntibus fossam efficit Fistorenam, ultima Padusae ostia facientem, apud Bondenum oppidum, ubi opinor fuisse Bondomacum, quod Plinius lingua Gallica ideo sic appellatum affirmat, quod immensum ibi Padus profundum habeat. Scultenna fluvius vetustum id nomen supra viam Aemiliam nunc retinet, infra Panarius appellatur. Est is fluvius, apud quem ad annum salutis sexcentesimum et septuagesimum proelio inter Ravennates et Longobardos commisso cecidisse in Ravennatium partibus octo milia ostendimus in Historiis.

# Seventh Region, Lombardy [356E]

In my last chapter, I took the region of the Romagna on one side up to the left bank of the Panaro river; on the other side to Melara, a village in Ferrarese territory, those being the region's definite boundaries on either side of the Po. Now I must turn my efforts to Lombardy. It is established that the Lombards used this name. For when Charlemagne and Pope Hadrian I named Romandiola, as I have mentioned, they wanted to distinguish this part of Italy, too, which had formerly been called Cisalpine Gaul, with the name Lombardy, because it had been occupied for nearly two hundred and eighteen years by the Lombards. And this is what the Roman church called the region in its documents from that point for six hundred and fifty years. Verona, Vicenza, Padua, the city of Treviso, and the entire territory of the church of Aquileia, had also been occupied by the Lombards: still, according to the procedure I have established, which I will use when I am ready to describe the regions, those four cities, along with several others, and the remaining part of Italy adjacent to it, including the former regions of Aquileia and of Friuli, have been named "the March of Treviso." [356F]

The boundaries of Lombardy are the Panaro and the Po rivers; the Apennines and the Alps on this side of the Po; and beyond the Po, whatever lies enclosed by the Po within the Alps, Lago di Garda, and the Po. To continue, then, the village of Bomporto is located on the right bank of the Panaro, where the stream Formico flows into it, mingled with the water of a canal which flows down from Modena. Below this is the town of Finale, where the mass of water I mentioned earlier, from the Reno, the Panaro, the Formico, and many other tributary streams, creates, at the town of Bondeno, the canal of Fistorena, which makes the last mouth of the Po. I think this is the site of the ancient Bodincomagus, which Pliny asserts was so called in the Gallic language because the Po there has great depth. The Scultenna river north of the Via Aemilia still retains its ancient name, but south of this road it is called the Panaro. It was near this river that, in 670 A.D., a battle took place between the inhabitants of Ravenna and the Lombards, and I related in my *Histories* that eight thousand men on the side of the Ravennates perished in it.

Cui interius ad sinistram adiacent Spilinbercum, Vignola, Maranum, et in Appennino Fananum, per quod oppidum arduus est in Etruriam ad Pistoriam trames. Formigo **[356G]** torrens apud Spezanum oriundus Mutinam attingit vetusti, et in Historiis frequentati nominis civitatem, quam Livius libro XXXIX dicit fuisse cum Pisauro et Parma deductam a Romanis coloniam. Et libro CXVIII idem Livius scribit M. Antonium obsedisse Mutinae D. Brutum; et cum missi ad eum de pace legati parum valuissent populum Romanum saga sumpsisse. Infra autem libro CXIX idem Livius,

> Causa malorum fuit, cum C. Octavius D. Brutum ab obsidione Antonii liberasset, senatus ipsi Bruto triumphum decrevit levi mentione habita militum Octaviani. Quare iratus, et Antonio ac Lepido reconciliatus Romam cum exercitu venit, et annos agens decem et novem, consul est creatus.

Tradit autem Plinius exire Mutinensi agro, statis diebus Vulcanum.

Eam Mutinam, quae nunc exstat novam esse et vetustae fundamenta pauxillum distare constat. Quis autem vel hanc aedificaverit novam, vel fuerit veterem demolitus, non invenimus; certum tamen habemus ipsam, quem nunc est tricentesimo quinquagesimo abhinc anno non fuisse, et utriusque solum annis ante reaedificationem quadringentis munitionibus in urbem coactis caruisse. **[356H]** In historiis enim Gothorum Longobardorumque nusquam eius nomen invenitur, cum Bononiae, Tanneti, Brixilli et Parmae nomina ibidem sint frequentia. Qua ratione in ea divisione terrarum Italiae, quam Carolus Magnus et Ludovicus, ac alii filii et nepotes Romana cum ecclesia fecerunt in neutrius partium sortem haec ipsa civitas venit. Unde nec pontifici Romano caesum pendet, nec ab imperatore aliquam dependentiam habet.

Fecit hactenus Padusa palus, ut sinistram Padi ripam a Primariis ostiis ad Bondenum describere nequiverimus. Post Bondenum quinto miliario in Padi ripa est Stellata vicus, arcem habens, unde catena in alteram trahitur e regione Pado appositam arcem, quibus praesidiis marchiones, Estenses, Padi integri, et utriusque eius ripae claustra communiunt et defensant.

Sermedum in hac Padi ripa sequitur vetusti nominis oppidum, per quod Antonini Pii itinerarius liber ostendit iter fuisse a Patavio *Atesto*que Con-

Moving inland along the river's left bank, we find Spilamberto, Vignola, Marano; and, in the Apennines, Fanano. A steep path leads through the mountains into Tuscany, to **[356G]** Pistoia. The stream named Formigine has its source at Spezzano and reaches Modena, a city with an ancient name much mentioned in my *Histories*. Livy, in book 39, says it, like Pesaro and Parma, was established as a colony by the Romans; and in book 118 he writes that M. Antonius besieged Decimus Brutus at Mutina, and since the emissaries sent to Brutus to obtain peace had had little influence, Antonius prepared for battle. And later on, in book 119, Livy writes,

> The cause of the trouble was that, although C. Octavius had freed Decimus Brutus from the siege, the senate decreed a triumph to Brutus, but made only slight mention of Octavian's soldiers. For this reason Octavian was angry; he reconciled with Antony and Lepidus, brought his army to Rome, and was elected consul at the age of nineteen.

Moreover, Pliny tells us that in the territory of Mutina, fire issues from the earth on days sacred to Vulcan.

It was well-established that the Modena which now exists is a new city, and the foundations of the old site are a short distance away. But I have not been able to discover who built the new city, or demolished the old one. I am, however, certain that the city that is now there, was not there three hundred and fifty years ago; and that the land of either city, forty years before the rebuilding, did not have a collection of fortifications sufficient to constitute a city. **[356H]** For the city's name is not found in the histories of the Goths and the Lombards, although they contain frequent mention of Bologna, Taneto, Brescello, and Parma. For this reason, Modena was not allotted to either side in the division of the lands of Italy made with the church by Charlemagne and Louis and his other sons and grandsons. Hence it neither pays homage to the Pope nor depends in any way on the Emperor.

Up to this point, the swamp of the Padusa has made it impossible for me to describe the left bank of the Po di Primaro from its mouth to Bondeno. After Bondeno, at the fifth milestone on the bank of the Po is the village of Stellata, which has a fortress from which a chain is drawn to another fortress placed on the opposite side of the Po. From these garrisons the Estense dukes fortify and defend the entrances to the Po, where it is uninterrupted, and both of its banks.

Next along this bank of the Po is Sermide, a town with an ancient name. The *Itinerary* of Antoninus Pius shows that there was a road through this

cordiam oppidum, et inde Bononiam accessuris; quae ratio facit, ut non dubitem ramum, qui sub Ficarolo ceteris maior a Pado scinditur, nedum per Antonini tempora, sed neque diu postea, sicut in Romandiola diximus, fuisse.

Post Sermedum in Padi ripa est Reverum novum oppidum e regione Ostiliae situm, quod Ludovicus Gonzaga Marchio Mantuanus validissimus communitum moenibus pulcherrima domo ornare perseverat. Intus est Mirandula, et interius Corrigia oppidum nobilis Corrigiorum **[357A]** familiae patria. Post est Carpum opulentissimum oppidum, nobilis Piorum familiae domicilium. Primus deinceps fluvios inter, solus Padum illabitur Sicla; cui ad sinistram imminet Nuvolaria vicus, Turris, Aqua Longa, Saxolum, et ubi torrente Dollo augetur Salcinium. Et ad Dollum sub Apennino Fraxanorium, et in Apennino Peregrinum, qua arduus item est in Etruriam et Lunensem agrum saltus. Apud Salcinium etiam altero Sicla dextrorsum augetur torrente, cui adiacent oppida Carponetum, Volognum, et in Apennino Piolum, ad Siclae dexteram est S. Benedicti celebre monasterium, a gloriosa Matildi comitissa aedificatum. Intus S. Martini oppidum, et ubi fossam Taram Crustulus illabitur torrens Regiolum. Interius ad dexteram Roberia, ad sinistram, Lora, Braesium, et sub Apennino Castrum Novum.

Ad Crustuli sinistram in via Aemilia est Regium Lepidum civitas; quam cum Mutina obtinet Estensis Marchio Ferrariensis. Et si vero haec civitas satis est vetusta, quam Lepidum per scelestissimi triumviratus tempora aedificasse constat, tamen sicut de Mutina diximus, nomen eius in nullis Gothorum aut Longobardorum historiis reperitur, cum Parmae, **[357B]** Tanneti, Bononiae, et Brixilli nomina eisdem in historiis frequentia inveniantur, ut non absurde videamur suspicari, ne aliquot saeculis destructa manserit, aut immunita. Frontinus enim in Strategematibus scribit:

> In legionem qua Regium Lepidum oppidum iniussu ducis diruerat, animadversum est; ita ut quattuor milia custodiae tradita necarentur. Praeterea Senatusconsultum cautum est, ne quem ex eis sepeliri, vel lugere fas esset.

town from Padua and Este to the town of Concordia; and from there you can get to Bologna. This makes me sure that the branch which is split off from the Po below Ficarolo, a branch greater than the others, neither existed yet at the time of the Antonines, nor came into being until a long time afterwards, as I mentioned in my chapter "Romandiola."

After Sermide on the bank of the Po is Revere, a new town in the region of Ostiglia. Lodovico Gonzaga, the powerful Duke of Mantua, has fortified it with walls and decorated it with a beautiful palace. Towards the interior is Mirandola, and farther inland is the town of Corrigo, **[357A]** the seat of the noble family of the da Correggio. After that is the wealthy town of Carpi, home of the noble family of the Pio. Then the first river, which flows in its entirety into the Po, the Secchia; perched over its left bank is the village of Novellara. Then come Turro, Acqualonga, Sassuolo, and where the stream Dolo flows into it, is Saltino. And next to the Dolo, at the foot of the Apennines, is Frassinoro. In the Apennines is Pellegrino, where a steep path leads into Tuscany and into the territory of Luna. At Saltino, the Secchia is joined by another tributary on its right-hand side, and next to it lie the towns of Carpineti, Vologna, and, in the Apennines, Piolo. On the right bank of the Secchia is the famous monastery of San Benedetto built by the glorious countess Matilda. Towards the interior is the town of San Martino; and where the stream Crostolo flows into the Taro river, is Reggiolo. Towards the interior on the right bank is Rubiera, and on the left, Lora, Bresio, and, at the foot of the Apennines, Castel Nuovo.

On the left bank of the Crostolo, on the Via Aemilia, is the city of Reggio Emilia. The Estense of Ferrara took possession of it along with Modena. Even if this city is old enough for it to be well-established that Lepidus built it in the time of the criminal triumvirate, still, as I said about Modena, its name is not found in any of the histories of the Goths and **[357B]** Lombards, although the names of Parma, Taneto, Bologna, and Brescello are frequently found there. For this reason I think it is sensible to posit that it was destroyed and remained so for several centuries, or that it was not fortified. And indeed Frontinus bears me out, writing in his *Stratagems*,

> He grew angry against the legion which had destroyed the town of Regium Lepidi without the general's order, and it is said that four thousand of the guard were killed. Furthermore, there was a decree of the Senate that none of them should be buried or mourned.

Superius sunt Palus et Sarcha, et ad dexteram Gypsum et Canossa, in quo oppido gloriosam Matildim comitissam in historia ostendimus VII Gregorium pontificem Romanum ab insidiis et violentia Henrici tertii imperatoris tutatam fuisse, et Henricum postea decalciatis pedibus, et nudo capite per mediam hiemem de nivibus et glacie veniam a pontifice impetrasse. Sequitur in ripa Padi Guardastallum olim, nunc Guastalla, quo in oppido miratus sum pontifices Romanos Urbanum et Paschalem utrumque nominis ordine secundum ante annos trecentos duo concilia celebrasse. Unde crediderim illo quod tunc fuerit oppido destructo, novum hoc postea aedificatum fuisse.

Deinceps est Brixillum, vetusti et in historiis celebrati nominis oppidum, **[357C]** nunc incivile; cuius arcem Corrigienses nobilis Lombardiae familia magnifici apparatus ornatam aedificiis inhabitant. Primus vero omnium Rotharis Longobardorum rex Brixillum, quod Ravennatibus suberat, cum vi cepisset demolitus. Eodemque bello a Longobardis materia, paucisque communitum, Ravennates iniecto igni penitus desertarunt.

Tannetum fuit oppidum Aemiliam inter viam et Brixillum Regio urbi propinquum. De quo Livius libro XXI infrascripta habet, quae potuerunt Mutinae esse communia:

> Triumviri ad deducendas colonias missi Placentiae moenibus diffisi Mutinam confugerunt. Legati ad Boios missi violati sunt; Mutina obsessa. Et simulatum de pace agi, missique ad eam tractandam a Gallis comprehensi. L. Manlius imperator effusum agmen ad Mutinam ducit, et in silvis, quae tunc circa Mutinam erant, caesi sunt Romanorum octingenti. Ceteri Tannetum petierunt.

Et libro XXI sicut in regione Romandiola Sassinam describentes Boiorum caput diximus, ostendit Livius Tannetum fuisse Boiorum oppidum his verbis, “Ita divisae copiae, Boisque in agrum suum Tannetum profectis.”

Apudque id oppidum, Longobardi equitum decem milia, quos Narses **[357D]** patricius copiarum Iustiniani imperator dux mercede conductos primum in Italiam duxit, Totilam Gothorum regem, sicut in historiis diximus, superatum interfecerunt. Eo denique paulo post in loco idem Narses Buccel-

Higher up are la Palude and Sarca, and on the right-hand bank Gesso and Canossa, the town where, as I showed in my *Histories*, the glorious countess Matilda kept Pope Gregory VII [*sic*; IV] safe from the plots and violence of the Emperor Henry III. And after this Henry, with his feet and head bare in the middle of winter, amid the snow and ice, begged pardon from the Pope. There follows on the bank of the Po the town once known as Guardastallum, and now as Guastalla, where, I was surprised to hear, the two marvellous councils held by Popes Urban II and Paschal II took place three hundred years ago. As a result I believe that the town which was there before was destroyed, and the new one built afterwards.

Then comes Brescello, a town whose name is ancient, **[357C]** celebrated in history, but now uncivilized. In its citadel, in splendidly decorated buildings, live the da Correggio, a noble family of Lombardy. Brescello was subject to Ravenna, but the first king of all the Lombards, Rothari, took Brescello by force and demolished it, because it was serving as a refuge for the inhabitants of Ravenna. And in the same war the men of Ravenna leveled this city, which was defended by a few Lombards, by fire.

Tannetum was a town between Brixillum and the Via Aemilia, near the city of Regium Lepidi. Livy, in book 21, wrote words which could be applied as well to Modena:

> The triumvirs had been sent to establish a colony at Placentia, but took refuge instead in Mutina because they had no confidence in the walls of Placentia. Emissaries sent to the Boii were mistreated and Mutina was besieged. The Gauls pretended to negotiate for peace, but seized the Roman envoys who were sent out to negotiate with them. The general Manlius led his army in disorganization to Mutina, and in the woods which surround Mutina 800 Romans were killed, and the rest fled to Tannetum.

Also in book 21, Livy shows in the following excerpt (as I noted on the region "Romandiola" when I described Sarsina, the capital of the Boii) that Tannetum was a town of the Boi: "So the troops were divided, and the Boii set out for Tannetum, in their own territory."

Near this same town, Totila, king of the Goths, was conquered and killed by the ten thousand Lombard cavalry led into Italy for the first time as mercenaries by the **[357D]** patrician Narses, general of the emperor Justinian (and I mentioned this in my *Histories*). And finally, a little later, in this same place, Narses defeated the Frankish prince Buccellinus, who had led

linum ducem Gallicum magnas regis Metensium copias adversum imperatorias legiones ducentem, magna in illius exercitu facta occidione superavit. Scribit Livius in censum Italiae, qui Vespasiani imperator edicto habitus est, virum unum Brixilli repertum fuisse, qui centum XX annos natus esset.

Post Brixillum Lentia fluvius Padum illabitur, ad cuius sinistram intus est Guardasionum, superius Rossana. Defluit postea in Padum Parma fluvius, ad cuius dexteram est Colornium tolleratae bis in aetate nostra durissimae obsidionis fama notum. Intus via Aemilia Parmam civitatem vetustam Romanorum coloniam, quam Livius libro XL simul cum Pisauro et Mutina deductam fuisse ostendit, idem fluvius Parma dividit. Viros habuit ea urbs praeclara praestantes, sed maxime duobus Cassio poeta, et altero centurione Cassio ornata fuit; Macrobiumque, cuius exstant doctrina pleni de Saturnalibus libri, Parmensem fuisse legimus, in cuius sepulcro Parmae celebri nostra aetate conditus est Blasius Parmensis philosophus non incelebris. Quattuor ipsa urbs ornata est magnatum familiis amplissimis, eius agri oppida ferme omnia ditione tenentibus, magnumque alentibus equitatum, **[358E]** Rossis, Corrigiensibus, Palavicinis, ac Vitalensibus. Qui cum uni domino parent, et Lombardiae aditum et ipsam custodiunt civitatem. Cum vero quicquam in provincia, aut inter seipsos acciderit disturbii, divisos secum quadrifariam cives, et omnem provinciam motibus involvunt.

Au[c]tor vero est Plinius, cum imperator Vespasianus Italiae populos describi faceret inventos fuisse duos Parmae, quorum uterque vigintiquinque supra centum annos vixisset. Et Martialis poeta ostendit agrum Parmensem semper antea, sicut nunc est, bene pascuum fuisse:

> Tondet et innumeros Gallica Parma greges.

Interius ad Parmae amnis sinistram Sapellum, Chaesta, et Brotium oppida; et sub Apennino Belforte. Ad dexteram Bagantiano torrenti, Parmam augenti Calestanum adiacet. Tarus exinde fluvius Padum illabitur. Intus ad sinistram, ubi Conio torrente augetur Fornovum; superius Complanum, Sancta Maria, et ad ortum fluvii Citium castella. Ad dexteram Solegnanum et Bargum, ubi Alpem Bardonis olim fuisse dictum invenio, in quo Luthprandus Longobardorum rex monasterium, quod Barcetum dicitur, aedificavit. Ad Conii sinistram, et ubi Ocha torrens illum influit, est Stopari-

the numerous troops of king Metensius against the legions of the emperor; and there Narses inflicted a great slaughter on his army.

Livy (*sic*) writes about the census of Italy conducted by the emperor Vespasian that one man was found at Brixillum who was one hundred and twenty years old. After Brescello, the Enza river flows into the Po. On its left bank, towards the interior, is Guardasone, and above it is Bossana. Then the Parma river flows into the Po, and on its right bank is Colorno, famous in my time for having endured two very harsh sieges. Inland on the Via Aemilia is Parma, an ancient city and a Roman colony; Livy, in book 40, says that it was established at the same time as Pisaurum and Mutina, and the same river, the Parma, runs through it. This famous city boasts some excellent men among its citizens, but is especially distinguished by two of them: the poet Cassius and the centurion of the same name. In Macrobius' *Saturnalia* (a work full of much learning), we read that the author was from Parma. In my time a famous philosopher, Biagio of Parma, was buried in Macrobius' tomb. The city has been distinguished by four important families who hold in their power its fields, towns, nearly everything, and support **[358E]** a great number of cavalry: the Rossi, Da Corregio, Pallavicino, and Vitagliani. All together obey the same ruler, and guard the entrance to Lombardy and the city itself. But when any disturbance takes place in the province or among them, they divide the citizens into four groups and engage them and the entire province in their operations.

Pliny reports that when the emperor Vespasian had a census done of the peoples of Italy, two men were found at Parma who were each one hundred and twenty years old. And the poet Martial indicates that the territory of Parma has always in the past been good pasture-land, as indeed it is now:

> Parma in Gaul shears innumerable flocks of sheep.

Towards the interior, on the left bank of the Parma river, are the towns of Sapello, Chesta, and Brosso. At the foot of the Apennines is Belforte. On the right bank of the Parma, next to its tributary, the stream Baganza, lies Calestano. From there, the Taro river flows into the Po. Farther inland on the left, where the tributary Ceno flows into the Taro, is Fornovo, and higher up Compiano, Santa Maria, and, at the river's source, the *castello* of Cisa. On the right bank are Solignano and Bardi, where I have found it reported in the past Bardone was located, where Liutprand, king of the Lombards, built a monastery called Berceto. On the left bank of the Ceno,

num. Post Tamugola et Cornus, **[358F]** et ad Conii ortum est Rumum, sub quo est Carisium.

Medio quod Tarum amnem et proximum torrentem Ardam interiacet spatio, in via Aemilia Burgus est Dononius nobile oppidum; infra est Buschetum novum oppidum, ad Lardae sinistram Scargia. Intus Columbanium, et in via Aemilia est Fidentiola oppidum nobile vetusti nominis, de quo Livius libro LXXXVIII: "Sulla Carbonem exercitu ad Clusium, ad Faventiam, Fidentiolamque caeso Italia expulit."

Ad dexteram est nobile oppidum Arquata, vinum habens omnium regionis suavissimum. Sequitur Nura fluvius, ad cuius dexteram intus Carminium, Ripa, et Ravengonum, ad sinistram Roncoverum; et sub Apennino Nucetum.

Post amnem Nuram primus Padum illabitur fluvius Trebia, ad cuius ostium est Placentia, quam Q. Asconius Pedianus tradit ordine quinquagesimam et tertiam coloniam Romanorum deductam fuisse a P. Masone Asina, a Cn. Pompeio Strabone, et P. Cornelio Scipione triumviris. Suntque eo missa sex milia hominum novi coloni, in quibus equites deducendi fuit causa, ut opponerentur Gallis, qui eam partem Galliae tenebant. Livius autem **[358G]** libro XXI: "Agro Gallorum capto coloniae deductae sunt Placentia et Cremona," et libro XXVII:

> Hasdrubal quod celeritate itineris profectum erat, id mora ad Placentiam, dum obsidet magis quam oppugnat, corrupit. Crediderat campestris oppidi facilem oppugnationem esse, et nobilitas coloniae induxerat eum.

Et libro XXVIII:

> Placentini et Cremonenses questi ad senatum de agri populationibus, quas fecerant Galli accolae, iussit senatus Manlio praetori, ut curaret. Et decrevit senatus, ut qui cives Placentini et Cremonenses erant, in colonias mitterentur.

Trebellius Pollio in Aureliani gestis rebus,

> Cum autem Aurelianus vellet omnibus simul Marcomannis facta exercitus sui constipatione occurrere, tanta apud Placentiam clades accepta est, ut Romanum paene solveret imperium.

where the stream Oca flows into it, is Stoparino. After that come Tamugola and Cornio, and at the Ceno's source is Rovina. Below it is Carisio. **[358F]**

In the area between the river Taro and the next river, the Arda, on the Via Aemilia, is Borgo San Donnino, a noble town; below that is Busseto, a new town. On the left of the Arda is Soarza, and farther inland S. Columbano, and on the Via Aemilia is Fidenza, a famous town with an ancient name. Livy writes about it in book 88: "After defeating his army near Clusium, near Faventia, and Fidentiola, Sulla expelled Carbo from Italy."

On the right is the noble town of Castell'Arquato, which has the best wine in the entire region. Then you come to the Nure river; on its right bank, towards the interior, are Camino and Rivergaro. On the left bank are Roncarolo and, at the foot of the Apennines, Niviano.

After the Nure, the first tributary of the Po is the Trebbia river. At its mouth lies Piacenza, which Q. Asconius Pedianus says was the fifty-third Roman colony established by the triumvirs P. Maso Asina, Cn. Pompeius Strabo, and P. Cornelius Scipio. Six thousand men were sent there as new colonists, and among them were cavalry, sent to oppose the Gauls who were then in control of that part of Gaul. Livy says in book 21, "When the Gallic territory **[358G]** had been captured, the Romans established colonies at Placentia and Cremona." And in book 27,

> Hasdrubal had set out quickly, but he wasted the time he had saved by delaying at Placentia, while he besieged it rather than attacking it. He had believed that a town surrounded by fields would be easy to take by attack, and the nobility of the colony had led him on.

And, in book 28,

> The inhabitants of Placentia and Cremona complained to the Senate about the devastation of their territory by their Gallic neighbors. The Senate ordered the praetor Manlius to see to the matter and decreed that those who were citizens of Placentia and Cremona should be sent into colonies.

Trebellius Pollio in his account of the achievements of the emperor Aurelian says,

> Moreover, when Aurelian wished to confront in battle the Marcomanni at the same time, with his army densely packed together, he suffered such a defeat at Placentia that the Roman Empire almost disintegrated.

Scribit etiam Livius XXI fuisse apud Placentiam emporium ope magna munitum, et valde firmatum praesidio, quod Hannibal expugnare nequivit. Id emporium fuerat a Romanis bello Gallico munitum, inde locum frequentaverant accolae, mixti undique ex finitimis populis, quos proelio superatos Hannibal crudelissime diripuit. Ornata fuit Placentia T. Tinca oratore Placentino, **[358H]** sicut Cicero in Bruto dicit, dicacissimo. Idemque Cicero pro Murena dicit patrem L. Pisonis eius qui fuit C. Iulii Caesaris socer, fuisse Placentinum, et bello Marsico faciendis armis praefuisse. Et diu post habuit Gregorium X pontificem Romanum, qui Lugdunense concilium celebravit. Isque pontifex celeberrimus post multa gloriose in ecclesia dei gesta, Arretii obiit et sepultus est, ubi saepe miraculis coruscavit. Scribitque Plinius, cum Vespasiani imperatoris edicto census Italiae haberetur, virum unum Placentiae repertum fuisse, qui XXX centumque vixisset annos. Eaque civitas ad annum XLIX supra ducentesimum et millesimum Palavicinis nobilibus subiecta fuit, cum numquam prius cuique alteri subdita fuisset, qui non Italiae omnis, aut saltem Longobardiae totius dominium obtineret.

Casus vero quos postea per aetatem nostram pertulit horrendos referre infinitum fuerit. Sed satis superque sit nunc clariores breviter explicare. Post mortem Ioannis Galeatii Vicecomitis, qui fuit primus Mediolani dux intra duos annos Placentia octies praedae exposita fuit, ad eamque tunc devenit calamitatem, ut nos ipsam perlustraverimus totam omni mortalium, praeterquam unius publici hospitatoris habitatione destitutam, et ad annum postea plus minus XL Philippo duce Mediolanensium tertio vita functo, cum populus Mediolanensis se liberum esse parum fortunato **[359A]** consilio quaesivisset, Placentiaque Venetis se dedisset, in eam Mediolanenses arma verterunt. Franciscusque Sfortia, Mediolanensis populi ductor exercitus, illam durissima pressit obsidione. Defensabatur autem urbs a Thadeo Estense, quem Veneti cum duobus equitum, totidemque peditum milibus praesidio immiserant, cum tamen populus inesset magnus milia virorum octo. Mediolanensium vero exercitui praeter Sfortianos milites decem milia inerant. Franciscus Piccininus, Guidacius Manfredus, Ludovicus Vermes, Carolus Gonzaga, et alii minores copiarum ductores, quos omnes constat supra XV milia equitum peditumque habuisset. Oppugnata vero est Placentia ali-

Livy also writes in book 21 that at Placentia was a supply-post with elaborate fortifications and a strong garrison, which Hannibal was not able to capture; this post had been fortified by the Romans during the Gallic War, and then the place had been densely settled by the various neighboring people from all around. After he had conquered these people in a battle, Hannibal sacked the town cruelly.

Piacenza has been distinguished by T. Tinca, an orator given to clever remarks, **[358H]** whom Cicero in the *Brutus* identifies as a citizen of Placentia. Cicero also, in *Pro Murena*, says that the father of the L. Piso who was Julius Caesar's father-in-law was from Placentia and, in the Social War, was in charge of making arms. A long time after this, Piacenza produced Pope Gregory X, who went to the Council of Lyons. After accomplishing many glorious achievements in the church, this famous pope died and was buried at Arezzo, and has been the cause of many miracles there. Pliny writes that when a census of Italy was taken in accordance with the edict of the emperor Vespasian, one man was found at Placentia who was one hundred and thirty years old. And this city, in the year 1249 A.D., became subject to the noble family of the Pallavicini. Never previously had it been subject to any other ruler; no one in all Italy or at least all Lombardy, maintained power over it.

It would be an unending task to relate the horrible misfortunes which Piacenza has suffered in modern times. But let it suffice to give a brief account of its more famous disasters. After the death of Giangaleazzo Visconti, the first Duke of Milan, Piacenza was in the space of two years left unprotected eight times, laid open to plundering; at that time it fell into such disaster that when I wandered through it I found it totally deserted, without any dwellings for inhabitants except for one inn. About forty years afterwards, Filippo, the third duke of Milan, died. The people of Milan asked to be free, **[359A]** a plan which had unfortunate results, and Piacenza put itself under protection of the Venetians; and the Milanese turned against the city. Francesco Sforza, leader of the Milanese, conducted a harsh siege against Piacenza; and to defend the city, the Venetians sent Taddeo d'Este with a force of two thousand cavalry and an equal number of infantry as a garrison, even though there was a great population in the city of about eight thousand. In addition to the Sforzas' men, there were ten thousand soldiers in the Milanese army. Francesco Piccinino, Guidaccio Manfredi, Lodovico dal Verme, Carlo Gonzaga, and other lesser *condottieri*, had in all over fifteen thousand infantry and cavalry. For several days, Piacenza was attacked by

quot diebus copiis bipartitis, quae unis castris Sfortiani, alii ceteri omnes tenderent, et muri utrobique bombardis aperti sunt.

Forte autem fortuna accidit Padum continuis aliquot dierum imbribus auctum adeo intumescere, ut naves ad moenia appellerentur. Quam ob occasionem tertio navali proelio urbs oppugnari coepta, et Guidatio Gonzagaeque id muneris est iniunctum. Capta est magno impetu urbs praeclara. Tanta autem in diripiendo fuit rabies, tam effrenis libido, ut nihil humani aut divini iuris aliter sit servatum, **[359B]** quam si in barbariem quandam publico dei principumque orbis Christiani edicto fuisset saeviendum. Et ne singulas percurram scelerum formas, ea quae alias in urbium direptione miserrima sunt visa, matronas violari, virgines parentum sinu evelli, inter minima Placentiae tunc sunt visa.

Secus Trebiam paulo supra Placentiam locus est insigni clade Romana Sempronio consule ab Hannibale inflicta notissimus, et Trebia intus ad sinistram habet Runchuverum; et superius Bobium monasterio beati abbatis Galli, quod ipse anno adventus Longobardorum in Italiam LXXXVII Addoaldi Theudelindae reginae filii et ipsius reginae impensa aedificavit clarum.

Ubi vero torrente Avanto Trebia augetur, est Argonastum; superius ad dexteram Octunum, Iovenum, et ad fontem Mombrunum, qua in Ligures supra Genuam est trames. Ad torrentis Avanti sinistram, ubi torrente Algretia augetur Sancti Ioannis oppidum, et in Apennino Talliolum est castellum. In Padi ripa sunt Tuni torrentis ostia, qui torrens in via Aemilia S. Ioannis agri Placentini oppidum attingit. Infra est ad dexteram Bosenasum. Ulterius ad Padum Stella, et ad torrentis Copae ostia Bricolanum. Ad huiusque torrentis sinistram intus est Clastidium illud Poenorum secundo bello Punico horreum nunc mediocre **[359C]** oppidum, de quo Livius XXI:

> Hannibal inopia quae per hostium agros euntes nusquam praeparatis commeatibus maior in dies excipiebat, ad Clastidium vicum, quo magnum frumenti numerum congesserant Romani, mittit. Ibi cum vim pararent spes facta proditionis, nec sane magno pretio

the two divisions of troops, the Sforza from one camp, and all the others; both companies broke the walls open by bombardment.

It happened by chance that the Po was swollen with continual rains for a few days, and flooded to the point of being navigable up to the city's walls. Due to this opportunity, the city was attacked a third time, this time in a naval battle, a responsibility given to Guidaccio and Gonzaga. The famous city was captured in a great assault. The victors vented their rage on Piacenza with such madness, such unrestrained lust for plunder, that no human or divine right was preserved; it was as if a barbarian people were being attacked in a holy war under **[359B]** an edict of God and of the princes of the Christian world. Not to rehearse the individual forms of wickedness, but those appeared which are most wretched when cities are plundered: the violation of women, the snatching of maidens from their parents'embrace, were among the least of the crimes seen at that time at Piacenza.

A little above Piacenza, along the Trebbia, is the place famous for the slaughter inflicted by Hannibal on the Roman consul Sempronius. And along the Trebbia on the interior, on the left, is Rivergaro, and above it is Bobbio, the famous monastery of the blessed abbot Gall, which he himself built eighty years after the Lombards came into Italy, at the expense of Adaloald the son of queen Theodelinda, and the queen herself.

But where the stream Àveto flows into the Trebbia is Ponte Organasco, and above it on the right are Ottone, Rovegno, and, at its source, Montebruno, where there is a footpath to the territory of Liguria north of Genoa. On the left bank of the stream Àveto, where the stream Algretia flows into it, is the town of Castel San Giovanni, and in the Apennines is the *castello* of Tagliolo. On the bank of the Po is the mouth of the Tidone stream, which flows past the town of Castel San Giovanni on the Via Aemilia, in the territory of Piacenza. Below it on the right is Bosnasco; farther on, on the Po, is Stella. And at the mouth of the Coppa river is Bricolano, and on this stream's left bank is Casteggio, a grain storehouse for the Carthaginians in the second Punic War, **[359C]** now an ordinary town. Livy wrote about it in book 21:

> The lack of food got worse from day to day as the Carthaginians advanced through hostile territory. Hannibal sent soldiers to the village of Clastidium, where the Romans had stored a great amount of grain. There, while they were preparing to attack the town, the Carthaginians began to hope that the town would be betrayed to them; and it was handed over to them, for the small price

> nummis aureis quadringentis datis P. Brundusino praefecto praesidii corrupto traditur Hannibali Clastidium. Id horreum fuit Poenis sedentibus ad Trebiam.

Illud autem oppidum, et adiacentes civitates per id secundi belli Punici tempus fuisse Ligurum ditionis ostendit Livius XXII:

> Q. Minucius in laevam Italiae ad inferum mare flexit iter, geminoque exercitu educto a Liguribus orsum est bellum, oppida Clastidium et Licubium utraque Ligurum, et duae gentis eiusdem civitates Celelates, Cordiciatesque sese dediderunt, et tum omnia cis Padum, praeter Gallos, Boios, Ligurum sub ditione erant.

Superius sunt Trochoneum et Turris; influit inde Padum Staffola torrens, ad cuius ostia est Albianum. Supra ad sinistram Nazzanum et Vorcum ad dexteram, intus Vogheria oppidum nunc opulentissimum.

Torrens inde habetur Coronus, ad cuius sinistram intus **[359D]** Cassium, ad dexteram superius Muleta et Castellatium. Fluvius sequitur Schirmia, supra cuius ostia ad sinistram Castrum Novum oppidum, et ipsum opulentissimum, quo insignem Borsium Estensem Philippus Anglus Mediolanensium dux donavit. Supra est Terdona civitas vetus, quam ad annum nunc LX supra ducentesimum Federicus imperator Barbarossus vastavit. Superius ad Schirmiae sinistram Servallis, quod oppidum Philippi Mediolanensium tertii ducis dono possidet Blasius Agereus Genuensis, quem res maritimis expeditionibus bene gestae clarum fecerunt. Et supra eam sunt insula Bissuda, et in Apennino Torilia. Sequitur amnis Tanarus duodecim auctus torrentibus, quorum quattuor ad sinistram, ad dexteram octo accipit.

Ad Tanarum amnem ora incipit celebris nunc Monsferatus appellata, cuius fines sunt hinc Padus, inde Apenninus. Et Tanarus ipse a fonte suo ad ostia, quibus fertur in Padum, et superiori in parte montes Moncalerio proximi, ubi Pedemontium incipit. Ferratensisque ora paene omnis marchionibus est subdita in Italia nobilissimis. Qui ex Palaeologis Constantinopolitanis imperatoribus oriundi quinquaginta iam et centum annis eam ora posse-

> of 400 gold pieces, by the commander of the garrison, the prefect Publius Brundusinus, who had been corrupted. That town was the granary for the Carthaginians as they remained encamped by the Trebia.

That Clastidium and the neighboring city-states were under the control of the Ligurians during that period of the second Punic War, Livy shows in book 22:

> Q. Minucius turned towards the left-hand side of Italy, towards the Tyrrhenian Sea, and after he had led his army out, the Ligurians started a war. The towns of Clastidium and Licubium, both Ligurian, and the two city-states belonging to the same tribe, Celelates and Cordiciates, surrendered. At that time all the area on this side of the Po, except for the Gauls and the Boii, were under the rule of the Ligurians.

Higher up lie Tronconero and Torre; from there its tributary the Staffora river flows into the Po, and at its mouth is Albiano; above it, on the left bank, are Rivanazzano and, on the right, Varzi. Farther inland lies the town of Voghera, now very wealthy.

The next stream is the Curone river; **[359D]** inland on its left bank is Casei Gerola, and on its right, higher up, are Muleta and Castellaro. Then comes the Scrivia river, above whose mouth on the left bank is the town of Castelnuovo, itself very wealthy, which Filippo Maria, the duke of Milan, gave to the distinguished Borso d'Este. Above that is Tortona, an ancient city-state, which the emperor Frederick Barbarossa destroyed two hundred sixty years ago. Higher up on the left bank of the Scrivia is Seravalle Scrivia, a town which Filippo Maria gave to Biasio Agereo of Genoa, famous for his successful naval expeditions. And above it are the island Busalla and, in the Apennines, Torriglia. There follows the Tanaro river, which has twelve tributaries: four flow into it on its left side, and eight on its right.

At the Tanaro river begins the famous region now called Monferrato. Its boundaries are: on this side the Po, on that the Apennines; and the Tanaro itself from its source to its mouth, at which point it flows into the Po; and on its higher side, the mountains next to Moncalieri, where the Piedmont begins. Almost the entire region is subject to the Marquis of Monferrato, the most noble marquises in Italy. Descended from the Paleologhi, who were emperors of Constantinople, they have by now possessed this region for

derunt. Supersuntque fratres quattuor Ioannes Guilielmus, Bonifacius et Theodorus sedis Apostolicae [360E] notarius. Etsi vero omnes litteris sunt ornati, tresque natu maiores arma cum laude tractarunt. Gulielmus tamen pluribus per Italiam bellis interfuit.

Locorum eius orae ordinem sequi, et simul digniora copiosius describere operosum fuerit atque impeditum nimis opus. Quare summatim quaecumque videbuntur digniora explicabimus. Ad Padi ripam sunt Bassignana, ubi ponte iunctus est Padus. Et Valentia, vel potius Valentium sicut Plinius, ubi primo Forumfulvii dicebatur; deinde Pomatum, Frassinetum, Casale Sancti Euasii, quod per aetatem nostram ornatum fuit Facino Cane praestantissimo rei bellicae ductore deinceps habentur Pons Sturiae, Camianum, Gabianum, Verrucula, Sanctus Raphael, Grassinum, et Moncalerium oppida, ac Salutia marchionum eius cognominis illustrium patria, in qua principem nunc habemus litteris, et omnimoda virtute conspicuum Ludovicum.

Et secundum amnis Tanari ripam post Bassignanam sunt Mons Castellus et Panonum oppida. Deinceps Bergolium, et altera potior eisdem civitatis pars Alexandria, quam Mediolanenses, Placentini, et Cremonenses, ut Papiensibus inimicis commodius obesse possent [360F] ad annum salutis LXV supra centesimum et millesimum aedificarunt. Et ut novae urbi ac facto suo maior accederet auctoritas, eam a tertio Alexandro tunc Romano pontifice Alexandriam vocaverunt. Supra quam sunt oppida Felicianum et Morum. Deinceps Asta civitas malo usurae quaestu opulenta, quam nunc obtinet dux Aurelianensis Francorum stirpe regia oriundus.

Et inde habentur oppida Guarene, Monticellum, Sancta Victoria, et Pollentum, ubi Cn. Plancus consul a M. Antonio superatus, interfectusque fuit. Superius sunt Ceva oppidum nobile, et sui marchionatus oppida, et castella, inter quae Tanarus fluvius ortum habet. Deinceps per Tanari sinistram descendendo obvia est Alba civitas Pompeiana a Plinio appellata. Inde Rocha Tanari oppidum, et supra ubi Burmida fluvius Tanarum amnem illabitur, sunt ad sinistram oppida, Castellatium, Castine, deinceps Aquae civitas. Supraque eam sunt Bastanium, Curtismilium, et Carium oppida nobilium Scaramporum, quibus locis oppida continentur, et castella marchionum Charrectensium in Appennino sita, et ad Genuensium occidentalem Riperiam continentia.

one hundred and fifty years. Four brothers survive: Giovanni, Guglielmo, Bonifacio, and Teodoro, a notary of the **[360E]** Apostolic See. Although all four are distinguished in the knowledge of literature, the older three have won glory in war; Guglielmo has taken part in many wars throughout Italy.

To follow in order the places in that region, to describe fully at the same time the things worthy of attention, would be too burdensome and would slow too much the progress of my work. So I shall explain only the main points. On the bank of the Po are Bassignana, where a bridge spans the Po, and Valenza—or rather, as Pliny calls it, Valentium—originally called Forum Fulvii. Then come Pomaro Monferrato, Frassineto, Casale Monferrato, which in our times has been distinguished by Facino Cane, a very powerful leader in war. Next come the towns of Pontestura, Camino, Gabiano, Verrua, S. Raffaele, Gassino, and Moncalieri, and Saluzzo, home of the famous marquises of that name. In that place we now have a prince, Lodovico, remarkable for his learning and every sort of virtue.

Continuing along the bank of the Tanaro river after Bassignana, we come to the towns of Montecastello and Panon. Then come Bergolium and the second and more powerful part of the same city, Alessandria, which was built in 1165 by the people of Milan and Piacenza and Cremona so they could more conveniently harm their enemies, the citizens of Pavia. **[360F]** So that more authority might accrue to their new city, they named it Alessandria after pope Alexander III. Above it are the towns of Felizzano and Mori. Next is the city of Asti, which gained wealth from the evil business of usury; it is now ruled by the duke of Orléans, of royal Frankish stock.

After Asti, one finds the towns of Govone, Monticello d'Alba, Santa Vittoria, and Pollenzo, where the consul Cn. Plancus was defeated and killed by M. Antonius. Above it is the noble town of Ceva, and the towns and fortresses belonging to its marquis. Between them is the source of the Tanaro river. Then, as you go down along the left bank of the Tanaro, you come to the city of Alba, called Pompeiana by Pliny; then, the town of Rocca di Tanaro; above it the tributary Bormida flows into the Tanaro. On the left bank are the towns of Castellazzo Bormida, Cassine, and then the city of Aqui Terme. Above the latter are the towns of Bistagno, Cortemilia, and Cairo, and the towns belonging to the noble family of the Scarampori; in these places are towns, and in the Apennines the *castelli* of the Del Carretto marquises, and those (towns) bordering on the western Riviera in Genoese territory.

Infra vero torrens Borbus ad dexteram Damianium, ad fontem habet **[360G]** Canachium, cui proximum est oppidum Carmagnola, quod aetate nostra ornatum fuit Francisco cognomine Carmagnola, quo excellentissimo rei bellicae ductore Philippus Mediolanensis, dux tertius, si diutius bene uti scivisset rem Venetam Florentinamque in maximum discrimen perduxisset.

Post supra dicta Padus in sinistro duorum cornuum, quae sub ortu suo efficit, habet Uncinum, in dextro Cricium, inter quae duo oppida est ipse Padi ortus, quem Plinius fontem Visundum appellat, dicitque eum mediis diebus aestivis velut interquiescentem semper arescere. Et arduus a quo fons ipse scatet Mons Vesulus a priscis est appellatus. Ex quo primum nasci, et ab Alpibus discedere incipit Apenninus. Padum amnem a Virgilio libro VI Eridanum appellatum Servius grammaticus scribit, ideo a poetis dici apud inferos nasci, quia nascatur in Apennino in mare inferum verso. Sed contrarium esse videmus, cum ea pars Apennini, ex qua ortum habet, sit in mare superum versa. Quod autem postea Servius subiungit, verum est, Eridanum fuisse dictum a Solis filio in curru fulminato, quem male regebat, postea sorores flentes versas in populos. **[360H]**

Sed iam transeundum est ad aliam Lombardiae partem, quem olim dicta est Italia Transpadana, de qua Plinius, "Transpadana Italia addita faba, sine qua nihil conficiunt"; et ubi de rapis libro XVII tractat, dicit: "Tertius hic Transpadanis fructus."

Primusque illi est in Padi ripa Mincius noti vetustique, et a Virgilio celebratissimi nominis fluvius lacu Benaco effusus. Mincio ad sinistram prope Padum Governum oppidum, apud quem locum primus Leo papa Athilam Hunnorum regem, qui flagellum Dei dictus est, ne ulterius Italiam ingrederetur suae sanctatis gravitate deterruit. Et ubi Mintius palude emittitur, Mantuam urbem circumdante, Formigosa est castellum. Mantuam urbem vetustissimam ab Etruscis conditam, et unam fuisse XII coloniarum, quas superius ex Livio Patavino docuimus trans Apenninum ab ea gente missas magis constat, quam ut alia indigeat probatione; praesertim cum poeta insignis Virgilius civis suus, id orbi faciat notissimum, diffusiusque eius urbis narrat originem: "Mantua dives avis, sed non genus omnibus unum." Livius libro XXII:

Below is the Borbera stream, on the right bank S. Damiano d'Asti, at the source is Canale, **[360G]** and next to it the town of Carmagnola, which in our times has been distinguished by Francesco Bussone (da Carmagnola). If Filippo Maria III of Milan had had the sense to use his services longer in war, he would have brought Venice and Florence to the point of crisis.

After the towns which I have mentioned, on the left of the two branches into which the Po splits beneath its source, is Oncino, and on the right is Crissolo. Between these two towns is the source of the Po, which Pliny calls Fons Visundus, and says that it always stops, as it were, in mid-summer, and dries up. The steep mountain from which this spring gushes up was called by the ancients Mt. Vesulus (Monviso). Here, at Monviso, the Apennines begin, and part company with the Alps. The grammarian Servius writes that the Po River was called Eridanus by Virgil in book 6; and that it is said by the poet to have its source in the underworld because it originates in the Apennines where they face the Tyrrhenian ("Lower") Sea. But I observe that the opposite is true: that part of the Apennines where the Po has its source faces the Adriatic. After the comment I have cited, Servius adds that the river was called Eridanus after the son of the sun god in the chariot which he failed to control and which was struck by lightning; afterwards his weeping sisters were turned into poplar trees. **[360H]**

But now I must cross over to the part of Lombardy which in antiquity was called Transpadane Italy. Pliny says about this region: "In Transpadane Italy they add [to millet] the bean, which they use in everything they cook." And about the bean in book seventeen, he says: "It ranks third [after wine and corn] among the products of the country north of the Po."

The first river on the bank of the Po is the Mincio: its name is famous, ancient, and celebrated by Virgil; it has its source in Lake Garda. On the left bank of the Mincio, near the Po, is the town of Governolo, where Attila the Hun, called the scourge of God, was kept by the holy authority of Pope Leo I from advancing any farther into Italy. And where the Mincio issues forth, from a swamp which encircles the city of Mantua, there is the *castello* of Formigosa. Mantua is a very ancient city, founded by the Etruscans and one of the twelve colonies which that race sent out across the Apennines, as I have shown above, based on Livy's account. This is too well-established to need any other proof, especially since the famous poet Virgil, a citizen of Mantua, made it well-known to the world when he told more fully his city's origins:

> Ita divisae copiae, Boisque in agrum suum Tannetum profectis Insubres Cenomannique super amnis Mincii ripam consederunt. Intra mille passuum et Cornelius consul eidem flumini castra applicuit.

Et libro XXIII, prodigia enumerans, quae anno V secundi belli Punici **[361A]** fuerunt dicit, "Mantuae stagnum effusum Mincio amni cruentum visum."

Passa est pridem Mantua calamitates maximas, praeter illas, quae Virgiliano versu sunt notissimae: "Mantua vae miserae nimium vicina Cremonae." Nam ab Athila, Gothis, Longobardis, et Chachanno Bavarorum rege eam quandoque dirutam, quandoque spoliatam, quandoque moenibus apertis immunitam fuisse relictam in Historiis ostendimus. Mantuae per Caroli Magni tempora sanguis Christi miraculosus apparuit, ad quem visendum II Leo Papa se contulit, et inde in Germaniam ad Carolum accessit. Carolusque Calvus Magni filius Mantuae veneno interiit, quod Hebraeus medicus pecunia corruptus dedit. Eadem quoque in urbe II Nicolaus pontifex Romanus concilium celebravit, in quo confirmata est constitutio de pontificis Romanis electione a cardinalibus facienda. Interfuitque concilio Mathildis gloriosa, in cuius potestate ea urbs tunc erat.

Obiit in ea nuper praestantissimus princeps Ioannes Franciscus Gonzaga bello et pace clarissimus, virtute cuius et proximarum Lombardiae civitatum infortuniis, per aetatem nostram opibus Mantua populoque quam multis ante fuerit seculis plenior est facta. **[361B]** Superestque Paula uxor, mulierum aetatis nostra a religionis sapientiae et humanitatis partibus celeberrima. Et huiusmodi parentum laudibus respondentes Ludovicus marchio, Carolusque frater, et si arma cum laude tractant litteris exornantur. Quibus eos et fratres et sorores imbuit vir doctissimus, ac omnimoda virtute conspicuus Feltrensis Victorinus. Episcopum item et civem nunc habet Mantua praestantissimum Galeacium Caprianum, litteris honestate et prudentia ornatissimum.

> Mantua, rich in its forefathers; but not all of the same race.

And Livy says in book 22,

> The troops were divided in the following way: the Boi set out into their territory, to defend it; the Insubri and Cenomanni settled across the bank of the river Mincius; within a mile the consul Cornelius set a camp on the same river.

and, in book 23, listing the prodigies which appeared in the fifth year of the second Punic War, Livy says, "At Mantua a pool flowing with gore was seen to ooze from the river Mincio." **[361A]**

On occasions in the past, Mantua has suffered great disasters in addition to the ones made famous in the line from Virgil,

> . . . Mantua, too close to wretched Cremona.

For I have told in my *Histories* how at one time or another Mantua has been destroyed by Attila, the Goths, the Lombards, and Chachannus king of the Bavarians: at one time the city was pillaged, at another its walls were breached, and the city was left undefended. In the time of Charlemagne a miracle took place: the blood of Christ was found. Pope Leo II came to see it, and from there went to Germany to Charlemagne. And Charles the Bald, Charlemagne's son, died of poisoning at Mantua; the agent was a Jewish doctor who had been bribed. Also in Mantua, Pope Nicholas II held the council at which they confirmed the arrangement for having cardinals elect the pope. Present at this council was the renowned Matilda who at that time had Mantua in her power.

Recently at Mantua, the most excellent prince Giovanni Francesco I Gonzaga died. He was famous in war and peace; because of his courage, and the misfortunes of the neighboring Lombard cities, Mantua flourished in wealth and population in our times more than she ever had in previous ages. **[361B]** His wife Paola survives, the most famous woman of our age in religion, wisdom, and philanthropy. And the marquis Lodovico and his brother Carlo equal their parents in glory: although they have won praise for their military exploits, they are also distinguished in learning; for they and their brothers and sisters were educated by Vittorino da Feltre, a very learned man outstanding in every virtue. Mantua also boasts now, as bishop and citizen, the most excellent Galeazzo Capriano, distinguished for learning, integrity, and wisdom.

Mincium amnem ponte iungit Valegium oppidum. Supra ad lacus emissorium est Piscaria magni portorii oppidum; arce et ponte magnifici operis a Scaligeris olim Veronensibus conditum. Isque pro Benaco Gardae lacus nunc appellatus est. Virgilius,

> Quos patre Benaco velatus arundine glauca
> Mintius infesta ducebat in aequora puppi.

Benacusque oppida et vicos habet ad dexteram Lagisium Gardamque, a quo nomen accipit, Turrim, Malsesinum, et Turbolum, sub quo illum intrat Sarcha fluvius in Tridentinis montibus oriundus. Estque is Turboli vicus turri munitus debilissima, ad quem primaria historiarum nostrae aetatis pars pro miraculo narrat triremes Venetorum Philippensi bello **[361C]** altissimis traductas montibus in Benacum fuisse dimissas.

Sarchiae item ad dexteram sunt castella et vici, Archus, Drenna, Madrusium, et ad parvi lacus quem in montibus facit dexteram Vocianum. Superius in valle Pontionum, et ad fluvii Sarchae fontem sancta Maria. Ad Mincii sinistram Goidum, Volta, et Capriana, ad lacus vero sinistram Rivoltella, Desentianum, Minervium, et in sinus quem facit lacus angulo Salodium. Post in circuitu Madernum, Gargnanum, Lucionium, et Riva nobilissimum regionis oppidum, quod in historiis Longobardorum legimus sic appellatum fuisse a rivo sanguinis, qui factus est, cum rex Longobardorum Grimoaldus Francos Italiam per Tridentum ingressos, magna occidione in proelio superasset.

Superius ad Sarchae sinistram Triennium et Cadarcionum. Estque in lacus insula Sermionum. Ultra Mincium per Padi ripam est Burgus Fortis, ubi Mantuanus marchio illum munitissimis hincinde custoditum arcibus catena claudit; paulo supra sunt amnis Ollii ostia. Is fluvius lacu Sebuino, quam nunc Isei vocant, effusus brevi supra Padum tractu, ad dexteram Clesio augetur fluvio, prope cuius ostia est oppidum Marcharia. Et ad ipsa **[361D]** ostia Calvatum castellum. Ad Clesii vero dexteram sunt Asola,

A bridge spans the Mincio at the town of Valeggio su Mincio. Above it at the lake's outlet is Pescheria, a town which exacts a high toll on goods passing through it. It was built with a magnificent citadel and bridge by the Della Scala, at that time citizens of Verona. This lake is now called Garda instead of Benacus. Virgil has the line,

> The figure of the river Mincius on the warship led them down to the sea, Mincius veiled in grey-green reeds, flowing from his father Benacus.

Lake Garda has towns and villages on the right hand side, Lazise and Garda, from which it takes its present name; and Torre, Malcesine, and Torbole, beneath which the Sarca river flows into it, which has its source in the Tridentine mountains. This is the same village of Torbole, fortified by a weak tower, where the Venetian triremes, [361C] in the war with Duke Filippo Maria, were brought over very high mountains and sent forth into Lake Garda. I tell about this miracle, as it were, in the first part of my *Histories*.

In addition, on the right bank of the Sarca are *castelli* and villages: Arco, Drena, Castel Madruzzo, and, on the right-hand side of a small lake which the river creates in the mountains, is Vociano. Higher up, in a hollow, is Pinzolo; and at the source of the Sarca river is Madonna du Campiglio. On the Mincio's left bank are Goito, Volta, and Capriana. On the lake's left shore are Rivarolo Mantovano, Desenzano del Garda, Manerba, and, in the bay formed in a corner of the lake, Salò. Then, as you go around the lake, Maderno, Gargnano, Limone, and Riva, the noblest town in the region. We read about Riva in the histories of the Lombards that it received its name from the stream of blood which resulted when Grimoald, king of the Lombards, defeated in a great slaughter the Franks who had invaded Italy through Trento.

Higher up on the left bank of the Sarca are Tione di Trento and Cavadeno; and in an island in the lake lies Sirmione. Beyond the Mincio, along the bank of the Po, is Borgoforte, where the marquis of Mantua has surrounded the town with well-fortified citadels and blocked it off with a chain. A little higher up is the mouth of the river Oglio. This river flows out of Lake Sebuino (now called Iseo) in a brief course above the Po, and on the right side the Chiese river flows into it. Near its mouth is the town of Marcaria, and right at its mouth [361D] is the fortress Calvatone. On the right bank of the Chiese are Asola, Casalmoro, and Montichiari; adjoining the

Morum, Mons Clarus, cui amplissima adiacet planities, et Lunatum oppidum. Ad eiusque sinistram Gavardum, Buarnum, Angosenium; superiusque Clesium tres augent torrentes, Toverus, Degnus, Biocolus. Ederum inde habet castellum, apud sui nominis lacum, quem sub Ludronio castello altissimis in montibus influit Chaffar torrens. Ad Clesii vero fontem Bargatium est oppidulum. At ad Ollii fluminis sinistram sunt, Pons Vicus, Urcei Novi, Urcei veteres oppida. Et supra ad Sebuinum est Isei oppidum, a quo lacus novum accepit. Supra ubi Ollius ipse lacum influit, est Pisognum castellum, et ubi torrente augent Grinia, Buenum. Superius Civitale et Brenum.

Ubi fontem habeat Ollius, difficile est diffinire. Nam cum a Frigidolfo lacu, qui est in Alpibus, torrentes decidant duo, qui ad sinistram est Frigidolfum nomen retinens Ollium influit; qui vero est ad dexteram, in alium cadit torrentem, a quo Ollium habere initium incolae affirmant. Cum item alter torrens apud Poggium castellum oriundus duorum, quos habet ramorum, altero ad sinistram per Dialengum, Sanctum Bartholomaeum, Armicumque, et Cusiam vallis solis loca Abduam, altero ad dexteram Ollium illabitur. Communem cum Abdua ortum Ollius habere videtur. Sed ad inferiora amnis Ollius paulo supra Clesii ostia ad sinistram habet Platinam, post Rebechum, inde Soncinum oppidum superius **[362E]** Palatiolum et Calebium. Ad lacusque sinistram Sarnagum, Pranorium, Loarium, Monticulum, Cemmium et Edolium.

Medio quod Clesium et Ollium amnes interiacet spatio Brixia est praepotens civitas, quam Iustinus ex Trogo dicit conditam fuisse simul cum Mediolano et pluribus aliis civitatibus a Gallis, qui urbem Romam ceperunt. Sed Livius velle videtur eam fuisse Cenomannorum olim, a quibus condita sit, caput. Est autem vetusto nomine, et rebus apud eam gestis clara, quam Livius libro XXI fuisse Romanis auxilio his verbis scribit:

> L. Aemilius imperator effusum agmen ad Mutinam ducit, et in silvis, quae tunc circa Mutinam erant, caesi sunt Romanorum LXXX. Ceteri Tannetum petiierunt. Sex signa militaria adempta. Fuere tunc auxilio Romanis Brixiani Galli, adversus alios Gallos et Boios.

Et libro XXII,

latter is a magnificent plain, and then the town of Lonato. On its left bank are Gavardo, Borno, and Agnosine; and higher up three tributaries of the Clesio flow into it, the Toverno, Degnone, and Abbiocolo. Then comes the *castello* of Idro, at the lake of the same name (Lago d'Idro); the stream Caffaro flows into it in the high mountains, under the *castello* of Lodrone. At the Chiese's source is the small town of Barghe. On the left bank of the river Oglio are the towns of Pontevico, Orzinovi, and Orzivecchi. And higher up towards Lake Iseo is the town of Iseo, which has given the lake its new name. Above where the Oglio itself flows into the lake is the *castello* of Pisogne, and where the stream Grigna flows into the Oglio, are Biennio, Cividate, and Breno.

It is difficult to locate the source of the Oglio. Two streams flow down from Lago Nero in the Alps. The one on the left keeps the name Oglio Frigidolfo and flows into the Oglio. The one on the right flows into another stream and the natives say that this is the beginning of the Oglio. Since the second stream likewise has its source at the *castello* of Poggio, of its two branches one goes towards the left through Ponte di Legno, S. Bartolomeo, Dimaro (?), and Cusiano, all places in the valley, and flows into the Adda; the other goes towards the right and flows into the Oglio. The Oglio appears to have a common source with the Adda. But further downstream, the river Oglio has, a little above, the mouth of the Chiese; on the left the town of Piadena, and after that Robecco, and then Soncino. Higher up are **[362E]** Palazzolo and Calepio. On the left of the lake are Sarnico, Parzanica, Lovere, Monticelli d'Oglio, Cemmo, and Edolo.

In the area between the Chiese and Oglio rivers lies Brescia, a powerful city. Justin, in his *Epitome* of Trogus, says that the Gauls who captured Rome founded it at the same time as Milan and many other cities. But Livy seems to think it was the capital of the Cenomanni and that they founded it. Whatever its origin, it has an ancient name, and is famous for the military actions which took place there. Livy, in book 21, says in the following words that Brixia helped the Romans:

> The commander L. Aemilius led his army in disorder to Mutina, and in the woods which then surrounded Mutina, eighty Romans were slain. The rest made for Tannetum; six military standards were taken from them. At that time the Gauls of Brixia helped the Romans against the other Gauls and the Boii.

And in book 22, Livy relates,

> Ita divisae copiae, Boisque in agrum suum Tannetum profectis, Insubres cum Cenomannis super amnis Mintii ripam consederunt; intra mille passuum et Cornelius consul eidem flumini castra applicuit, inde mittendo in vicos Cenomannorum Brixiamque, quae caput gentis erat, ut satis comperit . . .

et cetera. Nec tamen minus clara est reddita, per aetatem nostram obsidione, quam omnium durissimam Philippensi bello, et Francesco Barbaro insigni Veneto praefecto defendente **[362F]** pertulit.

Brixiam praeterlabitur fluvius Mella, scatentibus ubique per regionem fontibus et rivis potius quam torrentibus quattuor influentibus, non multis auctus aquis, quas ad nullum, proximorum amnium integer perducit. Habet Mella ad dexteram Mompianum, Concisum et Seretium castella, ad sinistram ubi crescere incipit Chorium, subinde Villam et Uncinum, et ubi influit Broccus torrens Broccium, et ad Broccii ortum Lodrium. Ad fontemque Mormae torrentis Pesacium, secusque Mellae ipsius alveum Boratum et Coium. Ad Padi alveum sequitur Dosiolum, et post Vitelliana oppidum, opibus populoque refertissimum, quod Vitellius imperator direpta Cremona, dum Ottonis Romae imperantis mortem cum proditoribus constitutam expectat, pro castris primo habuit, postea ut pro oppido habitaretur, reliquit communitum.

Superius est Sabloneta oppidum, quod familia in Cremonensibus nobilis comitum Persiceti, quae nunc habet Brocardum litteris ornatissimum, duxit originem. Inde quinto miliario in Padi ripa abest Casale, quod cognomine dicunt Maius, oppidum populo frequentissimum.

Inde milibus passuum triginta abest Cremona vetus Romanorum colonia simul **[362G]** cum Placentia, sicut Livius XXI scribit deducta, quae sicut Virgilio non de praeterito magis vere dixit, quam de futuro vaticinatus fuit, multas saepenumero calamitates incurrit, quae post tempora Virgilii a Vitelliano exercitu primum, ut diximus, direpta; et post annos circiter quadringentos a Gothis, inde a Gisulpho Longobardorum rege, et Sclavis illi militantibus per diem XII Septembris ad annum salutis circiter sexcentesimum et trigesimum eversa. Et annis postea plus minus sexcentis inde elapsis a

> The troops were divided in this way, and when the Boii had set forth towards Tannetum in their territory, the Insubri along with the Cenomanni took up a position above the bank of the Mincio. One mile away the consul Cornelius pitched camp beside the same river, and from there sent messengers into the villages of the Cenomanni and Brixia, which was the capital of that tribe, when he found out. . . .

etc. Brescia is no less famous in our age on account of the harshest siege it has suffered, in the war with Filippo Maria, when the city was defended by Francesco Barbaro the illustrious **[362F]** Venetian commander.

The Mella river glides past Brescia. Four streams, I would call them—rather than torrents—flow into it, from the springs which gush forth everywhere throughout the region. The Mella is not increased by many tributaries; undiminished, it does not lead its waters to any of the nearby rivers. On the right bank of the Mella are the *castelli* of Mompiano, Concesio, and Sarezzo; on its left bank, where it begins to widen, is Corio, and just after this Villa and Inzino, and Brozzo where the stream Brozzo flows into the Mella and, at the source of the Brozzo, Lodrino. At the source of the stream Marma is Pezzaze. Along the channel of the Mella itself are Burato and Collio. Next, near the channel of the Po, is Dosolo, and after that the town of Viadana, endowed with great wealth and many inhabitants. It was here that the emperor Vitellius first had his camp after he had plundered Cremona while awaiting the death of Otho (conspirators were planning his murder while he ruled at Rome). Afterwards, Vitellius left it strongly fortified so that it could be inhabited as a proper town.

Higher up is the town of Sabbioneta; from it a noble family among the inhabitants of Cremona, the counts of Persichetti, traces its descent. They now include Brocardo, distinguished in literature. Five miles from there, on the bank of the Po, is Casalmaggiore, a heavily populated town which is designated with a cognomen meaning "greater."

Thirty miles from here is Cremona. It was an ancient Roman colony established **[362G]** at the same time as Placentia, as Livy tells us in book 21. Just as Virgil spoke inspired words about the future as well as about the past of Cremona, the city has again and again met with disaster. After Virgil's time it was first, as I said, plundered by Vitellius' army, and then by the Goths about four hundred years later; then it was sacked on the twelfth day before the Kalends of September in about 630 A.D., by Gisulf, king of the Lombards, and the Hungarian soldiers in his service. Six hun-

Federico imperatore Barbarossa spoliata ac immunita fuit derelicta. Nunc autem Francisco Sfortiae per Blanchae Mariae uxoris dotem subiecta est.

Habuit ex vetustissimis M. Furium poetam cognomine Bibaculum, et postea Quintilium poetam Virgilio et Horatio familiarissimum, Eusebium quoque Cremonensem ecclesiasticorum dogmatum peritissimum. Habuit quoque Gerardum Sablonetum excellentem physicum, et astronomum, qui Chaldaeas Graecasque, sicut et Latinas edoctus litteras Avicennae et Rasis, sive Almansoris libros, qui nunc Latine leguntur, transtulit ex Arabico, et nuper habuit Ioannem Balistarium praeceptorem meum grammaticae, rhetoricae, et poeseos, quibus adolescens ab eo imbutus fui peritissimum. Habuit quoque tum multos iuri et medicinae **[362H]** deditos, tum maxime Nicolaum Placentinum episcopum Vincentium fratrem Amidanos cives eloquentia exornatos.

Supra ad dexteram est Machastorma castellum caede Cavalcaboum, quos Cabrinus Fundulus crudelissime ibi occidit, notissimum; deinde proximo loco sunt ostia fluminis Abduae. Intus ad dexteram paucis supra Padum milibus Abduam influit Serius amnis, ad cuius ostia imminet Abduae Picigitonum oppidum populo frequentatum arcem habens inter primas munitioresque Lombardiae numerandam. Et ad Serii dexteram sunt S. Sebastianus, Castilionum, Ruminengum, Martinengum, et in montibus Ghisalbaum Seriacumque, et inde vallis Seriana vicis plurimis frequentata.

Ad Serii fluminis sinistram primum est Crema oppidum nobile a Federico Barbarossa post afflictam Cremonam in eius civitatis damnum opprobiumque aedificatum, quod Veneti per foedera sunt potiti, quae cum Francisco Sfortia adversus Mediolanenses inierunt. Supra sunt Nemberium et Vertorium, et ad fluvii fontem Bardionum. Imminet ostiis Abduae ad sinistram castrum novum cognomine Bucca Abduae. Interius quinquagesimo secundum amnis decursum miliario est Lauda civitas, quam Federicus Barbarossus Mediolano destructo aedificavit, ornaturque ea civitas **[363A]** Am-

dred years, more or less, after this, the emperor Frederick Barbarossa plundered Cremona, leaving it undefended and abandoned. But now it has come under the power of Francesco Sforza as part of his wife Maria Bianca's dowry.

Among the noteworthy citizens of ancient Cremona were the poet M. Furius Bibaculus; and after him, the poet Quintilius, intimate friend of Virgil and Horace. Eusebius, very skilled in church doctrine, was also from Cremona. This city also boasts of Gerard of Cremona, the excellent physicist/naturalist and astronomer, learned in Chaldaean and Greek as well as in Latin: he translated from the Arabic the books of Avicenna and Rasi or Almansor, which can now be read in Latin. Recently Cremona counted among her citizens Giovanni Balestreri, my teacher in grammar, rhetoric, and poetry; this very skilled teacher introduced me, as a youth, to all these subjects. Cremona was also at that time home to many men who were devoted to law **[362H]** and medicine. Among her citizens especially distinguished at that time for their eloquence were the Amidani: Niccolò, bishop of Piacenza, and his brother Vincenzo.

Above Cremona on the right bank is the *castello* Maccastorna, very famous for the slaughter of the Cavalcaboi, cruelly killed there by Cabrino Fundulo. Then, in the next place is the mouth of the river Adda. Towards the interior on the right, a few miles above the Po, the river Serio flows into the Adda. At its mouth the town Pizzighettone overhangs the river; it is densely populated, and has a citadel numbered among the most important and strongly fortified in Lombardy. And on the right bank of the Serio are San Sebastiano, Castelleone, Romanengo, Martinengo, and, in the mountains, Ghiselba and Seriate; and then comes the valley of the Serio, thickly populated with villages.

On the left bank of the Serio river, the first town is Crema, a noble town; Frederick Barbarossa built it after the destruction of Cremona, as restitution and acknowledgment of the damage he had inflicted on that city. The Venetians took possession of it by virtue of treaties they entered into with Francesco Sforza against the Milanese. Higher up are Nembro and Verdello, and at the source of the river, Valbondione. Overhanging the mouth of the Adda on the left bank is Castelnuovo, with its additional name, Castelnuovo Bocca d'Adda. Fifty miles farther inland, following the river's course, is the city of Lodi, which Frederick Barbarossa built after the destruction of Milan, and this city is distinguished by Ambrogio Vignati, **[363A]** the most outstanding jurist of Lombardy, and a man devoted to the study of

brosio Vignatensi iureconsulto praestantissimo, bonarumque artium studiis deditissimo, et pariter Mapheo Veggio doctissimo atque optimo viro, aliquot editis operibus partim metro, partim oratione soluta claro.

Distat a praesenti Lauda civitate tertio miliario, altera Lauda Vetus dicta, quam vulgo ferunt Cn. Pompeius aedificasse, datis ibi colonis primariis piratarum, quos duxerat in triumphum, quod quidem nullo invenimus in loco. Quin potius Servius in Virgilii expositione est auctor, piratas partim in Graecia, partim in Calabria a Pompeio agros habuisse, nisi forte aliter voluisse videatur innuere Lucanus in primo, ubi facit Caesarem Arimini contionantem sic dicere:

> Quae sedes erit emeritis, quae rura dabuntur
> Quae noster veteranus aret, quae moenia fessis?
> An melius fient piratae, Magne, coloni?

Plinius vero velle videtur eam urbem fuisse conditam a populis nomine Laeviis et Maricis, qui fuerunt Transalpini, et tamen eam appellat Laudam Pompeianam. Raram autem in veteribus scriptis eius urbis aut loci vidimus fieri mentionem. Primusque praeter Plinium locus, in quo Laudae civitatis nomen legatus est, ubi nos Odoacris Erulorum regis adventum in Italiam describentes diximus, quod et aliunde accepimus Orestem patricium Augustuli imperatorem genitorem, apud Laudam Odoacri congressum, ab eoque superatum Papiam confugisse. **[363B]**

Supra Laudam Abduae imminet Cassianum oppidum. Post regio est Mons Brigantius appellata, multis habitata viculis, et vini optimi castanearumque feracissima. Ubi vero Abduae mons ipse imminet Brippium est oppidum quod Veneti obtinent. Et supra varios inter colles Abduam dextrorsum illabitur Brembus amnis, cuius convalli inter montes insunt castella et vici, S. Petrus, Menium, Augum, S. Peregrinus, S. Ioannes, et Platia.

Contra Brembi amnis ostia est Vavarium castellum, et intus Gorgontiola. Attrahit ex lacu Lario nunc Comi dicto Abdua sinum, quem Lauci lacum dicunt. Estque ad lacus ipsius emissorium, qua fluvius Abdua in mediterranea exit, Leucum oppidum, ubi pons eum iungit amnem. Et secundum lacus dexteram superius sunt Abbatia, Mandellum, deinceps Lernium, Varena, Bollanum, Corcenum, Prona, et ubi Abdua ipse ex Alpibus cadens

the liberal arts. The city also boasts as a citizen the learned and excellent Maffeo Veggio, famous for his works both in verse and in informal genres.

A second city, called Lodi Vecchio, is three miles distant from the modern Lodi. The common tradition is that Gnaeus Pompeius built it after he had given colonies there to the pirate chiefs whom he had led in his triumphal procession. But I have not found this anywhere; in fact, Servius, in his commentary on Virgil, tells us that some of the pirates got land from Pompey in Calabria, some in Greece; but perhaps Lucan indicates otherwise, when he has Caesar say in book 1 in his oration at Rimini,

> What homes will there be for the deserving veterans, what fields will be given for my veterans to plow, what wall will protect them when they are worn out? Or will pirates, Pompey, be better colonists?

Pliny, on the other hand, seems to think that Lodi was built by peoples named Laevii and Marici, who were Transalpines; and this in spite of the fact that he calls the city Laus Pompeiana. What is more, I have found in the ancient authors scant mention of this city or its location. And the first passage, except for Pliny, where the name of the city of Lauda is read, is where I mentioned it in my description of the arrival in Italy of Odoacer, king of the Eruli. From a different source I have heard that the patrician Orestes, father of the emperor Augustulus, fought against Odoacer at Lauda, was defeated by him, and took refuge at Pavia. **[363B]**

Above Lodi the town of Cassano overhangs the Adda. Beyond that is an area called La Brianza which contains many small villages and is very fertile land for vineyards and chestnut trees. And where this mountain towers over the Adda is the town of Brivio, now under control of the Venetians. And above, among the various hills, the Brembo river flows into the Adda on the right-hand side. In the valleys of the Brembo enclosed between the mountains are the following fortresses and villages: Ponte San Pietro; Almenno; Zogno (?); San Pellegrino; San Giovanni Bianco; and Piazzolo.

Opposite the mouth of the Brembo is the *castello* Vaprio, and inland is Gorgonzola. From Lake Larium, now called Lake Como, the Adda draws a body of water which they call Lago di Lecco. And at the outlet of this lake, where the Adda flows out into the interior, is the town of Lecco, with a bridge spanning the Adda. And following the right-hand shore of the lake, higher up, are the Abbadia, Mandello, then Lierna, Varenna, Bellano, Corenno Plinio, and Piona; and, where the Adda flows down from the Alps

Larium influit, est Colungum. Supra sunt Morbengum, Stationa, Tiranum, Machum, et ubi communem Abduae cum Ollio fontem esse diximus, sub Frigidolfo Burinum. Sunt etiam ad Abduae lacum [363C] influentis sinistram Postalesium, Xundrum, et supra lacunam, quae Abduae fons a multis esse creditur Posclavinum.

Medio quod Abduam influentes Serium, et Brembum fluvios interest spatio editissimis in montibus est Bergomum civitas vetusta, a Gallis simul cum Mediolano, et Brixia, et Verona, eodemque tempore sicut Pompeius Trogus dicit aedificata, quae Gasparino Bergomensi rhetore et grammatico exornata est. Eo item spatio quod Brembum, Serium, Abduamque amnes, et Bergomenses intercedit montes, regio est Glarea Abduae appellata. Insunt et castella Trivilium, Mozanica, et quae supra sunt dicta, Ruminengum, Martinengum, et Caravagium proelio insigne omnium aetatis nostrae memorabili, in quo Mediolanensis tunc rei publicae exercitus copias Venetorum equitum XII peditum IIII milia fregit, fuditque, vel potius maiori ex parte cepit.

Sequitur ad Padi dexteram Belgiosium villa opulentissima, quam Philippi Angli Mediolanensis tertii ducis dono obtinet Ludovicus Cunii comes, Albricum tertium et Malatestam comitum Cunii, sicut ostendimus clarissimorum reliquias in ea fovens. Postea habentur Umbronis fluminis, quod Eupilum lacus Larii sive Comensis partem exonerat ostia. [363D] Primum habet Umbro ad dexteram castellum Villalantem, post Sanctum Angelum. Et longe supra intus Canturium oppidum, superiusque Comum civitas vetusta lacui Lario, cui dat Comensem appellationem contigua, quae a Gallis cum Mediolano, Brixia et Verona, sicut Trogus scribit, condita fuit. Civem ea civitas habuit paterna origine Plinium, quem mutatus incolatus vacari fecit Veronensem, qui scribit Comum et Bergomum Oromoniorum stirpis fuisse, Catonem tradidisse, qui fassus fuerit se gentis originem ignorasse. Quam postea docuit Cornelius Alexander affirmans ortam fuisse eam gentem a Graecis, interpretatione nominis indicante, qui vitam in montibus degant.

Catullusque poeta innuere videtur Caecilium poetam fuisse Comensem hoc epigrammate:

> Poetae tenero, meo sodali,
> Velim Caecilio, Papyre, dicas

into Lago di Como, is Colico. Above this are Morbegno, Stazzona, Tirano, and Mazzo; and Bormio, where I said the common source lies for the Adda and the Oglio, below Frigidolfo. Also, on the left-hand side of the Adda as it **[363C]** flows into the lake, we find Postalesio, Sondrio, and Poschiavo, above the pool which many believe to be the source of the Adda.

In the middle of the area between the two tributaries of the Adda, the Serio and the Brembo, in very high mountains, is Bergamo. It is an ancient city, founded, according to Pompeius Trogus, by the Gauls at the same time as Milan, Brixia, and Verona. It boasts as its citizen Gasparino Barzizza da Bergamo, the orator and grammarian. Also in this same area situated between the Brembo, Serio, and Adda rivers and the Prealpi Bergomasche, is the region called Ghiara d'Adda. Here are found the *castelli* Treviglio and Mozzanica; and, as I mentioned earlier, Rominengo, Martinengo, and Caravaggio. In my time, among all these towns Caravaggio was famous for a memorable battle, in which the army of what was then the Republic of Milan defeated the troops of the Venetians, twelve thousand cavalry and four thousand infantry, putting them to flight or, more accurately, capturing most of them.

There follows on the right-hand bank of the Po Belgioioso, a very splendid estate which Lodovico, Count of Cunio, possesses, given to him by Duke Filippo Maria Visconti of Milan. As I have shown, he preserves there the remains of Alberic III, and Malatesta, the famous counts of Cunio. After this there is the mouth of the Lambro river, which flows into **[363D]** Lago di Pusiano, part of Lago di Como. On its right bank, the first on the Lambro is the *castello* Villanterio, and then S. Angelo. And far above it and inland is the town of Cantù, and farther above is the ancient city of Como, next to Lago di Como, to which it gives the name Comensis. Trogus asserts that it was founded by the Gauls along with Milan, Brixia, and Verona. Pliny, on his father's side, was a citizen of Como; he moved to Verona and called himself a Veronese citizen. He writes that Cato asserted that Como and Bergamo were of the stock of the Oromoni; but acknowledges that he does not know the origin of the tribe. Later, Cornelius Alexander asserts that this race had its origins among the Greeks, basing his claim on the name which indicates that these people lived in the mountains. And Catullus seems to hint, in the following epigram, that the poet Caecilius was a citizen of Como:

> Papyrus, tell my fellow love-poet and intimate friend Caecilius to leave the walls of New Como and Lake Como's shore, and come

Veronam veniat, Novi relinquens
Comi moenia Lariumque litus.
Nam quasdam volo cogitationes
Amici accipiat sui meique.
Quare, si sapiet, viam vorabit.

Isque Plinius Comi conversatus fontem esse dicit in Comensi, qui singulis horis semper intumescit ac residet. Et idem affirmat Abduam amnem lacum Larium supernatare, quodque nunc quoque usu cognoscitur, lapidem esse dicit in Comensi, qui cavatur, tornaturque coquendis cibis. Longobardorum quoque habent historiae in lacu Lario insulam esse, quem **[364E]** Comantina appellaretur, in qua legimus Francilionem primo ducem Romanum, postea aliquos Gothorum et Longobardorum reges multas conservasse divitias. Et forte maiores omnibus quae ab illo tempore alicubi in Italia fuerint congregatae, eaque insula nunc nobis ignota non longe a domo aberat, vel oppido, vel vico.

Scribit etiam Plinius Transpadanam Italiam iuxta Alpes Larium lacum habere amoenum arbusto agro, ad quem ciconiae non transvolant. Sunt ad eam lacus partem, quae a maioribus appellatur Eupilus, dextera in parte Fenium, Palantium, Ripa, Nesium, Lesenium, et qua se lacus in Abduam flectit Belasium.

Ab Umbronis fluvii ostiis parvo supra Padum tractu sunt S. Columbanus, post via Laudensi a Mediolano Melegnanum oppida, inde Vicus Mercatus populo frequentissimus, et superius Modoetia nobilissimum totius Lombardiae oppidum, in quo servat absurda consuetudo ab trecentis annis introducta, Caesares Germanos corona ferrea in Romanos reges imperatoresque insigniri. Id oppidum reddidit prius ex parvo amplissimum Theodoricus rex Ostrogothorum primus, palatio ibi magnificentissimi operis aedificato, et Theodelinda Longobardorum regina insignis, ad quam beatus Gregorius dialogorum libros **[364F]** scripsit, basilicam beati Ioannis Baptistae, ac palatium superbissimum sumptuosissimo opere in eodem exstruxit.

Supraque Modoetiam Umbroni fluvio adiacet Charrarum. Secus Comum ad Umbronis ex lacu Eupilo ortum Brixia influit torrens, ad cuius ortum castella sunt Murgum, Canossium, et Vatallum. Ad secundum latus Larii vel Comi sinistram sunt, Sennobium, Arcinium, Campus, et ubi torrens aqua Seria influit, Monasium, dehinc Rasonegum, Gundum, Gravidona, Damassium, Iera, Soregium, et ubi fluvius lacum influit est Senolegum. Supra torrentem sunt Larium, Victoria, et dehinc castellum Clavenna,

> to Verona. For I want him to hear certain thoughts of his friend and mine, so if he is wise, he will hurry.

Pliny, while he was living at Como (or so he writes), says there is a spring in Lake Como which, within an hour, regularly swells up and sinks down; and he also asserts that the Adda river floats on top of Lake Como. And now we also know from experience that a stone exists in Lake Como which is hollowed out and smoothed by cooking food. The Histories of the Lombards also say that there is an island in Lake Como called Comantina. Here, I read, first Francilio, **[364E]** the Roman general, and afterwards some of the Goth and Lombard kings, preserved much wealth, perhaps greater than any amount amassed anywhere in Italy from that time on. This island is not now known to us, but was not far from home, either town or village.

Pliny also writes that there is in Transpadane Italy, next to the Alps, a lake called Larium, pleasant with trees and fields; but storks do not fly over it. On that part of the lake which our ancestors called Eupilus, on the right-hand side, are: Fenium, Palanzo, Riva, Nesso, Lezzeno, and, where the lake turns towards the Adda river, Bellagio.

A short distance from the mouth of the Lambro river, above the Po, is the town of San Columbano, and after it on the road to Lodi from Milan, Melegnano. Then comes Vimercate, heavily populated; and farther above it Monza, noblest of all the towns in Lombardy. An absurd custom prevails here, introduced three hundred years ago: German kings are given iron crowns to distinguish them as Roman kings and emperors. Theoderic, first king of the Ostrogoths, made this town powerful, although it had previously been small. He built a magnificent palace there; and Theodelinda, the glorious queen of the Lombards, and addressee of the blessed **[364F]** Gregory's Books of Dialogues, built at Monza the cathedral of S. Giovanni Battista and a palace splendid with expensive workmanship.

And above Monza, next to the Lambro, lies Carate. Below Lake Como, at the source of the Lambro river, the Breggia stream flows from Lago di Pusiano into the Lambro. At its source are the *castelli* Muggio, Caneggio, and Vacallo. On the other side of Lake Como on the left-hand side are Cernobbio, Argegno, and Campo; and where the stream Acquaseria flows into it, Menaggio. Then come Rezzonico, Dongo, Gravedona, Domaso, Gera Lario, Sorico; and where the river flows into the lake is Samolaco. Above the stream are Lario and Vittoria; and after these, the *castello* of Chiavenna,

apud quam Plinius dicit curiam Rhetiarum fuisse. Ea vero montana regio cur olim Rhetia fuerit appellata, Iustinus in Trogo sic docet:

> Tusci a Gallis pulsi sedibus Alpes occupavere, et Rhetorum gentem sic ab eorum duce appellatam condidere. Fueruntque hi populi bifariam in primam et secundam Rhetiam divisi.

Ad alterum vero latus Casatium, et in extremo lacus angulo Megiulla castellum. Ad dexteram Padi ripam post Umbronem prima habentur Ticini ostia. Is fluvius Verbanum lacum, quem nunc Maiorem dicunt, exonerat. Adiacet huic amni ad dexteram quarto supra **[364G]** ostium miliario civitas nunc Papia Ticini nomine vetustior, quam Plinius velle videtur fuisse conditam a populis Leviis et Maricis, qui fuerunt Transalpini. Sed quantum licet ex Livii scriptis coniicere Ticinum urbs, quo tempore Hannibal in Italiam venit, nondum erat. Nam libro XXI sic habet, "Iam tamen Scipio Padum traiecerat ad Ticinum amnem motis castris." Et infra:

> Cum utrimque ad certamen accensi militum animi essent Romani ponte Ticinum iungunt tutandique pontis causa castellum superimponunt.

Et inferius: ". . . auxit pavorem consulis vulnus periculumque intercursu tum pubescentis filii propulsatum." Hic erat iuvenis Africanus. Dicimus itaque non potuisse abesse, quin si Papia tunc fuisset, aut Ticinum urbs, eius nomen aliqualiter Livius posuisset, nec pontem Romani fecissent, factoque castellum imposuissent.

Eam civitatem Athila rex Hunnorum direptam vastavit, et cum paulo post instaurata esset Odoacer Erulorum rex Orestem patricium, Augustuli imperatoris genitorem in eo obsessum vique captum interfecit. Ticinumque urbs crudeliter direpta atque vastata est, ubi tunc caedes maxima fuit civium Romanorum quanta numquam alibi post Romani imperii **[364H]** inclinationem commissa fuerat. Pariterque ad annum inde circa centesimum et vigesimum voverat se facturum Alboinus rex primus Longobardorum, nimia Papiensium resistentia fastiditus. Sed cum ipso ingressu equus sub eo col-

where Pliny tells us was the senate house of the Rheti. But why this mountainous region was in the past called Rhetia, we learn from Justin's *Epitome* of Trogus:

> when the Etruscans had been driven out of their homes by the Gauls, they settled in the Alps and founded a race which they called Rheti after their leader. These people were divided into two tribes, the first and second Rheti.

On the other side of the lake is Casate, and in the farthest corner of the lake, the *castello* Mezzola. On the right bank of the Po after the Lambro is the first mouth of the Ticino river. This river discharges into what is now called Lago Maggiore. Lying next to this river on **[364G]** its right bank, four miles above the river's mouth, is the city now called Pavia, formerly Ticinum. Pliny seems to believe it was founded by the Laevii and Marici, who were Transalpine peoples. But as far as I can conjecture from Livy's writings, the city of Ticinum did not yet exist at the time of Hannibal's invasion of Italy. For Livy writes, in book 21, "Scipio, however, had already crossed the Po, and had moved his camp up to the river Ticinus." And later on Livy writes,

> When the spirits of the soldiers on both sides had been inflamed for combat, the Romans built a bridge over the Ticinus; to protect it, they built a fort close by.

And later: "adding to their fear was the wound of the consul, who was only saved from danger by the intervention of his son, who was just reaching manhood." (This was the young Africanus.) And so I assert that it must be the case that if Pavia had existed at that time, or the city of Ticinum, Livy would have, somehow or other, given its name; and the Romans would not have built a bridge nor, after building it, fortified it with a castle.

Attila, king of the Huns, destroyed and sacked Pavia. And a little while after it had been rebuilt, Odoacer, king of the Eruli, besieged there, captured by force, and killed the patrician Orestes, father of the emperor Augustulus. The city of Ticinum was cruelly plundered and ravaged; at that time in that city there was a very great slaughter of Roman citizens, **[364H]** such as had never elsewhere been committed after the fall of the Roman Empire. About one hundred and twenty years later, Alboin, the first Lombard king, speaking disdainfully of the excessive opposition of the inhabitants of Pavia, vowed that he would do the same. But when he attacked, his horse fell under him and was unable to get up again. He was warned by one of his com-

lapsus, surgere nequiret, admonitus a bono viro comite suo mutavit propositum, equusque ilico surgens, illum in urbem detulit incolumem.

Rodulfo autem Burgundo Italiae regnum occupante, per VII Stephani pontificis Romani tempora Ungari Salodo duce Italiam ingressi, Papiam obsessam captamque, ferro ignique vastarunt. Alunda fuit adolescentula nobilis, et pulcherrima Papiae incerto nobis iure dominio potita, quam Ugo Arelatensis Italiae rex Lothario filio dedit uxorem. Eoque mortuo, tertius Berengarius Ugoni in Italiae regno successor Papia potitus, mulierem carcere tenuit. Interea Agapitus pontifex Romanus Italiaeque proceres et populi, Berengarii et Alberti filii tyrannidem exosi, Otonem primum ex Germani in Italiam vocaverunt. Isque cum armatorum milibus L veniens Berengario et Alberto deiectis, Alundam carcere eductam matrimonio sibi copulavit. Tumque Italia a malis, quae diu fuerat perpessa, respirare coepit.

Pertharis Longobardorum rex monasterium sanctae Agathae, et Theudelinda regina ecclesiam Sanctae Mariae ad Perticas in ea civitate construxerunt. Et Luthprandus [365A] Longobardorum rex ossa beati Augustini ex Sardinia Papiam, ubi veneratissime servantur, deferri curavit. Idemque rex monasterium beati Petri Cellula Aurea appellatum, et apud Holonam, ubi curiam saepe reges tenuerunt, monasterium S. Anastasii martyris aedificavit. Gondiberta regina eccelesiam S. Ioannis Baptistae, et Petrus episcopus Luthprandi regis consanguineus ecclesiam S. Savini Papiae construxerunt.

Eam urbem situ et aeris salubritate amoenissimam reges Ostrogothorum, et postea Longobardorum libenter incoluerunt, unde apud ipsam multa fuerunt praeclare gesta a nobis in Historiis praeter praedicta accuratissime scripta. Ornavit eandem maximisque prosecutus est spiritualibus adiumentis Epifanius episcopus Aquileia oriundus, qui sex milia captivorum Mediolanensium a Francorum rege liberari impetravit. Et duodevigesimus nominis ordine Ioannes pontifex Romanus qui a Bonifacio Ferrutii filio pontifice adulterino captus, in arcemque S. Angeli coniectus diem vi adhibita obiit, civis fuit Papiensis. Habet nunc Papia in gymnasiis multos iurium civilis et pontificii ac philosophiae et [365B] medicinae scientia claros. Sed ex civilibus Catonem Saccum, et Silanum civili deditos iuri et bonarum artium studiis exornatos.

panions, a good man, to change his intention, whereupon his horse immediately got up and bore him away unharmed into the city.

And when Rudolf of Burgundy had occupied the kingdom of Italy in the time of Pope Stephen VII, the Hungarians, led by Salodus, invaded Italy and besieged and captured Pavia, then devastated it with fire and sword. Adelaide was a very beautiful and noble young girl of Pavia, and by a right that is obscure to me she obtained the rule; Hugh of Arles, king of Italy, gave her as a wife to his son Lothar. When he died, his successor in the kingdom of Italy, Berengar III, gained control of Pavia and threw Adelaide into prison. Meanwhile, Pope Agapitus and the chief men and peoples of Italy who had come to hate the tyranny of Berengar and his son Adalbert, called Otto I from Germany to Italy. Arriving with fifty thousand armed men, he deposed Berengar and Albert, released Adelaide from prison, and married her. Then Italy began to breathe again, freed from the disasters she had suffered for so long.

Perctarit, king of the Lombards, built the monastery of Sta. Agata in Pavia; and Queen Theodelinda built there the church of Sta. Maria Pertica. And the Lombard **[365A]** king Liutprand undertook to transfer the bones of St. Augustine from Sardinia to Pavia, where they are reverently preserved. The same king built the monastery of S. Pietro in Ciel d'Oro, and at Corteolona, where the kings often convened their court, he built the monastery of San Anastasio. At Pavia Queen Gondiberta built the church of S. Giovanni Battista, and the bishop Peter, kinsman of King Liutprand, built the church of S. Savino.

The Ostrogoth kings, and after them the Lombard kings, were content to live in this very pleasant city with its good location and healthy air. For this reason, I have accurately reported in my *Histories* the famous deeds they accomplished at Pavia, more indeed than I have mentioned here. This city is distinguished by the bishop Epiphanius, who endowed it with great spiritual support; born at Aquileia, he obtained release from the Frankish king of six thousand Milanese captives. And Pope John the eighteenth was also a citizen of Pavia; he was captured by the antipope Boniface, son of Ferrucci, and thrown into the Castel Sant'Angelo, where he died a violent death. Pavia now has in its schools many men who are famous in civil law, religious law, philosophy, **[365B]** and medicine. But among those in public life, Catone Sacco and Silano Nigro are dedicated to civil law and distinguished in the liberal arts.

Adiacet Ticino amni intus ad dexteram et fossae manufactae ab eodem fluvio ductae haeret Abbiagrassum. Superius est Vigivanum Petri Candidi litteris Graecis edocti, ac Latinis, ac editis operibus clari patria. Inde Cuccionum et post Sextium lacui, propinquum, qua in parte Verbanum lacum duo minores augent lacus, quorum qui est ad dexteram Lugani, qui ad sinistram S. Iulii appellatur. Ad Verbani sive Maioris lacus dexteram Angleria primum est oppidum, a quo Vicecomitum familia originem traxit. Recedit vero intus ad dexteram eius lacus partem Varesium oppidum populo frequentissimum. Supra curvatus est bifariam Verbanus, sive Maior lacus Lugani ea in parte appellatus, cui adiacent, Brosivum, Portus, Caput Laci, Campronum, Ostenum et Porlectia, et ubi Lavenus influit amnis sunt ad lacus undas, Sessa, Morchum, et Luganum, a quo lacus nomen accepit.

Ticinum ad sinistram parvo supra Padum tractu torrens influit Gravalonus, ad cuius sinistram est Gropetum. Intus sunt Mortaria oppidum nobile, et Laumelum nunc exile, sed opulentissimum olim oppidum, multis celebratum, praesertim Longobardum historiis. **[365C]** Nam Theudelinda Autaris Longobardorum regis relicta Agillulfum Taurinenesem ducem apud Laumelium sibi in maritum, et Longobardis ut permiserunt, in regem ascivit. A Laumeloque nomen habet omnis peninsula regio aliquot oppidulis vicisque frequentata, in qua lignum gigni et multum et optimum, Plinius est auctor.

Interius est Novaria civitas, quae Albutio Silo claro oratore, sicut tradit Eusebius per Octaviani imperatoris aetatem ornata fuit. Et ad annum salutis VIII et terdecies centenum habuit Dulcinum haeresiarcham, in quem cum Clemens V pontifex Romanus animadvertendum censuisset, ipse in montes, qui Novariae altissimi imminent, cum sectatoribus quingentis se contulit, quos saltuosus natura, et paene inaccessibilis locus fuisset tutatus, ni superveniens solito maior nix plurimam eorum partem fame ac frigore mortem fecisset oppetere. Dulcinusque et Margarita uxor cum reliquis, eo confecti incommodo in potestatem venerunt. Nec tamen errori ut abrenuntiarent, adduci potuerunt, quin Margarita in conspectu mariti mutilata, et ipse item pari laceratus supplicio, in proposito pertinaces, tot paene mortes, quot habebat **[365D]** membra perpessi sunt.

Mons namque Bosus nomine, Cottiarum Alpium promontorium, ceteros superans Italiae montes, ad ipsum verticem, quem semper continuatis etiam aestate nivibus tectum habet omnino inaccessibilis est, cui haeret contiguus

Towards the interior, next to the Ticino river on the right bank lies Abbiategrasso; it is close to a man-made ditch which extends from that river. Higher up is Vigevano, the home of Pier Candido, famous for the works of Greek and Latin literature he has brought forth. From there, the next town is Cucciago (?) and after that is Sesto Calende, next to the lake where two smaller lakes flow into Lago Maggiore. Of these, the one of the right is called Lago di Lugano; the one on the left Lago d'Orta. On the right side of Lago Maggiore, the first town is Angera. The family of the Visconti trace their origins to it. But inland on the right side of this lake is the heavily populated town of Varese. Above this, Lago Verbano or Maggiore curves into two parts. Next to the branch called Lugano lie Brusino Arsizio, Porto Ceresio, Capolago, Campione, Osteno, and Porlezza. And where the Laveno river flows into it, beside the lake are Sessa, Morcote, and Lugano, which gives the lake its name.

On the left bank of the Ticino, above the Po, the Gravallone river flows into it in a short course. On its left bank is Gropello. Inland are the noble town of Mortara, and Lomello, now poor, but formerly a very wealthy town, famous and often mentioned especially in the **[365C]** histories of the Lombards; for Theodelinda, widow of Authari king of the Lombards, married Agilulf leader of the Taurinenses at Lomello, and as was permitted among the Lombards, claimed him as king. The entire peninsula takes its name from Lomello. It is crowded with little towns and villages, where much flax of high quality is grown, as Pliny tells us.

Farther inland is the city of Novara, distinguished in the time of the emperor Octavian by the famous orator Albutius Silus; so Eusebius relates. And in 1308 Novara had as a citizen the heresiarch fra Dolcino. Pope Clement V resolved to punish him; fra Dolcino fled with fifty followers into the high mountains which overhang Novara. The place was wooded and almost inaccessible, and they would have been safe if a greater than normal snowfall had not descended upon them. Most of them died from hunger and cold. Fra Dolcino and his wife Margarita, along with the rest, were worn out by this trouble and fell into his power. But they could not be induced to abandon their heretical views; Margarita was torn apart in full view of her husband, and he was punished in the same way. Stubborn in their beliefs, they suffered **[365D]** almost as many deaths as they had limbs.

There is a promontory of the Alpi Cozie named Monte Rosa, which towers over the other mountains of Italy, its summit completely inaccessible due to continual snows, even in summer. Next to it, a little lower in height,

paulo celsitudine demissior mons, nunc ab hoc Dulcini facto Gazaronum appellatus, in summo cuius vertice, et ad eum locum, in quo se continuerant haeretici, sacellum nunc est S. Bernardi vocabulo appellatum. Adiacentque eius montis radicibus ad aversam partem, Triverium, Cozola, et Crepacorum agri Vercellensis oppida et castella. Ad Ticini item undas est Castelletum, et paulo supra ad lacus Verbani, sive Maioris emissorium, a quo Gravalonus amnis ortum habet, sinum efficit ipse lacus, quem Mergotii lacum dicunt. Illabunturque torrentes duo Grais Alpibus defluentes, quorum unus Tonsa dicitur, alterque S. Iulii lacum transeat; eius lacus retinet nomen. Nam in eo lacu insula est a S. Iulii ecclesia, sicut et lacus appellata. Visunturque ibi confessoris Iulii reliquiae miraculis coruscantes.

Suntque ad lacus Mergotii sinistram Omagnum, Acabrium, Aimum, Boguinum, et ad dexteram Upaium atque Apelium. Ad Tonsae sinistram Vergonta, et supra in Alpibus Domussula, quam nunc Domodusulam appellant. Estque unus ex quattuor tramitibus, unde a Mediolano in Gallias sive Germaniam traiicitur. Ad Tonsae vero dexteram Mergotium, a quo sinus nomen accipit; et ad eandem sinus dexteram Palantia. **[366E]**

Sequunturque secundum Verbanum lacum oppida et castella, Canobium, Brisagum, Ascona, Carnium, Gardola, et ubi Ticinus ex Alpibus Graiis cadens lacum Sebuinum influit, castellum est nomine Magainum. Descripsimus supra duos amnes Padum illabentes, hinc Umbronem, inde Ticinum, et simul docuimus quibus in locis uterque amnis, ex Verbano hic, ex Eupilo ille, ortum ducat. Dumque loca explicuimus ipsis vel fluminibus, vel lacubus adiacentia, mediam liquimus intacta planitiem omnium Italiae populis frequentissimam. In qua Mediolanum est civitas potentissima, quam nostro iudicio insulse opinati sunt quidam inde dictam, quod in medio Padi, Ticini, Abduae et Umbronis amnium sita est. Sed alia est eiusdem nominis civitas in Gallia, cuius fines nullis amnibus similiter sunt coerciti. Originem vero habuit Mediolanum Lombardiae, cum Livius Patavinus et Trogus Pompeius narrant, a Gallis, qui duce Brenno in Italiam descenderunt; populique loca incolentes, in quibus est aedificata, Insubres appellabantur. De quibus L. Florus ex Livio dicit:

> Galli Insubres ferini et immensi corporis Alpium accolae saepe alias, sed Viridomaro duce iuraverunt se non soluturos balthea, nisi in Capitolio. Aemilius victor **[366F]** eos domuit.

is a mountain now called Gazzada to commemorate fra Dolcino. On its peak, at the place where the heretics stayed there is now a chapel named for St. Bernard. And next to the foot of this mountain on the opposite side are the towns and *castelli* of Trivero, Coggiola, and Crevacuore in the territory of Vercelli. Next to the Ticino is Castelletto, and a little higher up, at the outlet of Lago Maggiore, where the Toce river has its source, the lake itself makes a bay which is called Lago di Mergozzo. Two streams flow down into it from the Graian Alps. The first is called the Toce; the second, because it crosses the Lago d'Orta, keeps the name S. Giulio. In that lake is an island named after the church of S. Giulio, just as the lake is. The remains of Julian the Confessor are seen miraculously gleaming there.

And on the left side of Lago d'Orta are Omegna, Agrano (?), Ameno (?), and Boguinum, and on the right, Vapium and Pella. On the left of the Toce is Vogogna, and above it in the Alps is the former Domossula, now called Domodossola. It is one of four passes by which one crosses from Milan into Gaul or Germany. On the right side of the Toce is Mergozzo, which gives the bay its name; and still on the right side of the bay, Pallanza. **[366E]**

After Lago Maggiore come the towns and *castelli* of Cannobio, Brisaggo, Ascona, Camedo, Gordola, and, where the Ticino comes down from the Alps and flows into Lago Sebuino (d'Iseo), a *castello* called Magadino. I have described above the two tributaries of the Po, on this side the Lambro and on that side the Ticino; and I also showed where each river has its source, the latter from Lago Maggiore, the former from Lago di Pusiano. In the course of my description of the places lying next to the rivers themselves, or the lakes, I omitted the plain in the middle, which is the most densely populated of all Italy. Here is the city of Milan, very powerful; in my opinion the conjecture of certain men is absurd, that Milan is called *Medio*lanum because it is located *in the middle of* the Po, Ticino, Adda, and Lambro rivers. There is another city in Gaul with the same name, whose boundaries are not encompassed by rivers. Indeed, Livy and Pompeius Trogus relate that the Milan in Lombardy had its origin from the Gauls, who under Brennus' leadership came down into Italy, and were called Insubri by the local inhabitants among whom they built this city. Livy's epitomator Lucius Florus tells us,

> The Insubrian Gauls were savage and enormous; they lived in the Alps, and often in other places, but under the leadership of Viridomarus they took an oath not to unfasten their belts until they had reached the Capitoline. Aemilius defeated them. **[366F]**

Nec videmus alia fuisse Italiae loca, in quibus facilius coaluerit mortalium multitudo tanta, quantam Insubres primum post Mediolanenses per omne saeculum habuerunt. Roma enim non modo non genuit, quem habuit multo maiorem Mediolanensi populum, sed faciente aeris semper ab ipsa condita insalubris dispositione, confluentem ex tota Italia comportatamque, et vi ductam ex tota orbe mortalium exuberantiam male conservavit. Quae apud Insubres Mediolanensesque post eam conditam urbem historici gesta scribunt, hic referre operosissimum esset, sed nostro insistentes instituto, indices earum rerum ponemus.

Scribit Eusebius in temporum supputationibus Statium Caecilium comediarum scriptorem clarum fuisse Insubrem Gallum, et Ennii contubernalem, et quosdam existimasse ipsum fuisse Mediolanensem. Scribit Livius libro ab urbe condita XX exercitum Romanorum, tunc primum ultra Padum fuisse ductum, et Gallos Insubres aliquot proeliis superatos in deditionem tunc primum venisse, quod quidem ad annos Romanae urbis conditae CCCCLX fuisse videtur XXX inde Livii liber habet:

> Magonem Hannibalis fratrem in agro Insubrium vulneratum, **[366G]** dum in Africam per legatos revocatus navigaret, apud Corsicam obiisse.

Et libro XXXI habet L. Furium praetorem Romanum Gallos Insubres rebellantes, et Hamilcarem Poenum in ea parte molientem acie vicisse; Hamilcareque occiso milia hominum XXXVI caesa fuisse. Et libro XXXI habet Cornelium Cethegum consulem Gallos Insubres proelio fudisse; paulo post L. Furium Purpureonem, et Claudium Marcellum Boios et Insubres Gallos subegisse, Marcellumque triumphasse.

Post eum vero triumphum urbs Mediolanensis per annos ferme quingentos pacatissima, atque adeo florens fuit; ut illam principes Romani quod per occupationes licuit, inhabitaverint Nerva, Traianus, Hadrianus, Maximianus, Philippus, Constantinus III, Constans, et Constantinus IIII, qui dictus est Gallus, Iovianus, Theodosius, Valens et Valentianus. Iulianumque Galli fratrem Mediolani Caesarem appellatum fuisse tradit Eusebius. Post eam vero tam diuturnam felicitatem primas passum est molestias Mediolanum beato Ambrosio adhuc superstite, Arianis sicut ipse in Omeliis scribit infestantibus, quorum persecutiones ut declinaret in Illyricum exul se contulit. Post

I have not seen any other places in Italy where so great a population has come together more easily as in this place, first held by the Insubri, afterwards by the Milanese for the entire age. For Rome not only gave rise to a population smaller than that of Milan, but because of the unhealthiness of its air from the time of its foundation, Rome has maintained poorly the excess of population which has come together from all of Italy, and which has been brought, or compelled to move, there from the entire world. After the foundation of Milan among the Insubri and the Milanese, the historians write of the accomplishments achieved there; all that is much work to relate. But holding to my pattern, I shall adduce testimony of these matters.

Eusebius, writing the chronicle of his times, says that the renowned comic playwright Caecilius Statius was an Insubrian Gaul, and that Ennius was his close friend, and some men have thought that he was from Milan. Livy writes in his history, book 20, that the Roman army was then for the first time led across the Po, and the Insubrian Gauls were conquered in some battles and at that time first surrendered to the Romans, and that this happened four hundred and sixty years after the foundation of Rome. Further on, in book 30 of his history, Livy has the following:

> Mago, the brother of Hannibal, was wounded in the territory of the Insubri, **[366G]** and while he was sailing to Africa envoys were sent to recall him, but he died near Corsica.

And book 31 contains the information that the Roman praetor Lucius Furius conquered the rebellious Insubrian Gauls and Hamilcar the Carthaginian who was conducting maneuvers in that area, and when Hamilcar was killed, thirty-six thousand men were slain. And in book 31 he says that the consul Cornelius Cethegus routed the Insubrian Gauls in battle. A little later, he writes that L. Furius Purpureo and Claudius Marcellus put down the Boii and the Insubrian Gauls, and Marcellus was accorded a triumph.

After this triumph, the city of Milan was peaceful for almost five hundred years, and so flourishing that Roman emperors lived there, insofar as their affairs permitted them: Nerva, Trajan, Hadrian, Maximian, Philip, Constantine II, Constans, and Constantine IV, who was called Gallus, Iovianus, Theodosius, Valens, and Valentianus. Eusebius relates that Julianus the brother of Gallus was acclaimed as Caesar at Milan. But Milan went through its first disturbances after so long a period of peace while St. Ambrose was still alive. As he wrote in his *Homilies*, the Arians were hostile, and in order to escape their persecutions he went into exile in Illyria.

seram vero, sicut Eusebius tradit, Auxentii **[366H]** mortem Ambrosio Mediolani episcopo in sua sede restituto, omnis Italia ad rectam Christi fidem est conversa, paulo tamen post Athila Italiam ingressus, cum omnem afflixisset Venetiam Mediolanumque diruit.

Instaurataque tunc parum quievit bellis agitata, qua Ostrogothi cum Iustiniani imperatoris ducibus gesserunt. Quibus in bellis, ut Gothis resisteret, et in partibus Iustiniani imperatoris duraret, Mediolanum eas pertulit difficultates et angustias, quae hominibus vix tolerabiles esse videtur. Et tamen superante famis acerbitate deditionem tunc etiam, sicut et nunc, invitam fecit. A Longobardis autem eadem urbs non quidem destructa umquam, sed maximis molestiis agitata est. Illisque a Carolo Magno domitis regnoque privatis Mediolanum per annos LX et CCC sub Italiae et Romae regibus imperatoribusque quasi liberum floruit, nullas interim magnas passum agitationes, quousque Federicus imperator Barbarossa ad annum salutis LXV et undecies centenum eam diruit et solo aequavit. Populum autem in sex tribus portarum nomine divisum, sex loca decimo ad minus distantia passuum miliario habitare coegit. Sexto autem ab inde anno, cum Federicus bello a Franciae regibus pro tertii Alexandri pontificis Romani salute agitaretur, Mediolanenses a Parmensibus Placentinisque adiuti repetititam patriam tanto reaedificarunt **[367A]** animorum ardore, ut intra triennium ditior, populo frequentior potentiorque solito facta videretur.

Habuit vero per annos CV mirabile incrementum, adeo ut, nisi civilia obstitissent dissidia, Turrianorum Vicecomitumque omni Lombardia faciliter fuerit potitura. Anno autem salutis LXXVI supra duodecies centenum Vicecomites, pulsis Turrianis, Mediolani tyrannide sunt potiti. Et anno abinde LXXIIII sextus Clemens pontifex Romanus, cum a Ludovico Bavario imperatore adulterino multis agitaretur molestiis, in illius damnum dedecusque Luchinum Vicecomitum Romanae ecclesiae in Mediolano vicarium, et eius germanum Ioannem Mediolanensem archiepiscopum, creavit; annoque ab inde plus minus quinquagesimo Ioannes Galeacius Vicecomes primus ab imperatore dux Mediolani in ea familia est constitutus, princeps certe regno et imperio potius quam eo ducatu solo dignus, cum propter insignes alias virtutes, tum maxime cum doctrina et virtutibus excultos viros apud se habere, atque extollere curavit.

Omnium autem externorum quos dilexerit, primus fuit Petrus Cretensis patria Candianus, qui Novariensis episcopus, post Mediolanensis episcopus,

And after the late, as Eusebius says, death of Auxentius, Ambrose **[366H]** was restored to his see at Milan and all of Italy was converted to the Christian faith; but a little later Attila attacked Italy, and ruined all of Venice and destroyed Milan.

The city was rebuilt and enjoyed a brief period of peace before being disturbed a little later by wars, this time by the Ostrogoths against the generals of the emperor Justinian. In these wars, Milan paid a severe price, barely tolerable by human beings, for her resistance to the Goths and her loyalty to the side of the emperor. She nevertheless overcame famine and surrendered against her will then as she has in modern times. Milan was never destroyed by the Lombards, but was disturbed by the greatest troubles. When Charlemagne defeated them and took away their rule, Milan enjoyed a condition close to freedom for three hundred and sixty years under the kings of Italy and the emperors of Rome. In these year she suffered no significant disturbance until the year 1165, when the emperor Frederick Barbarossa destroyed the city and razed it to the ground. He divided the population into six tribes named after the city gates, and compelled them to live in six places at least ten miles distant from the city. Six years after this, when the kings of France, in support of pope Alexander the third, were harassing Frederick with war, the Milanese, with great courage and the aid of the people of Parma and Piacenza, rebuilt their city and went back to live in it. **[367A]** Within three years the city was wealthier, had a greater population, and was more powerful than it had been.

For one hundred and fifty years Milan sustained such remarkable growth that, if the civil dissension between the Della Torre and the Visconti had not stood in the way, Milan would have easily gained possession of all of Lombardy. In 1276 the Visconti drove out the Della Torre and established themselves in a tyranny over Milan. Seventy-four years later, Pope Clement VI was being attacked by the false emperor Louis of Bavaria; to his discredit he established Lucchino Visconti as a vicar of the church in Milan, and his brother Giovanni as the city's archbishop. About fifty years after this, the emperor established Giangaleazzo Visconti as the first of his family to be duke of Milan. He was certainly worthy to be the first man in the kingdom and the empire, rather than a mere duke, as in addition to his other virtues he made sure to have surrounding him, and to elevate, men who were erudite in learning and the virtues.

Of all of the foreigners whom he patronized, the foremost was Pietro Filargo, a native of Crete, who was named bishop of Novara, then bishop of

deinde Romanae ecclesiae cardinalis; et demum summus pontifex Alexander V nomine est appellatus. **[367B]** Isque omnium sui saeculi vir doctissimus, quo tempore Ioannes ipse Galeacius ducatu Mediolani a Venceslao Lucinburgensi Romanorum rege ornatus est, orationem habuit doctrina, et rerum variarum copia redundantem, quae inter multa ornamentum urbis Mediolani continentia haec habet:

> Mediolanum physico naturali situ suo ab incendiis caumatum et frigorum rigoribus aequaliter abesse, ac propterea locum totius orbis temperatissimum, aeremque serenissimum, et aquarum in puteis et fontibus salubritatem obtinere. Cum tamen lacus pulcherrimi decem et septem, et LXIIII flumina terrae superficiem irrigantia in illius agro reperiantur.

Dicitque idem pontifex Barnabam Pauli condiscipulum et comitem primum fuisse Mediolanensis ecclesiae episcopum, cui paulo post successerit beatus Ambrosius doctor ecclesiae celeberrimus, a quo S. Aurelius Augustinus doctor et ipse excellentissimus in ipso Mediolano ad fidem Christi conversus fuit.

Ioanne Galeacio, et post eum duobus filiis Ioanne Maria primum, et postea Philippo Maria, qui tertius dux fuit vita functis, populus Mediolanensis in libertatem se erigens, post asperam insignemque famem bello perpessam urbem dedidit Francisco Sfortiae **[367C]** Attendulo Cutignola Romandiolae Sfortia primo patre oriundo, cuius decorat robur atque principatum Maria Blanca uxor Philippo tertio duce nata, regio titulo fastuque dignissima.

Genuit Mediolanensis urbs Alexandrum secundum, tertiumque Urbanum ex nobili gente Cribella; ac Caelestinum IIII pontificem Romanum Datiumque episcopum suum, qui vir, si beato Gregorio credimus, sanctus et doctus patriae, cuius fuit amantissimus, plurimum profuit. Imperite vero scripsit Alexander V pontifex Romanus Valerianum et Galienum imperatores Mediolani genitos fuisse. Sed Aelius Spartianus scribit avum paternum Didii Iuliani imperatoris fuisse Mediolanensem. Et Iulius Capitolinus dicit Valerianum iuniorem non natum, sed sepultum fuisse Mediolani. Et Flavius Eutropius in alterius Valeriani gestis rebus tradit acceptam fuisse cladem sub Aureliano, a Marcomannis per errorem. "Nam dum is a fronte

Milan, and then cardinal, and finally reached the peak of his career as pope Alexander V. He was the most learned man of **[367B]** his century; at the time when Giangaleazzo was distinguished in his rule as duke of Milan by Wenceslas of Luxemburg, king of the Romans, he gave an erudite speech, full of diverse topics. Among many such passages, it contains the following praise of the city of Milan:

> Milan is in its natural location far from the fires of heat, and likewise from the stiffness of cold, and on account of this, it is the most moderate place in the entire world, its air the clearest, and it enjoys healthy waters in its wells and fountains. There are seventeen very beautiful lakes, and sixty-four rivers water the land in its territory.

Pope Alexander also says that Barnabas, fellow disciple and comrade of St. Paul, was the first bishop of the church of Milan, and a little later his successor was the famous father of the church St. Ambrose. It was at Milan that he converted to Christianity St. Aurelius Augustine, another excellent father of the church.

Giangaleazzo departed from this life, and after him his two sons died, first Giovanni Maria and afterwards Filippo Maria, who was the third duke. Then the people of Milan raised themselves up into freedom and after enduring a well-known and harsh famine as a result of war, gave the city over to Francesco Sforza, son of the first Sforza, Attendolo, **[367C]** from Cotignola in the Romagna. His power and reign have been enhanced by his marriage to Maria Bianca, daughter of Filippo the third duke, a woman worthy of the royal title and pride.

The city of Milan has also produced the popes Alexander II, Urban III, from the noble family of the Crivelli, and Celestinus IV. Bishop Datius, if the blessed Gregory is to be believed, was a holy and learned man from Milan, who was very patriotic and brought great benefit to his native city. But pope Alexander V showed his ignorance when he wrote that the emperors Valerianus and Gallienus were born at Milan. However, Aelius Spartianus writes that the emperor Didius Iulianus' paternal grandfather was from Milan; and Julius Capitolinus relates that Valerianus the younger was not born at Milan, but was buried there. And Flavius Eutropius, in his *Deeds of Valerianus the Second*, says that the slaughter under Aurelian by the Marcomanni has been incorrectly transmitted: "for the Marcomanni had suddenly broken out, and while Aurelian was not concerned to confront them, and

non curat, occurrerunt subito erumpentibus. Dumque illos a dorso persequi parat, omnia circa Mediolanum vastata sunt."

Fuerunt etiam patrum nostrorum memoria Mediolanenses iureconsulti excellentes Obertus de Orto, qui eam composuit iuris civilis partem, quae usus feudorum appellatur. Et Cristoforus Castilioneus iureconsultorum suae aetatis facile princeps. At **[367D]** Ioannes itidem Castilioneus episcopus Vincentinus, ac paulo post ad nostram pervenerunt aetatem viri duo eleganter docti, ordinis S. Augustini unus, S. Francisci alter, quorum ille Andreas Bilius, hic Antonius Raudensis appellati aliquot ediderunt opera, quid ipsi dicendo et scribendo valeant absque nostro testimonio ostendentia. Ornat quoque patriam Ioseph Biprius sacris saecularibusque litteris apprime eruditus.

Sed ad propositum iter nostrum: post Ticinum ostia Padus longo tractu, nullo flumine ad dexteram augentur. Est vero inter proximum Sicidam, et S. Iulii lacum torrens Gogna apud Cochium oriundus, et ad S. Martham Neblosamque cursum perdens. Ad Padi ripam, ubi Sicida fluvius ostia habet Bremide oppidum, et ad eius fluvii dexteram Palestrum, superiusque Romagnum oppida inveniuntur. Ad Sicidae autem sinistram priusque Sarvus influat torrens sunt Vercellae civitas vetus Apollineae a Martiali poeta appellatae, et quas Plinius a Salviis, Libicis ortas tradit. Tenuerunt autem Salvii populi montes Niceae supereminentes, de hac urbe Plinius:

> Extat lex censoria Vintimiliarum aurifodinae, quae in Vercellensi agro cavabatur, ne plus quinque M hominum in opere aurum faciendi publicani haberent.

Et Eusebius Caesariensis in temporum supputationibus tradit Eusebium Vercellensem **[368E]** episcopum sacrorum dogmatum peritia claruisse. Nosque Historiarum secundo ostendimus Valentinianum tertium Constantii comitis ex Galla Placidia filium misisse Ardaburum orientis praefectum adversus Castinum comitem Ioannis adulterini imperatoris ducem. Et proelio apud Vercellas commisso Castinum superatum captumque fuisse.

Superius ad eandem sinistram Sicidae adhaeret Burgus; Sarvoque ad dexteram Andurnum. Ad sinistram est Bedulum. Dehinc ad Padum est Triduum oppidum, Brolia patrum nostrorum aetate celeberrimo militum ductore

was preparing to go after them from the rear, the entire area around Milan was laid waste."

Even in our fathers' generation there was a memory of the outstanding Milanese jurists Oberto de Orto, who wrote the part of civil law which is called "usus feudorum"; and Cristoforo Castiglione, easily the foremost legal mind of his age. But Giovanni Castiglione was **[367D]** bishop of Vicenza, and a little while afterwards there came to the attention of my generation two men of elegant learning, one of the order of St. Augustine, the other a Franciscan. One of them, Andrea Bilio, and the other, Antonio da Rho, have edited works which show, apart from my testimony, how powerful are their speech and writings. Giuseppe Biprio also distinguishes his native city, a man especially learned in worldly literature.

But to adhere to my planned itinerary: after the mouth of the Ticino comes the Po in a long course; no tributary augments it on its right side. But between the next river, the Sesia, and Lago d'Orta, is the stream Agogna, which has its source at Cochium; and it dies out at Sta. Marta and Nebbiuno. On the shore of the Po, where the river Sesia has its mouth, is the town Breme, and on the Sesia's right bank are found the towns of Palestro and, higher up, Romagno. But on the left bank of the Sesia, before the stream Cervo flows into it, is the ancient city-state of Vercelli, which the poet Martial called Apollineae, and which Pliny says was founded by the Salvii and Libici. The Salvii also held the mountains which tower over Nice. Pliny writes about this city:

> There exists a law of the censors of Ventimiglia about the golddigging which is done in the territory of Vercelli, that the tax-farmers have no more than five thousand men engaged in this work.

And Eusebius of Caesarea, in his chronicle, relates that the bishop of Vercelli was famous **[368E]** for his knowledge of sacred doctrine. I too, in the second book of my *Histories*, have shown that Valentinianus the third, son of count Constantius and Galla Placidia, sent the prefect of the East, Ardaburus, as general against Castinus, count of the false emperor Ioannes. They came together in a battle at Vercelli, where Castinus was defeated and captured.

Higher up, on the same (left) side of the Sesia, Borgosesia lies next to the river; and next to the Cervo on the right side, Andorno Micca. On the left is Biella. Then the town of Trino is located on the Po river, distinguished in my parents' generation by the famous military leader Broglia.

ornatu. Et monasterio Locedi Duria Baltea proxime habetur amnis apud Hastubiam in Alpibus oriundus, cui amni inferius continet Crescentinum nobile oppidum, superius Salugiae, et paulo supra est Eporedia a bonis equorum domitoribus lingua Gallica, sicut Plinio placet appellata. Quam idem affirmat populum Romanum Sibyllinis libris admonitum, ac iussum condidisse.

Dehinc ascendendo per vallem Augustae Praetoriae itinere unius diei est mons Iovettus, et supra est Augusta Praetoria iuxta geminas Alpium fores sita Graias atque Peninas, quibus Herculem et Poenos transiisse Plinius asserit Graios opinari, apudque eam incisus fuit **[368F]** marmore titulus ille pergrandis populos enumerans, quos Caesar Augustus in Alpibus subegit. Dicitque Plinius Cottianas civitates XII non fuisse additas titulis Augusti, quia nil hostile commiserant.

Geminas autem fores Graias atque Peninas nunc appellant alteram montem Iovis, ubi monasterium est nobilissimum, S. Bernardo dicatum, alteram columnam Iovis, qua via iter est ad vallem Tarantasiae Allobrogum, quam quidem vallem Isera amnis excipit. Ad sinistramque Duriae oppidum est Mazadium. Orcus dehinc fluvius Padum illabitur, cui ad ostium est *Clavasium* nobile oppidum, et superius S. Martini ad dexteram. Ad sinistramque S. Benedicti de Fructeria habentur oppida.

Duriae Ripariae amnis Padum deinceps illabentis proxima haeret ostio Taurinum civitas vetustissima, per quam primum Hannibalem Italiam ingressum venisse, Livius XXI ostendit. Taurini Galli proxima gens erat in Italiam digresso, et infra:

> Peropportune Taurinis proximae genti adversus Insubres motum bellum erat. Inde ex stativis moverat Hannibal, Taurinorumque unam urbem caput eius gentis, quia volentis in amicitiam non venerat, vi expugnavit. **[368G]**

Duriae Ripariae fluvio ad dexteram oppida Lancium et Bellegerium, ad sinistram C*i*riacum et Druentum sunt proxima. Eoque in terrarum spatio quod Padum binasque Durias et Alpes interiacet, est regio Canapicium appellata, in qua tres nobilium familiae oppida possident et castella, Valpergani, S. Martini, et S. Georgii comites. Nec longe absunt a Taurino Sangoni amnis in Padum labentis ostia, cui ad dexteram haerent oppida Ripolum

The Dora Baltea river is next to the monastery of Lucedio and has its source at Entrèves (?) in the Alps. Below this river is the noble town of Crescentino, then above that is Saluggia, and a little above that is Ivrea, which Pliny tells us is named in the Gallic language from the word for good breakers of horses. Pliny also maintains that the Roman people were warned by the Sibylline books to found a city and did as they had been ordered.

Then, as you go up through Valle d'Aosta it is a day's journey to reach Monjovet, and above it is Aosta, which is located next to the two gateways to the Alps, the Graian Alps and the Pennine Alps; Pliny says the Greeks thought that Hercules and the Carthaginians crossed the Graian Alps. **[368F]** He relates the story that at Augusta Praetoria a huge inscription was cut in marble listing the people of the Alps whom Augustus subdued. Pliny also says that the twelve Cottian city-states were not added to this inscription of Augustus because they did not oppose him.

These two gateways to the Alps, the Graian and the Pennine, now give their names first to Mt. Iovis, where there is a noble monastery named for S. Bernard; and second, to the column of Jove, where lies the way to the valley of Tarantasia of the Allobroges. This valley is carved out by the Isère river. On the left bank of the Dora Baltea river is the town of Mazze. From there, the Orco river flows into the Po, and at its mouth is the noble town of Chivasso, and above it on the right San Martino. On the left is the town San Benigno di Fruttuaria. Then the Dora Riparia flows into the Po, and right at its mouth is Turin/Torino, an ancient city, the first Italian city which Hannibal passed through as he invaded Italy. About this Livy writes in book 21, "As he turned down into Italy, the Gallic Taurini were the next people on his route." And later he writes,

> The Taurini had conveniently started a war with the Insubri. Then Hannibal departed from his summer camp and attacked the only city and the capitol of the Taurini because they would not enter voluntarily into alliance with him. **[368G]**

On the right bank of the Dora Riparia are the towns of Lanzo and Balangero, and on its left the nearest are Ciriè and Druento. And in the area which lies between the Po, the Dora Riparia and the Dora Baltea, and the Alps is a region called the Canavese, where three noble families hold the towns and *castelli*; they are the counts of Valperga, San Martino, and San Giorgio. Not far from Turin is the mouth of the Sangone river which debouches into the Po, and on its right side lie the towns of Rivolo and

Aviliana, inter quae est celebre monasterium S. Antonii de Renverso; S. Ambrosius oppidum; et paulo supra civitas est Secusa. Superiusque ad Sangoni amnis ortum est Sesanna. Clusiola post hac amnis Padum illabitur, cui proximum ad sex milia passuum est Pinnarolum nobile oppidum, nobili item monasterio exornatum. Superius Petrosa oppidum, et ad fontem sinistrorsum est oppidum Pragellatum, cum amni Bricariasium primo post Mons Bobius dextrorsum haeret. Post Clusiolam Pelix fluvius Clusono auctus, Padum illabitur Panchalerium inter, et Villafrancham oppida populis frequentata. Fuitque Panchalerium Augusta Taurinorum antiquae Ligurum stirpis, apud quam Plinius dicit Padum primo navigabilem esse. Et **[368H]** Villafrancha primum ponte Padum sublicio est complexa. Pado autem fonti suo iam propinquanti oppida sunt proxima, Revellum et Pasana, et ad supremi ultimique torrentis illum illabentis fontem, ut diximus, oppidum est *Cricium*. Deinceps sunt Alpium iuga, et ea quidem quae Hannibal Italiam ingressurus aceto rupit.

Avigliana, and between them are the famous monastery of S. Antonio di Ranverso; the town of San Ambrogio; and a little above it the city of Susa. Above that at the source of the Sangone river is Sesanna. After that, the river Chisone flows into the Po, and next to it, six miles away, is the noble town of Pinerolo, distinguished by an equally noble monastery. Higher up is the town of Perosa, and at the spring on the left is the town of Pragelato; Bricherasio lies on the river, and then Monte Bobbio. After the Chiusella comes the river Pellice into which the Chisone flows, and the Pellice itself flows into the Po between the town of Pancalieri and the heavily populated town of Villafranca. Pancalieri was the ancient Augusta Taurinorum of the Ligurians, where Pliny says the Po first becomes **[368H]** navigable. Villafranca is the site of the first wooden bridge to span the Po. Towns next to the Po as one approaches its source are: Revello, and Paesana, and at the source of this farthest and highest stream, as I have mentioned, is the town of Crissolo. Then come the ridges of the Alps, and the places where Hannibal used sour wine to break a passage through rock in order to invade Italy.

# Regio Octava, Venetia

Lombardia ad finem perducta, si hactenus servatum morem sequi volumus, ad proximorum Pado amnium ostia revertendum esset. Sed cum ab ultimis Padi ostiis Ad Fornaces appellatis Venetiarum urbis ducatus fines Aquas Gradatas stagnantes mari Adriatico aquae salsae obtineant, in quas Athesis fluvius, post Meduacus, deinde Timavus defluunt amnes, ipsam Venetiarum civitatem eisdem salsis cicumdatam aquis, priusquam Marchiam Tarvisinam sive Foroiuliensem regiones describi necesse est. Postmodum namque ostia cursusque fluviorum in sicco melius prosequemur, secundum ripas quorum ex nostro instituto **[369A]** easdem regiones, et earum particulas certius invenimus.

Venetias civitatem in intimo Adriatici mari sinu sitam, ad annum salutis quinquagesimumsextum supra quadringentenum fuisse conditam, quo anno Athila rex Hunnorum Aquileiam diruit, docuimus in Historiis. Habet autem eius ducatus regio terminos longitudine milium octoginta ab Aquis olim Gradatis ad Lauretum oppidum a Vitali Faledro aedificatum. Nunc autem Pado proximum ubi Ad Fornaces diximus Padi ostia appellari. Latitudo autem varia nullos habet alios terminos quam quousque cedentes recedentesque maris aquae ad siccum stagnando perveniunt.

Eius regionis diverso modo nonnulli meminerunt vetusti scriptores. Antoninus enim Pius in Romani imperii provinciarum regionumque itinerario, cum a Ravenna Aquileiam per Altinum iter describeret: haec nunc Venetiarum stagna appellat Septem Maria quod a Ravenna Altinum usque septem vada essent navi transmittenda. Et Virgilius quod diffuse in Patavii descriptione infra ostendemus ubi Patavii aedificationem ab Antenore factam narrat sic habet:

> . . . Et fontem superare Timavi
> unde per ora novem vasto cum murmure montis
> it mare praeruptum et pelago premit arva sonanti. **[369B]**

Mare enim quod "per ora novem it praeruptum et premit arva pelago sonanti" est hoc totum quod a Pado ad Aquas Gradatas litus rumpens, colles

# Eighth Region, Venice

Now that I have arrived at the end of "Lombardy," if I were to follow my plan, I would have to return to the mouth of the rivers nearest the Po. But from the farthest mouth of the Po, called "The Ovens," salt waters occupy the territory of the dogado of the city of the Venetians, the Aquae Gradae (Grado) marshes to the Adriatic. Into these marshes debouche the river Adige, after it the Bacchiglione, and then the Brenta. Before describing the regions of the March of Treviso or Friuli, I need to describe the city-state of the Venetians, which is surrounded by those same salt waters. Subsequently, I shall follow the mouths and courses of the rivers better on dry land, following their banks, in accordance with my custom; **[369A]** that way I find more surely the same regions and their sub-regions.

As I have shown in my *Histories*, the city-state of Venice, located in the innermost bay of the Adriatic Sea, was founded in 456 A.D., in the year Attila, king of the Huns, destroyed Aquileia. The boundaries of this region are: longitude, eighty miles from the former Grado to the town of Loreto, built by Vitale Falier (now, however, it is next to the Po, where I said the mouth of the Po is, called "The Ovens"); its latitude varies, and has no set boundaries other than the ebbing and flowing sea waters as they reach dry land in the marshes.

A number of ancient writers mention this region in different ways. The emperor Antoninus Pius, in his *Itinerary* of the Roman provinces, when he describes the road from Ravenna to Aquileia through Altino, calls the Venetian marshes "Seven Seas" because a ship going from Ravenna to Altino has to cross seven shoals. And Virgil, I shall show later in detail in my description of Padua, when he tells about Antenor's founding of Padua, says,

> . . . [Antenor] was able to pass the source of the Timavus
> where the sea bursts forth through nine mouths, with an awesome roaring in the mountain rock, and covers the fields with its noisy waters. **[369B]**

Indeed, the sea which "breaks forth through nine mouths and floods roaring over the fields"—this all happens on the coast from the Po to Grado; it

eius poetice a Virgilio montes appellatos inter ipsa vada linquit, quae nunc litora appellamus.

Insulae eo conclusae spatio, quae habitantur, varios habuerunt conditores, qui in unicam hanc Venetiarum civitatem opes et consilia contulerunt. Unde hanc Venetiarum civitatem pro una regione non immerito a nobis positam esse intelleget, qui considerabit non modo opes eius cuiuscumque alterius regionis Italiae opibus aequiparandas esse; sed multas fuisse urbes, multa oppida, quorum excidio haec unica fit condita: Aquileiam, Altinum, Concordiam, Patavinum, Montemsilicis, Opitergum, Eracliam, Equilium, Gradum, Caprulas, et Lauretum. Quamquam et ex Vicentia, Verona, Mantua, Brixia, Mediolano, et Papia ab Athila afflictis, et ab aliis Italiae civitatibus, praesertim urbe Roma, diversis in persecutionibus nobiles et potentiores quosque Venetia a principio confugisse, in Historiis abunde docuimus.

Igitur Aquileienses primi Gradum, Concordienses condidere Caprulas. **[369C]** Altinates, sicut urbem suam in sex portas divisam habebant, sex quoque in stagnorum insulis oppida condiderunt, Torcellum, Maiorbum, Burianum, Amoriacum, Constantiacum, et Aimanum. Patavinorum pars, Rivumaltum, et postea Dorsum Durum, Montemsilicenses, Atestinique Methamaucum, Albiolam, Palestrinam, sive, ut Plinius appellat, Philistinam, et Fossam Clodiam, quae nunc est civitas Clugia.

Crevit autem ilico ab ipso conditionis initio Veneta civitas, quia non a pastoribus, sicut Roma, sed a potentioribus ditioribusque regionis olim Venetiae fuit a principio, sicut diximus, habitata. Primus externorum Venetiis ornandis attulit adiumentum Narses eunuchus patricius primi Iustiniani imperatoris copiarum in Italiam adversus Gothos missarum dux, qui quod Veneti eum traducendis a Tarvisio Ravennam copiis navigio iuvissent, postquam subegerat Gothos, ecclesias Sancti Theodori et Geminiani de capite Brolii in Venetiis aedificavit. Quin etiam anno ipsius conditae centesimo et trigesimo secundo Arnulfus rex Longobardorum Patavium civitatem **[369D]** post Tothilense excidium a praedicto Narsete eunucho, Ravennatibusque instauratam, igni ferroque absumpsit, et quotquot primae cladi superfuerant ac in patria coaluerant, Patavini secunda transmigratione in stagna Venetiarum confugientes, Rivumaltum implerunt, et Olivolense castrum, ubi nunc Castellanum est episcopium condidere. Atque eo tempore Sancti Martini et Sancti Ioannis in Bragula ecclesias construxerunt.

leaves hills—which Virgil poetically calls mountains—among the shallows, which we now call the shore.

The islands enclosed in that space, which are inhabited, had many founders, who brought their resources and advice to this single city-state of the Venetians. For this reason, my reader will understand my treating this city of the Venetians as an entire region, if he considers that not only is its wealth comparable to that of any other region of Italy, but that the single city was founded by the destruction of many cities and towns: Aquileia, Altino, Concordia, Padua, Monselice, Oderzo, Eraclea, Iesolo, Grado, Caorle, and Loreto; but also contributing to Venice were Vicenza, Verona, Mantua, Brescia, Milan, and Pavia, which had been attacked by Attila and by other Italian cities, especially by Rome, in various persecutions. That these cities' noble and powerful men fled to Venice for refuge, I have shown in detail in my *Histories*.

And so the first refugees from Aquileia founded Grado, those from Concordia **[369C]** founded Caorle. The people of Altino, just as their old city had been divided by six gates, built also six towns on the islands in the marshes: Torcello, Mazzorbo, Burano, Amoriaco, Constanziaca, and Ammiana. Paduans contributed Rialto and, later, Dorsoduro; the people of Monselice, and of Ateste, founded Malamocco, Albiela, and Pellestrina or, as Pliny calls it, Philistina; and Fossa Clodia, which is now the city of Chioggia.

The city of Venice grew from these beginnings, because it was inhabited from the start not by shepherds, as was Rome, but by the more powerful and wealthy men, as I said, of the region that was formerly Venetia. The first of the foreigners to bring aid and to enrich the Venetians was the patrician Narses the eunuch, leader of the emperor Justinian I's troops in Italy against the Goths. Because the Venetians had helped him cross with his troops from Treviso to Ravenna, after his defeat of the Goths he built the churches of S. Theodore and S. Gimignano in Venice. One hundred and thirty-two years after Venice was founded, after the city of Padua had been destroyed by Totila and restored by the Ravennates, Arnulf king of the Lombards **[369D]** took Padua from Narses by fire and sword. And the citizens of Padua who had survived the first slaughter and had come together in their homeland fled in a second migration to the Venetian swamps and settled in Rialto. And they founded the fortified place, Olivolense, where the bishopric of Castello is now located. At that time they built the churches of S. Martin and S. Giovanni in Bragora.

Mirum vero est et summo extollendum laudis praeconio potuisse a tot tamque diversis urbium et oppidorum populis conditam civitatem per annos propemodum mille hanc quam retinent rem publicam conservare. Nec tamen rerum humanarum conditionis adeo fuit expers haec civitas, quin per singulas quasque aetates suos, ut inquit poeta, "manes" fuerit "perpessa." Quamobrem eius incrementa summatim, sicut in ceteris facimus Italiae civitatibus, explicando, labores quoque et difficultates pariter ostendemus. Et ne in aliarum urbium quas in hac condenda destrui contigit, negotio ulterius laborandum sit, omnia simul contexemus ut facta inter condendum destruendumque variatio certius habeatur. Nec incongruum videtur a scissa patriarchali dignitate inchoare, quod eam scimus in rebus Italiae semper momenti plurimum habuisse.

Ad annum salutis sexcentesimum decimum Gisulfus dux Foroiulianus consensu Agilulfi Longobardorum regis elegit Ioannem abbatem in patriarcham veteris Aquileiae Candiano superstite patriarcha novae Aquileiae, qua apud Gradum fuerat a Romanis **[370E]** pontificibus constituta. Et anno inde quinto partium consensu constitutum est, ut qui esset Aquileiae patriarcha omnem continentis regionem moderaretur; qui esset apud Gradum, omni huic, quae nunc est Venetiarum ducatus regioni, praeesset.

Quartodecimo abinde anno cum Rotharis Longobardorum rex Opitergium civitatem diruisset, eius civitatis episcopus nomine Magnus ad stagna confugiens consensu et auctoritate Severini pontificis Romani ac Heraclii imperatoris civitatem condidit, quae ab ipso imperatore Heraclea est appellata. Eodemque anno Paulus Altini episcopus cum populo suo, qui cladibus superfuerat, Torcellum se conferens, sedem ibi Severini pontificis Romani auctoritate firmavit quae nunc exstat. Cuius pontificis consensu pariter Patavinus episcopus Arianam haeresim, quae tunc in multis Italiae locis fervebat, declinans sedem episcopalem in Methamaucum transtulit. Quo anno foedere inter Longobardos regem et duces ac Venetiarum civitatem icto declaratum est, ut tota terrestris Venetia ab Abdua ad Aquas Salsas Lombardia, et quicquid in ipsis esset salsis aquis Venetiae appellarentur. Ad annum vero salutis sexcentesimum et **[370F]** quinquagesimum Constantius imperator Heraclii filius Torcellum veniens ut Romam accederet, vicum qui est in Torcello Primarius Constantiacum de suo nomine voluit appellari. Heraclea civitate interim aucta eius populi pars in vicinam commigrans insulam Equilium condidit civitatem.

Cumque annis triginta duobus supra ducentos Venetiae variam sub tribunis habuissent gubernationis formam, primus earum dux in Heraclea et

It is indeed amazing, and most praiseworthy, that from so many populations of different cities and towns they were able to found this city and preserve it for nearly a thousand years. But this city has not been so free of the general condition of human affairs as to escape through each successive era, as the poet says, "suffering its own fates." For this reason I set out its stages of growth cursorily, and as I do for other Italian cities I shall show also its toils and difficulties. In order not to take more than the necessary effort in the case of other cities which happened to be destroyed in the process of founding Venice, I shall treat all of them together in order to ensure an alternation between creation and destruction. It seems appropriate to start from the schism between the bishops, which we know always to have been of the greatest importance in Italian affairs.

In the year 610, Gisulf duke of Friuli with the agreement of Agilulf the Lombard king chose the abbot Ioannes as bishop of the old city of Aquileia, while Candianus remained as bishop of the new Aquileia which had been established by the popes at Grado. **[370E]** Five years after this, with the agreement of the fathers, it was decided that whoever was bishop of Aquileia would govern the entire mainland region, while the bishop at Grado would be in charge of all the region now the dogado of Venice.

Fourteen years later, when Rothari the Lombard king had destroyed the city of Oderzo, the bishop of that city, whose name was Magnus, fled into the swamps and, with the agreement and by the authority of Pope Severinus and emperor Heraclius, founded the city now called Eraclea after that emperor. And in the same year Paolo, bishop of Altino, with the remnants of his people who had survived the slaughter, went to Torcello and there strengthened, with the backing of Pope Severinus, the settlement which now exists. Also by agreement with this pope the bishop of Padua, shunning the Arian heresy which was then widespread in many parts of Italy, transferred the see to Malamocco. In that year a treaty was struck between the Lombard kings and the leaders and city of Venice, stating that all Venetian *terra ferma* from Abdua to Aquae Salsae would be Lombard; and whatever was in salt waters would be called Venetian. In 650 the emperor Constantius, **[370F]** son of Heraclius, came to Torcello on his way to Rome. He desired that the neighborhood Primarius which is in Torcello be called Constantiacum after him. Meanwhile, part of the people migrated into the neighboring island and founded the city of Iesolo.

For two hundred and thirty-two years, the Venetians had a different form of government, that by tribunes. Their first leader in Eraclea was a

civis Heraclianus Paulinus anno salutis sexcentesimo nonagesimoseptimo a patriarcha episcopis clero tribunis, proceribus et plebeis creatus est, qui dux foedere cum Longobardis inito Heracleae fines a Plave maiore ad minorem produxit. Et anno inde undevicesimo Ursus item Heraclianus dux, mortuo Paulino, suffectus est, qui anno septimo ducatus civili in tumultu occisus est, sicque laborum suorum Veneti initia habere coepere. Nam eo ducatus nomine antiquato Dominicus Leo magister militum attributa ducatus potestate creatus est, cui post annum primum defuncto suffectus Felix Cornicula magister militum pariter est dictus. **[370G]** Et tertius item Iulianus Ceparius ac quartus Ioannes Fabriciacus magistri militum sunt dicti. Sed hic civili item tumultu magistratu depositus oculisque privatus est. Ad annumque salutis postea septingentesimum quadragesimumque secundum, Deusdedit Ursi quondam ducis interfecti filius mutata ab Heraclea in Methamaucum sede et magisterii militum nomine exploso dux est dictus.

Qui anno ducatus tertiodecimo, cum ad Brintae amnis ostia castellum aedificare coepisset, in tyrannidis suspicionem venit, et tumultu exorto depositus fuit excaecatus, eique in ducatu suffectus Galla, anno quartodecimo tumultu captus, oculosque est effossus, novaque subinde regiminis forma est facta. Nam creato duci Dominico Monegario, Methamaucensi duo annales tribuni ad annum pari potestate consessuri fuere creati, et tamen hic etiam dux post annum in tumultu oculos simul cum ducatu amisit.

Ad Heracleanosque item res Veneta rediit et Mauritius dux est factus, qui post annum malo exemplo filium ducatus consortem assumpsit. Quo anno primus Adrianus papa Obeliabatum Olivolensi ecclesiae primum dedit episcopum, a quo Sancti Moisi ecclesia aedificata est.

Iniecit vero **[370H]** Mauritius dux in Ioannem patriarcham Gradensem manus adeo violentas, ut brevi ille obierit, suffectusque patriarcha Fortunatus conspiratione contra ducem in praedecessoris sui ultionem inita, exorto tumultu pulsus in Franciam se contulit, deiecti tamen ducatu sunt Mauritius dux et filius, et illis unicus Obelerius tunc tribunus Methamaucensis in Venetiarum ducatu est suffectus, eodem anno qui erat salutis octingentesimus quartus Obelerius dux civili tumultu patria pulsus Tarvisium se contulit, ubi

citizen of Eraclea: in the year 697 Paoluccio was elected by the patriarch, bishops, clergy, tribunes, leaders, and common people. As leader he entered into a treaty with the Lombards that extended the boundaries of Eraclea from the greater to the lesser Piave. And nineteen years later in the same way, Orso Ipato duke of Eraclea succeeded on Paoluccio's death. He was killed in the seventh year of his rule in a civil uprising, and thus began the troubles of the Venetians. For Domenico Leo was elected military leader with power of command, with a title which reverted to an ancient term for military leadership. He died after his first year in office, and Felix Cornicula succeeded him, also called military leader or master of the soldiers. **[370G]** And the third such leader, Ceparius, and the fourth, Ioannes Fabriciacus, were likewise called master of the soldiers. But this last man was deposed in the same way, in a military disturbance, and his eyes were put out. Later, in the year 742, Deusdedit (Teodato Ipato), son of the late duke Orso, moved the seat of government from Eraclea to Malamocco and was called dux, duke or doge, and the title of master of the soldiers was abolished.

After thirteen years as doge, since he had begun to build a fortress at the mouth of the Brenta river, he was suspected of aiming at tyranny and, in an uprising, was deposed and his eyes were put out. Galla succeeded him in the office of doge. In an uprising in the fourteenth year of his reign, he was captured and his eyes put out and from this point on a new form of government began. For Domenico Monegario was elected doge. Two tribunes were elected, to be elected each year as colleagues with equal power, and still even this leader, after a year, lost, in a civil disturbance, his position, along with his eyes.

The Venetian state returned to the people of Eraclea and Maurice was elected doge, but after a year his son, who shared the rule with him, ascended to the title; this set a bad precedent. In this year, Pope Adrian gave the church of Olivolense a bishop, who built the church of S. Moisè.

But the doge **[370H]** Maurice brought such violence against Giovanni the patriarch of Grado, that the latter soon died, and the patriarch-elect, Fortunatus, entered into a conspiracy against the doge to avenge himself on his predecessor; a civil disturbance arose, and he went to France. Then the doge Maurice and his son were cast out of the government. Obelerius was then sole tribune. He succeeded in the same year to the office of doge of the Venetians. Obelerius, the fourth doge, was expelled from his country in civil unrest, and went to Treviso where he was elected doge a second time

ab exsulibus Venetis iterum dux creatus fuit, qui Beatum fratrem ducatus consortem accepit.

Interea Pipinus Caroli Magni filius, rex Italiae a primo Hadriano pontifice Romano constitutus, anno salutis LXXX in Italiam veniens, hinc patriarcha, Fortunato inde Obolerio et Beato instigantibus, bello Venetos agitare coepit, qui proelio apud Tarvisium commisso superati, cum Carolo Magno et Pipino filio Italiae rege per foedera convenerunt, quibus in foederibus actum est ut Obolerius Beatusque duces apud Methamaucum exsularent, nec tamen invenio aliquem a Carolo et Pipino magistratum administrandis Venetiarum rebus fuisse impositum. Eodem autem anno Heracleam Veneti destruxerunt, unde maxima nobilium pars, qui postea Venetias usque in haec tempora gubernarunt, in urbem confluens **[371A]** illam auxere, pariterque eodem anno Aquileienses in Venetiarum urbem populariter commigrarunt, ut tunc secunda Venetiarum urbis condicio fuisse videatur.

Eoque anno Agnellus Particiacus Heracleanus primus dux fuit, qui in Rivoalto insula electus palatium ducale nunc exstans aedificavit. Pariterque eodem anno apud Olivolense castrum exsistens cathedralis ecclesia ab eo castello appellata est Castellana, et pro Veneta Rivusaltus civitas dici coepta, Agnellus exinde dux tertio, qui secutus est anno, Heracleam reaedificans ambitu strictiorem appellavit Civitatem Novam, quod et nunc ratione episcopatus magis quam habitationum retinet nomen. Idemque Agnellus, filiis suis duobus assumptis in ducatus consortes, monasterium Sancti Zachariae aedificavit, inibique eiusdem sancti corpus reliquiasque locavit.

Ursus autem episcopus ecclesiam suam Castellanam Sancti Petri vocabulo decoravit, quo tempore eius consanguinei Sancti Severi et Sancti Laurentii ecclesias in geminis insulis construxere. Conspirarunt vero adversum hos tres duces, patrem et filios, Ioannes Tornaricus et Bonus Bragadinus, qui capti convictique et appensi patibulo interierunt, et tamen eorum de quibus sumptum erat supplicium **[371B]** agnati, per id temporis Sancti Danielis ecclesiam construxerunt.

Ad octingentesimum autem vigesimumseptimum salutis annum, defuncto Agnello Iustinianus Particiacus in ducatu solus est suffectus. Anno cuius secundo beati Marci corpus ex Asia est delatum, eoque qui secutus est anno, cum Iustinianus obiisset dux, Ioannes frater est suffectus, quo anno beati Marci ecclesia est aedificata.

Et per id temporis ducto in Methamaucum exercitu Obelerius ibi exul occisus et civitas est destructa, cuius demolitionis caedisque Obelerii causa factum est, ut vocatus in Franciam Ioannes dux accesserit, eoque absente

by the Venetian exiles. He took his brother Beatus into partnership in his rule.

Meanwhile Pepin, the son of Charlemagne, was established as king of Italy by Pope Hadrian I. In 800 (*sic*) [809] Pepin came into Italy, and the patriarch Fortunatus on one side, and Obelerius and Beatus on the other, incited him to war. He began to stir up hostilities with the Venetians. They were defeated in a battle at Treviso. They all entered into a treaty with Charlemagne and Pepin which decreed that the leaders Obelerius and Beatus would be exiled to Malamocco; I do not, however, find evidence that Charlemagne and Pepin imposed any magistracy upon the Venetians for administering their affairs. In the same year, the Venetians destroyed Eraclea. The greatest part of the nobles who governed Venice afterwards, and govern it even in these days, came into the city and **[371A]** increased its size; the people of Aquileia migrated into the state of the Venetians so that the status of Venice at that time appears to have been prosperous.

And in that year, Agnellus Particiacus (Agnello Participazio or Particiaco) was the first doge of Eraclea, and he built in the island Rialto the doge's palace that now remains. In the same year, the cathedral church which stood at the fort Olivolense was named after it, Castellana, and the city began to be called Rialto. And after that, the doge Agnello three years later rebuilt Eraclea in a smaller area and called it Cittanova, and it now preserves the name, more by reason of its bishopric than its dwellings. The same Agnello took his two sons as co-rulers; he built the monastery of S. Zaccaria and transferred the saint's relics there.

Bishop Orso adorned his church at Castello with the name of S. Pietro, and built churches of the brothers S. Severo and S. Lorenzo in the twin islands. Giovanni Tornarico and Bonus Bragadin conspired against these three doges, the father and his sons. They were captured, convicted, and tortured on the rack. Nevertheless, the relatives of the **[371B]** punished men then built the church of S. Daniel.

When Agnellus died in 827, the patrician Justinianus (Giustiniano Partecipazio) succeeded him as sole doge. In the second year of Giustiniano's reign, the body of St. Mark was transferred from Asia; in the following year, when Giustiniano had died, his brother Giovanni succeeded him as doge, and in this same year the church of St. Mark was built. In these times the army was led into Malamocco and there Obelerius was killed in exile. The city was destroyed. On account of its destruction and the murder of Obelerius, it happened that the doge Giovanni was called to France. In his

Castellanus episcopus duoque cives Rivialti civitatis curam administrationis ducali attributa potestate gesserunt. Ioannes autem, dux Francia reversus, civilique tumultu ducatu deiectus, et tonsoratus maestitia diem obiit.

Anno postmodum qui secutus est trigesimosexto et octingentesimo, Petrus Trundonicus Pola oriundus dux est creatus, qui Ioannem filium ducatus consortem habuit, ecclesiamque Sancti Pauli aedificavit. Quartoque abinde anno Sclavi Caprulas, Venetorum urbem, vi captam destruxerunt, Sergio, qui dictus est Os Porci, tunc **[371C]** pontifice Romano in quo anno episcopus Maurus ecclesiam Sanctae Margaritae exstruxit. Petro Trundonico vita functo, Ioannes filius ducatum solus obtinuit, quem a Sancti Zachariae ecclesia redeuntem populus tumultu concitato occidit, et in eadem ecclesia sepelivit anno salutis octingentesimoquarto.

Eratque Ursus Particiacus solenni tunc more electus, cum defuncti ducis famuli palatium populo non prius reddidere, quod Pupiliam sibi insulam certa cum immunitate habitandam impetraverunt. Ursusque dux anno ducatus sui tertiodecimo Ioannem filium ducatus consortem accepit, qui campanas duodecim anno salutis octingentesimo septuagesimo imperatori Graecorum misit. Fueruntque hae campanae, quas primum Graecia visit. Gessit vero Ursus iste dux maximas res non minus Italiae quam Venetis gloriosas. Nam Saraceni spoliata inflammataque Ancona omnem Italiae oram, quae inde ad Idruntum intercedit pariter afflixerunt, in quos sinus Tarentini oram vastare parantes cum Ursus duxisset superarunt Christiani, fugataque inde classis Saracena Gradum rubem invasit. Tuncque Ursus, qui illorum terga fuerat insecutus, repulsos a Grado non prius persequi **[371D]** destitit, quam omnis Italiae ora in superum mare versa reddita est pacatissima.

Urso duce mortuo, Ioannes filius dux solus Comaclum civitatem de Ravennatibus cepit, et anno inde tertio Petrum fratrem suum ducatus consortem habere obtinuit, qui novus dux ecclesias Sanctorum Cornelii et Cipriani in Methamaucensi litore aedificavit. Sed ambo duces intra tertium, qui secutus est annum, ducatu se abdicarunt.

Creatus est autem ad annum salutis octingentesimum octuagesimumseptimum Petrus Candianus vir praestantissimus, quem Sclavi, uno superati, altero redintegrato proelio, interfecerunt, Ioannesque Particiacus, quem ducatu se abdicasse ostendimus, ut seditioni occurreret in urbe fatiscenti ducatum resumpsit, cum eum sexto deposuisset mense suffectus est dux ad annum octingentesimum octuagesimumoctavum Petrus cognomine Tribunus,

absence the bishop at Castello and two citizens of the city of Rialto administered the government, holding the power of the doge. But Giovanni came back from France, was deposed as doge in a civil disturbance, became a monk, and died in sorrow.

In the following year, 836, Peter Trundonicus (Pietro Tradonico/Transdominico), a native of Pola, was elected doge. He made his son Giovanni his co-ruler and built the church of S. Paolo. Four years after that, the Slavs captured the city of the Venetians by force and destroyed it (during the reign of Pope Sergius, whose former name was Pig's Face). **[371C]** In this year, bishop Maurus built the church of Sta. Margarita. Pietro Tradonico died; his son Giovanni took sole power as doge. Indeed, Pietro was killed by the people in a riot as he returned from the church of S. Zaccaria, and they buried him in the same church. This happened in 804.

Then, according to custom, Orso Participazio was elected. When the attendants of the deceased doge did not give back the palace to the people, they obtained the island of Poveglia to live on in security and immunity. The doge Orso, in the thirteenth year of his rule, took his son Giovanni as consort in his office. Orso sent twelve bells to the emperor of the Greeks in the year 870; these were the first bells seen in Greece. This doge Orso performed very great deeds, glorious no less for the Venetians than for Italy. For the Saracens were disturbing the entire shore of Italy which lies between there and Otranto; Ancona had been burned and plundered, and they were preparing to devastate the gulf of Taranto, when Orso led out his army against them: the Christians were victorious, and the Saracen fleet was put to flight from there and invaded the city of Grado. Then Orso pursued them as they retreated, driving them out of Grado, and did not stop pursuing **[371D]** them until the entire coast of Italy facing the Adriatic and Ionian Seas had been returned to a peaceful condition.

When Orso died, his son Giovanni, who, as doge, was sole ruler, captured the city of Comacchio from the inhabitants of Ravenna, and three years after that he took his brother Pietro as consort. The new doge built the churches of S. Cornelius and S. Cyprian on the shore at Malamocco. But both doges abdicated within four years.

Pietro Candiano was then elected doge in 887, an outstanding man, who defeated the Slavs in one battle, but was killed by them when they renewed the fighting. Giovanni Partecipazio, whose abdication I mentioned, took up the rule again to oppose a rebellion, and because the city was growing weak. Within six months he had laid down the rule and, in 888, elected

quo anno reges duos Italia posthabitis Francis ex Italicis habere coepit, Berengarium Foroiuliensem, et Guidonem Spoletanum ducem. Anno autem qui inde tertius est secutus, hic dux Petrus Tribunus urbis Venetiarum partem muro cinxit a rivo castelli usque ad Sanctam Mariam in Iubanico, ibique Canale Maius ferrea clausit catena, cuius capita hinc in praedicta ecclesia inde in Sancto Gregorio observabantur, qui annus Italiae infelicissimus fuit, **[372E]** quod Ungaria Tarvisio Mediolanum usque omnia caedibus incendiisque foedarunt, et stagna Venetorum pelliciatis navibus tumultuarie fabricatis ingressi Civitatem Novam, Clugiamque et Caput Aggeris populati sunt. Eos tum Berengarius rex cum quindecim armatorum milibus aliquantulum repressit. Et tandem omni paene amisso exercitu ingenti data pecunia, ut in Ungariam redirent delinivit.

Petro Tribuno ducatus sui anno vigesimo tertio vita functo, successit Ursus Particiacus secundus, per cuius tempora Conradus Alemannus ex ea gente primus, licet papali confirmatione caruerit, imperium invasit, et rebus per Italiam fluctuantibus, Saraceni maiorem eius partem occupaverunt. Successitque huic post vigesimum annum in ducatu alter Petrus Candianus, qui nactus per debilitatem imperii, et Italiae occasionem primus Venetorum potentiam in Liburnis Dalmatisque auxit, et Genua tunc a Saracenis spoliata, Veneti in Italis mari potentiores esse coeperunt, quam quidem potentiam usque in haec tempora per imperii Romani, tam Graeci quam Latini inclinationem auxerunt. Nam Germani imperatores et si terra quandoque aliqualem, **[372F]** nullam tamen aliquando mari potentiam habuerunt. Itaque deinceps in hac Venetiarum regione brevitati consulentes nihil aliud, quod motus intestinos aut fabricas locorum, quod nostri est propositi attingemus.

Per Ottonis secundi imperatoris tempora ad annum salutis nongentesimum septuagesimum quartum Veneti Petrum Candianum ducem deiicere cupientes, cum ille se in palatio tueretur, iniecto igni pice et sulphure mixto, et palatium et ecclesias Sancti Marci, Sancti Theodori, Sanctae Mariae in Iubanico, et plusquam trecentas civium domus funditus combusserunt, duxque cum filio et complicibus est interfectus. Haecque omnia aedificia suffectus illi dux Petrus Urselos, vir optimus, instauravit, qui et Gradum civitatem instauratam muro cinxit, quo item tempore monasterium Sancti Georgii a Ioanne Mauroceno monacho est amplificatum.

doge in his place was Pietro, with the last name Tribuno. In this year Italy began to have two kings, from the Italians, the French being less esteemed; they were Berengar of Friuli and Guido duke of Spoleto. Three years afterwards, this doge fortified with a wall part of the city of the Venetians, from the canal of Castello up to Sta. Maria Zobenigo, and there closed the Grand Canal with an iron chain. Its capitals were fastened on one side in the previously-mentioned church, and on the other in the church of S. Gregorio.

This was the most disastrous year in Italy's history **[372E]** because the Hungarians overran with slaughter and fire every place from Treviso to Milan. With ships made of animal hide, they quickly invaded the marshes of the Venetians, the new city, Chioggia, and Cavarzere, and devastated them. Then King Berengar and fifteen thousand soldiers pushed them back a little. But since they had lost almost all of their huge army, he was able to entice them by a payment of money to return to Hungary.

After Pietro Tribuno died in his twenty-third year as doge, Orso Partecipazio the second succeeded him. In those days, the German Conrad, although he lacked papal confirmation, was the first of his nation to invade the empire. Italian affairs were precarious and the Saracens occupied a great part of the country. After twenty years as doge, Orso was succeeded by Pietro Candiano II, who, because of the weakness of the empire and the advantageous situation of Italy, became the first to increase the Venetians' power among the Liburnians and Dalmatians. At that time Genoa had been plundered by the Saracens, and the Venetians began to be powerful among the Italians on the sea. Because of the decline of the Roman empire, Greeks as well as Italians increased this power up to the present time. For the German emperors, although they were fairly strong on land, **[372F]** had no power on the seas. And so, then, in my treatment of the territory of the Venetians I shall keep it brief and, in accordance with my plan, not mention any events other than internal disturbances or the foundation of places.

In the time of Emperor Otto II, in the year 974, the Venetians wanted to depose Pietro Candiano, the doge. When he hid in his palace, they hurled a mixture of fire and pitch and sulphur, and burned down not only the palace but also the churches of S. Marco, S. Teodoro, Sta. Maria Zobenigo, and more than three hundred private homes. The doge was killed, along with his son and their confederates. And his successor was the doge Pietro Orseolo, an excellent man, who restored all these buildings as well as the city of Grado and surrounded the latter with a wall. At the same time, the monastery of S. Giorgio was enlarged by the monk John Maurocenus.

Ad annum vero salutis millesimum et nonum Adrienses magnae olim Adriae urbis reliquias apud Lauretum superatos Veneti tanta confecerunt occidione, ut dies ille ultimus fuerit civitati a qua mare Adriaticum est appellatum. Quo item anno Pepus patriarcha Aquileiensis Gradum civitatem dolo captam destruxit, [372G] quam Veneti iterum illico restaurarunt.

Anno inde XX dominicus Urseolus, pulso Petro Barbolano, per arma dux fit, et tertio die Ravennam metu confugit. Dominicusque Flabonicus tunc exul in patriamque revocatus dux est factus. Et ad annum XXXXIII supra millesimum Pepus patriarcha Aquileiensis noni Benedicti pontificis auctoritate atque consensu Gradum sibi subiicit, ecclesias diruit, urbem spoliat, et Veneti eiusdem pontificis auctoritate eandem instaurarunt. Annoque inde XXXX Dominicus Contarenus dux, monasterium Sancti Nicolai in litore et propinquo loco monasterium Sancti Angeli aedificavit.

Ad centesimum vero atque millesimum salutis annum incendia bina Venetiis fuerunt, quibus parrochiales ecclesiae ad viginti simul cum parrochianorum domibus arserunt, quo tempore Methamaucensis civitas inundatione maris atque incendio vastata et paene summersa est, terraemotusque superveniens Venetias ubique afflixit. Tertiodecimo autem abinde anno, quintus Henricus imperator Venetias veniens, situmque et regionem civitatis admiratus, Venetias regnum appellari decrevit, eoque qui secutus est anno Marcus Iulianus monasterium Virginis de Caritate exstruxit. Duodecimo deinceps anno Veneti Motonio Peloponensi sunt potiti, [372H] Petrusque Gatilosus ecclesiam Sancti Clementis, et hospitale in Canalis orphani ripa aedificavit, unde vicesimo inde anno turris campanaria Sancti Marci excitata est. Sed nec adeo continuare potuit quies inchoata, quin ad annum salutis LXXI supra undecies centenum Vitalis Michael dux fuerit interfectus.

Augebantur tamen in dies Venetorum opes mirabili incremento. Nam ad annum quartum de duodecies centeno Veneti Francis bello sociati urbis Constantinopolitanae dominio sunt potiti. Et anno inde XXXX ecclesia S. Francisci Venetiis, et monasterium S. Cipriani in Torcello aedificatum, undetrigesimoque inde anno pons Rivialti sublicius est constructus, quo tempore cum duplicatum esset Venetiis moliturae vectigal populus in tumultum concitus arma cepit. Sed his qui se duces incessoresque ingerebant captis eculeoque appensis, quies illico civitati reddita est. Maiorem vero plurimique faciendum anno inde undequinquagesimo tumultum urbs Veneta sensit, cum Baiamons Teupolus rerum novarum cupidus una cum Quirinis, Barociis, Doris, Badoariis et Basiliis regnum affectavit, in quos pro demeritis

In the year 1009, the Venetians conquered the inhabitants of Adria, and destroyed the remnants of the formerly great city of Adria at Loreto, with such utter annihilation that that was the final day for the city which gave its name to the Adriatic Sea. In this year, too, the patriarch Pepus of Aquileia captured by guile and destroyed the city of Grado. **[372G]** The Venetians restored it a second time in that very place.

Twenty years later, Dominico Orseolo became doge, through force, after driving out Pietro Barbolano. On the third day he fled in fear to Ravenna and Domenico Flabianico, who was then in exile, was recalled to his native land and elected doge. In the year 1043, Patriarch Pepus of Aquileia, by the authority and with the agreement of Pope Benedict the ninth, subjugated Grado, destroyed its church, and plundered the city. Then the Venetians, by the same pope's authority, restored the city. And forty years later, the doge Domenico Contarini built the monastery of S. Niccolò on the coast and, nearby, the monastery of S. Angelo.

In 1100, there were two fires in Venice, which burned twenty parish churches with the homes of the parishioners. At this time, the city of Malamocco was devastated by flooding from the sea and fire, and almost submerged; and on top of this there was an earthquake which afflicted all parts of Venice. What is more, the Emperor Henry V came from Verona to Venice. He admired the city's location and territory and decreed that Venice be called a kingdom. In the following year, Marco Giuliano built the monastery of the Virgin of Charity (S. Maria della Carità). Then twelve years later the Venetians took possession of Modon **[372H]** in the Peloponnese, and Pietro Gatiloso built the church of San Clemente and an asylum for orphans on the bank of the canal. Twenty years after that, the bell tower of San Marco was erected. The peace which had been established did not continue to this point, but in 1170 (1172) the doge Vitale Michiel II was killed.

The wealth of Venice grew steadily, with miraculous increase. For in the year 1204, the Venetians, allied in war with the French, took possession of the rule over the city of Constantinople. And forty years later, the church of San Francesco and the monastery of San Cipriano in Torcello were built, and twenty-nine years later the wooden bridge of Rialto. In that time the mill-tax at Venice had been doubled and the people took up arms in an uprising. But quiet was restored to the city after the leaders were captured and tortured on the rack. A greater disturbance, of more importance, afflicted Venice forty-nine years later, when Baiamonte Tiepolo, desirous of a revolution, joined with the Quirini, Barozzi, Doro, Badoer, and Basili, to attack

publico consilio animadversum est, quiesque civilis et concordia in haec usque tempora annis duodequadraginta atque centum Venetiis fuit.

[373A] Sed iam satis multa de Venetiarum origine ac inter ipsam constituendam rem publicam vel aedificatis vel dirutis civitatibus et oppidis sunt dicta. Ad viros itaque eiusdem ex nostro more institutoque veniamus. Habuit semper hactenus urbs Veneta viros maritimorum bellorum et mercaturae gloria claros. Sed ante patrum aetatem nullo decorata est viro litteris ornato, praeter quam Andrea Dandulo duce, quem Francesco Petrarchae testimonio doctum fuisse scimus. Patrum vero memoria Carolus Zenus vir inter Venetos non solum aetatis suae, sed priorum saeculorum litteris ornatissimus, et rebus bello gestis ita clarus fuit, ut alter Camillus merito a Venetis appelletur, quandoquidem Clugiensi bello, quod cum Venetis Genuenses difficillimum ac periculosissimum gessere, unico navali proelio felicissime gesto, Genuenses a Venetis etiam eo bello vinci posse primus docuit, et omni eo bello hostium ferociam sua fortitudine constantiaque compescuit, demumque Bucicardum regis Francorum navalis exercitus supremum ducem, dum opem Patavinis afferre cuperet, proelio ingenti gloriosissimoque superavit, quae omnia Leonardus Iustinianus funebri luculentissima [373B] oratione et Petruspaulus Vergerius elegantissimis duabus epistolis copiosissime prosecuti sunt.

Fuit et paulo post Zacharias Tarvisanus vir doctrina consilioque celeberrimus, oratio cuius exstans coram Gregorio pontifice Romano habita pro ecclesiae unione suadenda, illum eloquentissimum fuisse ostendit. Hoc autem saeculo multos praestantissimosque vidimus, Petrum Emilianum episcopum Vicentinum litteris multum, plurimum prudentia decoratum, Leonardum Iustinianum magni nobilisque ingenii virum, qui inter alia humanitatis Latina et Graeca studia musicae adolescens iuvenisque deditus dulcissimis carminibus et peritissime vulgariter compositis omnem replevit Italiam, et post natu grandior scripto, et pronuntiatione tam Latina quam vulgari eloquentissimus et senator gravissimus in administratione rei publicae potentissimus fuit.

Marcus quoque Lippomannus iureconsultus Graecas, Chaldaeas, Hebraeas litteras aeque ac Latinas egregie doctus erat. Paulusque Venetus religiosus dialecticos nostri saeculi superavit, qui et paucis in philosophia cedens, theologus quoque insignis est habitus. Franciscus Barbadicus gravis optimus ac propemodum sanctus, et Daniel Victorius [373C] cives splendidissimi fuerunt humanitatis litteris haudquaquam mediocriter eruditi. Petrum

the Republic. Public opinion turned against him, and quiet and harmony prevailed at Venice for one hundred thirty-eight years, into our own times.

**[373A]** But now I have said enough about the origin of the Venetians and the states either built or destroyed to establish the Venetian state. And so, according to my established pattern, let me come to its illustrious men. The city of Venice has always, up to this time, had men famous for their glory in naval warfare and in commerce; but before our parents' generation Venice was distinguished for no man of letters, except for the doge Andrea Dandolo, whose erudition we know about from Petrarch. In the memory of our fathers' generation, Carlo Zeno was a man most distinguished for literary learning among the Venetians, not only in his own age but among men of the generation before us; and in deeds of war he was so famous that the Venetians justly called him a second Camillus, as in the difficult and dangerous war with Chioggia, which the Genoese were waging with the Venetians, he was the first to show in a single fortunate naval battle that even in that war the Genoese could be defeated by the Venetians. And throughout this war he checked the enemy's fierceness by his strength and perseverance. Finally he defeated Jean II Boucicault, supreme commander of the fleet of the king of the French. (Leonardo Giustinian, in his very fine **[373B]** *Funeral Oration*, and Pier Paolo Vergerio, in two very elegant letters, describe all these matters most fully.)

Zaccaria Trevisan, who lived a little later, was famous for his learning and wisdom. His oration before Pope Gregory in favor of the union of the church shows him to have been most eloquent. But we have seen many outstanding men in this century: Pietro Emiliani, bishop of Vicenza, distinguished for literary learning and wisdom; Leonardo Giustinian, a man of great and noble talent who as a boy and a young man, among other studies of the liberal arts in Latin and Greek, was devoted to music, and filled all Italy with very sweet songs, composed most skilfully in the vernacular. After he grew older, he was most eloquent in writing and delivering speeches both in Latin and in the vernacular and, a most important senator, powerful in governing the state.

The legal expert Marco Lippomanno was remarkably learned in Greek, Chaldaean, and Hebrew, as well as Latin, letters. And the cleric Paolo Veneto surpassed the logicians of our century and yielded to few men in philosophy. Francesco Barbarigo was weighty, excellent, almost a saint; he and his fellow-citizen Daniele Vettori were most brilliant **[373C]** men, and of no mean learning in the liberal arts. My inclusion here of Pietro Loredan,

Lauredanum rebus bello gestis clarissimum, quem Veneti alterum Claudium Marcellum in sua patria appellare possunt, hoc in loco a nobis poni mirabuntur qui meminerint eum Latinas litteras grammaticales penitus ignorasse. Sed eius ingenium non duximus merita fraudandum laude, quod omnia quae per aetatem suam mari gesta sunt, quorum ipse magna pars fuit, et maris portuositates navigandique rationem vulgari scripto copiosissime prosecutus est.

Sed dum eos ex mortuis, qui in patria claruerunt, doctos perquirimus, dignitatem maximam Venetorum narrando postposuimus. Fuerunt ex gente Corraria XII Gregorius pontifex Romanus et Antonius nepos suus Romanae ecclesiae cardinalis ea uterque morum et vitae sanctimonia, quae privatos quoque celebres reddere potuisset. Fuerunt ex Maurocena et Landa gente cardinales duo virtutibus litterisque ornatissimi: Alterum vero pontificem paulo post habuere Veneti ex Condulmaria gente Eugenium quartum, cuius gesta per historias nostras orbi notissima, pontificem Romanum qui ante **[373D]** se fuerunt praestantissimis parem, et aliorum turbae multo digniorem eum reddiderunt.

Quantum autem ad doctrinam litterasque attinet, quibus hoc in catalogo primas partes tribuimus, et si Eugenius pontifex nec iuri, nec alicui scientiae particulariter perdiscendae animum adiecit, doctorum ecclesiae oratorum historicorumque Latinorum libros omnes et legit assidue, et quo erat mirabili ingenio subtilissime intellexit. Ornavit autem cardinalatus dignitate Petrum Barbum ex sorore nepotem, qui adolescens optimus tanta duodecim hactenus annis humanitate atque etiam integritate et simul liberalitate est usus, ut et alter Titus Vespasianus, et quod illi tribuebatur deliciae humani generis sit appellatus, vir autem factus, titulo sancti Marci est ornatus, et patrio cognomine cardinalis Venetiarum dictus.

Superque sunt Venetis dux Franciscus Foscharus omni virtutum praeterquam litterarum gloria ornatissimus, et cives Franciscus Barbarus excellentissimi vir ingenii, cuius litterarum Graecarum et Latinarum doctrinae an eloquentiae editis operibus celebratae, aut in administranda re publica sapientiae et pietatis, aut gestarum praesertim apud Brixiam rerum gloriam anteponas haud facile possis discernere. Andreasque Maurocenus bonarum artium studiis ornatus, sapientiae et gubernanda re publica habet, et Hermolaus **[374E]** Donatus et si gerenda re publica fuit occupatissimus in litteris adeo est imbutus, ut cum historiam teneat, tum heroicos versus saepe comp-

most renowned in deeds of war, whom the Venetians can call a second Claudius Marcellus in their fatherland, will amaze men who recall that he was thoroughly ignorant of Latin literature. But I have considered that his genius must not be cheated of its due praise, because he described in order and very fully, in the vernacular, all the naval exploits that were accomplished during his lifetime, in which he himself was an important participant; the harbors of the sea; and the science of sailing.

But while I search out learned men who have died, who were renowned in their fatherland for learning, I have put off telling of the greatest distinction of Venice. This is Pope Gregory XII, from the family of the Correr, and his nephew Cardinal Antonio: their purity of character and life could have made both of them famous. Two cardinals from the Morosini and Lando families were distinguished for their excellence and literary learning. The Venetians also had, a little later, Eugenius IV, from the Condulmer family; his exploits, well-publicized through my *Histories*, have made **[373D]** him equal to the most eminent previous popes, and worthier than a host of others.

I have allotted the foremost rank in this list to learning and literature; and although Pope Eugenius may not have not applied his mind specifically to learning thoroughly any branch of knowledge, he nevertheless diligently read all the books of the fathers of the church, orators, and historians. As he was endowed with a marvelous intelligence, he understood them in all their subtleties. He distinguished with the dignity of the cardinalate Pietro Barbo, his nephew, the son of his sister; an excellent youth, up to the age of twelve he was so kind, blameless, and generous that people called him a second Titus Vespasian, and ascribed to him all the charms of the human race. As a man he was distinguished with the title of St. Mark and the appellation Cardinal of the Venetians was added to his paternal surname.

Still living at Venice are the doge Francesco Foscari, endowed with every excellence except glory in literature, and his fellow-citizen Francesco Barbaro, a man of outstanding talent; you could not easily decide whether to prefer the glory of his learning in Greek and Latin literature, or that of his eloquence, famously employed in his published works, or again his wisdom and devotion in governing the state, or his exploits, especially at Brescia. Andrea Morosini, distinguished in the study of the liberal arts, possesses glory for his wisdom, and his skill in governing the state, and Ermolao **[374E]** Donato, even though very busy with the government, was so steeped in literature that not only did he compose history, but also often composed

suerit elegantes. Pariter Zacharias Trivisanus superioris Zachariae filius ac virtutis haeres Barbonus Maurocenus, Ludovicus Foscharenus, Vitalis Landus, Candianus Bolanus iureconsultissimi, Nicolausque Canalis et si iuri civili et simul rei publicae sunt dediti, tamen oratores poemataque et historias egregie callent. Laurus Quirinus magnae Graecarum Latinarumque litterarum peritiae iuris cognitionem addidit.

Ioannem vero Cornelium, sive ut nunc corrupte eam appellant vetustam gentem Cornarium doctum elegantemque moribus Venetiae habent. Et Paulus Barbus equestris ordinis germani fratris sui Petri Barbi Romanae ecclesiae cardinalis integerrimi humanissimique ac doctae ab Eugenio pontifice originis maternae gloriam bonarum artium, in quibus excellit studiis accumulat. Andreas Iulianus bono vir ingenio, Bernardus Iustinianus Leonardo genitus, Hieronymus Barbadicus Francisci praedicti filius, Nicolausque Barbus litterarii ornamenti gloriam, laudem habent.

Quid quod alterum in **[374F]** narrationis ordine errorem incurrimus, qui praelatos ecclesiae Venetos saecularibus postposuimus. Sunt ex Venetis Laurentius Castellanus, Fantinus Paduanus episcopi viri doctrina et gravitate ac sapientia venerandi, Gregorius patrui pontificis nomen referens sedis Apostolicae prothonotarius, Hermolaus Barbarus Francisci nepos Tarvisinus, Petrus Monteus Brixianus, Iacobus Zenus Feltrensis et Belunensis, Dominicus Torcellanus episcopi non modo iurium civilis et pontificii ac theologiae doctrina sicut eorum decet professionem abunde pleni, sed eloquentia quoque ornatissimi sunt, ut ei mancipatorum studio peritiorum multos aetatis nostrae scribendo dicendoque aequent. Petrus Thomasius medicorum non magis Venetorum quam ceterorum aetatis nostrae eloquentissimus habetur.

Sed iam non invidiae nimis exposuit brevitatis respectus, qui multos praeteriri facit, quos tanta civitas habet litterarum studiis, vel imbutos, vel operam impendentes.

elegant heroic verses. And in the same way Zaccaria Trevisan, the son of the Zaccaria I mentioned above, and the heir of his virtue; Barbone Morosini; Ludovico Foscarini; Vitale Lando; Candiano Bollani; and Niccolò Canal: dedicated to civil law and to the Republic, they still, as public speakers, have outstanding knowledge of rhetoric, poetry, and history. Lauro Quirini to his great skill in Greek and Latin letters has added knowledge of the law.

The Venetians boast Giovanni Cornelio (or, as they call the ancient family, Corner, since the name is now corrupted), a learned man of elegant manners. And Paolo Barbo crowns the studies in which he excels with the glory of his brother of equestrian rank, the cardinal Pietro Barbo, a blameless philanthropist, and the glory of his maternal origins in Pope Eugenius's family. Andrea Giuliani, a man of good talent; Bernardo Giustinian, son of Leonardo; Girolamo Barbarigo, son of the previously mentioned Francesco; and Niccolò Barbo, have the glory and renown of literary distinction.

But I have wandered again from the order of my narrative in **[374F]** favor of worldly matters, in deferring mention of the Venetian dignitaries of the church. Among these Venetians are Lorenzo bishop of Castello, Fantino bishop of Padua, bishops and men to be venerated for their learning, authority, and wisdom; Gregorio who recalls the name of the Pope, protonotary of the Apostolic See; Ermolao Barbaro, bishop of Treviso, nephew of Francesco; Pietro Monteo, bishop of Brescia; Giacomo Zeno, bishop of Feltre and Belluno; Domenico bishop of Torcello; they are all bishops not only full of learning in civil and pontifical law and theology, as is fitting for men in their profession, but also most distinguished in eloquence, so that through their study of the more skillful deliverers of speeches they rival in writing and speaking many men of our age. Pietro Tommasi is considered the most eloquent not only among the doctors of the Venetians, but also among all the remaining men of our age.

But now the wish to be brief will cause me to incur the ill-will of many, as I pass over a number of men whom this great Republic possesses, already imbued with literary studies, or poised to fulfill their promise.

# Regio Nona, Italia Transpadana, sive Marchia Tarvisina [374G]

Tribus earum quae supra a nobis descriptae sunt octo regionum continentem esse ostendimus Marchiam Tarvisinam, Romandiolae scilicet ad Melariae Brigantinique paludes, Venetae urbi ad aquas salsas, et Lombardiae ad Mintium et Benacum. Fecit tamen Benaci certius et copiosius describendi necessitas, ut ad eius dexteram litoralem sita oppida et castella Lombardiae regioni cuius esse non debent, adiunxerimus. Praedictis itaque trium regionum et Alpium et Padi atque limini amnis contra Caprulas insulam in mare Adriaticum defluentis finibus, conclusa erit Marchia Tarvisina. Eam regionem quandoque alias Galliae Cisalpinae quandoque Transpadanae Italiae partem quandoque Venetiam appellatam Romanae ecclesiae monumenta esse volunt partem Dalmatiae Supra Mare, ut nihil absurdius potuerit excogitari, cum nulla ex parte Dalmatia ad huius regionis fines umquam pertinuerit, quamquam par esse videtur absurditas barbaro Marchiae vocabulo [374H] maximas atque amplissimas urbes Veronam Pataviumque titulo subiici Tarvisio, quam civitatem illae opulentia potentatu et dignitate semper antea, sicut et nunc longissime anteierunt. Posterior tamen fuit indita ab ecclesia appellatio.

Nam Longobardi omnium qui Italiam invaserint externorum superbissimi Romani imperii et Italiae dignitatem evertere ac omnino delere conati leges novas, quae alicubi in Italia exstant condidere, mores ritus gentium et rerum vocabula immutavere, ut affirmare audeamus locutionis Romanae Latinis verbis qua nedum Italia sed Romano quoque imperio subiecti plerique populi utebantur, mutationem factam in vulgarem Italicam nunc appellatam, per Longobardorum tempora inchoasse. Idque incognitum nobis quando opus de locutione Romana ad Leonardum Arretinum dedimus. Postea didicimus visis Longobardorum legibus in quibus de mutatione facta multarum rerum vocabuli tituli tractatusque sunt positi. Quin etiam publicae administrationis et privatim vivendi instituta accuratissime ab eisdem sunt

# Ninth Region, Transpadane Italy, or the March of Treviso [374G]

I have shown that the March of Treviso is bounded by three of the eight regions I described earlier: Romandiola, of course, at the swamps of Melara and Bergantino; the city of Venice, at the salt water, and Lombardy, at the Mincio river and Lago di Garda. My need to describe Lago di Garda in greater detail caused me to append to the region of Lombardy towns and *castelli* located on its right shore which, strictly speaking, do not belong to it. And so, with the previously mentioned boundaries of the three regions, and of the Alps and the Livenza river and the Po river flowing down opposite the island of Caorle into the Adriatic Sea, I will have finished the region of the March of Treviso. This region is at times called part of Cisalpine Gaul, at times of Transpadane Italy, and at times Venetia; but the records of the Church insist that it is part of "Dalmatia above the sea." There is nothing more absurd than to think that any part of Dalmatia ever bordered upon this region; and equally absurd is the use of the barbarian word "March of Treviso" to describe the **[374H]** great and wealthy cities of Verona and Padua. These cities came into being long before this state, and always in past times surpassed it in wealth, power, and eminence, as they do now. Still, the Church gave this later name to the region.

I assert that the change from Latin to Italian began to take shape in the times of the Lombards. The most arrogant of all Italy's invaders, they sought to overthrow the Roman Empire and the eminence of Italy, and brought universal destruction. They established new laws which survive in some parts of Italy, and they changed the customs and ceremonies of her people, and the names for things as well, whereas most of the people who were subjects of the Roman Empire used to speak Latin. I was ignorant of this when I gave my treatise about the speech of the Romans to Leonardo Bruni. But afterwards I learned it, after seeing laws of the Lombards containing information about names, titles, and treatises in which there was mention of the changes in many things. The Lombards changed in great detail the institutions of public administration and private life, and so far did

mutata, et eo usque ipsius gentis processit insania, ut Romanorum charactere litterarum penitus postposito, novas ipsi et sua ineptia gentis barbariem indicantes cifras pro litteris adinvenerunt.

Econtra vero Ostrogothi aeque ac cives Romani Latinis delectati [375A] litteris, nullam in illis barbariem offuderunt. Nam Theodoricus rex primus Latine et Graece doctus, Amalasciuntha eius filia doctior, Theodatus rex tertius et primi nepos doctissimus fuere, quod Longobardorum vel regum vel principum virorum nemini contigit. Nullam vero aliam ab Ostrogothis factam fuisse mutationem hinc maxime credimus constare, quod Theodoricus et eum imitati reges ceteri Ostrogothorum cusi sua imagine numini ambitione abstinentes, aurum, aes, argentum, prisco cudi Romanorum signo voluerunt.

Sed ad rem. Longobardi in ea Italiae parte maxima quam optinebant regiones habuerunt quattuor a ducibus administratas, in quibus nullum successionis ius filiis et nepotibus competebat: Beneventanam, Spoletanam, Taurinensem, et Foroiuliensem. Duasque opulentia et amplitudine superioribus pares Anconitam atque Tarvisinam esse voluerunt ea affectas legis conditione: ut qui regum aut gentis Longobardorum concilii permissione et decreto impetrasset, eas filiis et agnatis successione possidendas relinquendi ius facultatemque haberet. Nomenque hunc significans perpetuum magistratum in Longobarda barbarie Marchionatus [375B] est appellatum.

Quo autem tempore Carolus Magnus, sicut supra diximus, nomine indito Romandiolae Lombardiam voluit appellari regionem, in qua regni sedem gens illa diutius habuerat. Romana ecclesia hanc, de qua nunc agimus, regionem de Longobardis sumptam appellavit, ut diximus Dalmatiam Supra Mare. Sed credo factum esse a minore nominis absurditate, ut haec ipsa manserit appellatio Marchiae Tarvisinae.

Mincio eiusque, ut inquit Virgilius, “Patre Benaco” ad sinistram relictis, nostrae descriptionis Padotenus initium faciemus. Cui primum ad Mincii ostia imminet Sachetta vicus familiae nobilis Caprianensium villa, quam successione annis ducentis in cognatione continuata possederunt. Inferiusque est Seravallis arx principum Mantuanorum munitissima, unde passus mille abest Ostilia oppidum in regione primarium, superbi operis arce moenibus et ductis in circuitu fossis conclusisque paludibus munitissimum, quod a Veronensi populo, cuius agri iurium fuit ad annum salutis quinquagesimum, deciesque centenum aedificatum Marchiones postea Mantuani

this race's foolishness go, that they even discarded Roman letters, and invented new symbols in place of letters, showing their primitive barbarian incompetence.

On the other hand, the Ostrogoths were like Romans in their **[375A]** delight in Latin literature, and did not spoil it with barbarisms. Theoderic, for instance, their first king, was learned in Latin and Greek, his daughter Amalasuntha more learned, and his grandson, the third king, was most learned of all, because he had contact with none of the Lombard kings or chief men. I believe it can be shown that the Ostrogoths didn't make any other changes to names, because when Theoderic and his Ostrogoth successors had coins struck with their images, they refrained from any claim to divinity and wanted them struck in gold, bronze, and silver, retaining the ancient insignia of the Romans.

But back to my topic. The Lombards occupied a great part of Italy, and divided it into four administrative districts governed by leaders who had no right of succession for their sons and grandsons: Benevento, Spoleto, Torino, and Friuli. They intended that two districts, Ancona and Treviso, which were equal in wealth and size to those mentioned above, be governed under the following terms: that whoever obtained them, by permission and decree of the kings or council of the Lombards, would have the right to leave them to their sons and successors in the male line. And the name that signified this continual right of governance, in the barbarian Lombard language, **[375B]** was "March."

But at this time Charlemagne (as I noted above) intended the Region called Romandiola to be called Lombardy, because it was here that that race had had for a long time its home. The church took this region I'm now discussing from the Lombards and called it "Dalmatia above the sea." But I believe that its lesser absurdity and lesser incongruity made the name "March of Treviso" stick.

Leaving the Mincio and, as Virgil calls it, "Father Benacus" to the left, I shall begin my description at the Po. Bordering on it, at the mouth of the Mincio, is the village of Sacchetta, an estate belonging to the noble family of the Capriani, which has been in their family for two hundred years. And below that is the strong fortress Serravalle, belonging to the princes of Mantua, and one mile from it is Ostiglia, the chief town in the region, well-fortified by its proud citadel and walls, and moats, and enclosed swamps. Built in 1250 by the people of Verona, who had jurisdiction over it, it has been for a long time afterwards in the holdings of the marquises of Mantua.

diutissime possederunt. Amplaque et recta est vigesimo inde miliario Veronam usque [375C] via aliquot apud Ostiliam locis succisa. Impositis pontibus arcibusque et castellis munitioni Ostiliensibus praesidioque futuris, pertinentque ad hos pontes paludis initia, quam in Romandiolae finibus descriptam Melariae Brigantinique agro diximus continere.

Augentque, sicut ostendimus, eam paludem Tartarus et Menachus amnes, quorum Tartarus in Veronensi agro ad Graecianum oriundus habet ad sinistram Nugarolum, quod nobili familiae Veronensi Nugarolae villa et primae originis patria fuit. Insulaque Porcaritia et Gagium vicus eidem fluvio dextrorsum adiacent. At Menacus amnis ortum ad Magnanum habens Ceretam vicum Praetellasque praeterfluit. Inferius vero eadem palus, sicut in Adriae urbis vetustissimae descriptione ostendimus, augetur ab Athesis fluvii scissura ad Castagnarium appellata, eamque nos scissuram pro nostro hactenus omni in Italia servato more pro ostio Athesis sinistrorsum cogimur accipere. Is autem Athesis famae celebris fluvius, de quo Virgilius in Bucolicis, "Athesim vel propter amoenum."

Primum habet ad sinistram vicum villam Bartholomaeam appellatum. Pauloque superius Athesi sinistrorsum haeret Liniacum oppidum populo [375D] opibusque plenum. Inde Athesi Zevedum adiacet, oppidum brassicae et multae et dulcissimae feracissimum, adeo ut Plinium credamus si suam nunc incoleret Veronam, nec Sabellam in admiratione, ut scribit, crispam, nec pullulantem cauliculis Aricinam, nisi a suis Veronensibus vellet dissentire praepositurum. Eos vero vicenos mille passus, quos Veronam Ostiliamque diximus intercedere, campi quaqua versum excipiunt amplissimi aequissimique, in quibus rectae imminet viae vicus insula Scaligerum appellatus, communito praesidio, ecclesiisque et Veronensium villis adeo ornatus ut accedente populi quem habet multitudine, urbis potius quam oppidi speciem prae se ferat.

Camposque hos, ut diximus, patentissimos manufacta ab agricolatore raro impedit fossa, adeo ut eam natura committendis maximos inter exercitus proeliis de industria fecisse ac complanasse sit visa. Estque hic locus, de quo Livius undeseptuagesimo ea habet, quae L. Flori breviatoris verbis libuit apponere:

> C. Marius Cimbros per hiemem Alpibus devolutos in campis Venetis usu iam vini et coctarum carnium mitigatos aggressus est. Et illis petentibus proximum diem pugnae statuit. Inde LX milia ce-

Spacious and straight is the way to Verona 20 miles from here, [375C] interrupted in some places near Ostiglia by bridges and fortresses and *castelli* built as a fortification and garrison for the people of Ostiglia. A swamp begins at these bridges, the swamp I described in the chapter "Romandiola" and said there bordered on the territory of Melara and Bergantino.

As I noted, the rivers Tartaro and Menago flow into this swamp. The Tartaro has its source in Veronese territory at Grezzaano; on its left bank is Nogarole, the estate and place of origin of the noble family of Verona, the Nogarola. Isola Porcarizza and the village of Gazzo lie on this river's right bank. The Menago river, on the other hand, has its source at Magnano, and flows past the villages of Cerea and Pradelle. Below this, a branch of the Adige river called Castagnaro flows into the same swamp (as I demonstrated in my description of the very ancient city of Adria); I am compelled to accept this branch, in place of the mouth of the Adige, on the left-hand side instead of keeping to my convention in Italy as far as this point. But it is this famous river, the Adige, of which Virgil wrote in his *Bucolics*, "or beside the pleasant Adige."

The first village on the left is called Villa Bartolomea. And a little above it, the town Legnago borders the left bank of the Adige, full of people [375D] and wealth. From there, the town of Zevio borders the Adige; it has such abundant crops of sweet cabbage that I believe Pliny, if he were now living in his native city of Verona, would not prefer to these the Sabellan cabbage with, as he writes, its curly leaves, nor those of Ariccia with their sprouting florets, unless he wished to disagree with his fellow citizens. Twenty miles separate Verona from Ostiglia, as I said, and everywhere along this route are wide and level fields, and among them along the road is the village called Isola della Scala. It has a garrison, and churches and estates of the Veronese, which augment its population to the point of appearing more a city than a town.

Man-made ditches frequently interrupt these fields, spacious, as I have noted, so that for great armies to join battle here seemed natural. It is this place about which Livy writes in his sixty-ninth book; I cite the words of the epitomator L. Florus:

> C. Marius attacked the Cimbri, who had come down for the winter from the Alps to the land around Venice; there they had grown soft from indulging in wine and cooked meat. At their request, he set the next day for a battle. On their side sixty thousand were

ciderunt, hinc tertio minus. Rex eorum Volerius pugnans interiit, non inultus; uxores eorum acerrimo bello captae libertatem non impetrantes suffocatis **[376E]** elisisque infantibus mutuis vulneribus et capistris capilleis se necarunt. Quae victoria eodem die Romae per laureatos Castorem et Pollucem scita et celebrata fuit. Tigurini qui Noricos Alpium tumulos insederant, fuga dispersi, in latrocinia evanuerunt.

Theodoricus quoque Ostrogothorum rex primus Odoacrem Erulorum regem, qui Romam et Italiam annis iam octo occupaverunt, apud Soncium amnem ubi primum occurrit recedere compulit. Deinde in campis Veronensibus ingenti proelio, quod tres continuatum est dies, superavit, factaque est maxima in utroque exercitu, sed in Odoacris partibus maior, caedes. Arnulfus etiam Bavoriorum dux ductis adversus Ugonem Burgundum Italiae regem copiis a Veronensibus in urbem receptus atque rex appellatus est, cumque Ugo ad Veronae recuperationem maximas duxisset copias, proelium his in Veronae campis est commissum, in quo superavit Ugo, et Arnulfus fugiens Veronae portis a civibus est exclusus. Veronenses vero rebellionis culpa in Racherium episcopum suum reiecta, veniam deprecati impetraverunt, et episcopus Papiam relegatus est.

Sed ut iam Athesim redeamus: is fluvius qui campi **[376F]** ad primos colles desinere incipiunt, Veronam dividit paene mediam, quam urbem auctor est ex Trogo Pompeio Iustinus Gallos qui urbem Romam ceperunt, et pariter Mediolanum Brixiam et Bergomum aedificasse. Nec tamen minus cingit quam dividit Veronam Athesis, ut custodiae simul ornamentoque, et subvehendis devehendisque mercibus et frugibus magno sit usui Veronensibus. Quandoquidem supra infraque et circum ager est praecipuae bonitatis multa gignens in urbem convehenda, olei vim maximam, frumenta incolis in mercaturam superabundantia, vinorum varietatem atque praestantiam, pomorum omnis generis copiam, et lanam ceteras Italiae subtilitate superantem, ut nulla sit Italiae regio quae partem inde non accipiat indumentorum oleumque.

Cum ceterae agri partes, tum maxime Benaci lacus dextera praestat ora, olearum consitis in silvae speciem amplissimae contecta. Frumentaque seminarius ager amplissimus undique patens mittitur. Vinorum praestantia

> killed; on the Roman side, only forty thousand. The king of the Cimbri, named Volerius, died in battle; but they avenged him, in that the wives of the Cimbri who were captured in the very fierce fighting did not beg for freedom, **[376E]** but rather killed their babies by suffocation and crushing them, and committed suicide by inflicting wounds on each other and strangling themselves in halters made of their hair. On the same day, they learned at Rome of this victory and celebrated it by wreathing the statues of Castor and Pollux. The Tigurini, who had taken possession of the hills of Noricum of the Alps, scattered in flight and disappeared into a life of robbery.

Theoderic, the first king of the Ostrogoths, on their first encounter at the Isonzo river also drove back Odoacer, king of the Eruli, a tribe who had occupied Rome and Italy for eight years. He then defeated Odoacer in a great battle which lasted three days in the area around Verona. There were extensive losses on either side, but Odoacer's faction suffered the worst damage. And the Bavarian king, Arnulf, led his army against Hugh of Burgundy, then king of Italy. The people of Verona welcomed him into their city and acclaimed him king. But then Hugh led back a great army to recapture Verona; the two armies met in the territory around this city, and Hugh was victorious. Arnulf fled, but the citizens of Verona shut him out of the gates. The Veronese, however, put the blame for the rebellion on their bishop Rather they obtained forgiveness, and the bishop was exiled to Pavia.

But to return to the Adige river: it divides Verona almost in **[376F]** half at the point where the plains meet the foothills. The founders of this city were the same Gauls who captured Rome; they also built Milan, Brixia, and Bergomum; so Justin tells us, basing his account on Pompeius Trogus. The Adige not only divides the city, but also encircles it, as if guarding it and decorating it. The river is very useful to Verona's citizens for the transport of goods and crops. There is scarcely a region of Italy that does not partake of clothing and oil from this area, on account of the extraordinary quality of the fields all around it. They produce crops that are brought into the city, especially oil, and grain which overflows in the marketplace, an excellent variety of wines, an abundance of every kind of fruits, and wool finer than that of other regions of Italy.

The right-hand shore of Lago di Garda in particular is so thickly planted with olive trees as to resemble a forest. The arable fields extending widely on every side produce grain. The outstanding quality of this region's wines

cum multis possit aliis ostendi rationibus, tum maxime uno extollitur argumento. Theodatus Ostrogothorum rex tertius, cum sciret in Veronensi agro esse vinum, sicut Cassiodorus appellat, **[376G]** accinaticum, odoris saporisque suavissimi, illud Romam navibus Athesi in superum mare delapsis comportari curavit. Libetque Cassiodori verba apponere:

> vinum etenim illud colore purpureo regium, sapore praecipuum, dulcedo cuius ineffabili suavitate sentitur, cum tamen tactus eius densitate pinguescat, ut carneus liquor aut potio edibilis videatur.

Pomorum copiam et si nonnullae habent aliae civitates Italiae Veronensi parem, nullo tamen in loco tam odorantia, tamque varia specie inveniuntur, quae perpetuitatem habent plurimi faciendam, cum senescentia tam serventur solida et illaesa, ut florentibus et novellis immixta manducentur. Lanae praestantiam greges a pastionis proprietate accipiunt, quam prata campique prospectu quoque amoenissimi naturaliter praestant. Cum tamen mons altissimus urbi supereminens Balbus nomine, et eandem herbis suis ingenitam, et multo maiorem virtutem praestet, quod herbilegi undique confluentes multa herbarum radicumque genera animantium saluti opitulantia inde legant.

Diversae etiam per agrum Veronensem, per quae oppida scaturiunt aquae, non minus ornamento a natura quam usui attributae, seu irrigationis **[376H]** seu innumerabilia artificiorum genera seu haustum ipse consideres, e quibus celebrem unius vim non reticendam esse censuimus. In valle, quam a telluris virtute et frugum praestantia Policellae appellant, ubi Negarinae loco est nomen, mammae ad iustam muliebrium formam de saxo fabre sunt ductae, sub quarum papillis perpetuae stillant aquae. Et si lactans mulier papillas asperserit atque laverit, exsiccatus aliquo, ut fit, vel morbo vel casu alio, illi humor lacteus revocatur.

Sed iam solidiora Veronae, sicut et ceteris urbibus, ornamenta viros omnis aetatis praestantes attigamus. Zenoque sicut religionem Christianam et suam ipsius decet sanctitatem primus erit, qui Veronae praesul celebris sanctimoniae multa scripsit exstantia sacras utriusque testamenti litteras declarantia et Ambrosianam quam imitatus est eloquentiam redolentia. Aemilium Macrum Veronensem poetam Eusebius in Asia obiisse asserit. Paulopost Catullus poeta, subinde uterque Plinius saepe a nobis hac in Italia celebrati Veronenses fuere. Et longe posteriores aetate genuit Verona Rainaldum insignem sicut F. Petrarchae placet grammaticum. Deinde Ioannem Madium iureconsultum non incelebrem. Isque Madium genuit nobis

can be praised in many ways, but this anecdote is most telling: when Theodatus, third king of the Ostrogoths, learned of the production around Verona of wine called (according to Cassiodorus) **[376G]** "accinaticum," of a most pleasant scent and taste, he made sure that ships could transport it to Rome by traveling down the Adige to the Adriatic. I am pleased to cite Cassiodorus' words here:

> The wine is the color of royal purple; it has an outstanding taste and an indescribably pleasant sweetness; when you touch it it thickens, so that it resembles liquid meat or an edible drink.

Some cities of Italy may produce an abundance of fruits comparable to those of Verona, but no place offers fruits of such fragrance, and diversity, and durability; when they are ripe they are still firm and unblemished, so that they can be eaten without admixture of fresher fruit. The meadows and fields, pleasant to look upon, offer excellent pasturage to the sheep, who produce outstanding wool. But there is a very high mountain which towers over the city, called Monte Baldo. It produces a superior kind of grass, so that people gather there to pick the grass, many kinds of grass and roots which are helpful to the health of living creatures.

The territory of Verona, and its towns, have many fountains which are decorative and useful, whether you consider drinking from them, or irrigation, **[376H]** or the countless types of employment that use them. There is one famous spring whose powers I do not blush to mention: in Valpolicella (so called from the quality of its land and excellence of its crops), in a place called Negarine, there is a rock formation in the exact shape of a woman's breast, and from the nipples water drips constantly. If a lactating woman sprinkles or washes her breasts from this fountain, if they have dried up for some reason (illness or accident, for example), her milk returns.

But now let me move on to the more substantial attributes of Verona, as with other cities: her famous men of every age. The first will be Zeno, as befits his religious devotion and holiness. As bishop of Verona he wrote many works famed for their holiness; those on the Old and New Testaments are still in existence, and resonate with the eloquence of Ambrose, whom he imitated. Eusebius says that the Veronese poet Aemilius Macer died in Asia. A little after that, the poet Catullus, and then the two Plinies, whom I have often praised in this treatise on Italy, were also from Verona. And long after them, Verona gave birth to the eminent grammarian Rainaldus, as Francis Petrarch says. Then Giovanni Maggi, the well-known legal expert,

adolescentibus familiaritate coniunctum iuri edisserendo defendendoque addictum, qui legum peritiae eloquentiam coniunxerat, adeo [377A] ut scriberet ornater, pronuntiaret suaviter, et in cunctis sese quantum nostrae aetatis nostrae patitur exigitque consuetudo, bonum ostenderet oratorem.

Medicosque genuit Verona sui saeculi praestantissimos Avantium et Iacobum Lavagnolum, cuius nomen refert et cognomen Iacobus equestris ordinis Lavagnolus humanitatis studiis et eloquentia exornatus. Bernardus quoque honesto genitus Campaniae loco, non parum Veronae attulit ornamentum, qui medicus et philosophus insignis tanta viguit memoria, ut Themistoclis instar nihil illi exciderit, quod aut discere, aut eum attentius legere contigisset. Ioannes etiam Salernus ad equestris dignitatis insignia doctrinam et facundiam socias addidit.

At res militaris praeclaros nobis ostentat viros, qui Veronae laudis accumulant, quorum memoriae altior repetitio efficiet, ut varios eius urbis casus referre cogamur. Floruerunt in ea praeclarae familiae Monticulenses et Sancti Bonifacii comites. Hique illos cum eiecissent Azzonem Marchionem Estensem urbis dominio praefecerunt. Isque ad annum duodecies centenum et duodecimum ab Ecelino de Romano per arma eiectus, armis Mantuanorum restitutus est. Qua in restitutione durissimum in Braida, Veronae vico, proelium est commissum. Azzone mortuo [377B] Ecelinus ad annum duodecies centenum et vigesimum quintum Veronam obtinuit.

Qui immanissimus omnium tyrannus ducentos Veronenses simul cum eo carcere, in quo tenebantur uno combussit incendio. Cumque sibi Veronae agenti, quod in Patavio referemus esset allatum Patavium sibi rebellasse, duodecim milia Patavinos, quos militiae praetextu obsides secum duxerat, diversis affectos cruciatibus in Verona occidit. Eo autem apud Soncinum Cremonensis agri oppidum interfecto, Veronenses reductis Sancti Bonifacii comitibus in libertatem erecti quietem nacti sunt, quae paucis continuata est annis, quod Scaligeri cives et ipsi Veronenses, sed novi per capitaneatus populi occasionem tyranni sunt effecti.

Primusque omnium Canisgrandis Scaliger Dantis Franciscique Petrarchae amicitia magisquam sua potentia notus, cum anno uno et quinquagesimo Veronae dominium tenuerit. Civitates interea Cremonam, Parmam, Regium, Vicentiam, Patavium, Feltrum, Civitatum, Tarvisium in potestatem redegit, Gonzagamque familiam ditioni Mantuae eiectis Passarinis imposuit.

whose descendant, Maggi, a friend of my youth, was devoted to explicating the law; he joined legal skill with eloquence, so that **[377A]** he wrote elegantly, spoke pleasingly, and in all that he did gave an example of the good orator, insofar as our generation's custom allowed and demanded.

Verona has also given birth to the outstanding physicians of their age, Avanzio and Jacopo Lavagnolo, whose name resounds also in the name of Jacopo Lavagnolo of the equestrian order, distinguished in eloquence and in the liberal arts. And Bernard, born in an honorable place in Campania, brought much distinction to Verona; this eminent physician and philosopher had such a powerful memory that, like Themistocles, nothing escaped from his memory once he had happened to learn it, or read it carefully. Also, Giovanni Salerno has added learning and eloquence to the badge of the equestrian order.

We see famous men who have brought glory to Verona in military affairs; the repetition of their memory compels me to relate the various fates of this city. In Verona the families of the Montecchio and the counts of Sambonifacio were prominent. After the latter had thrown out the former, they made Azzo, Marquis of Este, master of the city. And he was in his turn thrown out by Ezzelino da Romano in 1212, but restored to power by the forces of Mantua. During this restitution, they fought a bitter battle in Braida, a village belonging to Verona. Azzo was killed, and **[377B]** Ezzelino took possession of Verona in 1225.

He was the cruelest of all tyrants, and burned alive two hundred men of Verona by setting fire to the prison in which they were being held. When he heard in Verona the news that Padua had rebelled against him (an event which I shall narrate in my description of Padua), since he had taken twelve thousand Paduan hostages with him on the pretext of military action, he put these men to death by inflicting various tortures on them in Verona. He was, however, killed at Soncino, a town in Cremonese territory, and the people of Verona restored the counts of Sambonifacio and found liberty and peace, which they continued to enjoy for a few years, until the Della Scala, themselves citizens of Verona, were turned into new tyrants by assuming the title of Captain of the People.

The first of all of them was Cangrande della Scala, more famous for his friendships with Dante and Francis Petrarch than for his lordship; he held power in Verona fifty-one years. Meanwhile, he brought under his control the city-states of Cremona, Parma, Reggio, Vicenza, Padua, Feltre, Cividale, and Treviso, and threw the Passarini out of Mantua and placed the Gonzaga

Sed et Scaligeri cum annis LXX Veronae summo cum splendore dominati [377C] fuissent ob varias in familia divisiones ter quaterque subortas, quandoque a Vicecomitibus Mediolanensibus, quandoque a Charrariensibus Patavinis patria pulsi sunt, per quas contentionum occasiones Veneti ea urbe, quam annos iam XLV obtinent, sunt potiti. Luchinus Vermes Veronensis, vir bello insignis, Cretam insulam Venetis rebellem sua virtute recepit. Deinde in Turchos Christi Dei nostri hostes pugnans cecidit. Eiusque filius Iacobus Vermes, patri haudquaquam dissimilis, rem primi ducis Mediolani Ioannis Galeatii ab imminentibus periculis fortitudine et consilio saepe tutatus est. Qui Armeniaci comitem et Ioannem Haucut Anglicum adversus Mediolanum maximo cum exercitu ruentes proelio apud Alexandriam commisso profligavit, et maxima caede commissa Armeniacum cepit.

Ea quoque expeditione, in quibus Luchinus Vermes Cretam Veneto reparavit imperio Georgius Caballus Veronensis eques praestantissimus, militares ducens ordines navatae fortiter operae id retulit decus, ut senator a Venetis fuerit constitutus. Sed iam claudat Veronensium gloria digniorum aciem Guarinus, quem supra in eorum catalogo, quos eloquentiam [377D] in nostrum saeculum longo postliminio reduxisse ostendimus, merito laudum praeconio decoravimus. Pictoriae artis peritum Verona superiori saeculo habuit Alticherium. Sed unus superest, qui fama ceteros nostri saeculi faciliter antecessit, Pisanus nomine, de quo Guarini carmen exstat, qui Guarini Pisanus inscribitur.

Gesta vero sunt vario eventu Veronae multa a nobis in Historiis celebrata. Alboinum namque primum Longobardorum regem libro quarto ostendimus uxoris Rosmondae insidiis ab Helmechilde in Verona occisum fuisse et utrosque adulteros Ravennae quo confugerant veneno mutue dato interiisse. Et in octavo diximus Theudelindam Grimoaldi Bavarorum regis filiam, ad quam cum in praeclaram reginam devotissimamque Christianam evasisset beatus Gregorius dialogorum libros inscripsit, Veronae in Sardicensi campo desponsatam fuisse. Estque in XI Veronenses Aldegisio, Desiderii Longobardorum ultimi regis filio, civitate, quam firmo tenebat praesidio vi eiecto, Carolo Magno deditionem fecisse, quorum exemplo omnis regio Carolo et suis illico manum dedit.

Aedificiis Verona mediocribus publice privatimque ornata theatrum habet prae ceteris quae ubique exstent praeter Romanum amphitheatrum, nunc

in power there. But even though the Della Scala ruled Verona with much splendor for seventy years, **[377C]** dissensions arose several times in their family, and they were banished from their city by the Visconti of Milan, and by the da Carrara of Padua, and in this strife the Venetians obtained power over Verona and have now held it for forty-five years. A man distinguished in war, Lucchino dal Verme of Verona, recaptured the island of Crete when it had rebelled against the Venetians. And then he fell fighting the infidel Turks. His son Jacopo dal Verme, a man like his father, often by his courage and wisdom preserved the state of Giangaleazzo the first duke of Milan against threats and danger. When the count of Armagnac and the British John Hawkwood attacked Milan with a great army, Giangaleazzo Visconti fought them in a battle at Alessandria, inflicted great losses on them, and captured Armagnac.

In that same expedition of Lucchino dal Verme, when he took back Crete for the Venetian empire, Giorgio Cavalli, an outstanding knight of Verona, led an army which acted vigorously; for this he earned the glory of being named Senator by the Venetians. But let Guarino conclude this line of Veronese worthies, he whom I mentioned above in a list of those men who brought back after a long hiatus eloquence **[377D]** to our century, whom I have decorated with deserved commendation. In the previous century Verona boasted a skilled painter, Altichiero; but there is one who lives still, whose fame surpassed that of all the rest of our generation, named Pisanello, about whom Guarino wrote a poem, called the "Pisano" of Guarino.

I have celebrated in my *Histories* the many events which took place at Verona, with their various outcomes. I mentioned in my fourth book that Alboin, the first Lombard king, was killed by Helmechilde in Verona through the treachery of his wife Rosmonda; the two adulterers then fled to Ravenna, where they committed suicide together with poison. In my eighth book I wrote about Theodelinda, the daughter of Grimoald king of the Germans, and how she became a famous queen and devoted Christian, to whom St. Gregory addressed his books of *Dialogues*; and that she was betrothed in Campo di Sardi near Verona. And in my eleventh book, I told how Aldegisius, the son of Desiderius, the last Lombard king, was maintaining his grasp on the city-state with a garrison, but was thrown out, and the Veronese surrendered to Charlemagne, and due to their example the entire region gave power to Charlemagne and his people.

Verona has rather ordinary public and private buildings, a theatre, which is worth seeing in addition to a Roman amphitheatre, now a colosse-

colosseum operis magnificentia [378E] conspiciendum; habet et pontes quattuor superbi operis Athesi impositos, et cathedralem ecclesiam non minus vetere decoram aedificio quam novo insignem. Supra Veronam Athesis sinistrorsum Pontonem oppidum habet appositum, superius castrum Barchum nobile item oppidum. Inde Cadenium, et qua torrens Vallem Solis intersecans in Athesim labitur, Mecium est oppidum. Supraque illud Ignatum, superius Formigarium. Ad fontem vero Athesis in Alpibus parvo sub lacu, quem fons ipse efficit, est oppidum Lamium.

Diximus supra, sinistram Athesis ripam describentes, eius ostium ad Castagnarii scissuram, qua in Adrianorum paludes labitur necessario accipi designarique oportere. Nec aliter dicere, aut scribere, debuimus quia quicquid ab ea scissura ad mare pertinet in Romandiolae partibus est comprensum.

Dexteram vero eiusdem amnis ripam, ab ipso mari Adriatico ad fontem usque totam Marchiae Tarvisinae, cuius est, possumus applicare. Igitur qua Athesis in mare labitur, ostium efficit portuosum, ubi appellant Fossiones. Idque primum est eorum quae priscos Septem Maria diximus vocitasse. Adiacent intus huic amni paludibus stagnisque immixto, [378F] hinc turris nova praesidio et vectigalium custodiae apposita, inde Caput Aggeris, quod item praesidium ducatus Venetiarum finibus ea in parte institutae rei publicae initio fuit impositum. Interius Athesis bifurcatus peninsulam Rodigii efficit, quae sinistrorsum in Romandiola superius est descripta. Athesisque dextrorsum qua fluvius illabitur novus adiacet Castrum Baldum. Supra est Portus oppidum, quod Athesi a Liniaco divisum ponte illi coniungitur, ut unum idemque oppidum censeantur. Influit paulo supra Athesim amnis nomine Albus, cui dextrorsum Cereda haeret vicus in regione primarius. Sinistrorsum vero sunt Arcella, supra Sanctus Bonifacius oppidum, a quo nobili Veronensium familiae fluxit cognomen. Et superius Villanova.

Deinceps supra fluminis Albi ostium adhaeret Athesi Porcilae oppidum, a quo parum distat amnis, quem Montis Aurei nomine appellant ostium. Isque amnis fonte oritur uberrimo, cui in Montis Aurei vico omnium regionis amoenissimo villa est ea ratione superaedificata, ut fons ipse media in aula scatens, eam evomat vim aquarum, quae subito intra lapidis iactum,

um, magnificent in its construction. **[378E]** Verona also has four superb bridges over the Adige, and its cathedral is no less beautiful with its old building than glorious in its new one. Above Verona, on the left-hand bank of the Adige, is the town of Ponton; and above that is Castelbarco, also a noble town. Then comes Caino, and, where the stream cuts through Val di Sole and flows into the Adige, is the town of Mezzo Lombardo. Above that is Egno, and higher up Castello Formiano. But at the source of the Adige in the Alps, at the edge of a small lake made by the spring itself, is the town of Lamium.

I mentioned before, when I was describing the left bank of the Adige, a mouth of it at the fork of Castagnaro, where it flows into the swamps of Adria, that this fork ought to be noticed and described. I should not have said, or written, anything more, since whatever is included from this fork to the sea belongs in the chapter on the region Romandiola.

I can honestly append to the March of Treviso everything on this river's right bank from the Adriatic Sea to its source. So, then, where the Adige flows into the sea, it creates a mouth with a harbor, where they call it Fossona. It is the first of those mouths which I said the ancients were accustomed to call "Seven Seas." Towards the interior this river is mingled with swamps and stagnant pools, and next to it on this side is a **[378F]** new tower placed opposite a garrison and a customs house, and then comes Cavarzere, which is also a garrison of the Venetian Republic, placed on this side of the border when the republic was formed. Towards the interior, the Adige splits into two and creates the peninsula of Rovigo; I described what is on its left bank earlier, in the chapter on Romandiola. Castelbaldo lies on the right bank of the Adige, where the new river flows into it. And above it is the town of Porto, which is divided from Legnago by the Adige but is joined to it by a bridge, so that you would think them one and the same town. A little above it, the Adige is joined by a tributary, the Rioalbo river, on whose right bank the village of Cerea sits, foremost in its region. But on the left bank are Arcella, and above it the town of Sambonifacio, which gives its name to the noble Veronese family. Above that is Villanova.

Then, above the mouth of the Rioalba river, next to the Adige, is the town of Porcile, not far from the mouth of the river which they call by the name of "the mouth of Montorio." And this river has its source in a very abundant spring, and to take advantage of it a villa has been built above it in the village of Montorio; the spring gushes forth in the middle of its hall, and lets out a jet of water which when directed between stones is forceful

molis sufficit convolvendis. Suntque atterendo in farinam frumento et [378G] bombicinis in scriptum coagulandis tam frequentia amni superimposita aedificia, ut vix stadio colligendis aquis invicem separentur.

Sextoque inde abest Verona, supra quam dextrorsum item haeret Athesi Pelusium oppidum, a quo vallem vulgus dici existimat Pelosellam, licet eam a telluris virtute et frugum praestantia Pollicellam Guarinus existimet appellari. Licena deinceps est oppidum, et superius Roveredum, apud quod oppidum via scalpris monte excisa, arctum viatoribus praebet iter, validumque Veronensi agro ea in parte a Germanorum insultibus est munimen. Besenum deinde habetur oppidum, et superius qua fluvius a Perginae oppido defluens in Athesim cadit, est Tridentum, quam urbem Iustinus scribit a Gallis qui urbem Romam ceperunt, sicut et Veronam Vicentiamque fuisse aedificatam. Apudque eam urbem auget Athesim amnis iuxta Pineam oppidum in Alpibus oriundus. Cui dextrorsum haeret Secconzanum supra Parclasium et Vicum ac Chanazium.

Athesim item supra influit amnis apud Personorium oppidum nobile oriundus. Cui amni Valesium Foespergum et Cevedonum oppida dextrorsum. Sinistrorsum vero Clusa corrupte, sed Latino verbo Clausura, ubi arctissimo aditu trames Alpium est conclusus. [378H] Bolgianumque oppidum nobile parum ab Athesi recedens torrenti est appositum, qui a Sirentino oppido brevem cursum habet. Domus inde Nova oppidum, et superius est Maranum populo frequens oppidum, quod et si in Italia situm est, gentis locutione et moribus totum est Theotonicum potiusquam Italicum. Deinceps sunt Alpium iuga, quorum aditibus et quidem arduus in Germaniam est accessus.

Athesis cursu ab ostio in fontem undique descripto, amnem quo eum superius auctum esse diximus, et cui Novo flumini est appellatio, describi necesse est priusquam Meduacum sive, ut nunc appellant, Bachilionem assumamus ordine ostendendum. Is fluvius nomine Novus, quem apud Castrum Baldum Athesim illabi diximus, sinistrorsum attingit intus Coloniam, oppidum populo opibusque plenissimum, superiusque eidem haeret fluvio Mons Bellus, nobile item oppidum. Et ad fontem sunt Brendulae, oppidum populo opibusque refertum. Brendulisque paulo infra ad amnis dexteram propinquum est Leonicum, populi opumque exuberantia civitatulae aequi-

enough to turn them to grind grain. There are many buildings there, some for grinding grain into flour and some for **[378G]** making silk; they are placed so closely over the river that there is scarcely a stade's distance between them in which water can collect.

Six miles from there is Verona, and above it, also on the right bank of the Adige, is the town of Pelosa, from which it is commonly thought the valley of Pelesella gets its name, although Guarino thinks it is called Pollicella from the quality of its earth and crops. Then comes the town of Lizzana, and above it Rovereto; at this town there is a road cut out of the mountain by chisels, which presents a narrow route for travellers and has been a strong defense in this area for the territory of Verona against the attacks of the Germans. Then comes the town of Beseno, and higher up, where a tributary flows down into the Adige from the town of Pergine, is Trento, a city which Justin assigned to the Gauls who captured Rome, who also built Verona and Vicenza. And at this city a tributary which has its source in the Alps flows into the Adige next to the town of Pinè. On this tributary's right bank lies Segonzano, and above it Predazzo and Vigo and Canazei.

In the same way, there also flows into the Adige a river with its source at the noble town of Bressanono, and on the right-hand side of this river are the towns of Valese, Foespergum, and Cevedone. On the left bank is a town called by the corrupted name of Chiusa di San Michele, but the correct Latin name is Clausura; here a very narrow entrance hems in a footpath in the Alps. And the noble town of **[378H]** Bolzano is opposite it, a little way from the Adige, which runs in a brief course from the town of Sarentino. From there, one finds the town of Novale, and above that the densely-inhabited town of Merano, which, despite its location in Italy, is more German than Italian in its inhabitants' speech and customs. Then come the ridges of the Alps, through which is the difficult passage into Germany.

Now that I have described the course of the Adige from its mouth to its source, I must next describe the tributary I previously mentioned, before I resume my order and take up the Meduacus, now called Bacchiglione. This river, called "New," the Adigetto, which I said flows into the Adige at Castelbaldo, towards the interior on the left runs past Cologna. This is a town full of inhabitants. Higher up, on the same river, is Montebello, also a noble town. And at its source is Brendola, a town of many inhabitants and much wealth. Near Brendola, a little below it on the right bank of the river, is Lonigo, comparable to a small city in its abundance of population and wealth.

perandum, quod Omnebono cive ornatur litteris Graecis Latinisque apprime erudito, et prae se mores ferente quos a Feltrensi Victorino nutritus imbibit.

Ab Coloniaque in subiectas paludes Atesto oppido [379A] vicinas fossa est incurrentem fluvium manufacta, apud quam Roveredum et Montagnana, oppidum regionis primarium, sunt sita. Ad eiusque fossae ostia, quibus in paludes labitur, et paulo infra Locium castellum. Meduacus sive Bachilio amnis proxime a nobis describendus alterum habet ostium. Attingitque primo Bachilionem sinistrorsum Custodia oppidum, populo frequentatum, medio in cuius suburbio fodinas esse inspeximus, per quas longo tractu in subterranea penetratur. Estque lapidis eius montis minera Tiburtino lapidi adsimillima, ut quod nullo in loco scriptum invenimus, nequaquam dubitemus saxa construendae conservandaeque urbi Patavinae, vetustissimis olim temporibus inde excavata sumptaque fuisse. Et cum ea in caverna noxii olim servari consueverunt, Custodia inde vicus est appellatus.

Estque locus apud quem Bononienses milites, quorum opera Guilielmus, Ravennas archiepiscopus sedis apostolicae legatus, Ecelinum de Romano eiecerat Patavio, eundem deserverunt legatum, unde factum est ut paulo post Ecelinus, reassumptis viribus, vires ecclesiae retuderit, legatumque apud Gambaram, Brixiam agri oppidum, proelio superatum in carcerem coniecerit. [379B]

Superiusque Meduacus sive Bachilio Vincentiam dividit paene mediam, quae urbs a Gallis Romae incensoribus, sicut saepe supra diximus, cum Mediolano, Brixia, Bergomo, et Verona fuit principio aedificata. Et altero item fluvio urbem Vicentiam illabentem, Tesina appellato, apudque Landrigum oppidum oriundo Meduacus augetur amnis. Qui Tesina apud Luxianum oppidum scissus, alterum ramum cui Barcanum haeret oppidum facit. Isque Meduacum, priusquam Brentellas attingat, ingreditur. Genuit ex vetustis Vicentia Palaemonem, sicut Eusebio placet, insignem grammaticum, qui interrogatus quid inter stillam et guttam interesset, “Gutta,” inquit, “stat; stilla cadit.” Nostra autem aetate illustrata est Vincentia Antonio Lusco, qui vir doctissimus eloquentissimusque, et primus et solus in oratoribus M. Tullii Ciceronis duodecim, ars rhetoricae praticae, qua ratione a Tullio fuerit applicata, tam clare tamque diffuse commentus est ut nihil magis nostros

It boasts as its citizen Ognibene, learned in Greek and Latin literature, a man who displays the character inculcated in him by his mentor Vittorino da Feltre.

From Cologna into the swamps below and neighboring the town of Este, **[379A]** a canal has been constructed to run into the flowing river. Next to it are located Roveredo, and Montagnana, the chief town of the region. At the mouth of this canal, through which it discharges into the swamps, and a little below it, is the *castello* of Lozzo. The Meduacus or Bacchiglione, which it is my next task to describe, has another mouth; and the densely inhabited town of Costozza lies next to the Bacchiglione. I have myself inspected the ditches in the middle of its suburbs, which penetrate the earth far below. There is in this mountain a mineral like travertine, but I have not found it described anywhere. I am certain that rocks for constructing and preserving the city of Padua were in ancient times dug up and taken from this place. And since convicted criminals were accustomed in former times to be kept in *custody* in this cave, the village is called from this custom "Custodia," Costozza.

It was here that Guglielmo, archbishop of Ravenna and legate to the apostolic See, with the help of soldiers of Bologna, threw out Ezzelino da Romano from Padua. But the soldiers then deserted the legate's cause. Consequently, shortly afterwards Ezzelino regained his power, crushed the forces of the church and, defeating the legate in battle, threw him into prison at Gambara, a town in the territory of Brescia. **[379B]**

Higher up, the Meduacus or Bacchiglione cuts in half the city of Vicenza, which was first built, as I mentioned, by the Gauls who burned Rome, and also built Milan, Brixia, Bergomum, and Verona. There is also a second river that flows into the city of Vicenza, called the Tesina, which has its source at Landro and is a tributary of the Bacchiglione. At the town of Lusiano, the Tesina splits and along its other branch lies the town of Barche. Before it can arrive at Brentella, it flows into the Bacchiglione. Eusebius tells us that in ancient times Vicenza was the birthplace of Palaemon; he was the famous grammarian who, when asked the difference between a natural, liquid drop and a dense, viscous drop, said, "A natural, liquid drop stands still; a dense, viscous drop falls." In our generation Vicenza produced the learned and eloquent Antonio Loschi, who was the first and only commentator on the twelve books of Cicero on the orators, a guide to public speaking. Using the method of Cicero, he elucidated the work so thoroughly that it seems that men of our generation have mastered the art of rhetoric to no

homines perdiscenda eloquentia iuvisse videatur. Exstant etiam viri eiusdem heroica quaedam carmina Virgilianam maiestatem carminum redolentia. Mathaeusque Bissarius iureconsultus eloquentia [379C] et bonis artibus apprime eruditus patriam exornat.

Multa suppeterent in Vicentinorum laudem dicenda a ducentis annis gesta, dum Patavinorum Veronensiumque pariter paene vicinorum violentiae iniuriisque resistunt. Sed unicum eos facinus abunde reddit ornatissimos. Quandoquidem primi fuere, qui Venetorum imperio sese sponte sua subiicientes, praeclaras urbes Patavium, Veronam, Brixiam, Bergomumque, et quicquid aliud illi nunc optinent de Italia in potestatem venire plurimum adiuverunt.

Supra Vicentiam Meduaco adhaeret Caldogium oppidum, et superius fonti eius imminet oppidum Porcelletum. Meduacusque priusquam Custodiam attingat oppidum supra descriptum, altero scissus ramo fossas attingit, quibus Brentellis est appellatio, munimento Patavii circumductas. Inde apud Ingentionum delapsus, fertur ad oppidum Pubolentam. Defluens postea ad pontem longum continuato cursu stagnis se immiscet, a quibus alterno fluxu refluxuque retractus, vel repulsus in fossam Clodiam se exonerat. Quae urbis Clugiae ab ea fossa appellatae, portum efficit omnium regionis profundissimum. Plinius namque Meduacum amnem in fossam Clodiam labi docet.

Fuisse etiam [379D] Bachilionem amnem Meduacum Livii Patavini verbis ex decimo libet ostendere.

> Eodem anno classis Graecorum Cleonymo duce Lacedaemonio ad Italiae litora appulsa *Thuriorum* urbem in Sallentinis cepit. Adversus hunc hostem consul Aemilius missus proelio uno fugatum compulit in naves. Thuriae redditae veteri cultori, Sallentinoque agro pax parta. Iunium Bubulcum dictatorem missum in Sallentinos in quibusdam annalibus invenio, et Cleonymum, priusquam confligendum esset cum Romanis, Italia decessisse.
>
> Circumvectus inde Brundisii promontorium medio sinu Adriatico ventis latus, cum laeva importuosa Italiae litora, dextra Illyrici Liburnique et Histri, gentes ferae et magna ex parte latrociniis mari-

effect. Some epic poems by this same man also survive, which resonate with the majesty of Virgil. Matteo Bissario, the legal expert, learned in eloquence and the liberal arts, also distinguishes his native city **[379C]** of Vicenza.

I could relate many praiseworthy achievements of the citizens of Vicenza over the last two hundred years, during their resistance to the violence and insults of their near neighbors, Padua and Verona. But there is a single deed that brings them distinction. When they were the first to go voluntarily under the yoke of the Venetian empire, the citizens of Vicenza helped the famous cities of Padua, Verona, Brescia, and Bergamo, and whatever other places in Italy they now hold, to enter into Venetian power.

Alongside the Bacchiglione above Vicenza is the town of Caldogno, and higher up, the town of Porcelletum perches over its source. And before the Bacchiglione flows past the town of Costozza, which I described above, it splits into another branch and flows past the canals called Brentelle, which surrounded the fortifications of Padua. And from there the river flows down to Vighenzone, and to the town of Bovolenta. It then flows down, in an uninterrupted course, to a Pontelungo and flows into the swamps, and bends and turns back, and is drawn back or pushed out of these swamps and discharges into the Chioggia canal. This canal gives its name to the city Chioggia and creates a harbor which is the deepest in the region. Pliny shows that the Bacchiglione river flows into the Chioggia canal.

That the Meduacus was the **[379D]** Bacchiglione river, Livy shows in these words from his tenth book:

> In the same year a Greek fleet, under the command of Cleonymus the Spartan, put in on the coast of Italy and captured the city of Thurii which was located among the Sallentini. The consul Aemilius was dispatched against the Greeks, routed them in a single battle, and forced them back to their ships. Thurii was returned to its former inhabitants, and there was peace in the territory of the Sallentini. (I find in certain records that the dictator Junius Bubulcus was sent to the Sallentini, and that Cleonymus departed from Italy before he had to engage the Romans in battle.)
>
> From there he and his fleet sailed around the promontory of Brundisium and the winds in the Adriatic gulf carried them and pushed them off course. Knowing that, on the left (the Italian side) were no harbors, and on the right, the fierce tribes of Illyrici, Liburn-

> timis infames terrerent, penitus ad litora Venetorum pervenit. *Ibi* expositis paucis qui loca explorarent, cum *audissent* tenue *praetereundum* litus esse, quod *praetergressis* stagna ab tergo sint irrigua ostiis, maritimos agros haud procul proximos campestris cerni, ulteriora colles videri, esse ostium fluminis praealti, quo circumagi naves in stationem tutam *vidissent*-Meduacus amnis erat. Eo *iniectam* classem subire flumine adverso iussit. Gravissimas navium non pertulit alveus fluminis; in *minora* navigia transgressa multitudo armatorum ad frequentes agros, tribus maritimis Patavinorum vicis colentibus eam oram, pervenit. Ibi egressi praesidio **[380E]** levi navibus relicto vicos expugnant, inflammant tecta, hominum pecudumque praedas agunt, et dulcedine praedandi longius usque a navibus procedunt.
>
> Haec ubi Patavium sunt nuntiata (semper autem eos in armis accolae Galli habebant) in duas partes iuventutem dividunt. *Alteram* in regionem, qua effusa populatio *videbatur*, altera, ne cui praedonum obvia fieret, altero itinere ad stationem navium (milia autem quattuordecim ab oppido aberant) ducta. In naves *parvas*, custodibus interemptis, impetus factus, territique nautae coguntur naves in alteram ripam amnis traiicere. Et in terra prosperum aeque in palatos praedatores proelium fuerat, refugientibus ad stationem Graecis Veneti obsistunt.

Dicimus itaque praeteritum a Cleonymo tenue litus, transgressa stagna, ostium amnis praealti, in quem circumacta sit adverso flumine classis et ad quattuordecim milia oppido Patavio propinquata, satis ostendere Meduacum fuisse amnem descriptum, cui Bachilioni fuit postea estque nunc indita appellatio. Neque enim alium habet regio fluvium ex agro Patavino in stagna

ians, and Istrians, notorious bandits, he and his fleet sailed on until they arrived at the coastal settlements of the Veneti. After sending a few men ashore to reconnoitre, they heard that they had to pass over a narrow beach and that after they went around the port and when they had crossed it there would be lagoons behind it, flooded by the sea; and that fields were not far off, and beyond that were hills, and a harbor where a very deep river debouched, deep enough that the ships could be brought about and provided safe anchorage (this was the Meduacus river).

Cleonymus then gave orders for the fleet to sail up the river. But the riverbed would not float the heaviest ships, so the soldiers transferred en masse to lighter boats, and sailed towards the fields which were densely inhabited by three towns of the Patavini located beside the river. **[380E]** There they left a small defensive force with the ships and went ashore to plunder the villages, burn the houses, and drive off prisoners and cattle. The pleasure of plundering enticed them farther from their ships.

When this news was reported to the Patavini, they divided in two their force of young men (for they were always under arms due to the threat of the neighboring Gauls). One group proceeded to the region where the sporadic plundering had been reported; the other group went, by a different route so as not to meet the raiders, to the place where the Greek ships were anchored, fourteen miles from the town. The latter group attacked the light ships and killed their defensive force. The sailors were terrified and forced to move the ships across the river, to its other bank. The first group of Patavini also had success on land, in their struggle against the disorganized raiders, and every time the Greeks tried to retreat to the place where the ships were anchored, the Veneti blocked their way.

And so I assert that the narrow beach that Cleonymus crossed, and the lagoons, and the mouth of the deep river, where the fleet could be brought around against the river, and the approach of about fourteen miles to a town of the Patavini, is sufficient proof that it is the Meduacus river which Livy is here describing (which afterwards, and now, has had the name Bacchiglione). For there is no other river in the region which flows down from the territory of Padua into lagoons, or a mouth at the sea, unless someone thinks

marisve ostia delabentem, nisi forte eum quis proximum illi amnem nunc Brintam esse opinabitur, **[380F]** qui suam et ipse paucissimis cognitam fecit nominis mutationem.

Est enim Timavus priscorum scriptis, praesertim Virgilii celebratus, quem saepe miratus sum viros nostri saeculi doctrinae fama celebres in Istris et Liburnis quaesivisse, errore adductos atque ignoratione sensus Virgilii, quem volunt novem Timavo fontes in suo carmine attribuisse; cum potius Antenorem ille faciat a Troia Italiam petentem regna Liburnorum et Timavum superasse amnem, in ipso fontis nomine poetico more indicatum. Servius enim id verbum exponens sic habet:

> Fontem Timavi: amant poetae rem unius sermonis circumlocutionibus ducere, ut pro Troiam dicant urbem Troianam, sic modo pro Timavo fontem Timavi, et paulo post urbem Patavi pro Patavio, et ora novem multi septem esse dicunt.

"Superasse" autem ea parte "unde" pro qua "per ora novem mare it praeruptum," et "premit" stagnorum arva pro campis et planitie posita "sonanti pelago," sicut semper sonare videmus, cum litoris aut portus cuiuspiam fauces paulo violentior commotiorque ingreditur. Eaque novem ora etiam nunc notissima sunt litoris Veneti aperturae, quarum partem maximam a Ravennati agro in Altinum **[380G]** prisci et imprimis Antoninus Pius imperator in itinerario Septem Maria appellavere. Versus Virgilii licet notissimi sint subiciemus, cum prius Lucani de Timavo testimonium attulerimus:

> Euganeo si vera fides memorantibus augur
> colle sedens Aponus terris ubi fumifer exit
> atque Antenorei dispergitur unda Timavi.

Si ergo unda Timavi Antenorei dispergitur prope Aponum nunc etiam notissimum et Patavio propinquum, non oportuit in Histriis illum aut Foroiuliensibus a nostris hominibus requiri. Virgilius:

> Antenor potuit mediis elapsus Achivis
> Illyricos penetrare sinus, atque intima tutus
> Regna Liburnorum et fontem superare Timavi

of the river next to this one, which is now called the Brenta, **[380F]** having undergone an obscure change of name.

The Timavus river appears in the writings of the ancients, especially, and most famously in those of Virgil. I have often wondered at the error of my famously learned contemporaries who have sought this river in Istria and Liburnia, ignorant as they are of the import of Virgil's apparent attribution to the Timavus, in his poetry, of nine mouths. Virgil has Antenor, heading from Troy to Italy, penetrate to a point above the Timavus river, and in poetic habit he indicates the river by the very name of its source. Servius, commenting on this name, says the following:

> *The source of the Timavus*: The poets like to employ periphrasis, so that, for example, "Troy" becomes "the Trojan city," and so "the Timavus" becomes "the source of the Timavus," and a little after this "Padua" becomes "the city of the Patavi"; and many people say that the nine mouths are really seven.

In addition, "sail past" means in the direction from which "the sea rushes headlong through the nine mouths," and Virgil writes "roaring, pounds the lagoons" in place of the level fields on dry land, just as we notice it always roars, when it enters, in a violent and disturbed way, any mouth of the shore or the harbor. Those nine mouths are even now well-known; they are the entrance on the Venetian shore, the greatest part of which, extending from the territory of Ravenna to Altino, were called Septem Maria (Seven Seas) by the ancients and especially **[380G]** by the emperor Antoninus Pius in his *Itinerary*. Although I will cite Virgil's famous verses, Lucan's evidence about the Timavus may appropriately be placed first here:

> . . . if memory serves, the augur sitting on the Euganean hill
> where the smoke goes up from the earth
> and the wave of Antenor's Timavus spreads. . . .

So if the "wave of Antenor's Timavus spreads" near Abano (a place near Padua well-known even today), our learned men ought not to seek for it in Istria, nor in Friuli. Virgil's lines:

> Antenor was able to escape from the midst of the Greeks and reach the bay of Illyria, and arrive safely at the innermost parts of Liburnia and travel beyond the source of the Timavus, where the

Unde per ora novem vasto cum murmure montis
It mare praeruptum et pelago premit arva sonanti.

Exstant quoque carmina Musati Patavini poetae tragici sepulchro inscripta, Timavum affirmantia Patavii propinquum esse:

Condita a Troiugenis post diruta Pergama tellus
In mare fert Patavas unde Timavus aquas
Hunc genuit vatem.

Et Martialis:

Laneus Euganei lupus excipit ora Timavi.

Si ergo Timavus fuit Euganeus necessario erit Brinta nunc Patavii fluvius; nam idem Martialis appellatione telluris Aponae **[380H]** Patavium significat hoc versu,

censetur Apona Livio suo tellus.

Et L. Florus infrascripta habet verba ex quibus licet coniicere Timavum ab Arsia et finibus Italiae, in quibus nuper requirebatur plurimum distare, "Illyrici ab Alpium radicibus inter Arsiam et Timavum per Adriaticum litus effusi regnante Teutana muliere." Timavusque ubi salsas attingit aquas bifurcatus parte dextera Pupiliam Methamaucumque petit, ubi portum efficit cum amplitudine, tum etiam profunditate optimum.

Rectiore autem ad sinistram cursu Venetam urbem mediam scindere solitus portum efficit Venetum cui munitissimae arces duae hinc et inde praesidio sunt appositae. Sed haec pars occlusis pridem ad Luciafusinam meatibus in stagna paludesque diffunditur. Non fuisse autem Meduacum quem Timavum esse dicimus, aut econtra praeter rationes supradictas hinc maxime videtur constare, quod Plinius scribit contra Timavum amnem insulam fuisse parvam in mari cum fontibus calidis, qui pariter cum aestu maris crescerent minuerenturque. Et recto Brintae amnis cursui quem naturaliter per mediam urbem Venetam habebat, oppositam fuisse constat insulam cui castellum Olivolense appellatum fuit impositum, unde cathedralis ecclesia dicitur Castellana. Si vero calidi non apparent nunc fontes minime mirandum, quod nedum litoreis et maritimis locis in quae maris saepe desaevit

> sea bursts forth in a headlong course through nine mouths, with an awesome roaring in the mountain rocks, and covers the fields with its noisy waters.

There are also some poems of the Paduan tragic poet Mussato, inscribed on his tomb, which corroborate that the Timavo is near Padua:

> Built by the Trojans after the sack of their city,
> The land of Padua extends to the sea, from where the Timavo
> Bore this poet.

Martial too writes,

> The sea bass, with its flesh white as wool, swims up the Timavus in the land of the Euganei.

So, if the Timavus was "in the land of the Euganei," it will have to be what is now the river of Padua, the Brenta; for Martial also means **[380H]** Padua by "the land of Apona" when he says in this line,

> Livy calls the land of Apona his own.

And I append the words of L. Florus from which one can conclude that the Timavo is very far from the Arsa river, and the territory of Italy where some were recently looking for the river: "The Illyrici, whose queen is Teutana, are spread out across the Adriatic coast from the foothills of the Alps between Arsa and Timavus." And where the "Timavus" splits in two and reaches the lagoons on the right-hand side, it goes to Poveglia and Malamocco, where it makes an excellent harbor, both wide and deep.

The "Timavus" flows in a straighter course to the left and, cutting through the middle of the city of Venice, creates Porto Veneto, a harbor with two well-fortified citadels on either side protecting it. But the wanderings of this part are shut off, and it discharges into the lagoons and swamps at Lizza Fusina. In addition to the reasons I have given above, that the Timavus was not the modern Bacchiglione becomes clear from what Pliny writes, that opposite the Timavus river was a small island in the sea; it had warm springs which grew and diminished along with the tides of the sea. And it is definitely true that the Brenta river makes a straight course through the middle of the city of Venice and has opposite it an island which contains a *castello* called Olivolense and as a result the cathedral church is called Castellana. It is not surprising if the springs are not now observed to be warm, because we find that many springs have dried up: this happens much

violentia, [381A] sed in mediterraneis montanisque firmioribus multos aruisse fontes invenimus.

Timavusque supra Luciafusinam integer primum habet ad dexteram vicum Auriganum tabernis hospitatoriis frequentatum. Ibique Timavum illabitur Tegola torrens, cui adiacet Rus Peragum. Deinceps Timavo sinistrorsum adiacet Strata oppidulum, a quo sexto miliario fossa manufacta Paduam compendio navigatur. Eam urbem Italiae vetustissimam clarissimamque magis certum est Antenorem Troia profugum condidisse, quam ut indigeat testimoniis. Versibus enim, quos supra posuimus, sic addit Virgilius,

> Hic tamen ille urbem Patavi sedesque locavit.

Et Livius Patavinorum decus in primo idem seriose narrat. Cicero autem in Philippicis Patavinos dicit Romanis amicissimos fuisse, qui rei publicae difficillimis temporibus pecunia et armis iuverunt. Et Macrobius in Saturnalibus, ubi de fide servorum tractat, innuit Patavinos fuisse per humanos qui cum servis clementissime atque indulgentissime se habuerunt, quandoquidem asserit Asinio Pollione Patavinos cogente, ut tributa conferrent, et propterea dominis latitantibus, neminem servorum fuisse inventum, qui libertate proposita [381B] dominum proderet.

Fuit autem postmodum Padua perfelicissima stantis rei publicae tempora Romanorum colonia non eo modo deducta, quo ceterae deducebantur ductis novis populis in coloniam. Sed datum est Paduanis ius Latii, ut in designandis Romae magistratibus ferendi suffragii ius haberent, quod a Q. Asconio Pediano in expositionibus orationum Ciceronis habetur.

Ea vero describenda urbe si prolixiores erimus, sua nos dignitas excusabit. Nullam enim aedificiorum pulchritudine praesertim publicorum in Italia sibi similem esse tenemus. Sunt tamen nova quaecumque in ea nunc exstant vel publica, vel privata, quandoquidem ad trigesimum et quadringentesimum salutis annum Athila rex Hunnorum ferro ignique vastatam reliquit immunitam; et a Narsete eunucho Ravennatibusque instauratam anno a prima dirutione vixdum centesimo Longobardi incensam penitus desertarunt. Aucta vero est mirabili incremento per Caroli Magni et filiorum nepotumque imperii tempora. Nec aliquod postea incommodum sub Germanis imperatoribus accepit, quousque Federici primi Barbarossi temporibus Ecelinus de Romano, tyrannorum omnium qui umquam fuerunt crudelissimus, ad annum [381C] salutis trigesimum septimum et duodecies centenum eam sibi subegit, qui praeter commissas caedes alias, persecutionesque prope

more in the coastal and maritime places where the sea rushes in violently, **[381A]** but also in the solid land of the interior and mountainous places.

Where the "Timavus" is undivided above Lizza Fusina, the first settlement on its right bank is the village of Oriago, full of inns for travellers. Here its tributary the Tegola joins the "Timavus," and next to it is Peraga. Then on the left of the "Timavus" is the tiny town of Strà; six miles from here a manmade canal provides a passage to Padua. "This city is the most ancient and famous in Italy, and it is more certain that Antenor, in flight from Troy, founded it, than that evidence is lacking." For Virgil (continuing the lines of verse I cited above) says,

> But here he placed the city of Padua and his abode,

and Livy, the glory of the Paduans, relates this in abundant detail in his first book. In addition, Cicero in his *Philippics* says that the Paduans were very friendly towards the Romans, helping them with money and weapons in their times of difficulty. And Macrobius in his *Saturnalia*, in the passage about the trustworthiness of slaves, alludes to the humanity of the Paduans, in that they behaved mercifully and leniently towards their slaves, since he says that Asinius Pollio compelled the Paduans to pay tribute; but when the masters hid, no slave was found who would **[381B]** betray his master, even for the reward of his freedom.

Afterwards, however, Padua enjoyed good fortune while the Republic existed, for not only was it not made the site of a colony for a new population, which happened to other cities; but it was given the Latin rights, to have a right to vote at Rome in the election of its magistrates. Q. Asconius Pedianus mentions this, in his commentary on the orations of Cicero.

If I go on at too great length in describing this city, its prestige will excuse my prolixity. I consider Padua to have no rival in Italy in the beauty of its buildings, especially the public ones. But whatever buildings are now standing, public or private, are new, since Attila, king of the Huns, destroyed the city in 430 with iron and fire and left it defenseless. The eunuch Narses and the citizens of Ravenna rebuilt it, but scarcely a century after its first destruction the Lombards burned it thoroughly and left it a wasteland. In the times of Charlemagne and his descendants, Padua enjoyed a miraculous growth, and did not suffer any injuries afterwards under the rule of the German emperors. But in the time of Frederick the first, Barbarossa, Ezzelino da Romano, **[381C]** of all tyrants the most cruel, subjugated the city in 1237. In addition to his slaughters and persecutions of citizens, which I de-

innumeras civium ea usus est, de qua in Verona diximus, crudelitate raro alias audita, caedis per varia cruciatuum genera perpetratae, duodecim milium Patavinorum, quos Mantuanorum ingressurus fines sub militiae praetextu obsides secum duxerat.

Paulo tamen post quam is tyrannus apud Soncinum interiit, Charrarienses sub capitaneatus titulo rerum in Patavio potiti sunt, qui eam urbem annis paulo plus minus centum per varias successiones possessam opulentioremque ornatioremque reddiderunt. Nam gentis Charrariae opera maiori ex parte excitata ornataque fuerunt moenia, quibus triplici circuitu Patavium communitur. Et licet eam per urbem Timavus semper fuerit delapsus, quod Livius in decimo libro ostendit, multis tamen variisque fossis magno et ingenti opere manufactis aquae circum urbem et per diversa agri loca ornamento urbi commodoque futurae ab eisdem Charrariensibus sunt perductae, cum arx in urbe munitissima et coniunctum illi perductis brachiis palatium facile in Italis primarium superbique **[381D]** operis nonnulli in urbe pontes gentis eiusdem fuerint opera.

Henricus autem quartus imperator Germanicus cathedralem Patavii ecclesiam, quae exstat, aedificavit, praetoriumque quo nullum in orbe pulchrius esse tenemus, cum esset casu crematum, speciosius Veneti construxerunt, ossaque T. Livii conspicuo in eius fastigio collocarunt. Insignis vero et cui rarissimae sunt in Italia similes, beati Antonii basilica a Patavinis sub Romano imperio semiliberis aedificata est. Parrochiales ecclesias quadraginta et mendicantium quattuor loca, magnifici certe operis, cives Patavinos diversis aedificasse temporibus constat. Est ea in urbe Iustinae virginis templum, amplissimae cuius aedes mille in circuitu passus amplexae aquis circumluuntur, quod in vetustae aedis vestigio aedificatum fuisse hinc constat, quod effodientes ubique pulcherrima inveniunt lithostrata.

Eodemque in loco T. Livii sepulchrum aetate nostra repertum fuisse conspeximus, ut credere liceat vetustum Iovis templum ibi fuisse, in quo ipse Livius in X narrat spolia de Cleonymi Lacedaemonis piratae victoria Patavium reportata fuisse. Servat vero nunc idem templum Iustinae ipsius virginis, Lucae Evangelistae, Maximi et Felicitatis, Mathiae Apostoli, super quem sors cecidit, Prosdocimique tutelaris Patavinorum sancti corpora et reliquias.

Areas Patavium publicas quinque habet, nobilium scilicet et **[382E]** herbaticam, frumentariam, lignariam, palearem. In eius quoque gymnasio om-

scribed in the section on Verona, he committed an almost unheard of atrocity: twelve thousand men of Padua, whom he had taken with him as hostages on the pretext of military action when he was invading the territory of Mantua, he slaughtered by various types of torture.

A little while afterwards, this tyrant died at Soncino, and the Carrara took possession of the government in Padua, by virtue of their title of captain. In a little less than one hundred years of their successive tenures in the rule, they restored the city to opulence and splendor. The defensive walls of Padua, which surround the city in a triple circle, were for the most part raised and embellished through the work of the Carrara. And although the "Timavus" has always flowed through the city, as Livy shows in his tenth book, the Carrara also had many canals made, with great labor, to bring water around the city and through its contado, to be ornamental and useful. The same family also had built the strongly fortified citadel within the city, and the palace, easily the foremost in Italy, which is joined to the citadel by extended walls; and a **[381D]** number of bridges in the city, of splendid workmanship.

The present cathedral in Padua, however, was built by Henry IV, the German emperor. The palace, which I consider among the most beautiful in the world, although it was accidentally burned, was rebuilt more beautifully by the Venetians. They gave the remains of Livy a conspicuous place in its façade. The basilica of St. Anthony was built by Paduan freedmen under the Roman Empire; it is truly remarkable and there are few in Italy like it. The citizens of Padua built at different times forty parish churches and four cloisters for the mendicant orders, of magnificent workmanship. There is also in Padua the temple of Sta. Giustina, this extensive building in a circle of a mile surrounded by water; it is established that it has been built on the remains of an ancient temple, as when the builders were digging they found everywhere beautiful mosaic floors.

And in the same place I have seen the tomb of Livy, which was discovered in my lifetime. I therefore think it was the ancient temple of Jupiter, to which Livy himself (book ten) relates the spoils of the victory over the Spartan pirate Cleonymus were brought back. Now, the same temple happens to house the body and relics of Sta. Giustina, the apostle Luke, saints Massimo and Felicità, the apostle Matthew (to whose lot it fell), and of S. Prosdocimo, protector of the Paduans.

Padua has five public squares: **[382E]** the Piazza dei Signori, of course; and the haymarket, grain market, wood market, and straw market. Its gym-

nium Italiae celeberrimo aedes sunt amplissimae, studentium quibus opes sint tenuiores auxilio deputatae. Viros Patavium doctrina clarissimos genuit, T. Livium, cuius sepulchri priusquam Romam accederet, sibi et filiis duobus uxorique positi saxum nuper vidimus litteras haud quaquam elegantes inscriptum:

> T. Livius Caii filius sibi et suis Tito Livio Tito filio Prisco F. T. Livio. T. F. Longo F. Cassiae Sextiae Primae uxori.

Aliudque elegantiores maiusculas marmore incisum, sepulchrum etiam Patavi in Iustinae virginis vestibulo exstat titulis ornatum, et militiae cui ad decus utilitatemque fuit ascriptus, et virtutis suae qui diffidentes Patavinos cives, in patriam reversus ad concordiam revocavit:

> Vivens fecit T. Livius Liviae T. F. Quartae legionis Halys Concordialis Patavi sibi et suis omnibus.

Ratio autem quae nos adduxit, ut futuram in minore viro vanam huiusmodi diversitatis sepulchrorum curiositatem adhibuerimus, illa fuit quod in primo sepulchro omnes quos habuit Patavi degens uxorem et filios in successionem annotavit. In altero autem omnibus dixit, qui filia Romae esset auctus, quae Lucio Magio nupsit oratori Romano. **[382F]** De quo Seneca declamationum VIII sic habet,

> Non puto . . . quomodo Lucius Magius gener Titi Livii declamaverit, quamvis aliquo tempore suum populum habuit, cum illum homines non ipsius honorem laudarent, sed in soceri efferrent.

Fuitque is magnus vir Livius, ad quem nobiles ex ultimis Hispaniarum partibus venisse, et quos Romani nominis fama non moverat, eius hominis fama perduxisse beatus Hieronymus ex Plinio sumptum scribit.

Paulusque iurisconsultus apud vetustissimos celebratus fuit Patavinus. Et Martialis poeta duos dilexit Patavinos poetas, Stellam et Flaccum, his versibus:

> Verona licet audiente dicam,
> Vicit, Maxime, passerem Catulli.

nasium, the most famous in Italy, contains expansive buildings, and students of small means are given aid. Padua has given birth to men very famous for their learning: I recently saw the tomb of Livy: before he went to Rome, its stone was rather crudely inscribed, to him and his two daughters and wife, with the following:

> Livy, the son of Gaius, erected this for himself, and his family members: Titus Livius Priscus, son of Titus; Titus Livius Longus, and Cassia Sextia Prima, his wife.

Another tomb, also in Padua, in the vestibule of the temple of S. Giustina, was inscribed in marble with more elegant capitals, decorated with the titles both of his military service, to the glory and benefit of which he was enrolled, and of his own virtue, as he returned to his fatherland and recalled to harmony the distrustful citizens of Padua. This says:

> T. Livius Halys, freedman of Livia Quarta daughter of Titus, priest of Concordia, of the fourth legion, made this during his lifetime at Padua for himself and all his family members.

The reason I apply my curiosity, which would be useless in the case of a lesser man, to this discrepancy in the tombs, is that on the first tomb he makes note of all those whom he had when he was living at Padua, wife and sons in order. In the second, however, he said to everyone, he had at Rome a daughter who married the Roman orator Lucius Magius. **[382F]** Seneca, *Declamationes* 8, says about him,

> I do not think [that it is relevant], how Lucius Magius the son-in-law of Livy spoke, however great a following he had in another time; since men did not praise the honor of the man himself, but brought praise to his father-in-law.

This was the great man Livy, whom nobles from the farthest parts of Spain came to look at; even those who had not been aroused by the glory of a Roman name, this man's fame did so move them, according to St. Jerome, who took the information from Pliny.

Julius Paulus the jurist, also, was a citizen of Padua, famous among the ancients. And the poet Martial esteemed two poets from Padua, Stella and Flaccus; the following verses show this:

> Even though Verona may hear it, I shall say it:
> Maximus, it has beaten that "Sparrow" of Catullus.

Tanto Stella meus tuo Catullo
Quanto passere maior est columba.

Et infra,

O mihi curarum pretium non vile mearum
Flacce Antenorei spes et alumne laris.

Catullus vero Volusium poetam Patavinum, qui ad Ennii exemplar rerum gestarum populi Romani annales carmine scripsit, damnare et vituperare conatus est his epigrammatibus:

At Volusi annales Paduam morientem ad ipsam,
**[382G]** Et laxas scombris saepe dabunt tunicas.

Item alio loco:

Annales Volusi cacata charta,
Votum solvite pro mea puella.
Nam sanctae Veneri cupidinique
Vovit si sibi restitutus essem,
Desissemque truces vibrare iambos,
Electissima pessimi poetae
Scripta tardipedi Deo daturam
Infelicibus ustilanda lignis.
Et haec pessima se puella vidit
Iocose lepide vovere divis.
Nunc o caeruleo creata ponto,
Quae sanctum Idalium virosque apertos
Quaeque Anconam Cnidumque arundinosam
Colis, quaeque Amethunta, quaeque Aleos,
Quaeque Dyrrachium Adriae tabernam,
Acceptum face redditumque votum,
Si non illepidum neque invenustum est.
At vos interea venite in ignem
Pleni thuris et inficetiarum
Annales Volusi cacata charta.

Petrum etiam de Abano conciliatorem appellatum philosophiae et astronomiae usque ad magiae suspicionem peritissimum, Musattumque et Lovattum iureconsultos poesi ornatos Patavium cives habuit. Franciscus Zabarella iureconsultissimus et Pileus de Prata Romanae ecclesiae cardinales dignitatem litteris et prudentia ornaverunt. Marsilius quoque et paulopost Ioannes Galeatiusque et Guilelmus Sophilici, Ioannes quoque Horologius, et paulo

> My Stella is so much greater than your Catullus
> As the dove is greater than the sparrow.

And later in this same collection,

> O you who reward handsomely with your friendship my efforts,
> Flaccus, hope and child of the home of Antenor . . .

Catullus tried to disparage and insult with the following epigrams Volusius, a Paduan poet, who wrote a poem entitled *Annales* after the model of Ennius on the achievements of the Roman people:

> But the *Annals* of Volusius will perish in Padua,
> **[382G]** providing many loose wrappers for fish.

And in the same vein, in another poem:

> Befouled papers, *Annals* of Volusius,
> Pay a vow for my girlfriend.
> For she vowed to Venus and Cupid
> That if I were restored to her,
> And I stopped hurling fierce iambics at her,
> She was going to burn, on logs of ill-omen, to the slow-footed god of fire,
> The choicest writings of the worst of poets.
> And this wicked girl saw that she was making a clever joke in this vow to the gods.
> Now, Venus, born of the deep blue sea, you who take care of Mt. Ida and its men,
> Who dwell in Ancona and Cnidos full of swallows
> And Amethunta, and Alis, and Dyrrhachium the trading center of the Adriatic,
> Put to the torch, the vow repaid, if it is not lacking in wit and charm.
> But meanwhile, you, befouled papers of the *Annals* of Volusius, get into the fire, full of incense and coarse jokes. . . .

Peter of Abano was born in Padua, an author of philosophy and astronomy so skilled he was suspected of magic. Among the citizens of Padua were Mussato and Lovati, legal experts who were also poets. The city has been distinguished, too, by Francis Zabarella the legal scholar and Pileo da Prata; both cardinals who also honored the city in their literary knowledge and wisdom. Outstanding physicians who distinguished their birthplace of Padua included Marsiglio, and a little later Giovanni Galeazzo, and Gug-

post Antonius Cermisonus, **[382H]** excellentes medici, Patavium patriam exornarunt.

Agrum etiam habet Patavinum non minus quam urbis aedificia conspiciendum. Quandoquidem montes in illo sunt excelsi, nec Alpes et Apenninum quod nullo in Italiae loco alibi cernitur contigentes, et usque summa cacumina vinetis olivetisque et consitis tecti in quibus vina gignuntur, quae Plinius in intimo Adriatico sinu optima describit. Gemulam unum in cuius summitate mulieres Deo dicatae monasterium habent a Beatrice Estensi virgine nobili aedificatum, et Vendam alterum appellant monasterio ornatum, quod montis Oliveti fratres inhabitant. Hisque adiacent montibus colles Euganei fama apud Latinos vates notissimi. Eam enim vatibus sedem fuisse innuit Martialis poeta his versibus:

> Si prius Euganeas clemens Helicaonis in aras
> Pictaque pampineis videris arva iugis.

Et Lucanus in primo,

> Euganeo si vera fides memorantibus
> Augur colle sedens. . . .

Et cum vici villaeque multae hos contegant colles, tum maxime Arquatam populo frequentem vicum decorat Francisci Petrarchae praediolum, apud quod diutissime vixit, multaque scripsit. Estque eius sepulchrum, marmoreo in sarcophago columnis quattuor sustentatum. Balneaque apud rus Euganeum etiam nunc appellatum plurima visuntur, quae Theodericum regem Ostrogothorum muris conclusisse ac ornasse Cassiodorus est **[383A]** auctor. In eisque herbas gigni scribit Plinius, de quibus poeta Martialis,

> Nullae sic tibi blandientur undae,
> Ac fontes Aponi rudes puellis.

Quibus vero ea opitulentur morbis Michael Savonarola opere in id edito disseruit.

Sed iam ad Timavum est redeundum. Is fluvius supra Limivum vicum, ubi incipit esse integer, primum habet ad dexteram oppidum Citatellam, quod Patavini ad annum salutis quartum de duodecies centeno aedificarunt. Deinceps est Marostica, superius Bassianum, quae duo oppida populis sunt frequentia. Supraque Bassianum Timavus, ubi Cisinum est oppidum, Cesino

lielmo di Santa Sofia, and also Giovanni Dondi dell'Orologio, and shortly after him Antonio Cermisone. **[382H]**

The territory of Padua is no less worth seeing than the buildings in the city. Its mountains are high, and border on the Alps and the Apennines (a fact which is not true of any other place in Italy); they are covered up to their peaks with vines, olive trees, and covered structures for growing vines. Pliny describes them as the best in the deep gulf of the Adriatic. There is a mountain called Gemola, on whose summit is a monastery kept by women dedicated to God; it was built by the noble maiden Beatrice d'Este. Another mountain, called Venda, has a monastery where the brothers of Mount Olive live. And next to these mountains are the Euganean hills, famous among the Latin poets. That they were the seats of seers Martial implies in the following lines:

> Clemens, if you get to see before I do the Euganean shores of
> Helicaon, and the fields set with vines trained on trellises. . . .

And Lucan, in his first book, writes:

> If those who remember have reliable memory,
> The seer sitting on the Euganean hill. . . .

And not only are there villages and many estates bordering on these hills; but the estate of Francis Petrarch is an especially noteworthy ornament to Arquata (now Arquà Petrarca), a densely-populated village. Here he lived for a very long time, and wrote much. And here are his tomb, supported by four columns, and marble sarcophagus. The Euganean country, as it is called even now, has many baths; Cassiodorus tells us that Theoderic, king of the Ostrogoths, enclosed them with walls and decorated them. **[383A]** Among them, Pliny writes, grasses grow, and about them Martial writes,

> . . . no other waters will entice you as much,
> not even the springs of Aponus, untried by women. . . .

Michele Savonarola explained the usefulness of these springs to the sick, in a work published for this purpose.

But now I must get back to the "Timavus," or the Brenta. Where this river begins to flow undivided, above the village of Limena, there is on its right bank the town of Cittadella, built by the Paduans in 1196. Then comes Marostica, and above it Bassano, two densely-inhabited towns. Above Bassano, where the "Timavus" is joined by the Cismon river, the town Cismon

flumine augetur in quod Arcivagus Navoriusque torrentes exigui ex Alpibus delabuntur, Cisinusque apud Pemechum oppidulum habet ortum. Timavo supra Cisinum ad dexteram Grignum adiacet oppidum a torrente ibi augente dictum. Ulterius oppidum habetur Iuanum, supraque illud oritur Grignus. Et superius emissorium lacus incubat Tusopum. Caldonacium deinceps oppidum et uni imminet lacui, et aliis subiectum est binis lacubus, a quibus tribus originem Timavus habet.

Primus post Timavum Musio fluvius stagna Venetorum apud Mestre oppidum illabitur, cui ad sinistram **[383B]** Villa Nova primum est proxima. Supraque paulo remotius Campus Sancti Petri oppidum adiacet opulentum, eiusque fonti in montibus oppidulum imminet, Collis Musonis ab ipso fluvio appellatus. Ad dexteram vero Musoni intus continent Castrumfrancum nobile oppidum, superiusque Asola longe nobilius. Deinceps amnis est Silus, quem Plinius asserit oriri in montibus Tarvisinis, apud Torcellum in stagna cadens; Torcellumque civitatem, nunc episcopo ornatam doctissimo Dominico de Dominicis, supra Venetam describentes regionem diximus aedificatam fuisse ex ruinis excidioque Altini. Cuius vetustae urbis parva admodum vestigia ad eam continentis partem, quae sinistrorsum Sili amnis ostio est apposita, nunc cernuntur. Altinique nomen primus apud veteres ponit Plinius. Et post Martialis poeta tanti fecisse videtur Altini oppidi situm ut dicat,

> Aemula Baianis Altini litora villis.

Antoninus vero Pius in Itinerario vias describens a Ravenna Aquileiam, dicit aut Septem Maria recta Ravenna secundum Adriatici litus ad Altinum transmitti, aut eos qui per Bononiam Sermedum Athesum Pataviumque terrestri petant itinere, Altinum primo et post Aquileiam accedere.

**[383C]** In eo autem qui Musionem et Silum amnes interiacet spatio, Novale est oppidum nobile. Silusque supra in mediterraneis Tarvisium urbem dividit, cuius nomen prior inter vetustos habet Plinius per tempora vero Ostrogothorum dignitatem inchoasse videtur, quam nunc habet. Nam cum Totilae pater Veronam aeque ac Tarvisium dominio possideret, Tarvisium tamen continuo est moratus. Unde Totila, qui postea quintus fuit Ostrogothorum rex, et quidem praestantissimus Tarvisii natus educatusque est. Postea Longobardorum initio regni, cum Alboinus rex eius gentis primus

is located. Tributaries to the Cismon include the small streams Avisio and Navorius from the Alps. The Cismon has its source at the small town of Pemechum. Above Cismon on the right bank of the "Timavus" lies the town of Grigno, named after a tributary stream there. Further on is the town of Ivano, and above that the stream Grigno has its source. And higher up Tusopum sits over the lake's outlet. Then comes the town of Caldonazzo, and it sits above one lake, and lies beneath two lakes; from these three lakes the "Timavus" has it source.

After the "Timavus," the first river is the Musone, which flows into the Venetian lagoons at the town of Mestre. Next after Mestre comes **[383B]** Villa Nova on the left. And above it, a little farther away, lies the wealthy town of Camposampiero and, perched above the source of the Musone in the mountains, the little town of Colle Musone, named after this river. On the right bank of the Musone, towards the interior, are the noble town of Castelfranco, and above it the far more distinguished one of Asolo. And then comes the Sile river, which Pliny says has its source in the Trevisan mountains, and flows into the lagoons at Torcello. The city of Torcello is presently distinguished by the learned bishop Domenico Dominici. In my description of Venice, above, I said that Torcello was built from the ruins of the destroyed city of Altinum. Traces can now be seen of the old city bordering on that part which is on the left opposite the mouth of the Sile river. Pliny is the first among ancient writers to use the name Altinum. After him, the poet Martial grants such value to the site of Altinum that he says,

> Altinum's shores that compete with the villas of Baiae. . . .

Antoninus Pius, in his *Itinerary*, describes the roads from Ravenna to Aquileia, and says that either one traverses the "Seven Seas," following the Adriatic coast directly from Ravenna to Altino; or that travellers who go on land through Bologna, Sermide, Este, and Padua reach first Altino and after that Aquileia.

**[383C]** Between the Musone and Sile rivers lies the noble town of Noale. Inland and higher up, the Sile runs through the middle of the city of Treviso. Among the ancients, Pliny is the first to mention this name. The city apparently attained during the times of the Ostrogoths the prestige it now enjoys. When the father of Totila took possession of Verona and Treviso, he stayed at Treviso. For this reason Totila, afterwards the fifth and most eminent king of the Ostrogoths, was born and brought up at Treviso. After this, when the first Lombard king Alboin invaded Italy, he captured through sur-

Italiam esset ingressus, Aquileiamque qualisqualis tunc erat, et ceteras regionis urbes per deditionem cepisset, Tarvisium quia eius incolae deditionem tardiuscule obtulissent, spoliare ac diruere constituerat, nisi Felix illius episcopus, vir timoratus Ravenna oriundus, regis barbariae sua prudentia et precum instantia deliniisset. Ornataque nunc est ea civitas altero praestante episcopo Hermolao Barbaro, qui sicut decet episcopum populo magis prodesse adnititur quam praeesse.

Regionem vero quam nunc describimus sub nomine absurdo Marchiae Tarvisinae, et pariter proximam Forumiulium olim **[383D]** Galliae Cisalpinae partem Plinius in regione Italiae decima posuit, quam Carnorum fuisse affirmat. Nam cum multa dixisset de fluvio Silo, oppido Altino, flumine Liquentia, colonia Concordia, Taliavento, Anaxo, Alsa, Natisone, deque Aquileia colonia subiungit, Carnorum haec regio fuit, quod vocabulum regiones ipsae alicubi etiam nostra aetate retinent. Ad Sili fontem oppidulum est Casacorba, deinceps Anaxum est flumen, cui nunc Plavi vulgatissima est appellatio. Ad eiusque ostia Equilium est insula stagnis paludibusque a continenti divisa, fuitque ea insula civitas eiusdem nominis ab Heracliensibus vicinis aedificata; namque Heracleam in Historiis et in Veneta huius Italiae regione ostendimus fuisse post Aquileiae, Concordiae, et Altini demolitionem a dictarum urbium populis aedificatam, qui ab Heracleo illius tempestatis imperatore id nomen indiderunt civitati. Sed Heraclienses inde Venetias commigrarunt, ut nunc urbis vestigia requirantur, Equileique pariter, ubi mutato nomine civitas dicitur nova episcopio et quidem tenui nota, parvae et tenues reliquiae vix sciuntur.

Anaxo seu Plavi fluvio ad sinistram adiacent oppida Venetium, Limina, et Aquorium; et superius arduo in monte est Feltrum civitas, episcopo nunc Iacobo ornata Zeno non minus doctrina quam gentis nobilitate conspicuo. Ad dexteram Plavi primum haeret oppidulum Madirium, inde mediterraneis Vetorium. **[384E]** Superius ubi Varianus olim, nunc Calorius auget fluvius, est oppidum Tesega, eidemque amni Variano sive Calorio apposita est Belunum, civitas vetustissima quam Plinius ceterique scriptores Velunum appellant, eidemque nunc cum Feltro in eundem coniuncte episcopatum idem Zenus praeest episcopus. Varianum vero sive Calorium amnem in Alpibus oriundum, quas Germaniae incolunt gentes, quinque augent torrentes, quorum convallibus marginibusque castella vicique plures insunt barbaris nominibus appellati.

render Aquileia, such as it then was, and other cities in the region; but the inhabitants of Treviso offered their surrender too late, and he decided to devastate and destroy it. But its bishop Felix, a native of Ravenna and a man full of reverence towards God, soothed the king's savageness with his wisdom and insistent prayers. The city is now distinguished by the outstanding bishop Ermolao Barbaro, who fittingly cares more about helping the people than ruling over them.

Pliny placed in the tenth region of Italy this region which I am now describing under the ridiculous name of March of Treviso, along with the next one, Friuli, formerly part **[383D]** of Cisalpine Gaul. He claimed that this area was called the Carnic region; he went on at great length about the Sile river, the town of Altino, the Livenza river, the colony of Concordia Sagittaria, the Tagliamento, Piave, Ausa, and Natisone rivers, and added a part about the colony of Aquileia, and the name of this region was Carnea, a name used of these areas in some places even in our generation. At the source of the Sile is the little town of Casacorba; then comes the river Anaxus, whose modern colloquial name is Piave. At its mouth is the island of Iesolo, separated from the mainland by swamps and lagoons. This island was the site of a city of the same name which was built by the neighboring citizens of Eraclea. Indeed I showed in my *Histories*, as well as in this work's section on Venice, that after the destruction of Aquileia, Concordia, and Altino, Eraclea was built by the populations of these cities; they gave it that name after the emperor of those times, Heraclius. But the citizens of Eraclea migrated from there to Venice, and now one can hardly see the traces of the city, and the same is true of Iesolo, where the new city is called by a different name and is known for its bishopric, insignificant as it is; the sparse remains of the old city are not well-known.

On the left of the Anaxus or Piave river lie the towns of Venzone, Limina, and Quero, and higher up, on a hill, is the city of Feltre. It is now distinguished by Iacopo Zeno, famous for his noble family as well as for his erudition. On the right bank of the Piave, the first small town is Mandre (?), and inland from there is Vidor. **[384E]** Ascending, one finds the former Varianus river, now called Caorame, flowing into the Piave. Here is the town of Tesimo, and next to the river is Belluno, an ancient city called Velunum by Pliny and some writers. Zeno's see includes this town as well as Feltre. The Varianus or Caorame has its source in the Alps, where the German tribes live. It has five tributaries, and on their edges and in their valleys are many *castelli* and villages with barbarian names.

Sed et ubi Plavum diximus Variano sive Calorio incipere augeri alter influit Cordovalus amnis, et ipse ex summis defluens Alpibus, cui Falchachium Tabuliumque oppida, et quam plures vici Germanica potius quam Italica nomina habentes adiacent. Liquentia ad mare sequitur amnis vetusti nominis, quem ex montibus Opiterginis nasci Plinius est auctor. Eum nunc Liventiam appellant. Habetque ostii bifariam divisi partem ad easdem paludes, quibus Equilium insulam a continenti diximus separari; alteraque parte ad proxima Caprularum insulae stagna paludesque delabitur, ubi vero in dictas scinditur partes ad dexteram **[384F]** Turricium est castellum. Interiusque ubi Liquentiam sinistrorsum torrens auget Mutegus Opitergum est nunc oppidulum, quam vetusti nominis civitatem simul cum Aquileia, Altino, et Concordia ab Athila destructam, et postea cum esset reaedificata a Longobardis eodem anno quo et Forum Pompilii deletam fuisse, in Historiis ostendimus. Ad Mutegique amnis fontem Conilianum est, nobile ditissimumque oppidum.

Liquentiam item dextrorsum Meduna auget fluvius, supremis in Alpibus Iuliis oriundus. Cui dextrorsum Corva et supra ad Imeuli torrentis fontem Portoneum, superiusque Prata, et in mediterraneis Portilium, oppida sunt apposita. Prataque et Portilium duabus, ut in regione praestantibus nobilium familiis patrii cognominis exornantur. Ubi vero Liquentiam ipse auget Meduna amnis Sacilum nobile ditissimumque est oppidum. Ad Liquentiae sinistram supra Mutegi torrentis influxum est oppidum Buffolettum. Et supra ubi Mesulus auget torrens Civiolonum est oppidum, superius Seravalle. Sequitur Alsa vetusto nomine fluvius, nunc Liminius appellatus; quod nomen eum inde **[384G]** crediderim nactum esse, quod sicut huius regionis principio diximus, et eius et Foroiulii limes a barbaris fuit dictus. Habetque ad ostium quo in paludes stagnaque exoneratur Caprulas insulam, in quam Opiterginos Athilae saevitiam declinantes saepe alias ostendimus confugisse. Habetque Alsa sive Liminus ad sinistram oppidum nomine Sextum.

Where I mentioned the Varianus or Caorame flows into the Piave, another river is also its tributary, the Cordovole. It flows down from the peaks of the Alps, and next to it lie the towns of Falcade and Taibon, and very many villages with German, not Italian, names. The Livenza river then flows to the sea, a river with an ancient name (Liquentia), which Pliny tells us has its source in the mountains north of Oderzo; it is now called the Livenza. Its bipartite mouth is at the same lagoons which I mentioned separate the island of Iesolo from the mainland. Its other part flows down to the nearby marshes and lagoons of the island of Caorle, where it splits into the two forks I mentioned, and here is located the *castello* of Turricium. And inland **[384F]** from here, the stream Monticano flows into the Livenza on the left, and one finds the small town of Oderzo. This city with an ancient name was destroyed by Attila along with Aquileia, Altino, and Concordia, and then rebuilt by the Lombards in the year of the destruction of Forum Pompilii (I wrote about this in my *Histories*). At the source of the Monticano river is the noble and wealthy town of Conegliano.

Also contributing to the Livenza, on the right side, is the Meduna river, which has its source on the peaks of the Julian Alps. On its right is Croba, and above at the source of the stream Imeulis is Pordenone, and higher up is Prata, and inland is Porcia. Prata and Porcia are both distinguished by two of the region's noblest families, with the same name. Where it flows into the Livenza, the Meduna river has the noble and wealthy town of Sacile. On the left of the Livenza, above where the stream Monticano flows into it, is the town Portobuffole. Higher up, where the stream Meschio flows into it, is the town Civiolonum, and above that Seravalle. Next comes the Ausa, a river with an ancient name, now called the Lemene; **[384G]** I believe it got this name from the fact I mentioned earlier, that the border of both this river and of Friuli were named by the barbarians. Where the river debouches into the swamps and lagoons, at its mouth, it has the island Caorle. When they were trying to avoid the wrath of Attila, as I have written repeatedly elsewhere, the Opitergians escaped to this island. The Alsa or Lemene river has on its left the town of Sesto.

# Regio Decima, Forumiulium

Sequitur regio Foroiuliensium, quos Plinius dicit dictos esse cognomine Transpadanos. Id Foroiulii nomen notissimum, et quod ante C. Iulii Caesaris tempora in ipsa regione, inque supereminentibus eidem Alpibus Iuliis inchoasse constat, unde post factum Iapigum aut Cisalpinae Galliae mutationem habuerit originem ignoramus. Undecumque autem sit natum nostrae inhaerentes divisioni regionis ipsius quam tamen nonnulli Aquileiensem appellari volunt initium ad Alsae, seu Liminis, fluvii dexteram inchoabimus. Cui Portus Gruarius oppidum, post Cordevallum, et superius Porclanum oppida sunt apposita. **[384H]** Deinceps est Taliaventum prisci praesentisque nominis flumen, quod Plinius dicit maius minusque fuisse, cum nunc unico in Adriaticum ostio feratur. Sunt ei ad sinistram primum a ripa remotius oppidum Sanctus Vitus, post Valua castellum, et superius in montibus Spilimbergum natura loci munitionibusque validissimum, et populo frequentatum. Dextrorsum vero haeret Taliavento Tisana nobile munitissimumque item oppidum, et supra ab amnis margine semotum Cuchagna. Superius in monte arduo Sanctus Daniel praestans in regione oppidum, et ad fontem in Alpibus Dugonia est castellum.

In ea litoris ubique inaequalis et maiori ex parte stagnosi ora torrens est in mare cadens, cui Palazolum in mediterraneis castellum haeret et stagna magnum in sinum recessumque curvato piscosissimoque imminet Maranum oppidum populo frequentissimum. Torrenti autem id illabenti stagnum continet Castellettum. Interius in mediterraneis oppidum nobile est Belgradum, superiusque Coldroitum. At in maritimis est stagnis circumfusa Gradus insula alter Venetiarum regionis et urbis limes in quam et in Historiis, et ipsa in Venetiarum descriptione saepenumero diximus Aquileienses patria profugos sese cum opibus et sacra supellectile recepisse, et urbem aedificasse Gradensem **[385A]** quam pluries dirutam reaedificatamque tandem pauci nunc inhabitant.

# Tenth Region, Forumiulium

There follows the region of the people of Friuli, whom Pliny says have the surname of Transpadanes. The name of Friuli is a very old one, and it is established that it began to be used before the times of Julius Caesar in the region itself, and in the Julian Alps which tower over it. I do not know the source of the later change in its name to Iapydia or Cisalpine Gaul. I shall begin on the right bank of the Ausa or Lemene river. Located next to it are the towns of Portogruaro, and after that Cordovado, and higher up, Pordolane. [384H] Then comes the Tagliamento river (its name in ancient times Taliaventum), which Pliny says consisted of a Greater and a Lesser Taliaventum; but it now arrives at the Adriatic through only one mouth. On its left, the first town, rather far from the bank, is San Vito, and then comes the *castello* of Valvasone, and higher up in the mountains is Spilimbergo, densely inhabited and strongly fortified by both the nature of its location and man-made defenses. On the Tagliamento river's right bank is another well fortified and noble town, Latisana; and above that, farther back from the edge of the river, is Cucagna, and higher up on a high mountain is San Daniele del Friuli, the chief town of the region, and at the river's source in the Alps is the *castello* of Dignano.

That coastline is irregular everywhere, and for the most part swampy. Here a stream falls into the sea, and on its bank inland is the *castello* Palazzolo, and a lagoon, full of fish, withdrawn into a great bay; it has a curving edge and perched above it is the town of Marano, densely inhabited. On the stream which flows into this lagoon is Castellettum. Towards the interior lies the noble town of Belgrado, and above that Codroipo. But on the coast, surrounded by lagoons, is the island of Grado, the other island of the Veneto, which forms a boundary of the city. It was to this place, as I have said many times both in my *Histories* and in this work's description of the Veneto, that the exiled refugees from Aquileia fled, with their wealth, holy objects, and furnishings, and they built the city of Grado, [385A] which was destroyed a number of times, and rebuilt, and finally has now ended up sparsely populated.

Aquileia etiam urbium quondam Italiae Transpadanae primaria potentissimaque atque etiam pulcherrima quintodecimo, ut inquit Plinius a mari semota, nunc paene derelicta est. Nam praeter sacerdotes canonicos numero haud quaquam multos; ornatissima speciosissimaque in basilica divinae faciendae rei addictos, praeter pastores piscatoresque rarissimos, nulli nunc incolunt populi ut vix castellulum tanta olim urbs nunc possit appellari. Suntque et ecclesia superius dicta et patriarchale atrium et muri oppidulo circumducti et monasterium virginibus deputatum Peponis patriarchae operum reliquiae. Eam urbem qui prius condiderint non est memoriae proditum. Livius autem in bello Macedonico sic habet:

> Romae litterae Fabii magnam trepidationem fecerunt. Eo maiorem quam paucos post dies Marcellus tradito exercitu Fabio Romam cum venisset, exercitum in Ligures traduci posse negavit, quia bellum cum Histris esset prohibentibus coloniam Aquileiam deduci.

Et paulo infra, "Aquileia colonia Latina eodem anno in agro Gallorum est deducta."

Florere autem coepit quo tempore primum **[385B]** Romani subigendis barbaris ad Danubium incolentibus manum apponere coeperunt. Unde Octavius Caesar Augustus, etsi maiorem bellorum partem per legatos administravit, ut illis propinquior esset in his Italiae partibus frequenter obversatus est. Nam Suetonius:

> Reliqua bella per legatos administravit, ut tamen quibusdam Pannonicis atque Germanicis aut interveniret, aut non longe abesset, Ravennam vel Mediolanum vel Aquileiam usque ab urbe progressus est, et Iulia eum comitata Aquileiae abortu facto puerum amisit.

Gloriosissime vero de Aquileia scribit Iulis Capitolinus in vita duorum Maximinorum his verbis:

> Praetereundum ne illud quidem est, quod tanta fide Aquileienses contra Maximinos pro senatu fuerunt ut funes de capillis mulierum facerent cum deficerent nervi ad sagittas emittendas.

That Aquileia is the foremost city of what was once Transpadane Gaul, and very powerful and even beautiful, set back from the coast, Pliny tells us in his fifteenth book. But it is now nearly abandoned. For few men live there; its cathedral is decorated and beautiful and there are a few priests, clerics, and those dedicated to worship there. There are a few shepherds and fishermen, but now no inhabitant, so that one can hardly call a small *castello* what was formerly a great city. Some ruins of the works of the patriarch Pepus survive: the church just mentioned, and the hall of the patriarch, and walls surrounding the small town, and a convent. The long-ago builders of this city are lost from memory, but Livy writes of it in his section on the Macedonian War:

> Fabius' letter caused great fear at Rome. This was all the greater because after a few days Marcellus came to Rome after Fabius' army had been surrendered, and said that the army could not be betrayed to the Ligurians, because there was a war with the Istrians who were keeping a colony from being established at Aquileia.

And a little later, Livy says, "A Latin colony, Aquileia, was established in the same year in the territory of the Gauls."

Aquileia began to flourish, however, in the time when the Romans **[385B]** first began to set about subjugating the barbarians living on the Danube. Augustus used to frequent that part of Italy in order to be closer to his legates, whom he used for the most part to manage the wars there. As Suetonius tells us,

> He conducted the rest of the wars through legates. He wanted, however, either to participate in, or to be close to, the warfare with certain of the Pannonians and Germans; so he left Rome for Ravenna or Milan or Aquileia. Julia went with him, after she lost a son to a miscarriage at Aquileia.

Julius Capitolinus glorifies Aquileia in the following words from his *Life of the two Maximini*:

> I must not omit the faithfulness of the citizens of Aquileia to the side of the senate when fighting against the Maximini; they made ropes out of their women's hair to replace the bowstrings they lacked for shooting their arrows.

Et inferius asserit Capitolinus nuntium qui ex Aquileia ad significandam Maximini mortem Romam fuerat missus, tanto impetu mutatis apud Ravennam animalibus cucurrisse, ut quarta die Romam venerit.

Eius vero urbis amplitudo maxima unde processit non iniucundum, aut inutile fuerit explicare. Primum legiones Romanas ibi obversatas ut claustra Italiae tuerentur, [385C] eam non peperisse opum affluentiam, quae fuit Aquileiae. Hinc constare videtur quod nec Ravenna neque Mediolanum neque in Gallis Marsilia aut in Hispanis Taraco, apud quas urbes Romanae legiones diutissime fuerunt moratae, ad id opulentiae aut divitiarum potuerunt pervenire. Auxit igitur mirabili incremento et immense ditavit Aquileiam, orientalium occidentaliumque mercimoniorum mutua comportatio ibidem instituta quod nullus stante Aquileia locus alter circa Adriaticum mare fuit in cuius portu et diversorio occidentales orientalesque pro commutandis mercandis coemendisque et vendendis invicem rebus convenirent.

Eademque ratio Spinam olim urbem ut inquit Plinius iuxta Padum et Ravennam a Diomede conditam, et ea omnino destructa Adriam, quae mari Adriatico nomen dedit, et postremo diruta Aquileia Venetias crescere augeri et mirum in modum ditari fecit. Longum nimis atque superfluum fuerit res apud Aquileiam gestas ex nostro instituto recensere, quia id a nobis multis in locis diligenter est factum. Sed virorum eius urbis ornamenta non duximus omittenda. Evangelista Marcus dum a beato Petro Apostolorum Christi [385D] principe in Alexandriam mitteretur, navigaturusque naves illic ex more ut diximus operiretur. Aquileienses ad Christi fidem convertit, sanctumque Evangelium suum cuius codex manu exaratus sua Venetiis nunc veneratissime servatur scripsit. Hermacorasque et ipse sanctus ad Marci praedicationem conversus a beato Petro Aquileiae et omnis Venetiae protopraesul institutus omnem eam regionem deo nostro lucratus est. Quem Nero imperator et simul Fortunatum subdiaconem securi percussit. Syrus exinde vir Aquileiensis doctissimus Papiam ab Hermacora missus mira sanctitatis opera ibi edidit. Fuit et Aquileiensis Chromatius, ad quem gloriosus Hieronymus multa inscripsit opera multasque exstantes dedit epistolas. Nihilque fecisse videtur gloriosius Chromatius, quam quod beati Hieronymi notarios atque librarios sustentavit. Praestantem ultimo loco Aquileiensem virum ponimus Ruffinum presbyterum Latinum Graecisque litteris adeo eruditum,

And later he says that the messenger who was sent from Aquileia to Rome to announce the death of Maximinus changed horses so speedily at Ravenna and traveled so fast that he came to Rome in four days.

The story of the source of this city's expansion is not unpleasant or irrelevant to tell. The Roman legions were first stationed here to guard the key defense points of Italy, **[385C]** but they did not give rise to the wealth which Aquileia enjoyed. It seems to be generally agreed that none of the places where Roman legions stayed for a long time, neither Ravenna, nor Milan, nor Marseilles in Gaul or Tarraco in Spain, were able to reach that level of wealth. It was, therefore, the trade in import and export of goods from the Orient and the West which was established at Aquileia that enriched it with such marvelous growth. As long as Aquileia stood, there was no other place around the Adriatic Sea whose port both received western and Oriental merchants and enabled them to exchange their wares.

In the same way we can account for the growth and marvelous prosperity of the former city of Spina, which Pliny says was founded by Diomedes between Padua and Ravenna; and after Spina's destruction Adria, which gave its name to the Adriatic Sea; and finally after Aquileia's destruction Venice grew and prospered. It would be a lengthy and useless task to review here, in accordance with my method, the history of Aquileia; I have gone through it at length in many places elsewhere. But I consider worth including the distinction conferred upon the city by her famous men. The Evangelist Mark was sent to Alexandria by **[385D]** St. Peter, chief of Christ's Apostles, and while waiting to sail he fitted out his ships at Aquileia, as was the custom, and as I have noted. He converted the people of Aquileia to Christianity, and a codex of the holy Gospel in his own hand is reverently preserved now at Venice. Hermacoras, himself a saint as well, was converted by St. Peter to Mark's preaching at Aquileia. When he became established as chief patron of all Venice, he converted that entire region to our Lord. But the emperor Nero beheaded him along with his subdeacon Fortunatus. Hermacoras had sent Syrus, a learned man of Aquileia, to Pavia, where he published works of marvelous holiness. Chromatius, too, was from Aquileia, the addressee of many of the glorious saint Jerome's works; he gave him many letters which still survive. Chromatius' most glorious deed was to support St. Jerome's clerks and copyists. Finally, I mention an outstanding man of Aquileia: the presbyter Rufinus, so learned in both Latin and Greek

ut eius quae exstant cum opera tum translationes nullis cuiuspiam ecclesiae doctoris operibus secundas eloquentia ornatuque ducamus.

Visitur Aquileiae marmoreus lapis grandes elegantesque litteras huiusmodi incisus:

> Imperator Caesar Augustus Aquileiensium restitutor et conditor: viam quoque geminam a porta usque ad pontem per tirones iuventutis novae Italiae sui dilectus **[386E]** posterioris, longi temporis labe corruptam munivit ac restituit.

Adiacet sinistrorsum Aquileia Natisoni fluvio, cui nunc Lisontio est appellatio. Et eo qui ad Talliaventum amnem proximum intercedit campestri, in spatio supereminet Aquileiae ad triginta milia passus Utinum, praestans ditissimumque regionis oppidum novi nominis, quod nec in Gothorum, neque in Longobardorum aut proximioribus aetati nostrae rebus gestis id invenitur. Hinc quod vulgo fertur, Austrinos eum ad trecentesimum ab hinc annum condidisse credo. Eam enim regionem duces Austriae tunc temporis optinebant. Habet vero nunc Utinum Iacobum civem et Aquileiae canonicum eloquentia ornatissimum.

Suntque superius ad primos colles Fasagna, superiori loco in montibus Glemona vetusti quod Gothorum Longobardorumque historiae habent nominis oppidum. Et ad Natisonem est in montibus Ventionum. Natisoni sinistrorsum est propinquum Mons Falco, oppidum regionis egregium arduo in monte situm, quod Theodericus rex Ostrogothorum primus aedificavit. Superius celsos inter montes est Civitas Austriae nunc Cividale appellata, quam urbem et **[386F]** aspectu veterrimam, et ut montuosa in regione speciosam, civilique cultu habitatam fuisse crediderim oppidum illud a Gallis prope Aquileiam aedificatum, de quo Livius libro XXVIII sic habet:

> Eodem anno Galli Transalpini transgressi in Venetiam sine populatione et bello, haud procul inde ubi nunc Aquileia est locum oppido condendo ceperunt. Legatis Romanis trans Alpes missis responsum est neque profectos ex auctoritate gentis eos nec quid in Italia facerent se scire.

Dirimitque urbs ipsa Germanos ab Italis certiore atque etiam celebratiore modo ceteris omnibus limitaneis vel urbibus vel oppidis, quae aut Gallis aut

that I consider his surviving works, not only writings but also translations, inferior in eloquence and embellishment to none of the works of any of the church fathers.

At Aquileia, one can see a block of marble inscribed with the following, in tall and elegant letters:

> The Emperor Caesar Augustus, restorer and founder of Aquileia, built up and restored the double road from the gate to the bridge which was ruined by the decay of long duration, through the labor of recruits from the youth of Italy, recruits levied from his own centurions. **[386E]**

Aquileia lies on the left bank of the Natisone river, now called the Isonzo. And in the fields lying between it and the next river, the Tagliamento, towering over Aquileia, thirty miles away, is Udine—a modern name—an excellent town, the wealthiest in the region. The name is not found in the histories of the Goths, nor of the Lombards, nor in histories of more modern times. From this I deduce that the common tale is true, that Austrians founded the town about three hundred years ago. For the dukes of Austria held it at that time. But now Udine boasts as its citizen Jacopo the canon of Aquileia, famous for his eloquence.

Higher up, in the foothills, is Fasagna, and higher still in the mountains Gemona, a town with an ancient name which occurs in the histories of the Goths and Lombards. And on the Natisone in the mountains is Venzone. On the left bank of the Natisone the closest town to the river is Monfalcone, the preeminent town of the region, located on a high mountain; it was built by Theoderic, first king of the Ostrogoths. Higher up, among the high mountains, is the city now called Cividale del Friuli, a city **[386F]** very old even in its appearance, beautiful, because it is in the mountains, inhabited by a civilized people; I believe that town was built by the Gauls near Aquileia. Livy writes the following about it in book 28:

> In the same year, the Transalpine Gauls moved into Venetia, but did not cause war or destruction. Not far from there, where Aquileia is now located, they seized a place for establishing a town. Roman envoys were sent across the Alps, to whom the Gauls replied that they had not set forth under any official authority from their tribe, nor did their tribesmen know what they were doing in Italy.

The city separates the Germans from the Italians more surely and even more famously than all the other bordering cities or towns, which are contiguous

Germanis aut Sclavonibus ubique in Alpibus sunt conterminae, quod mores in illa et omnis vitae apparatus a Germanis omnino est dissonus.

Supra Civitatem Austriae Natisoni continet Sofimbergum. Turro amni sub Civitate Austriae Natisonem illabenti, et quem Plinius cum Natisone Aquileiam profluere dicit, ad fontem in Alpibus adiacet Vapochum. Et infra ad medium sui cursum celso in monte appositum est Dogrium. Et supra Montem Falconem celsiore item sub Alpibus loco Cormona est oppidum in nostris **[386G]** Longobardorum historiis celebratum.

Sed ad ea quae maris litoribus sunt propinqua: post Montem Falconem celso item in colle est Duinum, nobile munitissimumque oppidum, et minore in colle Mocolanum. Deinceps urbs Tergestum Romana colonia, cum vetusta, tum etiam apud vetustos scriptores C. Caesarem in commentariis, Plinium et alios cum historicos tum cosmographos celebrata, tertioque et tricesimo miliario ut inquit Plinius distans ab Aquileia. Ultraque Tergestum sex milia passuum esse dicit Plinius Formionem amnem, cui nunc Cisano est appellatio, et undecim de ducentesimo passuum miliario a Ravenna distantem, qui quidem amnis fuerit antiquus Italiae terminus. Labitur autem is amnis Formio sive Cisanus inter Muglam proximum Tergesto oppidum et Iustinopolim urbem, Caput Histriae haud quaquam improprie appellatum quando ad praedictum Formionem Histria inchoetur.

Sed priusquam novae huic nobis regioni manum apponamus paucula explicemus quae retro in montibus de Foroiuliensibus sunt omissa. In ea montium parte quae in Adriaticum e regione Duini oppidi est versa, Goricia est sub Alpibus, quod oppidum familiae **[386H]** nobili patrium comitatus titulum referenti subditum populo et opibus est refertum. Supraque Tergestum pariter sub Alpibus est Castrum Novum.

with the Gauls or Germans or Slavs everywhere in the Alps, because their customs and all their way of life are so completely discordant from those of the Germans.

Above Cividale del Friuli, next to the Natisone, is Soffumbergo (?). The Torre river flows into the Natisone below Cividale, and next to its source in the Alps lies Vapochum. Pliny tells us that the Turrus along with the Natiso flows to Aquileia. And below, at the midpoint of its course, on a high mountain, is Dogrium. And above Monfalcone, higher up but still lower than the Alps, is the town of Cormons, which is frequently mentioned in our histories **[386G]** of the Lombards.

But to return to the places next to the sea: after Monfalcone, also on a high hill is Duino, a noble and well-fortified town, and Moccò, on a smaller hill. Then comes the city of Trieste, a Roman colony, not only ancient, but also famous from the ancient writers, Caesar in his *Commentaries*, Pliny and others who were historians as well as cosmographers. It is thirty-three miles, so Pliny tells us, from Aquileia. Six miles beyond Trieste, according to Pliny, is the river Formio, now called the Risano. Two hundred miles from Ravenna, this river formed the ancient boundary of Italy. This river, the Formio or the Risano, flows between Muggia, the next town to Trieste, and the city of Justinopolis, which is appropriately called Capodistria, since Histria begins at the Risano river.

But before I set my hand to this new region (Histria), let me go briefly through the places which I omitted back in the mountains in Friuli. In that area of the mountains which faces the Adriatic, looking from the area of the town of Duino, there is Gorizia, at the bottom of the Alps, a town well-populated and wealthy, which is subject to a **[386H]** noble family bearing the title of Count. And above Trieste, also at the foot of the Alps, is Castronuovo.

# Regio Undecima, Histria

Histriam nunc non quidem novam, quae ante Caesaris Augusti tempora Italiae censebatur, sed inter ceteras oras ultimo additam inchoemus. Eam Plinius ut in peninsulam excurrere dicit latitudine quadraginta milium circuitu vigintiquinque et centum. Et quidem a Formionis sive Cisani ostio ubi ultima est Tergestini sinus pars, ad F[*l*]anatici sinus, quem nunc Carnarium appellant, intimam concavitatem, ubi est Castrum Novum sive Arsiae fluminis ostium, via difficilior quidem per arduos montes, sed brevior vix quadraginta milia passuum implet, cum circuitus mari secundum litora factus supradicta XXV et centum amplissime complectatur. Hinc pulchrum est cognoscere oram Adriatici maritimam supra a Venetiis Iustinopolim usque a nobis descriptam, ubique sinuosissimam et adeo tortuosam esse, ut dimidio brevius sit mari quam terra directum e regione centum milia passuum iter.

A Phormione autem fluvio ad F[*l*]anatici **[387A]** sive Carnarii promontorium ea sicut dicit Plinius peninsula Histriae se in mare Italiam versus dextrorsum flectit. Sed ad rem. Histriam regionem Iapydiam prius simul cum Foroiulio appellatam vult ex Trogo Pompeio Iustinus sic fuisse appellatam ab Histri amnis, qui et Danubius accolis, qui cum Argo navim ab Argonautis a Danubio in Adriaticum mare umeris deferri adiuvissent, in ea Iapydum regione consedentes Histriam de patriae regionis nomine appellarunt.

Plinius vero cum aliquorum confutasset errorem dicentium et quidem absurdissime Histriam dici a parte Histri fluminis in Adriaticum delabente; subinfert Argo navim flumine in mare Adriaticum descendisse non procul Tergesto, nec iam constare quo flumine, Alpinosque diligentiores affirmare umeris fuisse travectam, subiisse autem Histro, dein Savo, dein Nauporto, cui nomen ex ea sit causa, inter Emoniam Alpesque exorienti.

Primae Histriae urbs est ut diximus Iustinopolis, quam Iustinus Iustiniani primi imperatoris filius atque imperii successor in insula tunc Capraria sed prius Pullaria appellata aedificavit. Causam autem eius condendae urbis

# Eleventh Region, Histria

Before the times of Caesar Augustus, Histria was considered part of Italy; so it is not now a new region, but let me begin by adding it to the last among the other regions. Pliny says that, as it extends into a peninsula, its width is forty miles and it is one hundred and twenty-five in circumference. And from the mouth of the Risano river, where the last part of the Gulf of Trieste is, to the innermost recess of the gulf of Flanaticus, which is now called the Gulf of Quarnaro, where Castelnuovo, or the mouth of the Arsa river is, measures scarcely forty miles: a rather difficult road through high mountains but rather short. After going around the sea, following the shoreline I mentioned, it fully covers one hundred and twenty-five miles. From here there is a fine view of the Adriatic coastline above, from Venice to Capodistria, which I have described; the coast is curves and twists so that the one-hundred-mile journey out of this region is shorter by half by sea than by land.

From the river Formio to the headland of Flanaticus [387A] or Quarnaro, the peninsula, as Pliny calls it, of Histria turns to the right into the sea, towards Italy. But I return to my subject. Justin, relying on Pompeius Trogus, said that the region of Histria together with Forumiulium was formerly called Iapydia; it was named that by the inhabitants living near the river Hister, which is also called Danube, who, after they had helped the Argonauts carry the ship Argo on their shoulders from the Danube into the Adriatic sea, settled in that region, Iapydia, but called it Histria after their native region.

But Pliny, refuting the error of some who foolishly say that Histria is named for part of the river Hister which flows into the Adriatic, says that the ship Argo was carried into the Adriatic not far from Trieste, but it is not now established on which river; and that more careful authors report that men carried the Argo on their shoulders across the Alps, then proceeded up the Hister, then the Savio, then the Quieto which derives its name from this event and has its source between Emona and the Alps.

The first city in Histria is, as I said, Capodistria, built on the island then called Capraria, but Pullaria before that, by Justin, the son, and successor, of the first emperor Justinian. I mentioned in my *Histories* that his reason

in Historiis fuisse ostendimus, ut in eo natura loci munitissimo loco tuti essent **[387B]** Istriae populi, variis diutinisque barbarorum incursionibus agitati. Iungitur tamen continenti ea insula bracchio, mille passus longitudine et ad decem latitudine ducto, in cuius medio arx valida Leoninum appellata castellum oppidanis a terrestri oppugnatione praesidio est imposita. Magno fuit per aetatem nostram Iustinopoli ornamento Petruspaulus Vergerius iureconsultissimus et philosophus, quodque supra saepenumero diximus, inter primos huius saeculi eloquentissimus.

Primum a Iustinopoli V milia passuum semotum est Insula oppidum, et post tantundem inde distans Piranum civitas. Et tertio loco Salodi promontorium totidem abest passus, quartumque paris a superiori distantiae Humagum, nobile oppidum, cursu prope recto et ad Italiam transverso, per medium pelagus incurvari ferrique videtur. Deinceps aequaliore ad F[*l*]anaticum sive Carnarium promontorium, et tamen sinuosissimo inter se prospectu, cetera Istriae maritima oppida habentur, ab Humagoque quinque pariter milia passuum abest Emona civitas, cui nunc Civitati Novae est nomen, prope quam Nauporti sunt ostia fluminis, Quieti nunc appellati, in quem Alpibus exorientem **[387C]** Argo navim Plinius asserit fuisse dimissam.

Post Nauportum prima est Parentium civitas vetusta, cui Orsarium continet et mons et oppidum prominens illi impositum, post haec Ruvignum oppidulum, deinde sinu supereminet amplo colli imposita arduo naturaque loci munitissimo urbs Pola Romana colonia, et Histriae ac Italiae urbium postrema. Ab ea vero urbe incipiens F[*l*]anaticum promontorium postquam longo tractu contra Ariminum, vel sicut Plinio placet contra Anconem in mare se proripuit, sinum eiusdem nominis effecit quam nunc Carnarium diximus appellari. Estque eius sinus novum prisco correspondens vocabulum, quod F[*l*]anaticus a priscis a tempestatum frequentia atque, ut ita dixerim, insania, nunc vero Carnarius a multitudine cadaverum, quae frequentibus ibi tempestatibus fiunt, est appellatus.

Prius vero quam ea describimus quae F[*l*]anatico sinu apposita ad Arsiam amnem, certissimum atque notissimum Italiae ad Liburnos terminum pertinent mediterranea, quae altissimis in montibus a Iustinopoli ad Nauportum sive Quietum amnem interiacent explicabimus. Suntque in montibus Iustinopoli supereminentibus iurisdictionis suae castella Rasponum **[387D]** et Rogium. Sunt item in montibus a mari longius quam praedicta recedentibus in ea, quam diximus flectentis se ad Italiam peninsulae curvitate, Bulea,

for building this city was to provide a fortified place in that area to protect **[387B]** the people of Histria, who had long been harassed by various barbarian invasions. The island is joined to the mainland by a finger of land, one mile long and ten miles wide, in the middle of which is a stronghold, called Castel Leone, placed there to be a garrison for the townspeople against attack from land. Capodistria in our time boasts Pier Paolo Vergerio, legal expert and philosopher, and as I have often said in other parts of my work, among the foremost men of this century in eloquence.

The first town after Capodistria, five miles from it, is Isola. Equidistant from there is the city of Pirano, and the third in the series is the promontory of Salvore, and the fourth, equidistant from Salvore, is the noble town of Umago. The sea seems to be bent and to rush through the middle in an almost straight line pointing cross-wise towards Italy. Then on the same level as the promontory Flanaticus or Quarnaro, but on a winding curve, are the rest of the seacoast towns of Istria. Five miles from Umago is the city formerly called Emona, but which is now called Cittanova. Near this city is the mouth of the ancient Nauportus river, now called Quieto. It was into this river, where it has its source in the Alps, that Pliny claims **[387C]** the ship Argo was launched.

After the Quieto, the first city is the ancient one of Parenzo. Next to it is Orsera, the name of both a mountain and the town jutting out on top of it. After these places comes the small town of Rovigno, and then the city of Pola, a Roman colony, a well-fortified place which towers over the bay on a high hill; it is the last city in Istria and Italy. Here the promontory of Quarnaro begins; after a long stretch it juts into the sea opposite Rimini, or, as Pliny would have it, Ancona; and creates the bay of the same name which I said is now called Quarnaro. There is a new name for this bay which is not too different to the ancient name, because the ancient called it Flanaticus on account of its frequent raging storms, and, as I said, it is now called Quarnaro from the large number of bodies which appear there due to the frequent storms.

But before I describe the coastal towns on the Gulf of Quarnaro opposite the Arsa river, which is well-established as the border of Italy with the Liburnians, I shall lay out in detail the places which lie in between in the high mountains from Capodistria to the Quieto. In the mountains which overhang Capodistria, there are *castelli* in its jurisdiction named **[387D]** Raspo and Rozzo. There are also in the mountains (which go back from the sea farther than those previously mentioned), in that curve of the peninsula

Mimianum, S. Laurentius, Portulae, Grisana, et superiori loco, Pimontium, Pigmentium, et Petra Pilosa, quae omnia Iustinopolitanorum sunt oppida et castella. Medioque ferme eorum omnium spatio, Petram Pilosam inter et Portulam ac Primontem est oppidulum, nunc nomine Sdrigna, quod fuisse constat olim Stridonis oppidum. Unde gloriosissimus ecclesiae dei doctor illustratorque Hieronymus originem duxit. Et trans Nauportum sive Quietum amnem ad Arsiam usque amnem, castella nunc in montibus oppidaque extant vallis duo castra Iustinopolitanis supposita; superiusque Montona et Pissium.

Ne etiam superius promissum ulterius differamus, a F[*l*]anatico promontorio ad Arsiae amnis nostri limitis Italiae ostium, quo se in Carnarium sive F[*l*]anaticum sinum exonerat, oppida ipsi supereminent sinui, Albona et Terranova, quae duo et superius dictum Pisinum quod Arsiae et sinui F[*l*]anatico propinquent, Istriae atque Italiae ultima sunt censenda. Adhibita est nobis superiori loco describendis Istriae montium oppidis et castellis solito maior diligentia, quod quidem nulla alia fecimus ratione, quam ut rem minime nobis peritisque regionum dubiam, sed de qua multos ambigere vidimus praestantissimos Italiae, atque orbis Christiani **[388E]** aliarum provinciarum viros, doceremus. Stridonem oppidum gloriosi Hieronymi patriam in Italia, et quae nunc et quae Octavii Augusti imperatoris et multo magis Plinii atque etiam natalium ipsius Hieronymi temporibus erat, situm esse, ut tantum virum plane Italicum et non alienigenam fuisse constet. Idque verba sua de seipso scripta, in libro De viris illustribus certissimum efficiunt:

> Hieronymus presbyter patre natus Eusebio, ex oppido Stridonis, quod a Gothis eversum Dalmatiae quondam Pannoniaeque confinium fuit, usque in praesentem annum id est Theodosii principis quartumdecimum haec scripsit: vitam Pauli monachi, epistolarum ad diversos librum unum, et cetera.

Visitur vero apud Sdrignam sive Stridonem praedicti Eusebii genitoris Sancti Hieronymi sepulcrum, et fama per aetatis successiones tradita, et litteris laminae inscriptis plumbeae, in eo ut ferunt repertae notissimum. Videmus vero multis in eam de qua diximus opinionem ductos fuisse, ut crederent beatum Hieronymum Dalmatam fuisse, quia litteras illis adinvenerit composueritque a Latinis Graecisque diversas, quae sint postea appellatae Sclavonicaea Sclavonibus Germaniae olim populis, quos nunc appellant **[388F]** Boemos, a quibus sicut in Historiis ostendimus, regio Dalmatiae Histris contermina, paulopost functum vita ipsum beatum Hieronymum fuit oc-

which I said bends towards Italy: Buie, Momiano, San Lorenzo, Portole, Grisignana, and, higher up, Piedimonte di Taiano, Pinguente, and Pietrapelosa. All of these are towns and *castelli* in the jurisdiction of the people of Capodistria. Almost in the center of all of these, between Pietrapelosa, Portole, and Promontore, is a little town now named Stridone, and it is definitely the former city of Stridon, the birthplace of the glorious father and enlightener of the church, Jerome. And across the Nauportus (or Quieto) river up to the Arsa river there are *castelli* now in the mountains, and towns of the valley, two camps subject to the people of Capodistria; and higher up are Montona and Pisino.

Not to delay any longer what I promised earlier, from the promontory of Quarnaro to the mouth of the Arsa river, the boundary I am drawing for Italy, where it debouches into the bay of Flanaticus (or Quarnaro), two towns rise above the bay, Albona and Terranuova, and these two, together with the one higher up called Pisino, are close to the Arsa and the bay of Flanaticus, and are considered the last towns in Italy. I have been more diligent than usual just now in describing the towns and *castelli* in the mountains of Istria because I wanted to show something that is clear to me, but a point on which many disagree, and these the most outstanding men of Italy and of other areas of the Christian world. And that is that the town of Stridone, **[388E]** the location of the birthplace of the glorious Jerome, was and is in Italy, now and in the times of Augustus, and much more so in Pliny's time, and also in the time of Jerome's birth, so that it may be established clearly that such a great man was an Italian and not a foreigner. His own words from *On illustrious men* made this absolutely certain:

> Jerome, elder of the church, son of Eusebius from the town of Stridon which was destroyed by the Goths and was formerly a border town between Pannonia and Dalmatia, and up to the fourteenth year of the reign of Theodosius he wrote these works: A life of the monk Paul, one book of letters to various addressees, etc.

One can see at Stridon the tomb of Eusebius, the previously-mentioned father of St. Jerome; and the story handed down through the ages, and the inscription on a lead plate, found—so people say—in the famous tomb. I see that many men have been led to believe that Jerome was from Dalmatia, because he composed letters in a language different from Latin and Greek, afterward called Slavic after the Slavs, once a German people, who are now **[388F]** called the Bohemians. In my *Histories* I show that they occupied the area of Dalmatia, contiguous with Histria, a little after St. Jerome's death;

cupata, et semper postea sicut nunc quoque fit, Sclavonia est dicta. Et quidem non solum eas praedictis composuit, deditque Sclavonicas litteras, sed officium quoque divinum, quo catholici utuntur Christiani ex Graeco in id novum idioma traduxit, quod gloriosus pontifex Eugenius quartus, per nostras manus illis confirmavit.

Quo tempore apud Florentiam et Graecorum unio cum ecclesia occidentali est facta, et Armenii Iacobitae Nestorini ac Aethiopes acceperunt ab eodem Eugenio catholicae ecclesiae documenta. Illis vero, qui pertinaces contenderent beatum Hieronymum, si in patria sua idiomate ab Italico penitus alieno usus fuit, et suos contribules Histros uti docuit atque voluit, videri fuisse alienigenam, respondemus maiorem melioremque quam sit Histria partem esse Italiae Calabriam atque Bruttios, quibus in regionibus sine controversia Italicis et semper antea viguit, et nunc quoque viget Graecanicae linguae usus. Quinetiam circa Hastam Taurinos Eporedienses, et omnem eam Alpibus subiectam Italiae regionem, cui gentes diu **[388G]** praefuerunt Gallicae, alieno magis populi illi quam proprio idiomate Italico abutuntur. Pariter apud Vincentiam Veronamque praeclaras elegantissimasque moribus Italiae urbes, licet a Germani sint remotissimae, multi sunt vici, multa oppida ipsis subdita civitatibus, quorum populi Theotonica frequentius quam Italica locutione utuntur.

Sed etiam ad nostrum ordinem revertamur. Gesta in Histris particulatim referre non expedit, sed satis fuerit ea, quae supra diversis in locis sunt dicta, in suum hunc locum colligere. Primam scilicet invasionem factam in regionem ab Histris qui Iapydas vel expulerunt vel dominio oppresserunt. Teutanaque muliere praestantissima in Istris regnante, barbaros supervenisse, qui omnia in Istris ferro ignique vastarunt, tertiamque his populis fuisse maximam, et horribilem cladem illam a Visigothis illatam, de qua nos in Romanorum imperii inclinatione initio scripsimus, quae quidem clades illa fuit, de qua gloriosissimus ipse Hieronymus apud Bethleem degens voluit intelligi, et supradicto in libro De viris illustribus, et in expositionibus minorum duodecim prophetarum, ubi textum declarans prophetae Abacuch, **[388H]** multas in urbes provinciasque desolationes spiritu prophetico praedicentis, in hanc maxime sententiam commentatus est:

> Nonne hoc impletum esse audivimus, in nostrae originis regione finium Pannoniae atque Illyrici, ubi post varias barbarorum incursiones, ad tantam desolationem est perventum, ut nec humana ibi

and forever afterwards it was called Slavonia, as indeed it is now. Jerome composed not only the letters I mentioned above, and gave writing to the Slavs; he also brought them the divine office used by Catholic Christians, having translated it from Greek into their own new language. The glorious pope Eugenius the fourth has confirmed this to them by my hand.

When the union of the eastern and western churches was effected at Florence, the Armenians, Jacobites, Nestorians, and Ethiopians received documents of the Catholic church from this same pope Eugenius. But to those who stubbornly argue that St. Jerome taught and wished his fellow tribesmen the Histri to use them, if he used in his own country an idiom deeply foreign to Italian, and thus appears to have been a foreigner—I reply that Calabria and Cantazara are a greater and better part of Italy than is Istria; and in these regions, universally considered to be Italian, the use of Greek has always thrived, and is healthy today. But indeed around Asti, Turin, Ivrea, and all that region in the Alps under Italian jurisdiction, **[388G]** a region the Gallic races ruled for a long time, those peoples use a foreign dialect rather than their own appropriate language, Italian. In the same manner, at Vicenza and Verona, famous cities with elegant customs, although they are very far from Germany, there are many villages and many towns subject to those cities whose people use German rather than Italian.

But to come back now to my regular scheme. . . . It is not convenient to narrate here the details of Histrian history; it will suffice to bring together here the things I have already mentioned earlier at different points. The Histri made their first incursion into the region and either drove out or subjugated the Iapydes. While an outstanding woman, Teutana, ruled the Histri, the barbarians invaded, and laid waste to everything in Histria with fire and sword. The third invasion was the greatest, by the Visigoths, who inflicted a dreadful slaughter. I wrote about this in my *Histories*. Indeed, this was the disaster which the glorious Jerome, residing at Bethlehem, wished to make known, and in his book mentioned above *On Illustrious Men*, and in his explanations of the twelve minor prophets, where he sets forth the text **[388H]** of the prophet Habakkuk, who predicts with prophetic spirit great plundering in many cities and provinces, this observation of his is of particular interest:

> Have we not heard in our birthplace Pannonia and Illyria, where after various barbarian invasions, the desolation has reached such a point that no human being remains there, nor is any animal re-

manserit creatura, nec animal superesse conversarique dicatur, ex his, quae hominibus amicari et convivere consueverunt.

Quae quidem desolatio cum ad annos centum continuasset, Iustinum impulit ut sicut supra diximus, Iustinopolim munitissimo et tuto a barbarorum incursionibus loco, aedificari curaverit. Proximae vero aetati nostrae, in bello quod Venetos inter et Genuenses acerrimum fuit, et Iustinopolis de Venetis in potestatem Genuensium est facta, et ea adiacentesque urbes maxima calamitate aliquamdiu pressae et conculcatae fuerunt.

Finita iam ad hanc Alpium per milia passuum quadringenta et quinquaginta, ab Varo ad Arsiam amnem externis nationibus munimento Italiae oppositarum partem sit Italiae nostrae latitudo in recentem gloriosissimi Hieronymi doctoris commemorationem, qui sic eam et me sibi devotum ab omnibus tueatur adversantibus, sicut ad hos limites originem illum in ea habuisse ostendimus.

> ported to survive and dwell, of the species which usually live amicably with mankind.

When this desolation had gone on for a hundred years, Justin was motivated, as I said before, to build Justinopolis as a fortified place of safety from barbarian incursions. In a time very near to our own, during the fierce war between the Venetians and the Genoese, Capodistria changed from Venetian hands into the power of the Genoese, and it and the neighboring cities were for some time oppressed and crushed by great disaster.

Let my description of the breadth of our country now be finished, to this part of the Alps through five hundred and forty miles, from the Var to the Arsa river, part of the regions opposed as a bulwark against foreign invaders, in remembrance of the glorious father Jerome; thus may he keep Italy safe from all enemies and preserve me, his devoted admirer, as I have shown that he was born at these borders and in this country.

# Preface
# Commentary

This *Preface* was first written for B. by Francesco Barbaro (in A. Quirini, *Barbaro Diatriba praeliminaris in duas partes divisa ad Francisci Barbari et aliorum ad ipsum epistolas* [Brescia, 1741] clxxi–clxxiii) for the intended presentation of *It. ill.* to Alfonso of Aragon, King of Naples, at whose insistence B. had begun work on a treatment of famous men of Italy which was the first incarnation of the present work. In the summer of 1451 B., in Venice, met Alfonso's ambassadors and gave them to take to the king the part of *It. ill.* he had written, augmented by Barbaro's Preface, in which Barbaro had written for B., "I have traversed all of Italy so that I could not only be among the men of the present time in Italy, a thing which had been my goal from the beginning (*quod a principio quaesiveram*), but . . . so that I might live into the future also with men of later ages" (*Quod a principio quaesiveram* likely alludes to the work's genesis in Alfonso's request for a catalogue of illustrious contemporaries). B. later made changes to the *Preface*, and the revised version was published in the early printed editions of *It. ill.* (including this one; see Nogara, *Scritti Inediti*, 122).

**[293A]** *Alexander Antoni(n)us.* The emperor Severus Alexander (r. 222–235); see E. Hohl, ed., *Scriptores Historiae Augustae* 2 vols. (Leipzig: Teubner, 1927; repr. with additions and corrections by C. Samberger and W. Seyfarth, 1971) 2, 251–305. The biography (16.3) asserts that when deliberating important matters of war he consulted men who knew history for precedents among the Roman or foreign emperors. He was 13 years old when he acceded to the throne; his mother Iulia Mamaea was the real ruler for his entire reign. The *Life* (3.1) notes his frequent appellation, reflecting his subservience to his mother (*Alexander igitur, cui Mamaea mater fuit* [*nam et ita dicitur a plerisque*]). The *Life* calls him (63.6) *imperatorem optimum*, and B. agrees with this assessment possibly because he presented a popular and healthy relief after the reign of Elagabalus; because after Severus Alexander followed a military anarchy which contrasted with his reign;

and because he suited B.'s purpose so well here, in that he honored history and historians. See Clavuot 24, esp. n. 11, on B.'s similar expressions in his dedication of eleven books of his *Historiarum Decades* to Leonello d'Este.

*Fabius* . . . *Pictor* et al. An organizing principle in this list is difficult to discern. Fabius Pictor, Roman senator of the third century B.C., wrote in Greek a history of Rome and exemplifies the aristocrat involved in the events he is relating; he was the first to explain Rome to the Hellenistic world. Lucius Licinius Lucullus, cos. 74 B.C.; Aulus Postumius Albinus, Roman senator and consul. (151 B.C.) wrote a history of Rome in Greek; Gaius Asinius Pollio, 76 B.C.–A.D. 4, wrote *Historiae* in Latin; it is he who reproached Livy with *Patavinitas*, probably meaning dialectic Latin with a northern accent. Cornelius Nepos (c. 109–after 27 B.C.), well-known as a biographer mainly because his work is the earliest surviving Latin biographical writing; his universal history has been lost. Although not impressive for erudition, Nepos was important to fifteenth-century humanists because he provided an additional model of the biography of a single individual, an enhancement of the "Suetonian-Plutarchan tradition." (See Cochrane, *Historians and Historiography,* 405–407.)

*Caius Caesar* Julius Caesar wrote commentaries on his activities in two wars (*Bellum Gallicum* and *Bellum Civile*).

*Octavius Augustus* Augustus was the author of an autobiography and numerous works in prose, according to the *Vita* (85) in Suetonius.

*Hadrianus* Hadrian wrote his autobiography (Hohl v.1, 3 . . . *in libris vitae suae* . . . ). We know from Dio (69.3.1–2) that Hadrian also composed many works in both prose and verse; as to a specific work of history, neither Dio nor the *Historia Augusta* mentions one. See H. Benario, *A Commentary on the Vita Hadriani in the Historia Augusta.* American Classical Studies 7 (Atlanta: Scholars Press, 1979), 100. That B. used the *Historia Augusta* extensively for facts about the emperors' lives we can understand from *Roma triumphans* 149 B.C.:

> Hadrianus post eum et alii tres et viginti secuti sunt principes Augusti et plurimi Caesares et tyranni, quorum gesta a septem referuntur scriptoribus in unicam codicem (nescius a quo) ordini digesta suntque hi scriptores Aelius Spartianus, Iulius Capitolinus,

> Flavius Eutropius, Flavius Vopiscus Syracusanus, Trebellius Pollio, Helius Lampridius et Vulcatius Gallicanus. Imperatorum vero praeter tyrannos, qui inciderunt, et a dictis septem scriptoribus celebrantur hic est ordo.

Clavuot 171, n. 135, notes that B. frequently ornaments the text of *It. ill.* with mentions of Hadrian. His familiarity with details of this emperor's life may account for Hadrian's appearance in the *Preface* and elsewhere in *It. ill.*

**[293C]** *perductus ad litus* . . . An obvious, although to my knowledge previously unnoticed, imitation of Virgil, *Aen.* 1.118–119, the shipwreck of the Trojan ships off Carthage:

> apparent rari nantes in gurgite vasto,
> arma virum tabulaeque et Troia gaza per undas.

> There appear on the surface above the whirlpool a few survivors, swimming, and floating on the waves can be seen arms, men, and tablets, and the treasure of Troy. (Text for this and all subsequent citations of Virgil is R. A. B. Mynors, ed., *P. Vergili Maronis Opera* [Oxford: Clarendon, 1969]).

## EXORDIUM

**[294E]** *Hesperia in magna* Beginning with a citation from the seventh book of the *Aeneid,* from which he cites most heavily because of its frequent mentions of ancient Italian places and peoples, B. gives the opening address (*Aen.* 7.1–4) to Aeneas' nurse Caieta. As is usually the case in *It. ill.,* the context of the words appears to have little importance for him.

> Tu quoque litoribus nostris, Aeneia nutrix,
> aeternam moriens famam, Caieta, dedisti;
> et nunc servat honos sedem tuus, ossaque nomen
> Hesperia in magna, si qua est ea gloria, signat.

> You also, Caieta, nurse of Aeneas, have in your death given eternal fame to our shores; and your praise now preserves a place in great Hesperia, and marks your body and your name, if that amounts to any fame.

**[294F]** *querno folio adsimilis* B. adheres closely in language to his source, Pliny *NH* 3.43:

> Est ergo folio maxime querno adsimulata, multo proceritate amplior quam latitudine, in laevam se flectens cacumine et Amazonicae figura desinens parmae, ubi a medio excursu Cocynthos vocatur, per sinus lunatos duo cornua emittens, Leucopetram dextra, Lacinium sinistra. . . .
>
> (Italy) is in general similar to an oak leaf, much longer than it is wide. Where it bends to the left, at its end, it describes the shape of the shield of an Amazon, having a protrusion in the middle, called Cocynthos. From there, two gulfs with crescent shape create two capes: on the right Leucopetra, on the left Lacinium. (Text for this and subsequent citations from book 3 of Pliny's *Natural History* is H. Zehnacker, ed., *Pline l'Ancien Histoire Naturelle Livre III* [Paris: Les Belles Lettres, 1998].)

B. has lifted the measurements as well from Pliny, *ibid.,* 3.44. The miles indicated here are of course Roman miles, equivalent to 1480 metres or 1618 yards. 1020 miles equal 1509 kilometres.

*a barbarorum, ut inquit Cicero* . . . B. paraphrases, probably from memory, *de Provinciis Consularibus* 14.34:

> Alpibus Italium munierat antea natura non sine aliquo divino numine; nam si ille aditus Gallorum immanitati multitudinique patuisset, numquam haec urbs summo imperio domicilium ac sedem praebuisset. Quae iam licet considant! nihil est enim ultra illam altitudinem montium usque ad Oceanum quod sit Italiae pertimescendum.

See also *Phil.* 5.37 for the same image:

> Dubitaret, credo, homo amentissimus atque in omnibus consiliis praeceps et devius non solum cum exercitu suo sed etiam cum omni immanitate *barbariae* bellum inferre nobis, ut eius furorem ne *Alpium* quidem *muro* cohibere possemus. (This and all subsequent citations of Cicero's *Philippics* are from D. R. Shackleton Bailey, *Cicero: Philippics* [Chapel Hill and London: University of North Carolina Press, 1986].)

**[294G]** *ex Strabonis Cretensis geographia* How B. knew Strabo's work is an interesting question, for he was admittedly inexpert in Greek; he nevertheless relies heavily on Strabo for his description of Latium (in his third chapter, "Latina"). But the translation of Strabo's *Geography* into Latin was not accomplished until 1458, by Guarino, who began it in 1453; too late for B. to use for the first edition of *It. ill.,* although he might have had access to unpublished informal translations. See N. G. Wilson, *From Byzantium to Italy: Greek Studies in the Italian Renaissance* (Baltimore: Johns Hopkins 1992) 47; 55–56.

**[294H]** *diis sacram*. . . . With little regard for context, B. lifts out of Pliny summarized phrases that have lost in excision the connection they had in the original. Pliny concludes his rapid tour of the region of Italy, *NH* 3.138:

> Haec est Italia diis sacra, hae gentes eius, haec oppida populorum. Super haec Italia, quae L. Aemilio Paulo C. Atilio Regulo cos. nuntiato Gallico tumultu sola sine externis ullis auxiliis atque etiam tunc sine Transpadanis equitum LXXX, peditum DCC armavit, metallorum omnium fertilitate nullis cedit terries. . . .
>
> This is Italy, land sacred to the gods, these her tribes, these the towns in which her people live. In addition, this Italy, when in the consulate of Aemilius Paulus and Atilius Regulus the invasion of the Gauls was announced, marshalled on her own, without help from abroad or, at that time, even from Transpadane Gaul, eighty thousand cavalry, and seven hundred thousand infantry. This land yields to none in the abundance of mineral resources. . . .

By condensing this section in indirect statement, B. robs the original of its rhetorical embellishments, such as the tricolon and anaphora of the first sentence, and reduces Pliny's praise to a bare statement of the numerical strength of Italian military levies, in which the emotional *diis sacra* now sounds slightly ridiculous.

**[295A]** *equitum triginta, peditum octingenta milia* . . . B. has transferred the numbers erroneously, unless it is a matter of this edition's mistaken printing. Pliny states (*NH* 3.138) the figures at 80,000 cavalry and 700,000 infantry. See Clavuot, 188–190.

*pro[d]iderunt* I have adopted the reading of the Verona 1482 edition, instead of that in the Basel 1559 edition, *providerunt.*

*Guido presbyter Ravennas* With the name Guido, B. refers to an anonymous eighth-century geographer of Ravenna whom he has confused with his twelfth-century epitomator, Guido of Pisa. The anonymous Ravennate had digested the information in Hyginus' now-lost work on Italian cities; see Clavuot 161 n. 92; 189.

**[295B]** *Centumcellae ... Morlupo* Centumcellae corresponds to the modern Civitavecchia. See Clavuot 190 n. 204; he speculates that B.'s Morlupo is the modern Morlupum Castellum, but adds a question mark in parentheses, indicative of the difficulty in correlating modern sites with many of B.'s toponyms.

**[295C]** *Italiam peragratus ero....* This may be Barbaro's impression of B.'s method of work, or the impression he wished to make upon Alfonso. But as Jeffrey White notes, "Toward a Critical Edition," 274–5,

> the statement (made for him by Barbaro) ... must be understood metaphorically. We have no evidence (in the *It. ill.* or from elsewhere) of extensive peregrinations *for reasons of scholarship* for this period. Such on-the-spot investigations as Biondo did undertake in connection with the *It. ill.* must have been coincident with and subordinated to attempts to find employment—or they were reminiscences of earlier times put to a fresh application.... Though this is not to say that we do not discover our author in several places over the next three years, nevertheless the *It. ill.* smacks at least equally of the study as of the open road.

# First Region, Liguria Commentary

Biondo credits much of his information in this chapter to the treatise composed in 1442 by his friend, the Genoan Giacomo Bracelli (1390–1466 or later), important in the history of Ligurian humanism in the fifteenth century. This treatise, a small historical-geographical work entitled *Orae Ligusticae descriptio* (*Iacopo Bracellii Genuensis De Bello Hispaniensi Libri Quinque. Eiusdem de Claris Genuensibus libellus. Orae Ligusticae descriptio* [Rome: apud Heredes Antonii Bladii Impressores Camerales, 1573]), described the Ligurian coast from the Var river to the Magra river. In 1448 Bracelli had sent to Biondo a second edition, which Biondo reproduces almost literally here in this first chapter of *Italia illustrata* (cf. Fubini, "Bracelli, Giacomo," *DBI* 13 [1971] 652–653, for specific instances of B.'s dependence on Bracelli, see Clavuot, 244–249). This reliance sets the chapter "Liguria" somewhat apart from Biondo's treatment of other regions: because he follows Bracelli, B. neglects to orient the reader by hydrographic and orographic mark; because Bracelli described the coast of Liguria, Biondo does not venture to describe the topography and settlements of the interior (the well-developed portolan tradition, made for the use of seafarers, which depicted ports along the coast, also influenced this emphasis). Despite Biondo's lack of Greek, he could have acquired knowledge of the history of the region through Jacopo Angeli da Scarperia's translation into Latin of Plutarch's *Life of Marius*, an important source for Liguria's topography and history in the Roman period. (Angeli completed this translation in 1409 or 1410; see Roberto Weiss, "Iacopo Angeli da Scarperia," *Medioevo e Rinascimento. Studi in onore di Bruno Nardi*, 2 vols. [Florence 1955] II, 803–817, repr. in *Medieval and Humanist Greek: Collected Essays by Roberto Weiss* [Padua: Antenore, 1977] 255–277], 273.) *The Itinerarium Syriacum* (1358) of Petrarch, which gives information on the state of geographical knowledge in Petrarch's time, presents a description of the Ligurian coast similar to B.'s here in "Liguria," including many of the same names of cities and towns (see now Theodore J. Cachey, Jr., ed. and transl.,

*Petrarch's Guide to the Holy Land: Itinerary to the Sepulcher of Our Lord Jesus Christ* [Notre Dame, Indiana: University of Notre Dame Press, 2002]).

On Genoese culture, see Steven A. Epstein (*Genoa and the Genoese, 958–1528* [Chapel Hill and London: University of North Carolina Press, 1996] 246 and n. 85); and below on **[298G]**.

The region of Liguria was much wider in the time of the Roman republic than now or in Biondo's time. The ancients identified Liguria as extending to the Rhone at the western extremity, the Trebbia at its eastern; stretching across the Apennines through the valley of the Magra to the Mediterranean; in Gaul, extending from the coast inland to the level of the Isère; and in Italy up to the upper half of the course of the Po, and in the time of Justinian even beyond the Po, as Milan was considered the capital of Liguria; see W. H. Hall, *The Romans on the Riviera and the Rhone* (London 1898; repr. Chicago: Ares, 1974), ix.

**[295D]** Plinius Pliny names Liguria as his first region at NH 3.46–47:

> Nunc ambitum eius urbesque enumerabimus, qua in re praefari necessarium est auctorem nos divum Augustum secuturos, discriptionemque ab eo factam Italiae totius in regiones XI, sed ordine eo qui litorum tractu fiet; urbium quidem vicinitates oratione utique praepropera servari non posse, itaque interiore exin parte digestionem in litteras eiusdem nos secuturos, coloniarum mentione signata quas ille in eo prodidit numero. Nec situs originesque persequi facile est Ingaunis Liguribus—ut ceteri omittantur—agro tricies dato.
>
> I shall now go through the cities of Italy in a circuit. I must preface my account by declaring my intention to follow as my authority the divine Augustus and his division of the whole of Italy into eleven regions, but to take them in the order in which they come along the coast. In a summary like this one, it is not possible to keep the neighboring cities together; and so, in treating the interior, I shall preserve the alphabetical order of Augustus, and shall indicate the colonies with the classification which he published. It is not easy to specify their sites and foundations; for example, the Ligurian Ingauni, to mention just one population, three times received grants of territory.

*Pompeius Trogus* That Pisa was founded among the Ligurians, Trogus (20.1.6–7; 11) names *Pisae in Liguribus* as a city which retained traces of its Greek heritage. That Pompeius Trogus places Massilia among the Ligures and Gauls B. clearly founds upon *Hist. Phil. Epit.* 43.3, where Trogus, relating the history of the Etruscan monarchy at Rome, tells of the founding of Massilia by a band of Phocaean youth, *inter Ligures et feras gentes Gallorum.*

*Livius libro XLI* B. erroneously attributes this passage to Livy, book 41. It is to be found in the *Periochae*, book 60:

> M. Fulvius Flaccus primus transalpinos Ligures domuit bello, missus in auxilium Massiliensium adversus Salluvios Gallos, qui fines Massiliensium populabantur. M. Fulvius Flaccus was the first to overcome the transalpine Ligurians in war; he had been sent to help the people of Marseilles against the Salluvian Gauls, who were laying waste the territory of Marseilles.

*Livius ... libro nono* Livy's extant books indeed contain much material pertaining to the Ligurians, but B.'s citation of Livy here comes from 39.1.1,

> Dum haec, si modo hoc anno acta sunt, Romae aguntur, consules ambo in Liguribus gerebant bellum. Is hostis velut natus ad continendam inter. . . .
>
> While these affairs were being conducted at Rome [if indeed they took place in this year], both consuls were waging war with the Ligurians. This enemy seemed born to. . . .

**[296F]** *Servius Virgilium in undecimo. . . .* From *Aen.* 11.700, the slaying of Orsilochus by Camilla:

> incidit huic subitoque aspectu territus haesit
> Appenninicolae bellator filius Auni,
> haud Ligurum extremus, dum fallere fata sinebat.
>
> Frightened by this unexpected sight, the warrior son of Aunus the mountain-dweller stopped. (He was by no means the least skilled of the Ligurians at deception.)

**[296G]** . . . *Lucanus in primo* . . . 1.440–442 in A. E. Housman, ed., *M. Annaei Lucani Belli Civilis Libri Decem* (Oxford: Blackwell 1927), as are all my subsequent citations of Lucan. B.'s nonchalance about context appears clear here in his omission of line 440. When Caesar orders Roman soldiers to march on Rome, the various Italian peoples rejoice that the Roman troops stationed in Gaul are relinquishing their occupation of their territory and that they are free:

> tu quoque laetatus converti proelia, Trevir,
> et nunc tonse Ligur, quondam per colla decore
> crinibus effusis toti praelate Comatae. . . .

> You also rejoiced, Trevir, that the troops were moved, and you, shorn Ligurian, now rejoiced, you who formerly excelled all long-haired Gaul in the hair spread in beauty over your necks.

*Monoecus* Virgil *Aen.* 6.830–831:

> Aggeribus socer Alpinis atque arce Monoeci
> descendens, gener adversis instructus Eois!

> From the ramparts of the Alps, from the citadel of Monaco, the father-in-law will march down; the son-in-law will come against him with his Eastern army drawn up for battle.

**[296H]** *Torbia/Trophaea Augusti* (modern La Turbie). B. does not say on the basis of what evidence Bracelli concluded that Torbia, which is not shown on Berlinghieri's map of modern (*novella*) Italy, was the ancient Trophaea Augusti. B. apparently cites from *SHA Helvius Pertinax Iulii Capitolini* 1.2 and 3.3,

> natus est Pertinax in Appennino in villa matris . . . iussus est praeterea statim a Perenne in Liguriam secedere in villam paternam; nam pater eius tabernam coactili<a>riam in Liguria exercuerat. sed posteaquam in Liguriam venit, multis agris coemptis tabernam paternam manente forma priore infinitis aedificiis circumdedit; fuitque illic per triennium et mercatus est per suos servos.

> Pertinax was born in the Apennines on a farm which belonged to his mother. . . . Perennis ordered Pertinax immediately afterwards [i.e., after serving as consul four times and becoming wealthy] to withdraw to his father's farm in Liguria; his father had practiced the trade of clothmaking in Liguria. But after he got to Liguria, he bought many farms and added innumerable buildings on to his father's shop, which he preserved in its original structure. He stayed there for three years and kept the business going through his slaves. (Hohl, *SHA* 1, 115, 117)

But the information in 1–2 also occurs in Cassius Dio, 74.1, who specifies the place as Alba Pompeia in Liguria (the modern Alba).

**[296H]** *Abintimilium/Vintimilium* (modern Ventimiglia). See G. Petracco Sicardi and R. Caprini, *Toponomastica Storica della Liguria* (Genoa: Sagep Editrice, 1981) 11–12 and n. 5 (the capital of the Liguri Intemelii, Abintimilium takes its name from the ethnic Intemelii because it was the fundamental settlement of that tribe); 33 (Glossary #5); 54 (analysis of the linguistic elements comprising the name Ventimiglia).

**[297A]** *Album Ingaunum/Albinga* The modern Albenga lies southwest of Genoa on the Riviera di Ponente. Cf. Petracco Sicardi 11–12, 33, 54, and above on **[296H]**, Abintimilium.

**[297B]** *Vada Sabbati . . . Savona.* See Petracco Sicardi and Caprini 70 (Glossary #174, 175), who assert the etymological relationship between the similar roots of these two names. B. refers to Pliny, *NH* 3.48 and Mela 2.4.72.

*Thomas Fregosus* Tommaso Campofregoso (before 1370–1453), in the 15th century more commonly referred to as Fregoso, was doge of Genoa for 13 years (ruled from 1415–1421, regained the dogeship 1437, renounced the office in 1442), a record unique in the history of Genoa. In addition to his exceptional political qualities, he will have deserved B.'s mention here because of his well-known efforts in patronizing and encouraging humanist studies and literary men. See L. Amelotti, "Campofregoso, Tommaso," *DBI* 50 (1998), 448–451.

**[297C]** *Genua.* Modern Genova; in ancient times the capital and chief trading center of Liguria. B's dependence upon Bracelli is especially obvious here in the transferred details of the breakwater facing Africa and the uncertainty as to the reliability of the old stories about the city's foundation. The story of Phaethon is found in Hyginus, *Fabulae* 154: *Sorores autem Phaethontis, dum interitum deflent fratris, in arbores sunt populos versae*. The "absurd fiction about Janus," which B. says Bracelli does not reject, may be the "vulgar opinion" cited by the annalist Jacopo Doria (in Belgrano, Luigi T., ed., *Annales Ianuenses*, v. 1 Fonti per la storia d'Italia, n. 11 [Genoa 1890], 1099–1173. As Epstein, 64, summarizes it, "'Vulgar opinion' held that after the sack of Troy a certain Trojan inevitably named Ianus wandered into Liguria and built a castle on the present site of the archbishop's palace." A possible source is Jacopo da Varagine, *Cronaca* 4–5 [*Cronaca di Genova.*

Vol. 85, Fonti per la storia d'Italia. Rome, 1941]). *Pace* Biondo's *non improbat*, Bracelli (64) does withhold judgment (cf. Clavuot 90 and n. 233): *Cum antiquitatis suae multa sint argumenta; non illud in ultimis habendum puto, quod auctorem eius nemo satis affirmare ausus est.*

**[297D]** *Livius libro XXIX* B.'s Livy 29 is 30.1.10.

**[298E]** *Rotharis Longobardorum rex* B. must here be referring to the fact that in 641, Genoa was conquered by the Lombard king Rothari, the most competent of the Lombard kings, who conquered all of northern Italy and is known for the *Edictum Rothari*, the institution of Lombard law.

**[298G]** *Ludovicus Fregosius et al.* Lodovico Campofregoso, his mother Caterina Ordelaffi of Forlì, and her other son Giano Campofregoso.

*paucos habet egregie litteratos* ... Despite B.'s disparaging comment here and his naming of only three illustrious men of letters from Liguria, Bracelli named many; see Braggio, Carlo, "Giacomo Bracelli e l'Umanesimo dei Liguri al suo Tempi," *Atti della Societá Ligure di Storia Patria* 23 (1890), 5–295, who asserts (25) that B. comes to this conclusion because he limits himself to direct representatives of humanism. Braggio then proceeds to enumerate men who, although not purely literary men, participated nevertheless in the humanist movement, including the historiographers Giovanni Iacopo Spinola, the antiquarian Eliano Spinola, the archbishop Pileo De-Marini, *et al.* B.'s attitude here is in contrast to his generous assessment in his eighth chapter, "Venetia,"of many Venetian statesmen as distinguished in letters.

*Nicolaus Ceba.* A Genoese who was born between the end of the fourteenth to the beginning of the fifteenth century, and died sometime after 1475; he was more distinguished for counting numerous humanists among his friends than for his own activities, which were divided between business and culture. He was a friend of Giacomo Bracelli, Francesco Filelfo, and Ciriaco d'Ancona, and corresponded with Leonardo Bruni and Filelfo. Cf. M. Palma, "Cebà (Grimaldi), Niccolò," *DBI* 23 (1979), 186–187.

**[298H]** *San Fructuoso* Modern San Fruttuoso di Capodimonte, an example of a pagan cult frequented by Christians, and a Cluniac house from 984; see Epstein, 18.

**[299A]** *Sigestrum vicus in litore* B. correctly identifies Sigestrum with the ancient Sigesta Tiguliorum: cf. Pliny, *NH* 3.48, . . . *portus Delphini, Tigulia intus et Segesta Tigulliorum, flumen Macra, Liguriae finis.*

**[299A–299B]** *Mons Ruber, Vulneria, Manarola, Rivus Maior*. With the exception of the lack of a Latin equivalent for Corniglia, the modern Cinque Terre: Vernazza (Vulnetia was in the *volgare* Vernatia), Monterosso, Corniglia, Manarola, Riomaggiore.

*Luna*. Cf. Weiss, *Discovery*, 111 and n. 8:

> . . . it was only as late as 1442 that Giacomo Bracelli established in his *Description orae Ligusticae* that the Gulf of La Spezia was the harbour of ancient Luni . . . an identification which was accepted by Biondo in the *Italia illustrata* and Berlinghieri in the *Geographia*.

**[299C]** *Lunai portum* . . . In the satire cited here by B. (*Sat*. 6.6–11), a letter to Caesius Bassus asserting that wealth is for using, Persius cites a line of Ennius (in W. V. Clausen, ed., *A. Persi Flacci Satirarum Liber* [Oxford: Clarendon, 1956]):

> . . . mihi nunc Ligus ora
> intepet hibernatque meum mare, qua latus ingens
> dant scopuli et multa litus se valle receptat.
> "Lunai portum, operae est, cognoscite cives."
> cor iubet hoc Enni, postquam destertuit esse
> Maeonides Quintus pavone ex Pythagoreo.

> Now the Ligurian shore warms me, the sea here hibernates where the cliffs present their huge side and the shore bends inwards in many inlets. "Citizens, you must see the port of Luna and get to know it." This Ennius' heart commands him to say, after he has dreamed while snoring that he was the reincarnation of Homer, who was in a previous life (according to the Pythagoreans) a peacock.

B. shows no awareness that he has here cited Ennius and not Persius, although B. himself alludes unmistakeably to Ennius elsewhere in *It. ill.*

**[299C]** *Macra augetur, quod Lucanus* . . . Although reading *nullos* for *nullas, moratur for moratus*, and *prorumpit* for *procurrit*, B. cites Lucan 2.426, both a geographical source and a literary embellishment, from the digression on the Apennines and their watershed, and the rivers that run down to seas on either coast (2. 392–438):

> nullosque vado qui Macra moratur
> alvos vicinae prorumpit in aequora Lunae
> tesca Siler nullasque vado qui Macra moratus
> alnos vicinae procurrit in aequora Luna.

He misunderstands Lucan's literal meaning; see White, "Toward a Critical Edition," 269, n. 9,

> . . . discussing the capacity of the harbor of Luna for the traffic of large vessels . . . supposing the river capacious likewise . . . whereas it 'delays no alder-wood ships' precisely because it is too shallow to allow them to navigate in the first place.

But in the larger context of his use of sources, B. also fails to take in the import of Lucan's passage as a whole, and its implications as a precursor of his own endeavor in *It. ill.*, a misunderstanding which supports Clavuot's general assertion (e.g., 181) that B. depended on a thematically-arranged collection of excerpts. Departing from Pompey's taking up a position at Capua, Lucan describes Italy as a geographic whole and the Apennines as the source of the rivers of Italy. Although B. uses elsewhere in *It. ill.* Lucan's epithets for rivers, *rapax Crustumium* (Conca, **[342G]**); *Liris* (Garigliano, **[406E]**); *nocturnae editor aurae Sarnus* (Sarno, **[420E]**), he expresses no recognition of the similarities of his own undertaking to Lucan's; for example "a representation of Italy as a system of rivers flowing east and west," a "verbal map," in Elaine Fantham's brilliant analysis of Lucan's conversion of geography for his own purposes, with comments on the importance of rivers to classical geographers and literary writers (E. Fantham, ed., *Lucan De Bello Civili Book II* [Cambridge: Cambridge University Press, 1992], *ad* 392–438).

*Spedia est novum oppidum.* The modern La Spezia; cf. Weiss, *Discovery*, 111.

*pictura a maioribus facta* Clavuot, 246 n. 144 suggests Ptolemy as the likely author of this map.

*Bartolomaeo Facio viro doctissimo est ornatum.* B. probably before 1405, not after 1410; d. 1457. Consigliere and chancellor of Francesco Spinola at Genoa, he conducted missions to Naples and enjoyed contacts and friendships with humanists of the Aragonese court. Wrote *De Bello Veneto Clodiano* (1444), a poem on the 1377 war between Genoa and Venice; *De vitae felicitate* (1445), a philosophical dialogue. But his most important work is considered *De rebus gestis ab Alphonso primo Neapolitanorum rege*. See P. Viti, "Facio, Bartolomeo," *DBI* 44 (1994), 113–121.

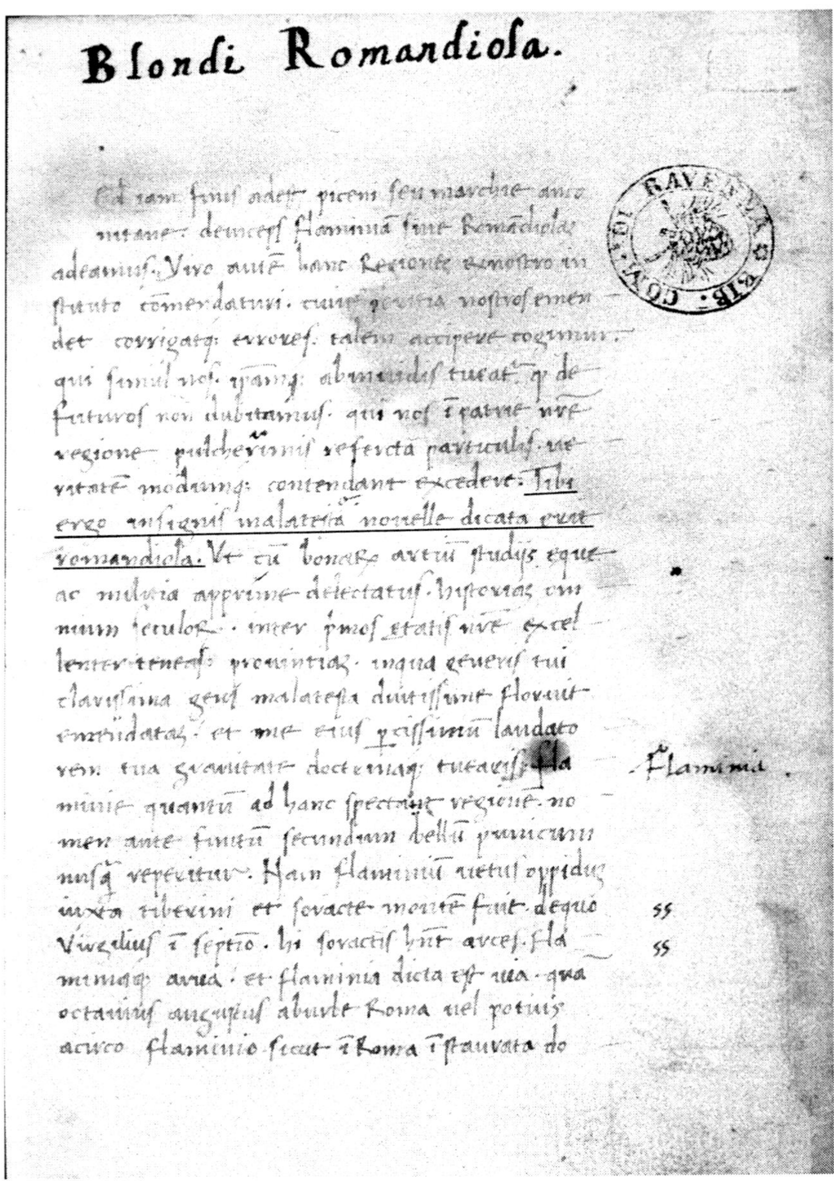
Blondi Romandiola.

Flaminia

Plate I. MS. Classense 203, fol. 6r, with dedication of the chapter "Romandiola" to Malatesta Novello (underlined; emphasis mine). Reproduced here by permission of Biblioteca Classense, Ravenna.

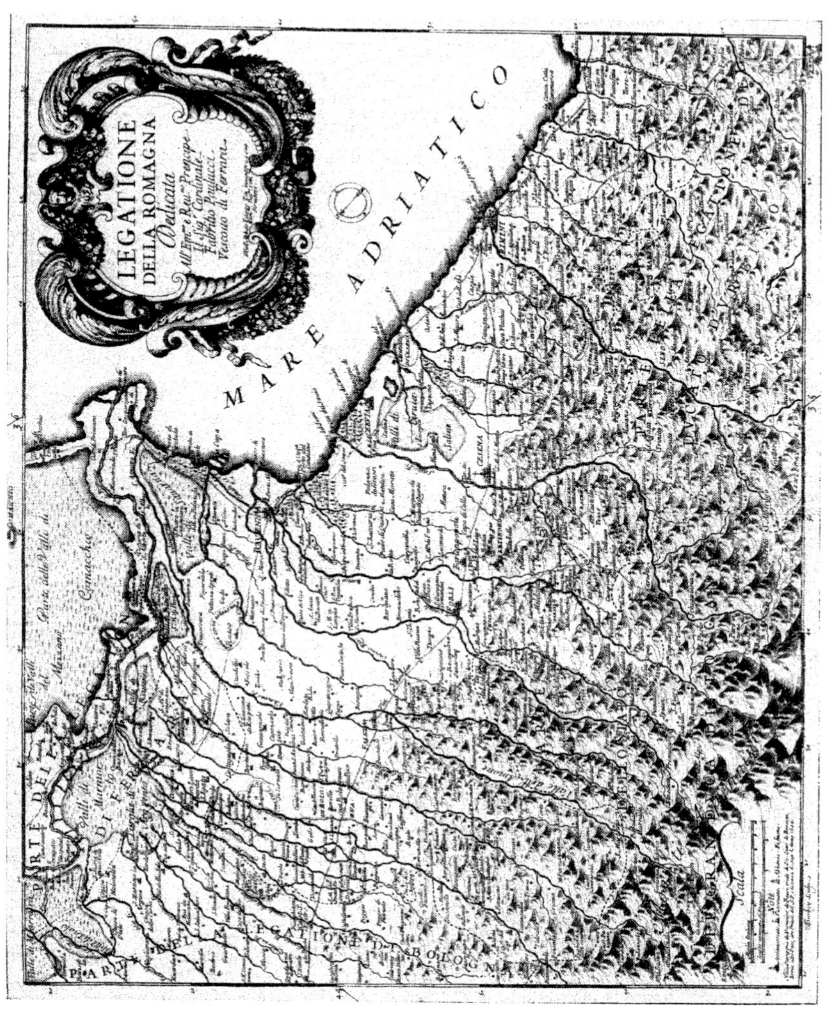


Plate II. Map of Filippo Titi, 1699. Archivio di Stato di Roma Coll. I, Cart. 96, N. 903. Reproduced by permission of the Archivio di Stato di Roma.

# Sixth Region, Romandiola
## Commentary

The modern district of Emilia-Romagna comprises the area described here and still corresponds to the area circumscribed by the boundaries mentioned by Pliny as the eighth region, Gallia Cispadana or Emilia: on the north, the Po; on the east, the shore between the Po delta and Gabicce; on the southwest, the watershed between Emilia and Tuscany. "Aemilia" is the name already used by Martial for the eighth imperial region, an area defined by Rimini, the Po, and the Apennines, corresponding to Gallia Togata. Under Hadrian, this area was divided between the ninth and tenth imperial regions. Paulus Diaconus described Emilia as ending at Imola (the ancient Forum Cornelii).

The name "Romagna" is a Byzantine appellation and appeared during Byzantine rule; it described citizens of the Roman Empire in Italy. Cf. John Larner, *The Lords of Romagna: Romagnol Society and the Origins of the Signorie* (Ithaca, NY: Cornell University Press, 1965), 205, who summarizes the boundaries of the province at different times in its history. A. Guillou identifies Romania as the official name in the era of the Franks for what had been the Exarchate of Ravenna; in "Esarcato e Pentapoli, regione psicologica dell'Italia bizantina," *Studi Romagnoli* 18 (1967): 297–319, Guillou claims a common mentality for this region's inhabitants during Byzantine domination (from 562 until 751). Guillou delineates, 298–299, the geographical boundaries of the region of the Exarchate and Pentapolis (the latter district), a name used by the Byzantines until 727, included Ariminum, Pisaurum, Fanum Fortunae, Sena Gallica, and Ancona, and identifies as its organizing principle its focus on Ravenna. For Biondo, the boundaries of Romagna were the rivers Foglia and Santerno; for his patron Pius II, however, Romagna included the whole of Emilia. The name *Romandiola* (*sc. terra*), derived from the adjective *Romandiolus*, is used by Latin writers (e.g., Dante, *de vulgari eloquentia* 1.10).

**[342E]** *Virgilius in VII* The relevant passage is *Aen.* 7. 691–697; the context, the catalogue of allies of Messapus. B. at 696 misreads or more probably mis-recalls "Flaminia" for "Flavinia."

> At Messapus, equum domitor, Neptunia proles,
> quem neque fas igni cuiquam nec sternere ferro,
> iam pridem resides populos desuetaque bello
> agmina in arma vocat subito ferrumque retractat.
> hi Fescenninas acies Aequosque Faliscos,
> hi Soractis habent arces Flaviniaque arva
> et Cimini cum monte lacum lucosque Capenos.

> Messapus, breaker of horses, son of Neptune, whom none had power to kill by fire or sword, suddenly called into battle his people, for a long time grown soft and unused to war; he drew the sword once more. The Faliscans came from hill and plain, from Mount Soracte, the Flavinian fields, Mount Ciminus and its lake, and from the groves of Capena.

*Hanc regionem Livius Patavinus ... Arimini verbo appellat* B. has paraphrased, rather than citing as he indicates, Livy 24.44.2–3, where assignment to the consuls of provinces, armies, and wars (213 B.C.) includes *P. Sempronio provincia Ariminum.*

**[342F]** *Livius ... libro XXXVIII* It is not in book 38 as B. supposes, but in 39, that we find the mentions of Aemilius' roadbuilding and the anecdote about Flaminius' mistress from Placentia; both in 187 B.C. At 39.2.10–22, Aemilius conducts war with the Ligurians:

> Pacatis Liguribus exercitum in agrum Gallicum duxit viamque a Placentia ut Flaminiae committeret Ariminum perduxit.

> After making peace with the Ligurians, he led his army into Gallic territory, and built a road from Placentia to Ariminum, in order to connect it with the Via Flaminia.

For the second anecdote B. mentions, he has mistaken Flamininus for Flaminius; the connection with the Via Flaminia is tenuous at best. Livy (39.43.2–4) reports Valerius' Antias version of a story about Flamininus' putting a Gaul to death (184 B.C.), which among other offenses caused Lucius Quinctius Flamininus' (cos. 192 B.C.) expulsion from the senate. Choosing to dwell on the disasters which afflicted Piacenza in his own times, and asserting direct observation of its site (*perlustraverimus*), B. has omitted any reference to this passage in his treatment of Placentia (in "Lombardia," **[358F–359B]**):

> Placentiae famosam mulierem, cuius amore deperiret, in convivium arcessitam scribit. Ibi iactantem sese scorto inter cetera rettulisse quam acriter quaestiones exercuisset et quam multos capitis damnatos in vinculis haberet, quos securi percussurus esset. Tum illam infra eum accubantem negasse umquam vidisse quemquam securi ferientem, et pervelle id videre. Hic indulgentem amatorem unum ex illis miseris attrahi iussum securi percussisse.
>
> [Valerius Antias] writes that at Placentia a notorious woman, with whom Flamininus was desperately in love, had been invited to dinner with him. He was boasting to the prostitute, among other things, about how tough he was in the prosecution of cases and how many persons he had on death row, whom he intended to behead. Then the woman, reclining below him, said that she had never seen a person beheaded and was very eager to witness an execution. At this, Antias reports, the generous lover, ordering one of the wretches to be brought to him, cut off his head with his sword.

**[342G]** *rapax Crustumium*, Lucan 2.406. The ancient name of the river now known as the Conca, which debouches into the Adriatic at the modern town of Cattolica, figuring in Lucan's description of Pompey's march to Capua to occupy the city. In an excursus on Capua Lucan writes,

> In laevum cecidere latus veloxque Metaurus
> **Crustumiumque rapax** et iuncto Sapis Isauro
> Senaque et Hadriacas qui verberat Aufidus undas . . .
>
> To the east flow the swift Metaurus and rushing Crustumium,
> the Sapis together with the Isaurus, the Sena, and Aufidus
> which pounds the waves of the Adriatic . . .

Cf. Pliny *NH* 3.20.115, on the eighth region of Italy, Gallia Cispadana or Emilia:

> Octaua regio determinatur Arimino, Pado, Apennino. In ora fluuius Crustumium, Ariminum colonia cum amnibus Arimino et Aprusa, fluuius Rubico, quondam finis Italiae.
>
> The eighth region is bounded by Ariminum, the Po, and the Apennines. On the coast, the river Crustumium, the colony of Rimini

with the rivers Ariminus and Aprusa, the river Rubicon, formerly the boundary of Italy.

**[342G]** *absorptum mari oppidum Concham* B. was the first to associate this legendary sunken city with the name Conca, an historically attested city whose site is in the environs of the modern Cattolica, a small resort town on the Riminese coast. The humanist's association of the two towns may be based on the fact that Cattolica appears as Conca in the "donation of Pepin," the transfer (754) to the papal state of towns that were in the exarchate, recovered for the Pope by King Pepin. B.'s belief in the existence of the sunken city and his association of it with the name of the historically-attested Conca perpetuated the myth in later historians and topographers who deferred to his authority as a Romagnol (Alberti [1567], Briet [1649], Sartoni [17th century], Muratori [1727], and most maps of early modern times [influenced by Alberti's account] which show the legend "Concha città profondata" in the sea opposite Cattolica; for an example, see Plate III, a seventeenth-century map showing the legend *Conca città sommersa* in the sea opposite Cattolica). For the identification and location of the original

Plate III. Detail of previous. Arrow in the Adriatic Sea on right indicates "Conca città sommersa."

town of Conca, its subsequent abandonment, and the meaning of the name Cattolica; and thorough recapitulation of previous bibliography on the subject, see M. L. De Nicolò, *La Strada e il Mare* (Villa Verucchio: LaPieve, 1993), 88–91; *Conca e Cattolica: La leggenda della città sommersa e le origini del nome* (Cattolica: Centro Culturale Polivalente, 1993); "I Caratteri della Storia di Cattolica: Miti, Leggende, Proverbi," (*Studi Romagnoli* 45 [1994]: 13–26); *Nuove Ricerche su Conca città sommersa.* Quaderni del Museo di San Giovanni da Marignano 1 (Marignano 1985); *Conca e Cattolica. La leggenda della città sommersa e le origini del nome* (Fano, 1993). The first mention of a sunken city in the ocean off Cattolica occurs in an anonymous fourteenth-century Florentine commentator on Dante's *Inferno* (*Commento alla Divina Commedia d'anonimo fiorentino del sec. XIV*, P. Fanfani, ed., 3 vols. [Bologna 1866–1874]). The Florentine commentator explains that Cattolica was "coperta dal mare," covered by the sea (1:606, cit. De Nicolò, "I Caratteri . . . ," 14 n.2).

The suggestive masses under water in the stretch of ocean opposite Cattolica are probably explicable as port structures from the promontory of modern Gabicce Monte, which are known to have washed away through erosion; very likely rocks and crumbled fortifications could be glimpsed from above from boats, and gave the appearance of a submerged city (see the sketch by the 18th century Luigi Ferdinando Marsili [Plate IV], who drew some objects in the sea opposite Cattolica which he calls "torazza," towers).

Also tending to vitiate the tradition begun by Biondo is the hydrogeomorphological reality of this area over the past several centuries: the tendency has been to silt up, for the land to encroach upon the sea, not for the sea to swallow up settlements on the land, making it still less likely that a submerged city was visible off Cattolica.

On the other hand, a 16th century priest described Cattolica as ". . . inghiottita dalla terra, e sommersa d'acqua che occultamente gli era di sotto, hora è niente . . ." (swallowed up by earth and submerged in water which was concealed under it), and connects Cattolica with a river much older than his times (cit. De Nicolò, *La Strada e il Mare*, 88–91). DeNicolò concludes that such significant hydrogeologic disturbances have taken place in the area (for example the existence earlier than the Renaissance of four rivers flowing to the sea at this point on the Riminese coast), and the topography has so moved and changed, that whatever Biondo's informants saw is lost to us.

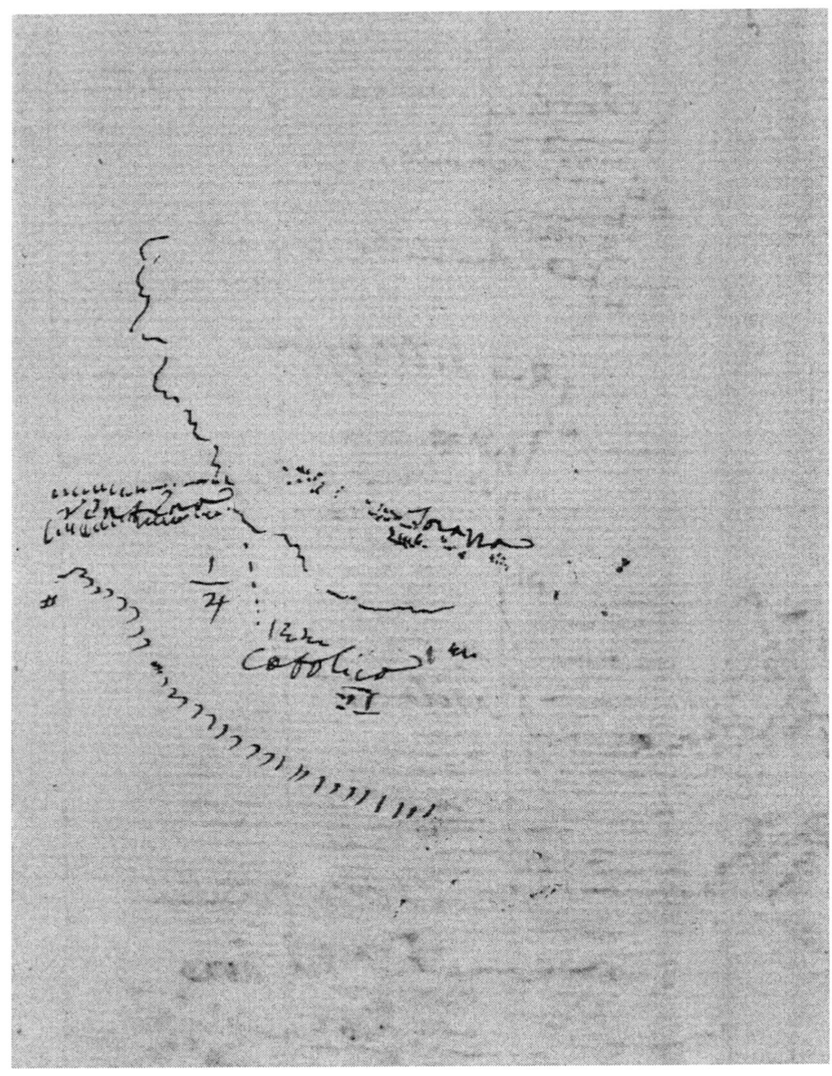

Plate IV. Luigi Ferdinand Marsili (18th c.), sketch of the coast near Cattolica (with annotation “torazza”). Biblioteca Universitaria di Bologna, ms. Marsili 72F/1, c.4. Reproduced by permission of the Ministero per i Beni e le Attività Culturali. Further reproduction or duplication by any means prohibited.

Biondo's son Gaspare was killed near Cattolica in a macabre coincidence reminiscent of the passage in *Inferno* (28, 76–90) which the abovementioned commentator glossed with the information that a submerged city could be seen off Conca: the account of the assassination of "i due miglior da Fano," Guido del Cassero and Angiolello da Carignano (see Augusto Vasina, "del Cassero, Guido," *Enciclopedia Dantesca* 2nd ed. [Rome: Istituto della Enciclopedia Italiana, 1984] 2: 345–346; the comparison is made by DeNicolò, *La Strada e il Mare*, 13; see also V. Fanelli, "Biondo, Gaspare," *DBI* 10 [1968]: 559–560). Perhaps the parallel was noted by later writers and reinforced their willingness to perpetuate the legend on which Biondo's status as a Romagnol authoritative on local topography had already conferred a certain credibility.

*Gradaria* See A. Polloni, *Toponomastica romagnola* (Florence: Olschki, 1966), 150, #634, for derivation of the name Gradara (B. uses Gradaria, a form attested before 1290) from the adjective *cretaria*, formed from *creta*, clay.

B.'s description softens the harsh military purpose of Gradara, rebuilt by Sigismondo Pandolfo Malatesta (1417–1468) and famous as a *castello*. See A. Campana, "Poesie Umanistiche sul Castello di Gradara," *Studi Romagnoli* 20 (1969): 501–520, for a detailed account of the conflicts in which Gradara was a prize. Campana enumerates its attractions and presents literary evidence from the 15th century, praise of Gradara linked to flattery of the Malatesta, which also constitutes testimony for Sigismondo's reconstruction of the *castello*. Campana notes that this passage of *Italia illustrata* is all we know about the building arrangement of Gradara in mid-fifteenth century under Sigismondo, and gives an appreciation of the passage's value: "è un testimone che si può a buon diritto chiamare *oculare* (italics mine), perchè si scrisse questa parte dell'opera sua proprio a brevissima distanza da Gradara," (516) referring to Biondo's residence at Montescudo (**[342H]**) while writing this part of *Italia illustrata*. Campana hypothesizes (517) that B. here uses *villa* in order to emphasize the pleasant and elegant characteristics of the fortress. Indeed, it is difficult for even the casual modern tourist to mistake Gradara for a *delizia*.

**[342H]** *Certaldum* ... The minute detail in B.'s treatment of the towns of the Riminese coastal area could be due, according to Campana, "Due Note su Roberto Valturio" (*Studi Riminesi e bibliografici in onore di Carlo Lucchesi* [Faenza: 1952] 11–24), 16, to either of two factors: the aid supplied B.

by Roberto Valturio's *De agro Ariminensi*, or personal observation resulting from B.'s sojourn near Montescudo in the time of composition of this chapter. But R. Cappelletto, "*Italia illustrata*," 685 n. 18, informs us that Campana subsequently abandoned the hypothesis that Valturio had compiled *De agro Ariminensi* for Biondo.

[343A] *Penna, Bilium,...* During the eighth century, mentioned with one name, Pennabilli was a defensive camp guarding access to the coast in the region of the Pentapoli; see Guillou 298–299.

*Livius XIIII libro* That Ariminum was, along with Beneventum, a Roman colony of ancient and famous name is well attested by other sources than Livy, whose fourteenth book cited here is, of course, among the lost. Ariminum was founded in 268 B.C.

*Iohannes Vitalianis* During the war against the Goths for the Byzantine restoration in Italy, John, nephew of Vitalian, had come to Rome in 537 to reinforce Belisarius; after seizing Ariminum he disobeyed Belisarius' order to abandon it. Vitigis then besieged Ariminum in 538; however, the Romans received reinforcements in northern Italy with which they dislodged Vitigis. See Procopius, *Bellum Gothicum* III. 11.32; 25.7, and J. R. Martindale, *The Prosopography of the Later Roman Empire* (3 vols. [Cambridge: Cambridge University Press, 1992]) 3, *s.v. Iohannes* 46.

*Sigismundo Pandulpho Malatesta vicariatus ecclesiae* The Church encountered difficulties, in the first half of the fourteenth century, in imposing papal sovereignty on all of north-central Italy; particularly in the Romagna, the local signori proved difficult to eliminate. Thus the papal vicariate was intended to transform lords like Sigismondo into official delegates of the Pope (P. J. Jones, *The Malatesta of Rimini and the Papal State* [Cambridge: Cambridge University Press, 1974]), 277. "Among the earliest of *signori* in the Papal States to receive the office of vicar, they were among the last to lose it. To trace the development of the institution under them is ... to trace a history of the institution itself" (Jones 262). The particular bull of investiture enabling Sigismondo Pandolfo to be described as B. does here was X of 1450, "confirmation of Rimini, Cesena, Fano, ... to Sigismondo and Malatesta Novello, and of Senigallia, Pergola, Gradara ... etc. to Sigismondo" (cited by Jones, 264 n. 2).

B.'s treatment of Sigismondo in *It. ill.* is clearly flattering in light of the preponderance of traditional negative evidence for his character and deeds. Although much of his unsavory reputation can be attributed to papal invective due to political conflicts (especially the charges of Pope Pius II), non-ecclesiastical sources show consistent flaws as well (see Jones 176–239). Sigismondo was apparently a hard ruler; see Pier Giovanni Fabbri, "Gli Inizi dell'Età di Malatesta Novello a Cesena," *Studi Romagnoli* 43 (1992): 281–306. B. does not mention, for example, the conflicts between the Malatesta and the Ordelaffi of Forlì, flattering both families in *It. ill.* G. Ricci, "Il Peso del Passato. La lenta evoluzione del quadro urbanistico," in *Dalla dominazione veneziana alla conquista francese* ed. Lucio Gambi, vol. 4 of *Storia di Ravenna* (Ravenna: Marsilio, 1994), 133–178, enumerating the many takings of Ravenna's building materials for reuse elsewhere, notes (154) that Sigismondo, when captain of the Venetian Republic, despoiled Sant'Apollinare in Classe of precious marbles in order to decorate his Tempio at Rimini. This was precisely the time of B.'s peregrinations while composing *It. ill.*, and he could have mentioned this act. Campana, "Poesie Umanistiche" (see above on **[342G]**), hypothesizes that B. was at Montescudo, writing *It. ill.*, perhaps in 1450, because he had thought to resolve his financial difficulties by accepting a position from Sigismondo.

**[343B]** *Et qui Tiberim item sub Ocriculo iungebat* It is likely that B. saw this bridge. See R. Cappelletto, *Recuperi ammianei da Biondo Flavio* (*Note e discussioni erudite* 18 [Rome 1983]), who believes that B. describes the bridge at Ocriculum from direct observation. For the bridge, see Leandro Alberti, *Descrittione di tutta Italia* (Bologna 1550), 92; T. Ashby and R. Fell, "The Via Flaminia," *Journal of Roman Studies* 11 (1921): 126–165, 162; C. J. Castner, "Direct Observation and Biondo Flavio's Additions to *Italia illustrata*: the case of Ocriculum," *Mediaevalia et Humanistica* N. S. 25 (1998): 93–113. The bridge at Rimini which was begun under Augustus and finished under Tiberius originally spanned the river Marecchia (B.'s Marida, in the fifteenth century, its course directed to the south of where it now flows).

**[343C]** *Ariminumque nunc habet* ... The independent version of "Romandiola," now Cod. Classense 203, dedicated to Malatesta Novello contained at this point (fol. 9r) a compliment to Roberto Valturio: *Ariminumque nunc habet Robertum Valturrem bonarum artium studiis ornatum, Petrum quoque ac Iacobum Perleones fratres....* See Augusto Campana, "Due note su Roberto Valturio," (16–17), who suggests that B. had asked Valturio, a noted Riminese humanist who had written a treatise *De agro Ariminensi*, for collaboration in the form of topographical information on his native region. The reason for striking the complimentary remark about Valturio in the edition which was published cannot be ascertained.

*Petrum* . . . Pietro Perleone, c. 1400–1463. Native of Rimini, first resident at Venice 1436–1441; educated with Filelfo in Florence and Siena; studied Greek in Constantinople under Joh. Argyropoulos, taught at Milan, Genoa and Venice (the latter 1457–1463). He shared with B. the patronage of Sigismondo Malatesta, for whom he worked as historiographer. See M. L. King, *Venetian Humanists in an Age of Patrician Dominance* (Princeton; Princeton University Press, 1986), 415–417.

*Iacobum Perleones* Iacopo Perleone. B. at Rimini, brother of Pietro Perleone and teacher at Bologna.

***The Malatesta.*** Sigismondo Pandolfo Malatesta, Galeoto Malatesta and his son Carlo Malatesta, Galeoto Roberto Malatesta. (See above on **[342G–H]**.) The Malatesta rose to power in Rimini in the thirteenth century; they were Guelphs, and Rimini was a center of opposition to the emperor. Sigismondo's *signoria* there lasted from 1429 to 1468, coinciding with the peak of power and status for Rimini. He supervised the building of the *castello* and *Tempio*, and at his court patronised important artists and men of letters. When Malatesta power yielded to the forces of Pope Pius II (1463, the year of B.'s death), Rimini became more and more marginalized and subordinated to the papal state. Galeotto Roberto ruled Rimini 1429–1432. See, in general, Jones, *The Malatesta of Rimini.*

**[343D]** . . . *magni quodam nominis torrens perexiguus Rubicon* (Pisciatello, Ruco) B.'s recognition of two names for the river here brings up a problem much debated by fifteenth century humanists, the identification of the actual Rubicon river crossed by Caesar; his addressing of this question exemplifies one of the *It. ill.*'s aims, the correlation of ancient sites with their fifteenth-century equivalents. The Pisciatello (most favored by humanists), Fiumicino, and Uso were candidates; modern opinion inclines to the Uso. The inscription B. cites, the *sanctio* on the bridge at Cesena, was a forgery (cf., *CIL* 11, 1, 30; 11, 7; and Clavuot 194 and 203). E. Bormann's note to *CIL* 11, 1, 30 (*Inscriptiones Falsae vel Alienae*. pt. 1 *Inscriptiones Aemiliae Etruriae Umbriae Latinae* [Berlin: Reimer, 1888]) lists a number of later writers who perpetuated Biondo's transmission of the forgery, as well as Leandro Alberti's comment, "Scrive Biondo lui haver veduto detta tavola

... ma io sovente quindi passando e diligentemente cercandola mai l'ho possuta vedere" (*Descrittione di tutta Italia* f. 269 [Bologna: Giaccarelli, 1550]). For fifteenth-century and modern bibliography on this question, see R. Weiss, *The Renaissance Discovery of Classical Antiquity* (Oxford: Blackwell, 1969), 111–112, 164 and n. 4.

[344E] *Cervia civitas ... civitas Cesena* The patron to whom B. dedicated "Romandiola," (Domenico) Malatesta Novello, son of Pandolfo Malatesta, exemplifies B.'s typically praiseworthy *signore*, a builder of cities and public works. B. here accords him also an idealizing portrait as supporter of art, literature, and scholarship. Pier Giovanni Fabbri, "Cesena e la signoria di Malatesta Novello," *Studi Romagnoli* 45 (1994): 233–257, on the documents of notaries recording acts of Malatesta Novello, reports (238) the ultimate (1463) fate of these salt-works: their sale to the Venetians due to this *signore*'s financial difficulties. Fabbri (257) also notes the verisimilitude of Biondo's comment here on Cervia, as the early version of this chapter in cod. Classense 203 does not mention the new enclosure of the city by walls; yet both the early edition of "Romandiola" and the later printed editions retain the expression *rarissimo habitata colono*, indicating that the population of Cervia did not change perceptibly in the course of the construction.

On the walls of Cesena, see Giordano Conti, "La ristrutturazione della cinta muraria di Cesena attorno alla metà del Quattrocento," *Studi Romagnoli* 31 (1963): 359–382, who shows in detail, through references to deliberations of the council of Anziani, the personal involvement of Malatesta Novello in this project ("... l'intensa attività di Malatesta Novello per il rinnovamento della cinta muraria," 376). Still incomplete at the time of Malatesta Novello's death, the project B. describes as "fortifying the city with new walls in some places" entailed the demolition and rebuilding of practically the entire perimeter; the purpose was to enclose new parts of the city, as well as replacement of walls which were old, in disrepair, and an ineffective defense. Conti, 372, mistakes B.'s earlier comment on Malatesta Novello's building activity at Cervia for a description of his public works at Cesena. When the walls were demolished in the 1860s, an inscription on marble came to light, "Mal[atesta] No[vello] Pan[dulphi] f[ilius] hoc dedit opus," which now resides appropriately in the entrance to the public library at Cesena.

In 1451 Malatesta Novello requested permission of Nicholas V to undertake the unification of the hospitals of Cesena into one large one, the project to which B. here refers (Fabbri 247); and Fabbri (248) deduces from documents of the Council that it was beginning to take shape in the beginning of 1453. Fabbri also (248 and n. 75) supports with documents B.'s report of the beginning of negotiations in 1450 for building the Malatesta library near the convent of S. Francesco.

**[344F]** *M. Cicero ... in ultima ad Lentulum epistola Ad fam.* 352.2.4–6 (in D. R. Shackleton Bailey, ed.: *Cicero: Epistulae ad Familiares* 2 vols. [Cambridge: Cambridge University Press, 1977], 207; all subsequent citations from this edition). In citing this letter of Quintus Cicero to Tiro, in which he criticizes the consuls Hirtius and Pansa as not worthy of responsibility for any important matters, B. conflates *Cossutianarum tabernarum* into a toponym. Shackleton Bailey comments, 493, "... what put this locality into Quintus' head there is no knowing."

> nam isti duo vix sunt digni quibus alteri Caesenam, alteri Cossutianarum tabernarum fundamenta credas
>
> Those two worthies could hardly be trusted, one with Caesena, the other with the bottom floors of Cossutius' taverns.

*Plautum ... ad molas manuarias se locasse ...* That Plautus had to find work in a mill is now recognized as a biographical fabrication built upon the fate of slaves in his comedies.

**[344G–H]** In three supposed citations of Livy, B. paraphrases and summarizes with some inaccuracy or perhaps misrepresentation intended to suit his topographical purpose. First, indicating book 22 as his source, he composes a summary of 32.29.6, 29.8, and 32.30 3–4, Livy's account of Cornelius Cethegus' campaign against and subjugation of the Insubrian Gauls. Where our texts of Livy read *tutandum*, ("the Boii went to defend their own territory") B. wishes to see Tannetum, because he wishes to corroborate Pliny's statement that the Boii possessed the area around the present Modena and Reggio. He then accurately summarizes or creates a pastiche of fragments of 21.25.2–13. Finally, he combines part of Livy's account at 36.40.3 of Scipio Nasica's moves against the Gallic Boii and their surrender to him, with his bald statement (36.40.10–11) of this consul's triumph over the Boii.

**[345B]** *Butrium* A clear instance of B.'s reading a corrupt ms. of Pliny.

**[345C]** *ad Portam eius clausam quem aurea dicitur....* The Porta Aurea at Ravenna, originally a triumphal arch erected in 43 A.D. by the emperor

Claudius, granted a triumph by the city of Ravenna, the fleet, and the praetorians after defeating the Britons. The arch became a gate when it was incorporated into the walls built in the fifth century. It was drawn by Sangallo in 1552, about thirty years before it was destroyed. The original drawing is in the Uffizi; for a reproduction, see G. Savini, *Le mura di Ravenna* (Ravenna 1905), 15.

**[345D] Famous men of Ravenna.**

*Vitalem et eius filios Gervasium et Prothasium* Vitalis and his sons Gervasius and Prothasius. With St. Apollinaris, all martyrs; the two principal churches in Ravenna, St. Apollinare in Classe and San Vitale, are named for them.

*Urcinum medicum* Urcinus, bishop of Ravenna in the mid sixth century

*Ioannem . . . decimumseptimum pontificem Romanum* Pope John XVII; this obscure pope, actually of Roman origin, ruled for only five months in 1003.

*Cassiodorum urbis Romae senatorem . . .* Flavius Magnus Aurelius Cassiodorus Senator (before 490–580) lived at Ravenna while holding political office under the Goths until the Byzantines conquered the city in 540. He was born at Squillace in Calabria and died there after returning to found a monastery. B. cites him sporadically in *Decades*; see below on **[376F–H]**.

*Faustinum, ad quem Martialis* Martial 10.51.5–10. B.'s assignment of Faustinus to Ravenna is based on a reading now disputed:

> quos, Faustine, dies, quales tibi Roma +Ravennae+
> abstulit! o soles, o tunicata quies!
> o nemus, o fontes solidumque madentis harenae
> litus et aequoreis splendidus Anxur aquis,
> et non unius spectator lectulus undae,
> qui videt hinc puppes fluminis, inde maris!

> What days, Faustinus, what pleasant days of Ravenna has Rome stolen from you; O sun, O rest in comfortable dress! You groves, and springs, and shore of hard moist sand, and Anxur gleaming with ocean waves, and a couch with a view of two bodies of water, that on one side looks on ships in the river, on the other looks on ships on the sea!

The apparent equation of Ravenna with Anxur, on the opposite coast south of Rome (near the modern Terracina), indicates the problem with the reading *Ravennae* in l. 5. Perhaps it was the name of Faustinus' villa; the description of ships visible both on a river and on the sea, a prospect possible from Ravenna, may have led to the suggested reading; or Martial may have intended to name Auser in Dalmatia, perhaps visible from Ravenna whereas Anxur could not by any stretch of the imagination be seen from Ravenna.

*Gulielmum physicum* Guglielmo da Ravenna; in the century preceding B.'s activity, a physician from Ravenna, and addressee of Petrarch's *Rerum Senilium* 3.8.

[346E] **The rebirth of eloquence and letters from a man of the Romagna.**

Here begins the digression on cultural conditions in the fourteenth century and a catalogue of famous men of the Romagna, in which B. exhibits his patriotism and love of his native region. Throughout this catalogue, he credits the Romagna with the origins of humanism's impetus to study and value Cicero and the discovery of classical texts. The disciples mentioned here are not Romagnols, but several of them are Florentines, pointing to the importance of the circle of Florentine humanists in B.'s intellectual development, during his residence there in 1434–1443 due to the Curia's removal to Florence after Eugenius IV's exile from Rome; chief among these influences on B. was of course Leonardo Bruni, whose new concept of historiography shaped B.'s own writings in that genre and then, through them, *It. ill.* The list of writers and teachers of classical studies is followed by an encomium of the great military leader Alberico da Barbiano, which credits the Romagna, through this leader, with reforming the military customs of Italy.

*Ioannem grammaticum rhetoremque doctissimum* Giovanni da Ravenna. Scholarly opinion has been divided as to the identification of this teacher, crucially influential on the generation of humanists before Biondo. He is thought to have been either Giovanni Malpaghini, Latin scholar, teacher, and historian (1346–1417), who as secretary and copyist for Petrarch copied for him Latin translations of *Iliad* and *Odyssey*; or Giovanni Conversini (1343–1408), humanist, poet, and teacher of rhetoric. Both were referred to as Giovanni da Ravenna; for analysis of the evidence and summary of the controversy, see Ronald G. Witt, "Still the Matter of the two Giovannis," *Rinascimento* 2nd ser. 35 (1995): 179–199, who decides for Malpaghini. Whichever of the two is B.'s subject here is of interest to B. both as a source of pride in the Romagna and as teacher of the following generation of humanists, who first restored culture at the end of the medieval period. The general problem of identification is addressed by R. Sabbadini, *Giovanni da Ravenna insigne figura d'umanista (1343–1408)*, (1924; repr. Turin 1961), who assumes that Giovanni da Ravenna is Giovanni Conversini; he includes as an Appendix a short biographical notice of Giovanni Malpaghini da Ravenna, basing his distinction of the latter from the former on Malpaghini's long service with Petrarch, reported by Salutati (*Epistolario* 3, p. 537). Sabbadini believed B. had conflated the two figures. Fubini, "Biondo, Flavio," *DBI* 536, follows Sabbadini's interpretation in seeing B.'s Giovanni here as an emblematic creation honoring the Romagna, "in cui si confondono i due omonimi G. Malpaghini e G. di Conversino." W. K. Ferguson (*The Renaissance in Historical Thought: Five Centuries of Interpretation* [Boston: Houghton Mifflin, 1948], 41) and Clavuot advocate identification with Malpaghini; Viti discusses the controversy surrounding this figure's identity and supports the Conversini identification (P. Viti, "Umanesimo letterario e primato regionale nell 'Italia illustrata' di F. Biondo," in G. Varanini and P. Pinagli, edd., *Studi filologici, letterari e storici in memoria di Guido Favati. Medioevo e Umanesimo* 29 [Padua 1977] [2 vols.] 2: 711–732; 721–23). Viti notes that B. neglects the three great writers of the Trecento (Dante, Boccaccio, and Petrarch) in assigning the merit of primacy in the rediscovery of literature after the middle ages; and that attributing this primacy to the poets and scholars of one's home region was a characteristic of the fifteenth century, as was the humanist tendency to slight Petrarch in favor of Chrysoloras, whose re-importation of Greek into Italy provided a new cultural stimulus. For a clear analysis of this section, see A. Mazzocco, "Decline and rebirth in Bruni and Biondo," 262–263. See also B. Kohl, "Conversini, Giovanni," *DBI* 28 (1983): 574–578; and the introduction in Vittore Nason, ed., *Giovanni Conversini da Ravenna, Rationarium Vite* (Florence: Olschki, 1986), 7–39.

**[346F] Students of Giovanni.**

*Iohannes autem Ravennas Petarcham senem puer novit* . . . It is difficult to know exactly what B. means by this sentence. For as clear an interpretation of this passage as I have seen, see Ronald G. Witt, *"In the Footsteps of the Ancients": The Origins of Humanism from Lovati to Bruni. Studies in Medieval and Reformation Thought* 74 (Leiden, Boston and Cologne: Brill, 2000), 340–341. Witt translates, "Giovanni da Ravenna knew the old Petrarch as a boy, *and he did not have these books in any other way than Petrarch did*, nor did he write anything that we know of"; (italics mine) and explains the import of the passage:

> Petrarch did not yet know all of Cicero's most important works or have access to a complete manuscript of Quintilian. *Nor had Malpaghini, Petrarch's young assistant, been in a better position.* Nevertheless, while Malpaghini himself had lacked the ability to recreate Ciceronian style, his desire to imitate Cicero had been realized by his own students, who comprised a majority of the great humanists of the early fifteenth century. (italics mine)

*Leonardus Aretinus* Leonardo Bruni, called Aretino from his native city (b. Arezzo 1370, d. 1444), Florentine humanist, historian, and (from 1427 to his death) chancellor of Florence. At the urging of Coluccio Salutati, his mentor and close friend, Bruni collected, edited, and translated into Latin many works of Greek literature, and is thus responsible for the transmission and survival of much of ancient Greek writing. After service in the Curia, he entered active political life at Florence, holding many important offices. An intense participant in the political and intellectual life of Florence, he was an important member of, and friend to, the first generation of humanists. His masterpiece, *Historiae Florentini Populi* (treating the city's history from the origins to 1404), revolutionized the writing of history and greatly influenced the historical work of his friend Biondo, in its rejection of the traditions of universalist history and the chronicles (e.g., divine providence as a motivation of events) in favor of rigorous critical and philological research. He also wrote treatises and orations and developed the commentary (*Rerum Suo Tempore Gestarum Commentarius*) into an important form of historical writing. See C. Vasoli, "Bruni, Leonardo," *DBI* 14 (1972): 618–633, who, by the way, identifies Malpaghini as the Giovanni with whom Bruni studied rhetoric.

*Petrus Paulus Vergerius* Pier Paolo Vergerio (1370–1444), follower of Petrarch, educated to an advanced level in medicine and law, teacher of logic (at Bologna) and dialectic (at Florence). For extensive biographical information, see John M. McManamon, *Pierpaolo Vergerio the Elder: The Humanist as Orator. Medieval and Renaissance Texts and Studies* 163 (Tempe, Arizona: 1996). His connections with humanists, especially the Florentines, and his production of works in various genres are numerous, including the edition of Petrarch's epic *Africa* (1396). Most active in oratory in the classical style, but a reformer of education as well, with emphasis on moral philosophy, perhaps his most significant work is his treatise on education, *De ingenuis moribus et liberalibus studiis* (1403), which prescribes a program of study in the liberal arts, ethics, and physical and military exercise; his ideas had enormous influence on the development of humanist culture.

*Omnibene Schola* Ognibene Scola, born c. 1374. Trained in medicine and the law, taught in the *studium* of Padua, then married an illegitimate daughter of Francesco Novello at Padua and served as diplomat and official in that court.

*Robertus Rossus* Roberto de' Rossi, Florentine humanist and teacher (1355–1417); pupil of Chrysoloras and one of the circle around Coluccio Salutati, he was noted for his knowledge of classical Greek and facilitated the study of Greek in Florence.

*Iacopus Angeli filium* Iacopo di Angelo da Scarperia (c. 1360–1410/11), translated (1409) Ptolemy's *Cosmographia* (although B. mentions him as translator of Plutarch's *Life of Cicero*). For his importance, see R. Weiss, "Jacopo Angeli da Scarperia," *Medioevo e Rinascimento: Studi in onore di Bruno Nardi* (Florence: Sansone 1955), 2: 801–824:

> The first Italian humanist to go to Constantinople in order to master Greek, he also played some rôle in establishing the regular teaching of this language in Florence. The settling of Emanuel Chrysoloras in Florence in 1397 was partly the outcome of his efforts, and he was perhaps the first Italian scholar of his generation who collected Greek manuscripts. Furthermore his translations of works by Plutarch and Ptolemy set an example which, though admittedly mediocre, proved nevertheless stimulating to his fellow humnists. (803)

*Poggius* Poggio Bracciolini, 1380–1459; this most famous humanist and collector of ancient manuscripts needs, in B.'s assessment, no surname or epithet. Like Leonardo Bruni, he followed a career in the Curia until, in 1453, he became chancellor of Florence. As a result of his travels to ecclesiastical councils and explorations of the libraries of convents and cathedrals, not only in Italy, but in Switzerland, Germany, and France, he was responsible for the discovery and transmission of many ancient Latin texts. He devised a new script and also wrote dialogues, letters, and a sylloge of inscriptions; see A. Petrucci, "Bracciolini, Poggio," *DBI* 13 (1971): 640–646.

*Guarinus Veronensis* ... Guarino da Verona; Guarino Guarini (1374–1401), often called the originator of humanist pedagogy, was the first Italian to bring Greek studies to Italy. He traveled in 1403 to Constantinople, where his studies with Manuel Chrysoloras conferred upon Guarino a level of expertise in Greek unprecedented among Italian humanists. Upon his return to Italy, he taught in Venice, Padua, and Verona, before finding permanent employment in 1410 in Florence. In 1414, at the call of his patrician friends there, he returned to Venice. From 1419–1429 he taught at Verona, most of that time publicly; he fled the plague at Verona and went to Ferrara where he taught both privately and publicly until his death. Guarino's pedagogy, based upon Greek and Latin languages and literature, was intended to inculcate virtues in his pupils and prepare them for public life. He was also a collector of classical Greek and Latin manuscripts; author of grammatical and pedagogical works and commentaries on classical works; and he left a substantial correspondence. His contribution to the development of the humanist *contubernium* influenced the formation of the boarding school for instruction in classics. See P. Viti, "Guarino da Verona," *DBI* 52 (1999): 466–470; Giulio Bertoni, *Guarino da Verona, Fra Letterari e Cortigiani a Ferrara (1429–1460)* (Geneva: Olschki, 1921), 160–175 (L. Carbone's funeral oration for Guarino); and A. Grafton and L. Jardine, "Humanism and the School of Guarino: A Problem of Evaluation," *Past and Present* 92 (1982): 51–80.

*Victorinus Feltrensis* Vittorino da Feltre, 1378–1446. One of the most influential teachers in Western educational history, Vittorino followed advanced courses in Padua including rhetoric, logic, and natural philosophy. In 1415 he began to study Greek with Guarino. He taught in Mantua at a school established by its rulers the Gonzaga, where his choice of ancient authors marked by an emphasis on Greek authors set the course of the classical curriculum for the next centuries. See Witt, "Two Giovannis," 191, and N. G. Wilson, *From Byzantium to Italy: Greek Studies in the Italian Renaissance* (Baltimore: Johns Hopkins University Press, 1992), 34–41.

*Emanuel Chrysoloras* The first Greek to teach the language in Italy; 1397, the date of the beginning of his lectures in Florence, is a landmark in Renaissance acquisition of classical learning; the next is 1453, the fall of Constantinople to the Turks, which resulted in the flight of many Greeks to Italy and their subsequent occupation in teaching Greek and copying Greek texts. See L. D. Reynolds and N. G. Wilson, *Scribes and Scholars* 2nd ed. (Oxford: Clarendon, 1974), 131–132.

[346G] *concilium ... apud Constantiam Germaniae* The Council of Constance 1414–1417, intended to end the Great Schism; ended in the election of Oddo Colonna who established his seat at Rome as Martin V in 1420. Biondo identifies this occasion as an opportunity for Italians who traveled to the Council to discover manuscripts in Germany.

*secutaeque sunt incerto nobis datae libertatis patronae Ciceronis ad Atticum epistolae. . . .* Translation of the Basle reading is impossible (the Verona edition [1482] repeats this wording). Fauno's (137v) translation is not helpful: "furono medesimamente ritrovate le epistole di M. Tullio ad Attico *da non so chi altro. . . .*"

*Gasparinus Bergomensis* Gasparino Barzizza, who was born in approximately 1360 and died in approximately 1431. B.'s emphasis conforms to the general assessment of Gasparino's importance primarily as a teacher, the high point of whose humanist activity was his encounter with the codex of Cicero discovered at Lodi by Gerardo Landriani. B. could not, of course, enjoy the perspective from which we now view Gasparino as one of the founders of humanist Ciceronianism, a tradition which culminates in Valla's *Elegantiae*. Grammarian and teacher of rhetoric and literature, Gasparino taught at Bergamo, Milan (where he was summoned by Giangaleazzo Visconti at the beginning of the Quattrocento, and returned in 1421 at the summons of Filippo Maria Visconti), Pavia (1403–1407), Venice (1408–1411, where he gave private instruction to Francesco Barbaro and Andrea Giuliano), and Padua (1407–1421). As B. recounts, Gasparino had his student Cosmo Raimondi of Cremona transcribe the early medieval ms. of Cicero's rhetorical works. Gasparino's influence was crucial in the development of the pedagogy of his friends Guarino da Verona and Vittorino da Feltre; his most important role in the evolution of humanism consists in the number, quality, and reputation of his students. His library was notable especially for its copies of Livy and the Livian *Periochae*; he wrote a number of scholarly and pedagogical works, including treatises on rhetoric, stylistics, and etymology of Latin words; and correspondence, accessible today in, e.g., G. A. Furietti, *Gasparini Barzizii et Guiniforte filii opera* (Rome 1723); R. Sabbadini, "Lettere e orazioni edite e inedite di Gasparino Barzizza," *Arch. stor. lombardo* 13 (1886): 363–836. For many more references, including works on Gasparino's relations with other humanists, the contents of his library, and documentation of his teaching career, see G. Martellotti, "Barzizza, Gasperino," *DBI* 7 (1965): 34–39.

**[346H]** *Gerardus Landrianus*. Gerardo Landriani, bishop of Lodi (1418–1424) who found in 1421 the codex (now lost) of Cicero's *de oratore, Brutus de oratore*, and *Orator ad M. Brutum*. B.'s transcription from the Lodi archetype is now in cod. Vat. ottob. lat. 1592, which contains (ff. 14–58) the text of the *Brutus*, and preceding that (ff. 1–11) the text of *De militia*, a minor treatise of Leonardo Bruni, both signed and dated by B., Milan, October 1422. See Nogara, *Scritti Inediti*, XXXVI–XXXVIII for details (e.g., the suspicion that B. may have transcribed the last part, the first fifteen pages having been copied by someone else, probably under Barzizza's supervision).

*Cosmos . . . Cremonensis* Cosmo of Cremona. Cosmo Raimondi transcribed three books *de oratore*. When Landriani sent the codex of Cicero mentioned above (containing *De inventione, Rhetorica ad Herennium, De oratore, Orator*, and *Brutus*) to Gasparino Barzizza in Milan, the latter sent back a copy made by Cosimo; see R. Sabbadini, *Storia e critica dei testi latini* 2nd ed. (Padua 1971), 77–108, cit. Viti, 728 n. 36.

**[347A–B]** *Guarinus . . . Ferrariae . . . Ferrarienses . . . principes erudierunt*. Cf. above on **[346F]**. In praising Guarino, B. praises not only the Romagna but also obliquely the Este of Ferrara, because Niccolò III d'Este called Guarino to Ferrara to teach his son Leonello. B. declares Niccolò lacking in literary expertise, and notes that Borso did not attain this either (**[354H–355A]**). Bertoni, 7, n. 3, remarks that Niccolò neglected his other sons in comparison with Leonello, providing Borso as teachers Giacomo Bisi and Guglielmo Cappello. The State Archive in Modena contains testimony, in the form of letters to contemporaries, of Leonello's love of books, and many humanists dedicated their works to Leonello, as B. did his *Historiarum Decades*.

**[347B]** *Georgius Trapezuntius* George of Trebizond (1395–1472 or 1473), a Greek who preferred to write in Latin, is one of the most important connections in the transmission of Greek literature, especially Byzantine rhetoric, to the West. He emigrated from Crete to Italy, probably in 1416, through the sponsorship of the Venetian humanist Francesco Barbaro. Close association with Vittorino da Feltre was instrumental in George's acquisition of Latin eloquence. Teacher of Greek in Venice, Mantua, and Vicenza, he served in Rome in the Curia under Eugenius IV and Nicholas V: as protonotary, apostolic secretary and scriptor of the apostolic letters he was Biondo's colleague. B. refers here to the fact that George of Trebizond taught in the Studio Romano during the papacy of Nicholas V, who pressed him for increased production of translations and whose favorite translator George was. Even an incomplete list of George of Trebizond's prodigious production of translations from Greek to Latin would include among classical works Aristotle *Rhetoric*, *Physics*, *de anima*, *de caelo*; *de generatione et corruptione*; Demosthenes, *On the Crown*; and Plato, *Laws*; he also translated patristic authors. George also authored his own scholarly works (including the first full-scale *Rhetoric* of the Italian Renaissance), exegesis of patristic works, and theological treatises. For extensive biography, see John Monfasani, *George of Trebizond: A Biography and a Study of his Rhetoric and Logic*. Columbia Studies in the Classical Tradition 1 (Leiden: E. J. Brill, 1976), at 3–235. Monfasani, 37, notes B.'s suppression in this standard edition of a passage (included at **[344F]** in MS Ravenna, Biblioteca Classense 203) which praises Gerardo Gambacorta of Pisa, in connection with B.'s description of Bagno di Romagna, for having engaged George of Trebizond as teacher for his children. On this deleted passage, see Augusto Campana, "Passi Inediti dell' «Italia illustrata» di Biondo Flavio," *La Rinascita* 1 (1938): 91–97.

*Franciscus Philelphus* Francesco Filelfo (1398–1481) studied in Constantinople under Chrysoloras; taught Greek in a number of cities but spent most of his professional life in Milan as professor at Pavia and poet at the court of the Sforza. He left collections of poetry, translations of Greek works into Latin, commentaries, dialogues, and an enormous production of letters, including to his friend and correspondent Biondo. See P. Viti, "Filelfo, Francesco," *DBI* 47 (1997): 613–626

*Laurentius Valla* Lorenzo Valla (1407–1457), professor, translator of Greek texts into Latin, philologist, textual critic, and historian. He was active at the court of Alfonso V of Aragon in Naples; later entered the Curia under Nicholas V, then became papal secretary. The work B. mentions here, *Elegantiae* (1471), on Latin grammar and style, appeared in many editions, as B. asserts (*per omnem Italiam*).

*Porcellius* The historian Giannantonio de' Pandoni (1405–after 1476) was known as Porcelli; taught rhetoric at Rome and Naples; and shared with B. the patronage of the Malatesta, Pope Pius II, and King Alfonso of Aragon, king of Naples. See Eric Cochrane, *Historians and Historiography in the Italian Renaissance* (Chicago and London: University of Chicago Press, 1981), 147 and bibliography in n.70.

*Seneca Camertinus* Tommaso Seneca; also, Tommaso da Camerino. Professor of rhetoric and poetry who taught in various cities.

*Sed Martialis contra* B., probably influenced by his immediately previous citation of Pliny (*NH* 19.151), seems to misunderstand the import of 3.56:

> Sit cisterna mihi quam vinea malo Ravennae,
> cum possim multo vendere pluris aquam.

> I prefer a cistern at Ravenna to a vineyard, seeing that I can get a much better price for water.

The epigram emphasizes the scarcity of water at Ravenna, not the inferiority of its wines.

**[347C]** *asparagum* Pliny *NH* 19.19.2; Martial 13.21:

> Mollis et aequorea quae crevit spina Ravenna
> Non erit incultis gratior asparagis.

Again B. seems to misunderstand Martial, whose couplet on cultivated vs. wild asparagus is not a confirmation of Pliny's judgment that the cultivated asparagus of Ravenna's gardens is the best; Martial's poem seems to downgrade the cultivated type.

*Martialis* vero *indicat* . . . B. again pairs Pliny and Martial, this time without much point. Noting that Pliny (*NH* 9.144, 9.169?) judges the turbot from the sea at Ravenna to be the best, B. then cites three lines (6–8) from Martial 3.93, insults to a certain Vetustilla:

> cum conparata rictibus tuis ora
> Niliacus habeat corcodilus angusta,
> meliusque ranae garriant Ravennates. . . .

with the comment that Martial proves that in ancient times as in his own, there were many frogs at Ravenna. In the context of the first two pairings, which B. obviously intends as opposing or complementary pairs (**[347B]**, *sed Martialis contra* . . . ; **[347C]**, *quod Martialis confirmat* . . . ), this third pair is not a clear example of either type. However, the introduction *Martialis vero indicat* seems to suggest a relationship of opposition; perhaps that the

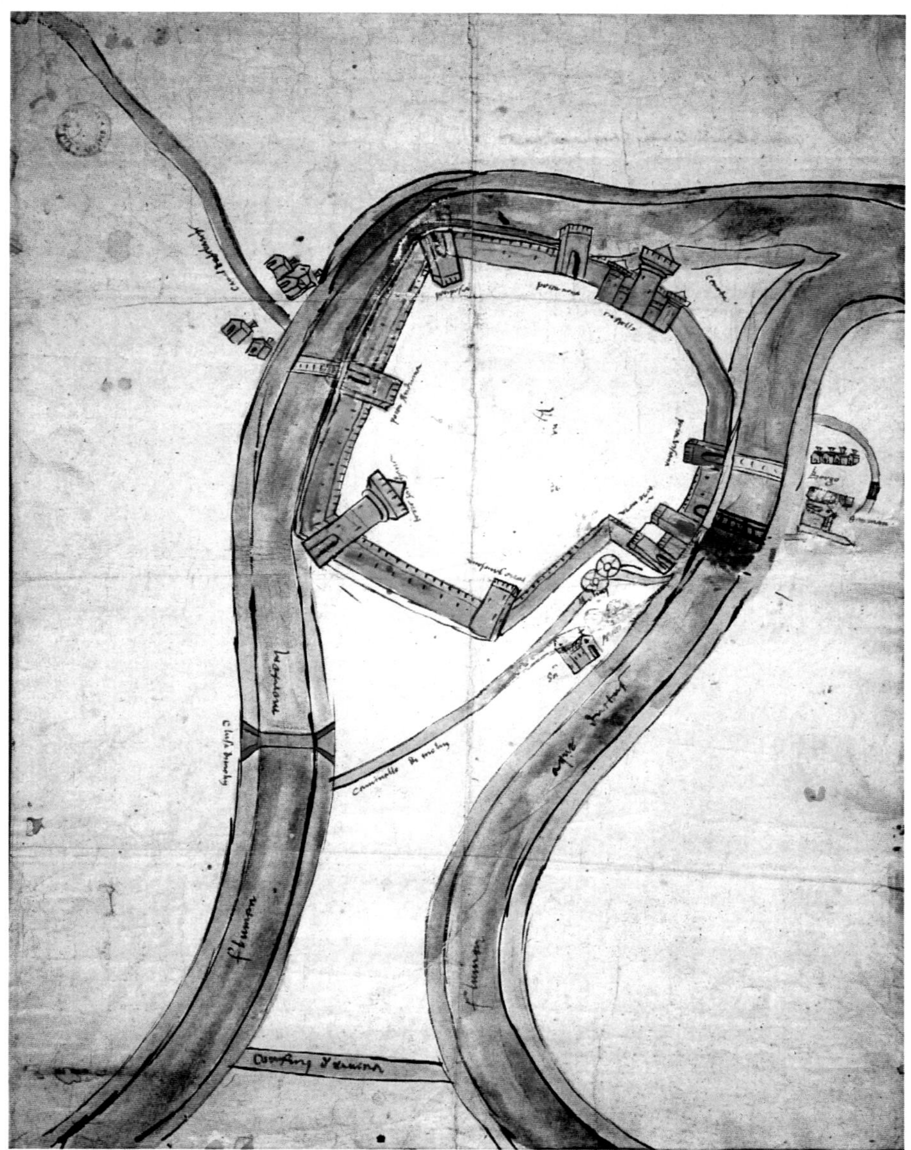

Plate V. Map of Ravenna from second half of fifteenth century. ASCRA Mappa 61, reproduced by permission of Biblioteca Classense, Ravenna.

fame of Ravenna for having the best turbot is balanced by the presence of frogs, an unattractive form of marine life.

*Cingunt Ravennam amnes duo Bedisum facientes. . . .* The Bedisus was a river at Ravenna formed of the confluence of the Montone and the former Vitis, until the 15th c. the Aqueductus, lastly the Ronco. These two rivers flowed close to the walls of Ravenna. In 1739 was completed the project of diversion of the Ronco and Montone, planned as a remedy for their frequent flooding of the city. Plate V (Archivio di Stato, Ravenna, Piante topografiche, 61) is the earliest map of the city, from the second half of the fifteenth century. For the importance of these rivers to the character of the city, see Ricci, "Il Peso del Passato," to which the following comments are indebted.

B.'s description corresponds in part to the map exemplifying the Quattrocento conception of Ravenna's topography: the Montone and Ronco were brought in a circle around the city; the city was considered safer, from a military-strategic point of view, for being thus encircled; the map focusses on the rivers' confluence and the defensive walls and towers, while the city's interior remains a blank space, an empty container to be filled by the mapmaker's bias. But B. betrays no recognition of the probable cause for this cartographic bias, the influence of the Venetian sovereignty (1441–1509) which most likely led to portrayal of the city as a machine of war (Ricci 133–134). Ricci characterizes (142–146) subsequent cartographic representations of Ravenna as emphasizing the city's many problems with water, its cartography experiencing a retarded evolution, due to the prevalent Italian view of Ravenna as ancient, isolated, and ranking low in status and interest, a bias which repressed the growth of an urban cartography. His article explains in terms of the city's history the slowness of cartographic development in regard to Ravenna, "fra campagne cartograficamente eloquenti una città cartograficamente quasi muta" (146).

As it did for the mapmaker, so for Biondo Ravenna serves as empty container. Despite his profound familiarity with Ravenna, founded on citizenship, family connections, and personal observation, B.'s written description of the city's topography, like the Venetian map, omits peculiar detail to fulfill its own agenda, emphasis on the cultural primacy of the Romagna. The superficiality of B.'s treatment of Ravenna highlights the importance of issues of patronage in shaping *It. ill.*, in view of Sigismondo Pandolfo Malatesta's captaincy of the Republic of Venice at the time B. was composing *It.*

*ill.* In 1449 Sigismondo appropriated marbles from St. Apollinare in Classe to decorate his Temple at Rimini, a construction project of which B. was surely aware, despite his omission of it from *It. ill.* Perhaps mention of this despoliation would have ill accorded with the obligatory-sounding praise of Sigismondo earlier in this chapter ([342G], praise of Gradara).

*Eusebium ... Gallum poetam* See Nogara, CXCII–CXCIII, who reveals an early modern debate as to whether Biondo "corrected" a ms. of Eusebius in order to claim Gallus as a compatriot.

**[347D] Famous men of Forlì.**

In general on this topic, see L. Avellini and L. Michelacci, edd., *La cultura Umanistica a Forlì fra Biondo e Melozzo, Atti del Convegno di Studi* (Forlì: Il Nove, 1997), esp. R. Fubini, "La geografia storica dell'Italia illustrata di Biondo Flavio e le tradizioni dell'etnografia," 89–112.

*Guido Bonactus* The astronomer, astrologer, and mathematician Guido Bonatti, born at Forlì probably in first decades of the thirteenth century; died at Forlì at the end of the same century; see C. Vasoli, "Bonatti, Guido," *DBI* 11 (1969): 603–608. He was the most authoritative medieval Italian writer of astrological treatises; especially well-known was his *Tractatus de astronomia* (actually a collection of twelve treatises).

*Rainerius Arsenus* Raniero Arsendi, b. at end of 13th c., d. Padua 1358. A jurist and teacher from Forlì in the thirteenth century, a prolific author of legal writings and professor at Pisa and Padua; see R. Abbondanza, "Arsendi, Raniero," *DBI* 4 (1962): 333–339.

*Checo Rubeo* Cecco di Melletto Rossi, secretary to Francesco Ordelaffi. A friend of Petrarch and a poet, he and Boccaccio exchanged eclogues when Boccaccio was residing at Forlì (1247–1248), probably as a Florentine ambassador.

*Nereo Morando* From Forlì, man of letters of the fourteenth century and friend of Petrarch.

*Iacobo Alegreti* The family of the Allegretti were prominent at Forlì in the eleventh to fifteenth centuries; Iacopo was the author of *Bucolics* and famous for having found a fragment of the poetry of Cornelius Gallus, also commonly attributed to Forlì.

*Ugolinus Urbeventanus* Ugolino da Orvieto, author of musical treatises, born approximately 1380, died at Ferrara 1457. The family of the Ugolini of Forlì were prominent from the fourteenth to the sixteenth century; this musical composer was a canon and archdeacon at the cathedral in Forlì. Exiled from Forlì in 1430 as a result of Guelph-Ghibelline strife, he moved to Ferrara where he held the position of archpresbyter in its cathedral.

*Ioannes Ordelaffus* The Ordelaffi of Forlì were the city's most prominent family from the ninth to the sixteenth century. Ghibellines, they ruled several towns in the Romagna in addition to Forlì but ended up losing Forlì in 1359 to Cardinal Albornoz' campaign to return the area to papal rule.

*Brandolinus* 1) Brandolini Brandolino, military leader b. after 1350, d. 1396. See A. Esch, "Brandolini, Brandolino," *DBI* 14 (1972): 28–29.

2) Tiberto Brandolini was a *condottiero*, probably born in Romagna between 1401 and 1420, died probably in Milan, 1462; see P. Partner, "Brandolini, Tiberto," *DBI* 14 (1972): 43.

*Mostarde*. Paolo Orsini, condottiere.

*Nicolaus Hasteo Recenetensis* The bishop Niccolò dall'Aste, from a noble family of Forlì, trained as a physician, but became bishop of Recanati and Macerata. Perhaps related is: Bishop Angelo Asti of Recanati, a curialist who helped bring Lapo di Castiglionchio (1405–1438) into papal service.

**[348E]** *Galli . . . Guidone Appiensi ductore* Dante, in *Inferno* 27, 43–44, referred to the siege in 1281–1282 of Forlì by combined papal and French forces intent on recovering for the church the rebellious city of Forlì. Jean d'Eppes led the besieging army of French and papal troops which was slaughtered by defenders of Forlì under Guido da Montefeltro. Here B. has apparently confused the names of Guido Bonatti, who was astrologer of Guido da Montefeltro in Forlì; and Giovanni d'Appia, rector of Romagna leading the papal forces. See Augusto Vasina, "Forlì," *Enciclopedia Dantesca*, 2: 967–969.

**[348F]** *Ambrogio Camaldulensi principe monacho* Ambrogio Traversari, 1386–1439, became general in 1431 of his order of Camaldolensian monks and lived in the monastery of Santa Maria degli Angeli in Florence. Chiefly known as a translator of Greek patristic texts into Latin, he played an important role at the Council of Florence. See Wilson, *Byzantium to Italy*, 31–33.

*Padusa . . . palus vetusti nominis* Although Pliny, *NH* 3.16.119–20, says of the water in the canal at Ravenna called *fossa Augusta*: *Ravennam trahitur ubi Padusa vocatur, quondam Messanicus appellatus* (the canal of Augustus takes it [the Po] to Ravenna, where it is called the Padusa, and was formerly called Messanicus), B. applies the name Padusa to the swamps of the Po delta. Memory fails him in his attempt to assign the Virgilian phrase *piscosove amne Padusa* to its correct source, *Aeneid* 11.457. The context (454–458) describes the enraged assembly of Italians inciting Turnus to prepare for war:

> . . . hic undique clamor
> dissensu vario magnus se tollit in auras,
> haud secus atque alto in luco cum forte catervae
> consedere avium, piscosove amne Padusae
> dant sonitum rauci per stagna loquacia cycni.

> . . . the shouting went up on every side,
> from the conflict favoring now one faction, now the other,
> just as when a flock of birds have settled in a deep grove,
> or in the Padusa, full of fish, harsh-throated swans
> fill the stagnant pools with their clamor.

*Piscosove amne Padusa* is one of two instances (the other at [375C]) of B.'s misquoting Virgil (specifically by attributing to the *Georgics* a phrase from the *Aeneid: propter Athesim amoenum*, from *Aen.* 9.679 [the heroes Pandarus and Bitias are likened to mighty oaks along a river's banks, perhaps the Po or the Adige]). In both cases, B. is clearly "guessing from memory," and logically assumes that a description of the countryside occurred in a "bucolic" work. Each phrase occurs in a simile in the latter books of the *Aeneid* (as we might expect, since these books are full of Italian place names), and each presents an alternative example of a rustic scene. Here in book 11, the bellicose peoples' discordant voices are likened to those of crowds of birds in a grove, or to the harsh sounds of swans in the marshes of the Padusa, which Virgil calls *amnis*.

L. Gambi, *Cosa Era la Padusa?* (Faenza: Fratelli Lega, 1950), esp. 4 and 10, provides a thorough discussion of the problematic assumption of writers after Pliny, including B., that the term "Padusa" refers to a swamp, when evidence shows that it was a channel or minor branch of the Po which ensured a passage from Ravenna to the Po. Vibius Sequester (a geographer active around A.D. 500) applied the term Padusa to a swamp (*palus Gal-*

*liae*); from him Boccaccio, like B. a resident of Ravenna, took the term Padusa referring to a swamp in his topographical work *De montibus, sylvis, fontibus, lacubus, fluminibus, stagnis seu paludibus, de nominibus maris* (now in the modern edition of Manlio Pastore Stocchi, v. 10 in Vittore Branca, ed., *Boccaccio Tutte le Opere* [Verona: Mondadori, 1998]). In addition to Gambi's assertion that B. took from Boccaccio this application of the name Padusa, I suggest that B. was perhaps also misled by Virgil's *stagna.* He often privileges literary sources of topographical information without recognizing that poets may use toponyms for purposes other than geographical accuracy; he takes as serious and authoritative topographical descriptions in Virgil and Livy, showing little recognition of the possibility that they could be using toponyms for aesthetic purposes.

Gambi (10) juxtaposes the facts of B.'s residence near this area when composing *It. ill.* with his carelessness in affirming the Padusa as *palus*, in contrast to Pliny's description. According to Gambi, as with other mistakes perpetuated by his followers (see my discussion above *ad* **[342G]**, B.'s description of the "sunken city" Conca off Cattolica), B.'s origin and residency gave him authority with later compilers, especially Leandro Alberti. But, as Gambi notes (10–12), D. Spreti and Gerolamo Rossi diverged from B., and did not call these swamps by the precise name of Padusa; nor did the German cartographer Abraham Ortelius perpetuate B.'s mistake.

**[349B]** *Albricum Cunii comitem* . . . Alberico da Barbiano, inspired by patriotism and sympathy for the devastation of Italy he had witnessed, to which B. alludes in this passage. He became the first native Italian to form his own company of soldiers, the Compagnia di San Giorgio. B. refers to the battle (Marino, in 1379) during the Schism when, with his Italian soldiers, Alberico fought in support of the Roman pope and defeated the Breton mercenaries supporting the Avignonese pope. This was the beginning of the exclusion of foreign mercenaries and the domination of native Italians in the fighting forces in Italy. The heroic status of Alberico, and the claims of his priority in leading an Italian company, are questioned by Michael Mallett, *Mercenaries and Their Masters: Warfare in Renaissance Italy* (London, Sydney, and Toronto: The Bodley Head, 1974), 41–43. See P. Pieri, "Alberico da Barbiano," *DBI* 1 (1960): 639–642.

**[349D]** *Testantur Cesena Faventiaque crudeliter direptae* . . . Cf. Mallett, *Mercenaries*, 40.

**[350F]** *Fomesque id et origo quaedam fuit omnium rei militaris ducum* . . . D. Hay and J. Law, *Italy in the Age of the Renaissance* (London and New York: Longman, 1989), credit B., and this passage, with originating the tradition of the Italian peninsula's domination by two Italian schools of warfare: that of Braccio da Montone, and that of Muzio Attendolo Sforza.

**[350H]** *Gregorius XI natione Lemovicensis* Gregory returned to Rome in 1377. He was a native of Limoges, Latinized by B. to Lemovicensis.

**[351A]** *Zaniolum* This is the Zeno, and I take the citadel B. mentions here (*magnifici operis arcem*) to be the "Bastia dello Zaniolo," whose location is known from its bridge which remains at the modern S. Biagio di Argenta. Not only did B. possess a farm on the Zeno (*Blasianus, in quo villam habemus locupletam e regione Zanioli sitam, in qua horum partem scripsimus*— **[353C]**); documents in the Archivio di Stato, Modena, show B. selling materials for the building of the Bastia dello Zaniolo. See A. Franceschini, *Artisti a Ferrara in età umanistica e rinascimentale: Testimonianze archivistiche*, Parte I dal 1341 al 1471 (Ferrara and Rome: Gabriele Corbo, 1993), 334, and, for the original which Franceschini transcribes, see Plate VI, reproduction of the original records with "Misser Biondo da Furlì"'s name clearly visible.

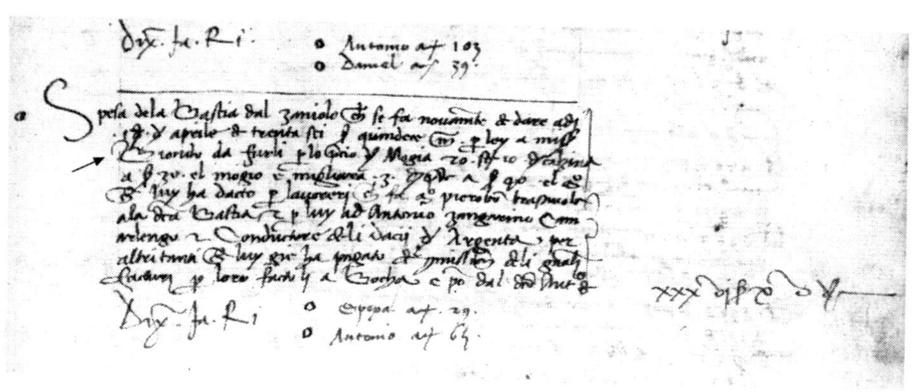

Plate VI. Bookkeeping records from Modena showing Biondo's sale of materials for construction of a fort at S. Biagio. Protocollo No. 2867/ V.9, Archivio di Stato, Modena. Reproduced by permission of Archivio di Stato, Modena. Arrow indicates "Misser Biondo da Furlì."

Franceschini's transcription:

> Spesa dela Bastia de Zaniolo che se fa novamente, de dare adi 17 d'aprile lire trenta sei, soldi quindece marchesani, per lei a Misser Biondo da Furlì per lo pregio de mogia 20, stari 10 de calzina, a soldi 30 el mozo, e migliara 3 de prede a soldi 40 el miaro, che lui ha dacto per lavoreri che fa Maistro Pierobono Brasavolla ala deta Bastia.

**[351B]** *Benvenutum ... grammaticus et ludi magister* Benvenuto da Imola, born in the third decade of the fourteenth century, died 1387–1388; his best-known work, *Comentum super Dantem*, is one of the most important commentaries on Dante of the fourteenth century. He also glossed Virgil's *Bucolics* and *Georgics*. B. refers here (*historias*) to Benvenuto's work as a historiographer, *Augustalis libellus*, a review of the emperors from Julius Caesar to Wenceslas. See L. Paoletti, "Benvenuto da Imola," *DBI* 8 (1966): 691–694.

*Ioannes Imolensis* Giovanni da Imola, famous for his knowledge in canon and civil law, held the chair of canon law at Bologna, taught at Ferrara, Padua, and then returned to Bologna, where he died in 1436. His works on canon law included commentaries on the Decretals, and those on civil law, commentaries to the Digests. See G. Ermini, "Giovanni da Imola," *EncIt* 17:243.

*decimum Ioannem Romanum pontificem* Pope John X r. 914–928.

*Ioannes Ferrariensis episcopus* Giovanni Tavelli di Tossignano, elected in 1432 bishop of Ferrara, for whose election Guarino Veronese delivered an oration. Tavelli died in 1446. See Pius Bonifacius Gams, *Series Episcoporum Ecclesiae Catholicae* (Regensburg: Josef Manz, 1873–1886; reprint, Graz: Akademische Druck-u. Verlagsanstalt, 1957), 695, who notes Tavelli as beatified.

*Caput Silicis* Conselice. Imola was primarily an agricultural center, for which Conselice functioned as the port. From 1084 Conselice was the arrival point for shipping between the Po di Primaro (at Argenta) and the Romagna. The name comes from its position at the head of the ancient Via Selice, which led to Imola. For detailed treatment of this and related waterways, see Mauro Calzolari, "La Navigazione interna in Emilia Romagna tra l'VIIII e il XIII secolo," in *Vie del Commercio in Emilia Romagna Marche*, ed. Giuseppe Adani (Cinisello Balsamo: Silvana, 1990), 115–124.

**[352E]** *Bononiam urbem vetustam* Bologna; see Franco Bergonzoni and Giovanna Bonora, edd., *Bologna Romana*. Vol. 1, Fonti per la storia di Bologna. Testi 9 (Bologna: Istituto per la Storia di Bologna, 1976), 14–21 for thorough modern collection of the ancient sources for the history of Bologna (in contrast with B.'s group).

**[352F]** *de Censorio* Censorinus; in Trebellius Pollio, *Tyranni Triginta* (the Thirty Pretenders to the Throne); Hohl, *Scriptores Historiae Augustae* 2, 133 (33.4–5):

> Exstat eius sepulchrum <circa Bononiam> in quo grandibus litteris incisi sunt omnes eius honores; ultimo tamen versu ads<c>rip<tum> est:
>
> "felix omnia, infelicissimus imperator."

B.'s omission of the inscription's final word negates the meaning; as Hohl prints it, it reads "Happy through all events, but most unfortunate as emperor," alluding to Censorinus' seven-day reign which ended with his soldiers putting him to death.

*Sergii pontificis Romani os porci prius appellati* Pope Sergius II; the Frankish king Lothar I ruled 822–55. As B. had explained in *Decades* 174H, this pope's family name was Bocca di Porco; forced by the clergy and the people to discontinue this undignified name, he took the name of Sergius, and began the tradition of popes' changing their names upon election.

**[352G]** *Sequenti anno orta civili dissensione. . . .* The Lambertazzi, an important Bolognese family in the thirteenth century, headed the Ghibelline faction. They were forced into a mass exile from Bologna in 1274, but returned briefly in 1279. The Asinelli, who built and gave their name to one of the two famous towers extant today in Bologna, were also very influential. The Carbonesi, one of the most ancient families of Bologna, were prominent in the Ghibelline faction.

*Venetorum monumenta* B. refers to the chronicles of Andrea Dandolo, cited by Clavuot 109 n. 286.

**[352H]** *Ioannem Andreae Calderinum* Giovanni Calderini, d. 1365, from an illustrious Bolognese family with a strong professional tradition in the law.

Professor of canon law at Bologna, he published a number of works of jurisprudence, but was also active in public life: magistracies at Bologna and embassies to the Curia at Avignon. See H. J. Becker, "Calderini, Giovanni," *DBI* 16 (1973): 606–608.

*Nicolaum Albergatum* Nicolò Albergati, b. 1357. B.'s effusive praise may have something to do with this important religious reformer's connections with B.'s mentor Eugenius IV. Bishop of Bologna (1417–1443), Albergati was also a patron of humanists. Interestingly, Pope Nicholas V, Tomaso Parentucelli, was Bolognese, a secretary to Albergati, then his successor as Bishop of Bologna (1444–1447), even taking the name Nicholas as pope in Albergati's honor. Much of Albergati's professional effort was expended upon laborious mediations between Martin V and the Comune of Bologna, yet B. does not hint at the hostilities between Bologna and the papacy over papal rule. See E. Pasztor, "Albergati, Niccolò," *DBI* 1 (1960): 619–621.

*Antonius Bentivolius* Antonio Bentivoglio (early 1400s), from one of the most distinguished families of Bologna, with whom the story of the Bentivoglio power begins; this family held the ascendancy at Bologna through most of the Quattrocento. B. does not mention his organization in 1416 of the uprising against papal rule; Bentivoglio's successful coup to make himself signore; his exile in 1423; and, upon his return to Bologna in 1435, assassination by order of a papal governor. See O. Banti, "Bentivoglio, Antonio," *DBI* 8 (1966): 603–605.

[353A] *Nicolaus Faba* Niccolò Fava, born c. 1380, died 1439. Humanist, teacher of medicine and philosophy in the *studio* of Bologna; he was likened to Aristotle by his admirers. B. here repeats his popular name of "most famous philosopher." See M. Muccillo, "Fava, Niccolò," *DBI* 45 (1995): 420–422.

*Gaspar . . . episcopus Imolensis* Caspar Sighigelli, O. S. D., elected 1450, d. 1457; see Gams, *Series Episcoporum*, 702.

*Ludovicus de gente Lodovisia* I print the reading in Vat. lat. ottob. 2369, *Lodovisia* following Nogara's (*Scritti inediti*, 224) note that the Basel edition's reading *Ludosia* does not correspond with this manuscript's reading. The reading of Vat lat. ottob. 2369 is preferable, as Lodovisi is a name attested in Bologna.

*Bornius Salensis* Bornio da Sala, d. 1469, was a jurist and literary man who taught the law and held various civil offices; he was briefly exiled in civil conflicts. Like B., he dedicated a treatise (*De Principe*) to Borso d'Este.

**[353C]** *Primum ea dextera Padi ripa* ... B. describes the branch of the Po called the Primaro, now a dried-up riverbed. Next, he narrates the history of the fort built in the middle of the twelfth century by the Venetians, Marcamò (which B. calls Marcomama; see Plate VII, bottom left), as a blockade against commerce with Ferrara and Ravenna. The Ferrarese tore it down in 1309 and then built on the opposite bank of the river a new fort to operate against the Venetians.

*villa Belreguarda* Belriguardo was the first of the d'Este pleasure villas outside the city walls. Niccolò d'Este had the first version of it built in 1435; B. died before Borso added to it in 1469–1472. Leonello d'Este died at Belriguardo in October 1450.

**[354E]** *Fossadalbarum* Fossadalbero was a country estate of the d'Este.

*Codeghorum* is the modern Codigoro, a name derived from *Caput Gauri*, used to describe the confluence of the small branch of the Goro with the Po di Volano, a result of silting-up in the late Roman period.

**[354G]** *post donationem de exarchatu Ravennate factam Romanae ecclesiae* The act to which B. here refers, the "donation of Pepin" of 754, granted to the church many cities and towns in the exarchate of Ravenna and was the beginning of the papal states. See above on **[342G]**.

**[354H]** *tali domino felix* If B. is correct that these events took place in Clement V's papacy (1305–1341), he is omitting a number of conflicts, including excommunications, between the Este and the popes in the 14th century. After 1314, the last year of Clement V's rule, for example, in 1323 the pope accused the d'Este of heresy; and Obizzo III d'Este participated in the Ghibelline league against Pope John XXII in 1324. B. "whitewashes" history to present it to his patrons in a pleasing light, also glossing over the interference of Venice in Ferrara, which in the early fourteenth century led Pope Clement V to intervene. Before the Este took control in 1317, for example, the papal forces had taken Ferrara from the Venetians and put it under the control of Robert, King of Naples, as papal vicar.

For the Biblioteca Estense and especially Leonello's relations with Renaissance humanists, see Anthony Grafton, *Commerce with the Classics: An-*

*cient Books and Renaissance Readers* (Ann Arbor: University of Michigan Press, 1997), 19–49.

[354H–355A] *Nicolaus Estensis ... Leonellus ... Borsius* Biondo's assessment of Niccolò III d'Este, marquis of Ferrara and Modena (1383–1441), accords with modern biography (see A. Menniti Ippolito, "Este, Niccolò d'," *DBI* 43 [1993]: 396–403) in emphasizing Niccolò III's strengths in the political and military spheres, especially his skill at mediation between the more powerful developing regional states of Venice and Visconti Milan. Niccolò's brilliant diplomatic activity and the territorial expansion achieved under him in the first decades of the Quattrocento assured his small state a disproportionate role among the courts of the Po delta. That he was not lacking in intellectual sensibility is evident from his reopening of the University at Ferrara (1402); his presiding over the birth of the University of Parma (1412); and his patronage of Guarino Veronese, the driving force of Ferrarese humanism, and his school at Ferrara which welcomed many foreign students. In 1438 he welcomed to the Council of Ferrara eminent dignitaries of the Greek and Roman churches. The institution of the Biblioteca Estense at Modena exemplifies the activity of Niccolò III's principate in the development of the court of Ferrara, and the city's buildings, into one of the foremost centers of Renaissance culture.

Niccolò's favorite son and heir Leonello, 1407–1450, marquis of Ferrara, Modena, and Reggio, was instructed by Guglielmo Capello and Guarino Veronese, who arrived in Ferrara in 1429. Leonello continued his father's successful policy of peace-making. B.'s assessment of Leonello as a strong supporter of humanist culture comports with modern biography; see G. Brunelli, "Este, Leonello (Lionello) d'," *DBI* 43 (1993): 374–380. Leonello strove to exemplify the ideal of the philosopher-king and an equilibrium between the *vita activa* and the *vita contemplativa*. He fostered the hiring of eminent intellectuals to the Ferrarese Studio as well as acquisitions for the Biblioteca Estense. Among the intellectuals he welcomed to his court were Giovanni Aurispa and Teodoro Gaza; Leonello corresponded with the foremost humanists of his time: in addition to Biondo, Pier Candido Decembrio, Ambrogio Traversari, Lorenza Valla, Poggio Bracciolini, Francesco Barbaro, and Leon Battista Alberti. A promoter of the discovery of classical texts and a student of classical authors, he was the dedicatee of many works and translations; his interests extended to the visual arts.

Leonello shared his rule with his brother Borso, who succeeded him in 1450 and was marquis of Ferrara, Modena, Reggio, and Rovigo. As B. indicates, Borso's cultural orientations were more limited; a soldier, he trained in military science under Braccio da Montone.

**[355A]** *Roberto, Niccolò, Tito Strozzi* For this family of men of letters at the Estense court, see L. Carbone's funeral oration for Guarino in Bertoni (cf. above on **[347B]**). Niccolò Strozzi was a student of Guarino and a historian. His more famous brother Tito Vespasiano Strozzi (1424–1505), educated in the school of Guarino, was entrusted by Borso d'Este with diplomatic missions, but his principal fame came from his role as poet: an imitator of classical poets, he was influenced also by Petrarch. He wrote in Latin in a variety of genres, of which his elegies were the best-known.

*Lippus Platesius* Lippo Platesio, fifteenth-century poet and student of Guarino Veronese; mentioned in Carbone's funeral oration for Guarino (Bertoni, 166).

*Hieronymus Castellus* Girolamo Castelli, born at Ferrara in the first years of the fifteenth century, died approximately 1482. A student of Guarino Veronese, Castelli became a highly-esteemed physician at the Estense court. A classical scholar and poet as well in the humanist circle at Ferrara (addressee of elegies by Tito Vespasiano Strozzi), he counted among his friends and associates the greatest cultural figures of his age, e.g., Filelfo and Decembrio. See M. Palma, "Castelli, Girolamo," *DBI* 21 (1978): 729–730.

**[355D]** *ramus scinditur Ficaroli* The branch of the Po in the neighborhood of Ficarolo, commonly referred to as the "rotta di Ficarolo," "rotta di Sicardo," or simply "la rotta," resulted in 1152 when a portion of the waters of the Po broke through the banks, making a new course north of Ferrara (from this branch developed the modern Po, the Po di Venezia) and ultimately a new mouth near the present Loreo (a good map of the Po is included by Hans Philipp, *s.v.* "Padus," *RE* 18 pt. 2, 2178–2202; 2184). As a method of proof that this branch did not come into being until around 1350, B. employs, again to infelicitous result, an *argumentum ex silentio*, as he did in the cases of Modena and Pavia (see below on **[356G–H]** and **[364G]**). Unlike the long-lived legend of the sunken city of Conca (see above on **[342G]**), and the application of the name Padusa to a swamp (see above on **[348F]** and reference there to Gambi, *Cosa Era la Padusa?*), B.'s error in the case of the *rotta* was not perpetuated; for Leandro Alberti, relying on Riccobaldo da Ferrara's *Chronica Parva Ferrariensis* (early 14th c.), transmitted the correct date for this event (*Descrittione di tutta Italia* [Bologna: Giaccarelli, 1550], 306v, cit. L. Gambi, "Per una rilettura di Biondo e Alberti, geografi," in *Il Rinascimento nelle Corti Padane: Società e Cultura* [Bari: De Donato 1977], 259–275; 269–270).

Plate VII. © Biblioteca Apostolica Vaticana. MS. Vat. lat. 1960, fol. 267r, map of Fra Paolino Minorita (1330s). This map of the lower course of the Po river includes on far right the legend *"rota Figaroli"* (indicated by arrow).

Of the many regions of Italy in which he lived and traveled, we would most expect B. to have inspected personally and in detail, and to know the history and topography of, the Ferrarese; in Adriano Franceschini's words, B. had the area of the rotta "sotto gli occhi" and had every reason to be accurate in what he wrote about it. For B.'s well-attested purchase of property in 1442, residency in Ferrara in 1444, in S. Biagio near Argenta in 1449–1450 (*Blasianus, in quo villam habemus locupletam e regione Zanioli sitam, in qua horum partem scripsimus*, [353C]) as well as later residency in Ravenna and purchase of burial rights there, see A. Samaritani, "Il 'Vicus Blasianus' tra Bessarione e Biondo Flavio," *Atti e Memorie della Deputazione Provinciale Ferrarese di Storia Patria* ser. 3, 13 (1973): 157–172; and S. Bernicoli,

"Flavio Biondi in Ravenna," *Il Ravennate Corriere di Romagna*, 4 December 1900, 68. But although B. acknowledges (**[354F]**) that the ramifications and changes in the riverbeds of the Po near Ferrara cause *locorum confusionem*, an unwillingness to fully take into consideration the same topographical indeterminacy condemns his method to failure in this instance.

B. places this event *intra centum proximos annos*, around 1350, basing his *argumentum ex silentio* on the absence of the *rotta* on the map of King Robert I of Naples and Petrarch, and in 400-year-old documents of the church of S. Salvatore di Ficarolo and its successor S. Lorenzo delle Caselle which describe boundaries of properties in Ficarolo conceded to the church. The map is no longer extant, but its omission of the *rotta* is meaningless as evidence in the face of the inclusion of the *rotta* on the map of fra Paolino Minorita from the 1330s (Plate VII: on this map, B. could have seen the *rotta*, noted on the far right-hand side of the map [center right on Plate VII] as "rota Figaroli"). As Clavuot (197–198) notes, B. does not apply critical judgement to the map of Petrarch; not asking whether it illustrates correctly and completely the condition of Petrarch's own time (for example, this map of the entire Italian peninsula might simply have omitted details too small for inclusion on such a large scale). B.'s second source, the document from the church of San Lorenzo delle Caselle (*vetusta annorum quadringentorum iurium suorum monumenta*, **[355D]**), describes property boundaries in the area of the *rotta*, on the basis of which B. correctly concludes the branch's non-existence in the eleventh century. But the value of these documents as evidence for this conclusion must also be called into question from a modern standpoint.

Research into the records of medieval Italian churches in the area around Ferrara can of course be accomplished more efficiently now, thanks in great part to the work of Samaritani and Franceschini. Their collections allow us to form a more complete picture of the inconsistency of descriptions of church property leased to individuals: some mention the *rotta* in delineating boundaries, but others do not; inclusion or omission of any specific topographical feature appears to mean very little. Although I was unable to find the precise documents to which B. refers here, it is not difficult to find records relating to the same church which disprove B.'s assumption that any property description after 1152 would have mentioned the *rotta* if it had then existed. (Most of these documents describe church property let by the church on long term leases [*enfiteusi*]; many of them are copies of earlier leases, copied and re-copied through the years without taking into account topographical changes. The custom seems to have been to demarcate boundaries by careless and inexact topographical references; the prevailing attitude was likely that, *grosso modo*, residents of the area knew what was church land.) From 1172, a diploma of Pope Alexander III in favor of the monastery of S. Salvatore di Ficarolo confirms the church's exemptions and rights over a property of which *inter confines numeratur rupta Padi* (in A. Samaritani, *Regesta Pomposiae* I. Deputazione Provincia Ferrara di Storia Patria Serie Monumenti 5 [1963], 199, #673). A decree of bishop Amato from 1158 grants a privilege over some land to the church of San Salvatore di Ficarolo and a prior who officiated there and defines the property at one point with *rupta Padi* (L. Muratori, *Antiquitates Medii Aevi diss*. LXX, cit. Francesco Ravelli, *Pagine Storiche di Ficarolo* [Bologna: Zanichelli, 1883], 23–24). Finally, Fondo S. Benedetto cartello A1 47, in the regesta of A. Franceschini, a permission at Ficarolo from 1356, shows a description of property at Ficarolo without mention of any rivers or their branches, attesting that later documents describing *beni* of the church in the same area contain no mention of the *rotta* among topographical marks used to define the properties. Proof of B.'s familiarity with such documents is afforded by a very interesting coincidence: a document from 1446 shows a concession to the Ravennate Carmelite Alessandro de Guarino, a property over which the monastery had rights, which was referred to as *la possessione de la rota*, and its concession to de Guarinis was on condition that it not be rented or in any way conceded to our author or another person (Chiappini, Alessandra, "Manfredo Maldenti forlivese tra Biondo Flavio, Civis Ravennae, Venetiae et Ferrarie e Ludovico Carbone," in Dante Bolognesi, ed., *Ravenna in età Veneziana* [Longo Editore: Ravenna, 1986], 227–244; 229).

Many realities and circumstances must be invoked to explain why it is generally only in the 1600s and 1700s that we begin to see maps of this area consistently use the *rotta* as a boundary. The area of the Ferrarese was for centuries upset by *rotte* and displacements of riverbeds; it also, like the area around Cattolica, has underground rivers. Not a single event, but many successive *rotte*, or breaks in the banks of the Po, would have to take place before a new river bed could be sharply defined; the *rotta di Ficarolo* took about 150 years to define itself. This hydrologic indeterminacy is attested in local cartography and history: early maps, such as that in A. Franceschini, "I Sostegni Rossettiani di Polesella" (in *Uomini, Terre ed Acque: Politica e Cultura Idraulica nel Polesine tra '400 e '600*, edd. Cazzola, Franco, and

Achille Olivieri, [Rovigo: Minelliana, 55–89]), 68, fig. 1, depict a *canale morto*, an indication of the precarious status of canals in swampland.

B.'s assumption is thoroughly flawed, that one could not have delineated church property in Ficarolo without referring to an existing *rotta*. We can perhaps see in this rigorous attention to documentary sources and concomitant refusal to attend to local tradition, personal observation, and common sense, B.'s focus, in the years of composition of *It. ill.*, on the development of a historical method which privileged documents and research and sources chronologically close to the event under discussion. In this case, a reverence for Petrarch might have contributed as well to B.'s choosing his map and the church records over the more trustworthy chronicle of Riccobaldo.

# Seventh Region, Lombardy Commentary

Biondo's "Lombardia" comprises the region in the west, formerly Cisalpine Gaul but including part of the ancient Gallia Transpadana as well as northern Liguria (since B. limited his "Liguria" to the coastal strip described by Bracelli, much of the interior area comprised in Pliny's Liguria falls in B.'s Lombardia), the western part of Emilia, and the western part of Venetia. B. uses for this region a name commonly used in the language of the church since the end of the 8th century (see Clavuot 58). The name "Marca di Lombardia" became current when the Carolingian empire ended (888), applied to the area from the Alps and the Ticino river to the territory of Modena. As B. admits, the cities of Verona, Vicenza, Padua, and Treviso might seem more appropriately attributed to Lombardy, but his method necessitates placing them in the March of Treviso.

B.'s procedure in this long chapter (a procedure summarized by Clavuot, 81–82) is to describe the tributaries of the Po with their affluents, presenting inhabited places on their banks. He begins with the southern tributaries of the Po and moves from east to west; then the northern tributaries from the Mincio. Then he ranges beyond the rivers to discuss regions between them.

**[356F]** *Bondenum* Here B. must refer to Pliny, *NH* 3.122, yet he actually confuses Pliny's assertion based on Metrodorus of Scepsis that the Ligurian name referred to the river's depth, with a Gallic name derived from the word for pine tree (*padus*); cf. Zehnacker 246. The passage from Pliny,

> Pudet a Graecis Italiae rationem mutuari; Metrodorus tamen Scepsius dicit, quoniam circa fontem arbor multa sit picea, quales Gallice vocentur padi, hoc nomen accepisse, Ligurum quidem lingua amnem ipsum Bodincum vocari, quod significet fundo carentem. Cui argumento adest oppidum iuxta Industria vetusto nomine Bodincomagum, ubi praecipua altitudo incipit.

> I am ashamed to borrow from the Greeks explanations of Italian toponyms; but Metrodorus of Scepsis says that the Po acquired this name because around its source there are many spruce trees, of a type called *padi* in the Gallic language; and that in the language of the Ligurians the river itself was called *Bodincus*, which means "bottomless." This hypothesis is supported by the neighboring town of Industria, its ancient name Bodincomagum, which is located where the river's greatest depth begins.

### [356G] Mutina (Modena)

*. . . exire Mutinensi agro, statis diebus Volcanum.* With no transition from or to the historical/political contexts preceding and following, B. inserts this mention from Pliny (*NH* 2.240) of the marvelous fire that issues from the earth on days sacred to Vulcan.

> Quid quod innumerabiles parvi, sed naturales, scatent? . . . (flamma) exit in Mutinensi agro statis Volcano diebus.

> What of the many small fires which naturally shoot forth (from the earth)? . . . in the territory of Modena, fire shoots forth on the days sacred to Vulcan. . . .

*Mutinam quae nunc exstat novam esse. . . .* We saw B. privileging documents to the exclusion of personal observation and common sense in his discussion of the "rotta di Ficarolo" ([355D], p. 106). Although here in the discussion of Modena he relies again on an *argumentum ex silentio*, and although he confuses the two settlements, B.'s research has led him to the correct conclusion about the transfer of the original population. But he is mistaken about the recent foundation of the late medieval city. As Clavuot, 193–4 n. 215, and J. K. Hyde (*Society and Politics in Medieval Italy* [New York: St. Martin's], 1973), 22–24, point out, the original settlement on the site of Roman Mutina, damaged by floods and war, was abandoned in the 5th and 6th centuries. In the first half of the eighth century the Lombard king Liutprand built a new fortified town more to the west, so as to control the Via Emilia and the crossing of the Secchia river, called Cittanova or Città Geminiana (after the patron saint of the diocese, whose bones were entombed there), and the two settlements continued to exist side by side until in the late ninth century bishop Leodoino obtained the right to fortify the "ecclesiastic" city (on the original site of Mutina), and so the city was reborn. Hyde draws on the *Mutinensis Urbis Descriptio*, which B. apparently could not—or neglected to—consult.

**[356H]** *Reverum . . . Ostilia* Modern Ostiglia is a town opposite Revere on the left bank of the Po; this was the foothold of the d'Este upon the Po. The Gonzaga ducal palace at Revere was built between 1450 and 1460, so B. must here report on a work in progress.

**[357A–B]** *Regium Lepidum* The d'Este took possession of Modena and Regium Lepidum/Reggio Emilia. B. refers here to Borso's investiture (1452) by Emperor Frederick III.

**[357C]** *Brixillum* Clavuot, 224, cites Pliny *NH* 7.162–3 parallel with Biondo on Brixellum as an example of B.'s use of sources, specifically his concentration on single passages which he exploits intensively.

*Tannetum* B.'s treatment here is an example of his purposeful shortening of longer passages to a few lines according to his interests (cf. Clavuot 219–220), here the retreat of the Romans and the allusion to the long since disappeared forest around Modena. Parts of the passage in Livy, 21.25.3 (218 B.C.), which correspond to B.'s summary:

> Ipsi triumviri Romani, qui ad agrum venerant adsignandum, diffisi, Placentiae moenibus Mutinam confugerunt. C. Lutatius C. Servilius M. Annius . . . legati ad expostulandum missi ad Boios violati sint . . . Mutinae cum obsiderentur . . . simulari coeptum de pace agi . . . comprehenduntur. L. Manlius praeter ira accensus effusum agmen ad Mutinam ducit. Silvae tunc circa viam erant plerisque incultis.

Polybius relates one ambush, Livy two. B. may mistake *Romani Tannetum, vicum propinquum Pado, contendere* for *Bois in agrum suum Tannetum profectis*. B. reworks this Livian passage to extract from it the necessary topographical indications; see *infra* on **[362E]**, where B. quarries it for evidence on the location of the ancient Tannetum.

*Sarsina* Modern Sassina, an ancient town in Umbria and birthplace of the comic poet Plautus. B. elsewhere **[344E]** accepts the (generally discredited) story in Eusebius of Plautus' working in a mill.

*Alpes Bardonis/Barcetum/Berceto* Clavuot (272–273) identifies this passage as an example of B.'s noting place names in the margin of Paulus Diaconus' *History of the Longobards*. B. marked Paulus Diaconus' account of Venantius Fortunatus because of the topographical information it contained.

**[357D]** *Livius* Clearly B. here means Pliny (*NH* 7.136).

*Blasius* Biagio of Parma, the philosopher and astronomer Biagio Pelacani (d. 1416). B.'s error in interpreting the inscription on Biagio's tomb at Parma, which mentioned both Biagio and Macrobius, led him to conclude that both were buried in the same tomb. Weiss notes, *Discovery*, 122:

> the sculptor responsible for [Biagio's] tomb, still to be seen on the front of the Cathedral, represented Pelacani on the right end of it and Macrobius on the left. With the result that already not so many years later, scholars like Ciriaco d'Ancona and Flavio Biondo were led to believe that the tomb was that of Macrobius, to which Pelacani's remains had been added.

**[358E]** *Martialis poeta* ... B. cites 5.13.8, on the poet's poverty in comparison with the wealth of his friend Callistratus; the poem is not about this region, but uses Parma as an example of a place from which Callistratus derives part of his revenue. Perhaps more appropriate would have been Martial 14.155.1, concerned with wool production:

> Velleribus primis Apulia, Parma secundis
> nobilis: Altinum tertia laudat ovis.

> Apulia produces the best wool, Parma produces the next best,
> and the sheep of Altinum obtain the third place.

**[358F]** *Burgus ... Dononius ... in via Aemilia est Fidentiola* B. names Borgo San Donnino and Fidentiola as if they were two distinct towns; he "sees" two towns and uses the "decadent" name Fidentiola, which suggests that he might have used an old map at this point. But Borgo San Donnino substituted the Roman *municipium*. The ancient name of the Augustan *municipium* was Fidentia. "Fidentiola vicus" was its name in the third century A.D., a form which reflects its decline. Borgo San Donnino arose in the eighth or ninth century, as a result of the location there of the relics of San Donnino, martyred in 303 A.D. B.'s confusion is recorded in his paraphrase or citation of Livy, in which he gives the toponym "Fidentiola," whereas Livy (or the author of the *Periocha*), gives the name Fidentia. It is clear from B.'s wording here that his source is Livy, *Periocha* 88, *Sylla Carbonem, eius exercitu ad Clusium ad Faventiam Fidentiamque caeso, Italia expulit.*

Pier Luigi dall'Aglio, "*Fidentia*—Borgo San Donnino-Fidenza," *JAT* 7 (1997): 37–48, rejects the hypothesis, similar to B.'s description, that a village called "Fidentiola vicus" arose near the city, concluding (48) that Fidentiola was swallowed up by the Diocese of Parma, and that in the era of the communes Borgo San Donnino attained a size to encompass the area once occupied by the Roman city.

*Gian Galeazzo Visconti* b. 1351, first and one of the greatest dukes of Milan. The account of his acquisition of power figured prominently in B.'s *Historiarum Decades* and ensures his frequent mention in B.'s chapters on northern Italy.

*Placentia* Clavuot, 111, notes B.'s treatment of Placentia as an example of his repeated breaking through the limits of local and regional history with episodes of high politics. Placentia opposed Hannibal in the second Punic War. In the third century A.D. it saw the Marcomanni defeat Aurelian, which according to Trebellius Pollio put the Roman empire on the verge of destruction.

**[358G]** *Trebellius Pollio* The author we now identify as Vopiscus, in Hohl, *SHA*, 2, 164 (26.21.1).

*Scribit . . . Livius XXI* B. here, as often, cites erroneously and abbreviates his model, Livy 27.47.6–7.

**[358H]** *Tinca* Cf. Cic. *Brut*. 46, 172; see G. V. Sumner, *The Orators in Cicero's* Brutus: *Prosopography and Chronology* (Toronto and Buffalo: University of Toronto Press, 1973), 102.

**[359A]** *bombardis* One of B.'s few lapses in the *It. ill.* into post-classical Latin. The new phenomenon of firearms intensified the humanists' debate on whether or not neologisms should be introduced into otherwise Ciceronian Latin; Biondo compromised by using new terms for new realities. See O. Besomi and M. Regoliosi, "Valla e Tortelli," pt. 1, *IMU* 9 (1966): 75–189, 85.

**[359B]** *Clastidium* In Livy's time, a fortress in Gallia Cisalpina (21.48.9).

**[360E]** *Alexandria* After its foundation in the thirteenth century, this city assumed an important military role in the affairs of the Lombard League.

**[360F]** *Asta* The modern Asti is now in Liguria. Cf. Pliny *NH* 3.49; and Clavuot's (155.n.72) citation of the city-description *Chronicon Astense* from the end of the 13th c., in L. Muratori, *Rerum Italicarum Scriptores* (Milan 1727), 11.149–152. The modern towns Monticello d'Alba and Pollenzo, which correspond to B.'s Monticellum and Pollentum (modern Pollenzo and the Roman Pollentia), and Morum (La Morra), which B. appears to locate between Asti and Alba, are actually beyond Alba as one travels southwest along the Tanaro from Asti. This inaccuracy is typical of B.'s observations about towns in very mountainous regions and suggests that the very regions for which his following local maps results in a knowledge of dialectal toponyms are also those whose mountainous topographies yielded inaccurate relations between locations. However, see below on **[360G]** on the source of the Po between Crissolo and Oncino.

*Aqua civitas* The modern Acqui Terme (the modern name reflects its importance from Roman times for its thermal springs).

**[360G]** *Carmagnola* B.'s summarizing comments on the Milanese defeat of Carmagnola exemplify his practice, an aspect of the new historiography, of following heathen ancient historiography, with its emphasis on human behavior as cause, as opposed to the moralizing Christian interpretation of such events as manifesting God's working in human lives (Clavuot 25 n. 14).

*Padi ortus . . . Uncinum . . . Cricium* B. agrees with Pliny (*NH* cited below), Virgil (*Aen.* 6.6), and Servius on the identification of the Po with the Eridanus. Probably due to the severely flawed ms. of Pliny he used, he interprets as a toponym Pliny's appositive *visendo fonte* (a spring well worth seeing).

*Padi fons mediis diebus aestivis velut interquiescens semper aret.* B. recognizes Mt. Vesulus as the location of the source of the Po, today narrowed down to a reservoir in meadows on the mountain Monviso. B.'s accuracy here is striking when his description is compared to a modern map; he has pinpointed exactly what modern cartography shows. We must conclude that the source of the Po was such an object of interest that his contemporaries had spent enough time and effort defining it to have arrived at a near-modern level of accuracy. Uncharacteristically, however, he fails to cite Virgil, *Aen.* 10.707–709,

> ac velut ille canum morsu de montibus altis
> actus aper, multos Vesulus quem pinifer annos
> defendit. . . .
>
> Just like the boar driven by snapping dogs down from the high mountains, protected for many years by pine-covered Vesulus. . . .

**[360H–361B]** B. announces his strategy of returning to the East to the border of Lombardy above the Po. He is one book—and one vegetable—off in citing Pliny on the turnip (B. has *faba*, the bean), NH 18.34.125–126: *quamquam prius de rapis dixisse conveniat ... si iustus ordo fiat, a frumento protinus aut certe faba dicendis, quando alius usus praestantior his non est*; and 18.34.127–128: *a vino atque messe tertius hic transpadanis fructus*.

**[360H]** *Mincius* A tributary of the Po in Cisalpine Gaul, the modern Mincio runs past Mantua.

*Mantua* Modern Mantova/Mantua, on the river Mincio which surrounds it on three sides. B.'s treatment is weighted towards its medieval disasters and those of his own times. The first section of Livy to which B. alludes is not known. Virgil is thought to have been born in neighboring Pietole (see R. Sabbadini, *Le scoperte dei codici greci e latini*, 132 n. 25: the first direct notice [independent of the Dantean tradition], on Pietole, found in Benzo d'Alessandria, identifies it as the supposed birthplace of Virgil). A treatment exemplary of B.'s brief summary descriptions (cf. Clavuot 127 n. 345); his similar uses of generals and politicians on the one hand and literary men and scholars on the other (cf. Clavuot 132, on Giovanni Francesco I Gonzaga); and his functional use of Virgil and almost *verbatim* citations of this poet (cf. Clavuot 234). Where the Basel edition reads *Virgilius civis suus ... diffusiusque eius verbis narrat originem*, the reading from the Verona 1482 edition, *urbis*, is preferable to *verbis*.

B. first cites verbatim Aen. 10.201,

> Mantua dives avis, sed non genus omnibus unum.

B.'s next citation, from Livy, is not from book 22, but 32.30.5–6; his third citation of Livy is not from book 23, but 24.10.6, *Mantuae stagnum effusum Mincio amni cruentum visum*.

**[361A]** *Mantua vae miserae....* The final quotation is taken verbatim from Virgil *Ecl*. 9.27–28.

**[361B]** *Virgilius, Quos patre Benaco....* The variant here suggests that B. is citing Virgil from memory. B. has *ducebat in aequora* puppi; Virgil's lines are (*Aen*. 10. 205–206):

> quos patre Benaco velatus harundine glauco
> Mincius infesta ducebat in aequora pinu.

B., like Virgil, is surprisingly often correct: "The illustrations testify to the fidelity of Vergil's writings to the topography and nature of the land" (Alexander G. McKay, *Vergil's Italy* [Greenwich, CT: Graphic Society 1970], 16; in general, McKay provides thorough identification of Virgil's toponyms and descriptions). But unlike Virgil, B., despite his own obvious sentimental and patriotic attachment to another part of northern Italy (the Romagna), shows little awareness or appreciation for Virgil's (or Martial's) emotional connections to northern Italy as an ideal landscape, homeland, and escape from Rome.

**[361B]** *Gonzaga* Giovanfrancesco I Gonzaga (1395–1444), the first marquis, and his wife Paola Malatesta (1393–1453) were married in 1410. In addition to this mention, B. alludes to their marriage at **[335D]**. The presence of Vittorino da Feltre at his court, invited to teach his children, conferred prestige upon Gianfrancesco's court, assuring it a prominent position in Renaissance culture. Gianfrancesco was most famous for his military exploits, but exercised a cultural policy befitting a humanist prince, and Vittorino acquired many classical texts for his library. See also Nogara, 175, B.'s letter to Galeazzo Sforza which according to Fubini ("Biondo, Flavio," *DBI*, 538), possibly indicates B.'s being known at the court of Mantua in his poorly-attested years 1410–1420.

*Lacus Benacus* The largest lake in Italy; B. recognizes its present name of Garda derived from the town on this lake. B. is accurate in the location of Piscaria (Pescheria), where the Mincio has its outlet; and Turbolum (Torbole), location of the debouching of the Sarca river into the lake (the Sarca flows into Lake Garda, the Mincio flows out of it).

**[361C]** *Desentianum* . . . *Salodium* . . . *Madernum* . . . *Riva* Modern Desenzano del Garda, on the eastern shore of Lake Garda, corresponds to B.'s mention of Desentianum on the lake's left shore, assuming that he is looking north from the south.

*Sermionum* B. mentions in connection with Pescaria the citadel and bridge built there by the della Scala at Pescheria; he may indicate the Rocca Scaligera which is located on the peninsula of Sirmione. Associations for modern classicists are of course with Catullus, whom B. does not mention in this connection although he has clearly read his poetry, for he cites it elsewhere.

*Lacus Sebuinus/Iseus* B. refers to the new name of the lake (Lago d'Iseo).

**[361C]** *Riva* An example of B.'s confident use in *It. ill.* of medieval sources, here Paulus Diaconus, *Hist. Long.* 5.5. This methodology contrasts with his procedure in *Roma instaurata* (cf. Clavuot 297, who cites both passages and notes B.'s willingness here to endorse the medieval historiographer's explanation).

**[361D]** *Ubi fontem habeat Ollius. . . .* B. could not determine this river's source on the basis of maps alone, and thus relies on the somewhat peculiar statements of the inhabitants (cf. Clavuot 191, n. 207).

**[362E]** *Loarium* The modern Lovere, in dialect Loer. Clavuot (143 n. 18) asserts that B. must have worked with regional maps for this area, as only they could have possessed the preciseness desired in *It. ill.*

*Brixia* The modern Brescia, familiar to B. from his service here in 1427. Cf. Nogara XLVII–XLVIII; Fubini, "Biondo Flavio," *DBI*, 539. For the seven cities of northern Italy B. describes—Milan, Como, Brescia, Verona, Bergamo, Trento, and Vicenza—he regularly recurs to the same five passages in Justin's *Epitome* of Pompeius Trogus (on the areas settled by the Gauls). Clavuot (165) concludes from this that Justin is B.'s major source here; despite Livy's (32.30.5–6) disagreement with Justin about the origin of Brescia, B. opposes both without deciding in favor of either source.

B's first "citation" (*his verbis*) from Livy is indeed from book 21, but is a brief paraphrase of 21.25.9–14, with L. Manlius changed to L. Aemilius. The second citation, from Livy, which B. notes as from book 22, is from book 32, cited above on **[360H]**, with the addition of the subsequent sentence (32.30.6; cf. 5.35.1), *Inde mittendo in vicos Cenomanorum Brixiamque, quod caput gentis erat. . . .*

**[362F]** *Vitelliana* Modern Viadana, listed by Clavuot, 100–101 and n. 267, among examples of B.'s more reliable explanations for etymologies of city names associated with their foundations (as opposed to cases like that of Siena where B. appears to disregard ancient evidence for its foundation in antiquity).

**[362G]** *Cremona* An example of B.'s habit of stating briefly and without proof or reference to Livy, the importance of a number of northern and mid-Italian cities to the stability of the Roman Empire (cf. Clavuot, 91). B. might have appealed to Livy 21.25.2. This passage also, according to Clavuot (104), exemplifies B.'s interest in, and frequent mention of, the suffering of

Italian cities during the Middle Ages at the hands of Goths, Lombards, Saracens, and Hungarians.

*Gerardus Sablonet(i)us* The two main books in Islamic medicine cited by philosophers like Roger Bacon and Albertus Magnus. Avicenna wrote the *Canon of Medicine*. Rasi is Rhazes (al-Razi), Iranian physician and philosopher, b. 864 A.D., d. 925 or 932; he wrote a work which, when translated into Latin, was given the title *Liber Almansoris*. See Clavuot, 131 and n. 360, on B.'s evaluation of knowledge of Greek as part of a cultural ideal.

**[362H]** *Machastorma* The *castello di Maccastorna* still standing today near the ferry stop of Crotta d'Adda is likely that mentioned by B.

**[363A]** *Ambrosius Vignatensis* Ambrogio da Vignati. G. Vinay, *L'Umanesimo subalpino nel secolo XV* (Turin: Gabetta, 1935), asserts that due to his success as a lawyer Vignati is often named in the Piedmontese history of his era.

*Mapheus Veggius* Maffeo Veggio (1407–1458), most famous for writing a "Thirteenth Book of the *Aeneid*"; he held positions in the pontifical bureaucracy and was acquainted at Rome with B. and other major humanists.

*Lauda* Modern Lodi and ancient Laus Pompeia. B. here takes issue with Pliny (*NH* 3.124), ... *ex quibus (sc. oppida) Laevi et Marici condidere Ticinum non procul a Pado, sicut Boi Transalpibus profecti Laudem Pompeiam, Insubres Mediolanum.*

He mentions that common opinion declares Lauda Vetus to be a Pompeian foundation destined for the pirate chiefs Pompey had conquered, but cannot decide between the opinion of Servius, that this city was settled by Pompey to give land to the pirates, and that of Lucan, who depicts Caesar decreeing that the land around Ariminum (Rimini) be allotted to his veterans. Odoacer, murdered by Theoderic in 493, dethroned in 476 Orestes' son Romulus Augustulus, the last Western Roman emperor. Odoacer was the son of Edeco, Orestes' colleague.

**[363C]** *Bergomum civitas vetusta.* B. repeats his use of Justin as source for Italian cities founded by the Gauls. For Gasparino Barzizza, see commentary above on **[346H]**.

**[363D]** *Comum civitas vetusta. . . .* At the end of the south-western curve of the modern Lake Como. Here B. is certainly paraphrasing Pliny, *NH* 3.21.124:

> Oromobiorum stirpis esse Comum atque Bergomum et Licini Forum aliquotque circa populos auctor est Cato, sed originem gentis ignorare se fatetur, quam docet Cornelius Alexander ortam e Graecia interpretatione etiam nominis vitam in montibus degentium.
>
> Cato says that Como, Bergamo, Forum Licinii, and some of the surrounding peoples are of the race of the Oromobii, but he acknowledges that he does not know the origin of this tribe, although Alexander Polyhistor asserts that it came from Greece, by way of interpreting their name as "mountain dwellers."

See Zehnacker, ad *NH* 3.124, for modern correction of Pliny on the history of Como and Bergamo.

*incolatus* "residing, dwelling": an example of usage of post-classical words, relatively infrequent in B. Clavuot (128 n. 350) explains that Veronese local pride amplified Pliny's application to Catullus of *conterraneus* (*NH* praef. 1) into evidence that Pliny too came from Verona.

*Caecilius* Catullus' addressee Caecilius was a minor poet. Compare B.'s text of Catullus 35.1–7 with that of the modern edition of Fordyce:

> Poetae tenero, meo sodali,
> uelim Caecilio, papyre, dicas
> Veronam ueniat, Novi relinquens
> Comi moenia Lariumque litus.
> nam quasdam uolo cogitationes
> amici accipiat sui meique.
> quare, si sapiet, uiam uorabit. . . .

B. seems unaware of the name Novum Comum, acquired in 59 B.C. when Caesar resettled the town with 5,000 colonists (cf. Appian, B.C. ii.26; Suet. *Jul.* 28, and C. J. Fordyce, *Catullus* [Oxford: Clarendon, 1961], 176).

*Plinius Comi conversatus* B. abbreviates Pliny here; the original sentence, *NH* 2.232, reads: *In Comensi iuxta Larium lacum fons largus horis singulis semper intumescit ac residit lapidem* Pliny *NH* 36. 159:

> lapis est qui cavatur tornaturque in vasa vel coquendis cibis utilia vel ad esculentorum usus, quod et in Comensi Italiae lapide viridi accidere scimus. . . .
>
> (On the island of Siphnos) there is a stone which one hollows out and shapes into a round contour for vessels for cooking or the table, and we know that it is the same with the green stone from Como in Italy. . . .

[364E] *Modoetia ... basilica beati Ioannis Baptistae* Monza, important in the seventh century under the Lombards, whose queen Theodelinda converted her Arian subjects to Roman Catholicism. The iron crowns of Monza were the instrument of the Italian coronation of kings. Their tradition says that Theodelinda, daughter of a Bavarian king, widow of Authari king of the Lombards and then married to Agilulf, the Lombard duke of Turin, endowed the cathedral she built (the Johannes Church) with her Lombard treasures, which included an iron nail from the cross of Christ. A Lombard after Theodelinda had this nail beaten into a thin circle, which became the base of the golden and bejewelled crown used to confer the rule over Italy in the medieval period. B.'s judgement here inspired Muratori to undertake his first research in medieval history, in which he also called the iron crowns an absurd habit: *De corona ferrea* (1698).

[364F] *Senolegum* B. uses here the name in dialect; cf. Olivieri, *Diz. di top. lomb.*, s.v. *Senolegum.*

*Rhetia* Rhetia, the third and fourth regions of Italy according to Diocletian's division, as opposed to Pliny's, which B. follows. Cf. Justin 20.5.9, *Tusci quoque duce Raeto avitis sedibus amissis Alpes occupavere et ex nomine ducis gentem Raetorum condiderunt.*

[364G] *Papia/Ticinum* Modern Pavia was the metropolis of the Lombards, formerly the Roman Ticinum. On this change in place names cf. O. Besomi, ed., L. Valla, *Gesta Ferdinandi regis Aragonum* (Padua, 1973), 1.2.3. In an *argumentum ex silentio* here (*si Papia tunc fuisset, aut Ticinum urbs*), B. dismisses Pliny's assertion of Pavia's foundation by the Laevi and Marici, placing all reliance instead on the authority of Livy, and arguing from his silence that Pavia must not have existed in 218 B.C. The relevant sections of Livy are 21.39.10 and 21.45.1–2.

Attila invaded Italy and sacked Pavia in 452, along with Milan and other cities. Clavuot, at 111, notes that the fate of Italy was decided in Pavia when, in 951, Otto I had freed Adelaide from the hands of Berengar II, had elevated himself to kingship over Italy, and had thus ended a long period of misery for the peninsula (but see Clavuot 111, n. 290, who notes that Adelaide had already succeeded in recovering her freedom before Otto's arrival in Italy). For a detailed account of medieval Pavia in the eighth century, see Jan T. Hallenbeck, *Pavia and Rome: The Lombard Monarchy and the Papacy in the Eighth Century*. Transactions of the American Philosophical Society 72, pt. 4 (Philadelphia: American Philosophical Society, 1982). In general, B. gives a minimal sketch of Pavia, omitting the city's important role as capital of the Lombard kingdom, because he is condensing from *Decades* 102H (cit. Clavuot 292) information taken from Paul the Deacon's *History of the Lombards* (2.27). Hallenbeck provides a modern treatment of this city which relies on many sources available to B.

**[364H]** *Alboinus ... resistentia* Late Latin for the classical *repugnantia*. Pavia was the first Italian city to resist the Lombard king Alboin (572). At *Decades* 102H B. condensed this episode from Paulus Diaconus (*Hist. Long*. 2.27), as he used in both *Decades* and *It. ill*. many of the passages he marked in manuscripts; see Clavuot 292. Paulus Diaconus has *Ad cuius viri boni vocem et mutavit mentem Alboinus et surgenti equo illaesus insedit.*

**[365A]** *Epifanius* Epiphanius was bishop from 467–497 and, as B. notes, politically active and powerful.

*duodevigesimus nominis ordine Ioannes* B. must actually have intended to write *quatuordecesimus*; he describes here John XIV (Clavuot does not correct the error, 125 n. 336). Peter Canepanova was bishop of Pavia when in 983 he was appointed Pope by Otto II; he held on to his office only a few months. Deposed by the antipope Boniface VII, as B. correctly relates, John XIV starved to death in prison.

*Catonem Saccum, et Silanum* Vinay, *L'umanesimo subalpino*, 34, asserts that Catone Sacco was an outstanding representative of humanism in a jurist; and, 183, names a *Sillanus iureconsultus* recommended to Cristoforo Vellate by Antonio Astesano.

**[365B]** *Lacus Verbanus, Luganus, S. Iulii* Lago di Maggiore is even today given the alternate name of Verbano. But B.'s description of two smaller lakes flowing into Lago Maggiore, the one on the right named Lugano, the one on the left, S. Giulio, does not correspond to the modern map of this area of Italy, according to which Lago di Lugano is separated about 24 km.

from Lago Maggiore, and Lago di Orta (the obvious match with S. Giulio) is separated from Lago Maggiore by what looks like fairly mountainous territory. Lago di Mergozzo is almost continuous with Lago Maggiore, so is a good candidate for S. Giulio. But the town named Orta S. Giulio right on Lago di Orta seems to show an association between the names Orta and S. Giulio. It seems obvious that B. is following a map here, or else the topography would have to have changed so drastically in the last five hundred years that lakes which were contiguous are now separated by land and mountain masses.

[365C] *Theudelinda* Authari reigned 584–90, and died leaving a fairly recent marriage with the Bavarian princess Theodelinda. For additional information, see Chris Wickham, *Early Medieval Italy: Central Power and Local Society 400–100* (Ann Arbor: University of Michigan Press, 1989), 32.

*Novaria* The heresiarch *Dulcinus* is fra Dolcino, a leader of the Apostolical sect, whose members, in addition to trying to live the apostolic life in spiritual poverty, also advocated the destruction of the church and its leaders; its practice was limited for the most part to the area in and around Lombardy. The heretics waged war for two years against the troops of Pope Boniface VIII, not Clement V as B. writes. Fra Dolcino and his partner Margaret were taken prisoner and executed at Vercelli in 1307. Fra Dolcino appears also in Dante, *Inferno* 28, 55–60.

[365D] *Cottiarum Alpium promontorium. . . .* The Cottian Alps, the Alps west of the present Turin, were named for Cottius, prefect under Augustus in the region.

*Omagnum, Vergonta, Mergotium* B. has misplaced these towns in reference to Lago di Mergozzo. Omegna, for example, if it is B.'s Omagnum, is at the end of Lago di Orta rather than "on the left side of Lago di Mergozzo" (B.). Pieve Vergonte, on the other hand, corresponds well to Vergonta "on the left of the Tonsa" (B.) if by the Tonsa we mean the Toce, and to the following description of Domo(do)ssula as "above Vergonta in the Alps." The Toce could well be the "Gravellonus river"—we see at its mouth the modern town of Gravellona Toce. In this mountainous area, again, accurate direct observation would be difficult and accurate mapmaking next to impossible in the fifteenth century. Here, B. possibly relies on maps which are not very accurate.

**[366E]** *Mediolanum* Milan receives the second-longest (after Verona) description accorded any city in *It. ill.*, attention not surprising in view of the city's importance and B.'s familiarity with it. The length of the descriptions of Verona and Milan are probably due also to the existence of models in medieval descriptions of these cities. J. K. Hyde, "Medieval Descriptions of Cities," *Bulletin of the John Rylands Library* 48 (1968): 309–340, discusses these and other *descriptiones*; see also Clavuot 122 and n. 326. B. would have known not only the speech of Filargo which he cites (**[367B]**), but also *De situ urbis Mediolanensis* (from the ninth or tenth century) and Bonvesin della Riva's *De Magnalibus Urbis Mediolani* (begun around 1288).

**[366G]** *L. Furius* Furius was as praetor allotted the province of Gaul for 200 B.C. B. here turns into *oratio obliqua* part of *Periocha* 31 of Livy. He then mistakes book 31 for *Periocha* 32, *Cornelius Cethegus cos. Gallos Insubres proelio fudit* (197 B.C.) and follows this with what he represents as a paraphrase of 31.49.2, but which is actually from the *Periocha* of book 33 (196 B.C.), *L. Furius Purpureo et Claudius Marcellus coss. Boios et Insubres Gallos subegerunt. Marcellus triumphavit.*

Procopius is the source for Milan's rank as the second city to Rome in area and population when it was besieged in 535 by the Goths, who allowed the troops in the city to escape before killing the city's male population and giving its women as slaves to the Burgundians.

**[366H–367A]** Frederick I razed Milan in 1162; the Visconti defeated their rivals the Torrini in 1287.

**[367A]** *pontifex Alexander V* Pietro Filargo (also known as Pietro di Candia) technically became the antipope Alexander V (1409–1410), elected by the council of Pisa whose authority was not officially recognized. Archibishop of Milan in 1402; the speech cited here on Milan (1394) before King Wenceslaus in Prague can be found in *Annales mediolanenses* (*RIS* 16, 821 c–d), cited in Clavuot 122 n. 122.

*Datius* Archbishop of Milan at the time of its conquest by the Goths in 535.

**[367C]** *Alexander II, Urbanus III, Celestinus IIII* B. is correct about the Milanese origins of Urban III (Umberto Crivelli, archbishop of Milan, whose refusal to crown Henry VI was perhaps the most notable conflict of his pontificate [1185–1187]) and Celestine IV (Goffredo da Castiglione, a cardinal bishop whose pontificate lasted only 16 days [1241]). Alexander II (1061–

1073) was Anselm, bishop of Lucca, before his elevation to the pontificate; his birthplace was Baggio, north of Pistoia, seemingly difficult to confuse with Milan. B. may have had in mind another Alexander, as he at times errs in the numbering of popes.

[367C] *Obertus de Orto* Oberto dall'Orto, famous jurist of the 12th c. The work B. refers to as *usus feudorum* is better known today as *Libri feudorum*, a collection which formed the foundation of feudal law for much of Europe.

[367D] *Antonius Raudensis* Antonio da Rho, c. 1395–1447, a student of Antonio Loschi; learned in poetry, rhetoric, and theology, he wrote about education and taught rhetoric at the *studium* in Milan. For biographical information see D. Rutherford, "A Finding List of Antonio da Rho's works and related primary Sources," *IMU* 33 (1990): 75–108.

*Extat lex censoria....* B. closely paraphrases Pliny 33.4.21 #78,

> Extat lex censoria Victumularum aurifodinae in Vercellensi agro, qua cavebatur ne plus quinque milia hominum in opere publicani haberent.
>
> The text of the censorial law exists, having to do with the gold mine of Victimulae in the territory of Vercellae, prohibiting the state tax-farmers from employing more than five thousand men in its exploitation.

[368E] *Augusta Praetoria* The modern Aosta; founded in 25 by Augustus. Pliny 3.43, the famous and influential comparison of the shape of Italy to that of an oak leaf, takes Praetoria Augusta as the northern boundary from which he begins to trace the longitude of Italy. B. seems not to know of the Roman bridge at Aosta which spanned a stream which changed course in the thirteenth century.

The inscription is that called the trophy of La Turbie, *CIL* V, 7817. For discrepancies in the numbers of the *civitates* between this inscription and that on the Arch of Susa (*CIL* V, 7231), see H. Zehnacker's notes *ad NH* 3.136–137.

*Alpium fores ... Graias atque Peninas* The Graian Alps (Petit-St. Bernard pass), which extend to Mont Blanc, and the Pennine Alps, between Vallais and upper Italy. Pliny, *NH* 3.134 transmits the mistaken majority opinion associating this first section of the Alps with Greeks. The reference is to Hercules crossing the Alps with the cattle of Geryon; his comrades became inhabitants of the Graian Alps. But see Lewis and Short *s.v.* "Alpes," for the Graian Alps, "the western division between Italy and France . . . a Celtic word of uncertain significance, sometimes falsely referred to Hercules Graius," and, for the Pennine Alps, "East of [the Graians], as the northern boundary of Italy . . . so called from the deity Penninus, worshipped there."

**[368G]** *celebre monasterium S. Antonii de Renverso* S. Antonio di Ranverso, a name derived from *rivus inversus*, was founded in the early twelfth c. by monks of the Antonian order of hospital brothers, and can be visited today.

*Plinius dicit* . . . From **[368E]** to this point, B. depends heavily upon Pliny, *NH* 3.123:

> Transpadana appellatur ab eo regio undecima, tota in mediterraneo, cui maria cuncta fructuoso alveo inportat. Oppida Vibi Forum, Segusio, coloniae ab Alpium radicibus Augusta Taurinorum —inde navigabili Pado—antiqua Ligurum stirpe, dein Salassorum Augusta Praetoria iuxta geminas Alpium fores, Graias atque Poeninas—his Poenos, Grais Herculem transisse memorant,—oppidum Eporedia Sibyllinis a populo Romano conditum iussis.

# Eighth Region, Venice Commentary

As Denis Hay notes ("Italian View of Renaissance Italy," 8), B.'s dedication of a separate chapter to Venice reflects the mid-fifteenth-century recognition of Venice as a major territorial power. This chapter imparts some sense of Venice's famed isolation and independence from mainland Italy. It is also, due to the city's foundation in late antiquity, almost completely lacking in the citations of classical authors so profuse in the rest of *Italia illustrata*. As he describes the mainland in "Lombardia" and "Marchia Tarvisina," this chapter dispenses with describing—or even acknowledging—the extent of Venice's conflicts and dominions on the mainland (her taking possession of Vicenza in 1404, for example, an act which B. portrays as benevolent, [**379C**]).

B.'s sources for this region were chronicles whose unmediated stylistic influences permeate this chapter of *Italia illustrata*, written before the great development of the Venetian image: "beauty, religiosity, liberty, peacefulness, and republicanism" (as expressed by Edward Muir, *Civic Ritual in Renaissance Venice* [Princeton: Princeton University Press, 1981], 21, and in general the first chapter, "The Myth of Venice," 13–61). As Clavuot, 179, demonstrates, B. has so summarized his major source, Andrea Dandolo, as to produce an account that itself reads like a chronicle. Andrea Dandolo (1306–54, doge 1343–1354), whom B. praises at the end of this chapter (see below on [**373A**]), wrote two Chronicles of Venetian history (ed. E. Pastorello, *Rerum Italicarum Scriptores*, 2nd ed. [Bologna 1938]). The *Chronica Altinate* is also an important source for Venice in this period (R. Cessi, ed., *Origo civitatum Italie seu Venetiarum [Chronicon Altinate et Chronicon Gradense]* [Rome 1933]), as is John the Deacon for Venetian history up to the 11th century; B. also uses Ademar's *Chronicle*, to which we have B.'s own marginalia (see Clavuot 325–337). Cochrane, 62, summarizes the chronicle tradition in Venice. Clavuot, 177–182, compares in detail Dandolo and B., and analyzes B.'s use of sources in "Venetia": primary reliance on Dandolo supplemented by his own *Decades* (although he cites

Dandolo only once, at **[298F]**). When Dandolo's chronicle stops (1280), he gives attention indirectly to more recent history of Venice through the descriptions of great Venetians.

B. later approached an inspired treatment of Venice at the end of the protreptic *De origine et gestis Venetorum* (**[292E]**, *divina potius quam human ope condi, ... salutis arx et domicilium sine muro, sine portis die noctuque pateret ...* ). For further discussion of B.'s connections to Venice and its intellectual history, see F. Gilbert, "Biondo, Sabellico, and the beginnings of Venetian official historiography," in J. G. Rowe and W. H. Stockdale, eds., *Florilegium historiale: Studies in Honor of W. H. Ferguson* (Toronto: University of Toronto Press, 1971), 275–293.

**[369A]** *ad annum salutis quinquagesimumsextum supra quadringentenum fuisse conditam* ... 456 A.D.; the traditional date of the founding is 421 A.D.

**[369B]** *Et Virgilius ... sic habet* ... Cf. my comments above on **[380F]**, where B. attempts to prove, mostly on the basis of ancient sources, that the ancient Timavus is the Brenta. Most modern authorities side with Biondo's contemporaries in identifying it with the modern Timavo in the area of Istria, which flows into the Gulf of Trieste. Virgil alludes at *Aen.* 1.242–6 to the tradition that the Trojan Antenor, cited by Venus as an example of an easier migration to Italy, founded Padua:

> Antenor potuit mediis elapsus Achivis
> Illyricos penetrare sinus atque intima tutus
> regna Liburnorum et fontem superare Timavi,
> unde per ora novem vasti cum murmure montis
> it mare proruptum et pelago premit arva sonanti.

**[369D]** *Olivolense* Olivolo was a fortified island; as a result, it later became known as Castello, and its church is still known as San Pietro in Castello.

*manes fuerit perpessa:* Virgil, *Aen.* 6.743, *quisque suos patimur manis*, of the souls in the underworld who are to be reincarnated but must first be cleansed of the contaminations of their previous lives. An echo cited for its literary value, this type of citation is rare in *It. ill.* (Clavuot 233 n. 108). B. reclaims the pathos of Virgil's souls by applying the line to cities which have suffered destruction and some of which have been rebuilt. The cycle of destruction and rebuilding is noticeable in the case of the cities of northern Italy.

*scissa patriarchali dignitate....* The transfer of the episcopal see from Aquileia to Grado in 569, and the beginnings of the complicated conflicts around the patriarchate of Aquileia. Grado and Aquileia are rather far, about sixty miles from Venice, at the extreme end of the Adriatic on the Gulf of Trieste. But, as B. seems to realize from his frequent interspersed inclusion of these conflicts in his summary of Venetian history, the relation of this division is extremely important in the history of the Venetian Republic.

After the Lombard invasion in 568 had caused the archbishop of Aquileia, Paolo, to flee to Grado, the bishops of Grado (Candianus) and Aquileia (John) each claimed to be his rightful successor. The solution B. mentions here was reached at the Synod of Pavia (683) and had the effect of making Grado the ecclesiastical center of Venice, thus confirming Venice's religious independence from the mainland. B. is in error at **[370E]** when he locates the new Aquileia at Grado. For Candianus and the division in the patriarchate, see Foulke-Peters, *Paul the Deacon History of the Longobards* 175–6 n.6. B. writes Candianus for Paul's Candidianus.

**[370E]** *Heraclea, Methamaucum, Equilium* Methamaucum-Malamocco, the center of government for the lagoon in the eighth century, was destroyed in 1105 by inundation from the sea and earthquake; see **[372G]**. Modern Malamocco on the southwest part of the Lido is not in the location of the original city. Malamocco, modern Eraclea on the mainland north of the present site of Venice; and Equilium (also called Jesolo, its ruins identifiable today near Cava Zuccherina) were the major settlements of the Venetians outside of the present site of Venice.

**[370G]** *Deusdedit* Elected in 742. The Byzantine emperor customarily appointed a military leader for the Venetian lagoons. The title was dux (doge). With the election of Deusdedit to the office, and the transfer of the seat of government to Malamocco, the Venetians brought about a change from appointed to locally elected ruler.

Here begins a series of chronological inconsistencies between B. and modern historians; I have not identified every one. Examples: Galla Gaulus, who deposed and blinded Deusdedit, was himself deposed and blinded after one year, not fourteen, of his reign; the doge Domenico Monegario, who ruled with tribunes as colleagues met the same fate after six, not one, years in office, etc.

*Adrianus papa ... dedit episcopum* In 774, not one year, but 10, after the election of Maurice as doge, the creation of the bishopric of Olivolo due to the growth of the islands' populations and prestige.

**[370H]** *Iniecit ... Mauritius dux* Expression of the beginnings of tensions between a party sympathetic to the Franks (John, patriarch of Grado), and the conservative allegiance to Constantinople (the doges, here Maurice).

*Pipinus ... bello Venetos agitare coepit....* Yet another event which contributed to the independence of Venice. See Clavuot 300–301 for B.'s manipulation of his sources in order to arrive at this conclusion, less damaging to Venetian prestige than would be a flat assertion of military defeat. The city's present site was chosen for its high bank (rivo alto) by the Venetians fleeing before the advent of Pepin in 810, who was charged with subjugating the Veneto to the restored Empire of the West.

**[371A]** *Agnellus Particiacus dux* The beginning of the dynasty of the Participazio or Particiaco, the first great Venetian ruling house.

**[371B]** *beati Marci corpus* B. omits the sensational and fundamentally important legend (and of course its political uses); see Muir, 80–83, with the admonition that it "seems to be a thirteenth-century fabrication" (80 and reference, n. 39 to Patrick J. Geary, *Furta Sacra: Thefts of Relics in the Central Middle Ages* [Princeton: Princeton UP, 1978], 140–142).

**[371D]** *Berengarium Foroiuliensem* Berengar I, Duke of Friuli, Frankish king of Italy and emperor (r. 888–924; emperor 915–924). See Wickham 221; Arnaldi, "Berengar," *DBI* 9 (1967), 1–26.

**[372E]** *Petro Tribuno ... vita functo* B.'s chronology corresponds fairly closely to the conclusions of modern historians based on the chronicles. In 912 Pietro Tribuno died, and was succeeded by Orso II Participazio; he reigned twenty years and was succeeded by Pietro Candiano, who ruled seven years until his death in 939; then came Pietro Participazio, who ruled 939–942; then Pietro Candiano III, who ruled for 17 years.

**[372F]** *Petrus Urseolus* With Pietro Orseolo II (r. 991–1008), begins the acquisition of empire, with the conquest of Dalmatia. Clavuot, 179, notes that B. conflates the two Orseoli (Pietro I, r. 976–978; Pietro II, r. 991–1009), into one person in his efforts to compress his source, Dandolo.

**[372H]** *urbis Constantinopolitanae dominio sunt potiti* This event (1204, despite B.'s dating of 1196), and the acquisition of Modon (**[372G]** above, *Veneti Motonio Peloponensi sunt potiti*), are the only events outside of Italy B. describes in his summary of Venetian history.

*Baiamons Teupolus* The conspiracy of Bajamonte (or Baiamonte) Tiepolo and members of the Quirini family failed in 1310 to bring down the doge Pietro Gradenigo. The consequences were that Tiepolo was exiled to Dalmatia, and, more importantly, Venice brought into being the Council of Ten, originally as an emergency temporary measure in times of unrest, but successively renewed until in 1334 it was made a permanent body.

**[373A] Famous men of Venice.**

Here B. begins his summary of the famous men of Venice; as he writes before the height of Venetian humanism at the end of the Quattrocento, he has missed many of the most famous figures or even the later careers of contemporaries. His descriptions are generally conventional: that is, they correspond with the emphases and portrayals found in contemporary sources. Indispensable for this section is the work of M. L. King, especially *Venetian Humanists in an Age of Patrician Dominance* (Princeton: Princeton University Press, 1986), with its valuable "Profiles"; and, for the early years of the Quattrocento, the second appendix ("Prosopographie") of Dieter Girgensohn's two-volume *Kirche, Politik und adelige Regierung in der Republik Venedig zu Beginn des 15. Jahrhunderts* (Göttingen: Vandenhoeck and Ruprecht, 1996). King's general observation (275) holds good for B.'s portraits here: "Venetian humanism is . . . naturally characterized by the participation at a modest level of a great many patricians whose main commitment is outside of intellectual life." An interesting comparison with B.'s description of the rebirth from the Romagna of Italian learning (**[346E–347B]**) is afforded by Benjamin G. Kohl and Ronald G. Witt, eds., *The Earthly Republic: Italian Humanists on Government and Society* (Philadelphia: University of Pennsylvania Press, 1978), 179, who adduce as two of the three factors shaping Venetian humanism the Petrarchan influence transmitted through Giovanni Conversino da Ravenna to his Venetian students; and the close rapport with Greek scholarship in Constantinople and the influence of Emmanuel Chrysoloras.

*Andrea Dandulo duce . . .* Andrea Dandolo 1306–1354. Doge 1343–1354, a period of crisis in Venetian history; his later reputation suffered somewhat as a result of the disasters of his times. Although central questions of his political career revolve around the degree of responsibility he bore for Venice's war with Genoa, these comments will confine themselves to B.'s concern here, Dandolo's erudition. Two letters of Petrarch, in which he portrays Dandolo as fundamentally peaceful and studious, testify to Dandolo's education and his knowledge of literature, philosophy, and history; of the two recorded letters (in Latin) of Dandolo to Petrarch, one is of questionable genuineness. Dandolo wrote works on Venetian law and foreign relations, but his most famous and important works are historical: he wrote a *Chronicon brevis*, a history of Venice from its origins to 1342; and a larger chronicle, *Chronica per extensum descripta*, which treated Venetian history from 48–1280 A.D. For modern bibliography on Dandolo, see G. Ravegnani's contribution in "Dandolo, Andrea," *DBI* 32 (1986), 432–440, which includes several items addressing the specific topic of Dandolo's relations with Petrarch and humanism.

*Carolus Zenus* Carlo Zeno (Zen): hero of Chioggia, later disgraced; in retirement, took up the *studia humanitatis*. See King, *Venetian Humanism*, 4, and her bibliography n.4. B. here refers to L. Giustiniani, *Funebris oratio pro Carlo Zeno* (1418) in *RIS*, new ed., XIX, Parte VI, fasc. 2 (Bologna: Nicola Zanichelli, 1941), 141–146.

**[373B]** *Petruspaulus Vergerius* Pier Paolo Vergerio. See above on **[346E]**.

*Zaccarias Tarvisanus* Zaccaria Trevisan, 1370–1414. Venetian statesman and humanist at Padua and mentor of Francesco Barbaro. He declined to pursue an ecclesiastical or academic career in favor of service to foreign powers. In addition to holding high political offices in Venice, he performed embassies for Venice and papal commissions. In 1413 he was Captain at Padua when the supposed remains of Livy were discovered in S. Giustina, and advocated the building of a mausoleum for the writer. See Girgensohn, 2:983–998.

*Petrum Emilianum* Pietro Emiliani, 1362–1433. After beginning a successful political career, he turned to ecclesiastical service. Although his ecclesiastic ambitions seemed favored when a Venetian became Pope Gregory XII, at the papal court Emiliani's relations with Antonio, nephew of the Pope, became strained to the point of conflict, and Emiliani had to abandon the papal court. (This B. of course omits, mentioning only his literary learning and wisdom.) After returning to Venice in 1407, he was in 1409 named bishop of Vicenza. Emiliani's education left him a lover of ancient literature with good knowledge of Greek rare for his times. Well-connected among the humanists and a patron of many, he was a collector of manuscripts; although born Pietro Miani, he insisted on using the Latinized form of his surname, as the aristocratic Venetian tendency was to claim that Venice was the legitimate successor of Rome.

*Marcus ... Lippomannus* Marco Lippomano. Doctor, celebrated by others in addition to B. for his learning. See King, *Venetian Humanism*, 389–390.

*Paulus Venetus*. Originally Paolo Nicoletti, better-known as Paolo Veneto, philosopher and expert on Averroes and member of the faculty at the University of Padua. See King, *Venetian Humanism*, 264, and bibliography there.

*Franciscus Barbadicus* Francesco Barbarigo (b. 1380 or later, d. 1448), ambassador and military man, who held various high offices at Venice; a correspondent with Guarino interested in ancient authors. See G. Cracco, "Barbarigo, Francesco," *DBI* 6 (1964): 62–63.

[373C] *Daniel Victorius* Daniele Vitturi, born late fourteenth century, died before 1441. Probably a student of Gasparino Barzizza, he was a "[m]ember of the first-generation learned circle that also included Barbaro, Andrea Giuliani, Leonardo Giustiniani ..." (King, *Venetian Humanism*, 445–446).

*Petrus Lauredanus* Pietro Loredan, Venetian admiral and statesman; in 1427, B. was his secretary in Brescia.

*XII Gregorius pontifex Romanus* Pope Gregory XII, formerly Angelo Correr. Elevated 1406.

*Antonius nepos* Antonio Correr, nephew of Pope Gregory XII.

*Pontificem ... Eugenium quartum* Pope Eugenius IV (Gabriele Condulmer). Although Francesco Condulmer is the person most often suspected as blamed by B. for his plans to plagiarize the unpublished ms. of *It. ill.* loaned to him in good faith by B., his kinsman Eugenius IV was B.'s generous patron, whose death left B. without support in the Curia. B. here echoes almost *verbatim* Cic *Q. fr.* 3.4.4, *in scribendo priores partes alicui tribuere.*

*Petrus Barbus* Pietro Barbo (1417–1471), Pope Paul II. Nephew of Eugenius IV and student of George of Trebizond, he was bishop of Cervia, Vicenza, and Padua before being elected pope in 1464. More interested in artistic than literary patronage, he was nevertheless the dedicatee of many humanist works: King, *Venetian Humanism*, 331–332, notes the contradiction inherent in his moralistic hostility to some aspects of humanist thought and his activities in manuscript collection and restoration of antiquities in Rome.

*Franciscus Foscarus* Francesco Foscari, 1373–1457. Doge 1423–1457; his brilliant political career expressed the policy of the expansionist movement, but he also surrounded himself with humanists, to whose influence his eloquence was probably due. See G. Gullino, "Foscari, Francesco," *DBI* 49 (1997): 306–314; Girgensohn, 2: 757–774.

*Franciscus Barbarus* Francesco Barbaro, 1390–1454. See G. Gualdo, "Barbaro, Francesco," *DBI* 6 (1964): 101–103. Educated at the school of Giovanni da Ravenna, whom Gualdo believes to be Giovanni da Conversino (see comments above on **[346E]**), then studied at Padua, and upon returning to Venice learned Greek from Guarino Veronese; moved to Florence in 1415 and joined the circle of humanists there. Considered among the greatest of Venetian humanists, impressive for his knowledge of Greek at a time when devotees of Hellenism were few, in 1419 his literary and philological interests, like those of many of his aristocratic Venetian contemporaries, shifted to public life and he began a brilliant administrative and political career. B., Barbaro's greatest protegé, was his secretary between 1422 and 1435.

*Andreas Maurocenus* Andrea Morosini, podestà of Padua and addressee of a philosophical dialogue by Lauro Quirini; see King, *Venetian Humanism*, 164, 419.

*Hermolaus Donatus* Ermolao Donato (Donà, Donato, Donado). Born at end of 14th c., died 1450. A patrician intensely involved in politics whose diplomatic missions took him far from Venice, he had humanist contacts, expressed in a distinguished collection of books and epistolary exchange with Francesco Barbaro. B.'s attribution to him of *heroicos versus . . . elegantes* may refer to the history of his times attributed to him. See P. De Peppo, "Donà, Ermolao," *DBI* 40 (1991): 722–724.

**[374E]** *Barbonus Maurocenus* Barbone Morosini, born c. 1414, died 1457/1458. A skilled lawyer and orator, he is praised as exemplifying the ideal of humanist studies in the service of the Republic. See King, *Venetian Humanism*, 407–408.

*Ludovicus Foscharenus* Ludovico Foscarini, 1409–1480. B. groups him with five other men he summarizes as dedicated to civil law and the state, while still having knowledge of rhetoric, poetry, and history. A patrician, his prestigious career was spent in service to his country. Remarkable among his class for having earned two university degrees, in philosophy and in law. After publication of *It. ill.* in 1450, B. and L. F. spent time together at the Diet of Mantua in 1459, where Foscarini conceived the idea that B. would be ideal writer of an ideological history of Venice portraying Venice as the Christian heir of ancient Rome. B. portrays Foscarini conventionally as admirable for his skill in the law, as did contemporaries Ciriaco d'Ancona and Pope Pius II. See G. Moro, "Foscarini, Ludovico," *DBI* 49 (1997): 383–388.

*Vitalis Landus* Vitale Lando, born c. 1421; died 1482 or after. Lando held the doctorate in laws and arts from Padua and was governor of Ravenna; in addition to B., Foscarini and Pietro Perleone praised Lando for his learning. See King, *Venetian Humanism*, 385–386.

*Candianus Bolanus* (Candiano Bollani, Bolano, Bollanus, Bolanus) 1413–1478. A military and political man as well as a man of letters, he moved in the same circles as B. For example, he negotiated in 1452 at Ferrara with Borso d'Este, and in 1463 with representatives of Malatesta Novello, lord of Cesena. Among his works were a commentary on the first three chapters of the book of Genesis (extant); a commentary on the *Rhetorica ad Herennium* (lost); an oration in Ciceronian style on election of doge Cristoforo Moro. His political activity continued long after B.'s death in 1463. See G. Pillinini, "Bollani, Candiano," *DBI* 11 (1969): 287–289.

*Nicolaus Canalis* Niccolò Canal 1415–1483. See A. Ventura, "Canal, Niccolò," *DBI* 17 (1974): 662–668. Studied literature and law at University of Padua; due to his knowledge of literature, won friendship and esteem of humanists like Francesco Barbaro, Ludovico Foscarini, Francesco Filelfo. He was involved in diplomatic initiatives with B.'s patrons Borso d'Este (1455) and Sigismondo Pandolfo Malatesta of Rimini and Malatesta Novello of Cesena (1462). But B. writes about Canal before the most sensational event of his life, seven years after B.'s death (1470), when Canal, commander of the Venetian fleet in the war against the Turks, was found responsible for the loss of Negroponte; prosecuted by Bollani and sentenced to death, he was allowed to serve a commuted sentence.

*Laurus Quirinu* Lauro Quirini, Querini. 1420–c.1475–79. See King, *Venetian Humanism*, 419–421 for details of his political career and bibliography. B. is aware of his learning and specifically his training in the law. Quirino had studied canon law at Padua between 1443–1448, taught in Venice in 1449. B. wrote and published *It. ill.* before Quirini had moved to Candia in Crete in 1452, where he lived until his death.

*Ioannes Cornelius . . . Cornarius* Giovanni Corner, born c. 1370, died 1452. He was known less for his political career than for his connections with humanists (Ciriaco d'Ancona and Pietro Perleone dedicated translations to him); he was a patron of Filelfo and an early collector of ancient manuscripts. See King, *Venetian Humanism*, 354–355.

*Paulus Barbus* Paolo Barbo, born 1416, d. 1462, he was brother of Pietro Barbo, the future Pope Paul II (elected in 1464). Both received many honors and benefices from their uncle Eugenius IV, upon whose death Paolo Barbo returned to Venice from Rome, administered his brother's property in the Veneto, and entering political life rose to the highest levels of the Venetian hierarchy. Among the diplomatic initiatives entrusted to him was an embassy to the court of France to motivate Louis XI to take a military role against the Turks; Barbo returned unsuccessful in 1462. See S. Borsari, "Barbo, Paolo," *DBI* 6 (1964): 254–255.

*Andreas Iulianus* Andrea Giuliani, born approximately 1384, died 1452, held political offices and was entrusted with embassies, but was most famous for his funeral oration for Manuel Chrysoloras in 1415, widely circulated thereafter. He was a student, friend and correspondent of Gasparino Barzizza and Guarino Veronese. It was Giuliani who in 1420 presented the young Biondo to Guarino. See King, *Venetian Humanism*, 3–4, 379–381.

*Bernardus Iustinianus* Bernardo Giustinian,1408–1489. A student of Francesco Filelfo and Guarino Veronese, the majority of Giustiniani's sixty-year political career took place after the composition of *It. ill.* He simultaneously pursued international commercial activity. Giustinian was famous for his erudition and was praised as an orator. He delivered important orations to rulers and popes, many of which contained exhortations to crusades against the Turks. In the custom of Venetian humanists' concern to provide the ruling class of their Republic with exemplars of public life, he translated an oration of Isocrates into Latin. From 1471–1474 he was involved in writing a biography of his uncle, (S.) Lorenzo Giustinian, *Vita beati Laurentii.* His literary activity most relevant to *It. ill.* drew on B. as a model of historiographical and archaeological research: *De origine urbis Venetiarum rebusque eius ab ipsa ad quadringentesimum usque annum gestis historia* was published posthumously in 1492. See King, *Venetian Humanism*, 381–383; G. Pistilli, "Giustinian, Bernardo," *DBI* 57 (2001): 216–224.

*Hieronymus Barbadicus* Girolamo Barbarigo: born to Francesco Barbarigo around 1410, he died in 1467. In addition to following the government career customary to the son of an aristocratic Venetian family, he also became a great orator; most of his important diplomatic missions took place after the publication of *It. ill.* See G. Cracco, "Barbarigo, Girolamo," *DBI* 6 (1964): 66–67.

*Nicolaus Barbus* Niccolò Barbo, 1420–1462. A student of George of Trebizond and Paolo della Pergola, he was a true man of letters some of whose letters and an oration remain. In addition to a career in public life, his literary distinction is attested by his relations with Biondo and many other men of letters, including Guarino Guarini. See F. Gaeta, "Barbo, Niccolò," *DBI* 6 (1964): 252–253.

**[374F]** *Laurentius Castellanus* Lorenzo Giustinian, uncle of Bernardo Giustinian, was elected bishop of Castello in 1433, patriarch of Venice in 1451 (after the establishment of the new patriarchate of Venice from the defunct patriarchate of Grado and see of Castello), and was beatified in 1472; the process of canonization began in 1474. See Gams, *Series Episcoporum,* 782.

*Fantinus Paduanus* Fantino Dandolo, 1379–1459; son of doge Andrea Dandolo. After a political career followed by an ecclesiastical career, he was bishop of Padua from 1448 to his death. He was an early Venetian humanist, a collector of manuscripts respected for his learning by contemporaries in addition to Biondo; see King, *Venetian Humanism*, 357–359; Girgensohn, 2:709–724.

*Gregorius patrui pontificis nomen referens* Gregorio Correr, 1409–1464, was nephew of cardinal Antonio Correr and great-nephew of Pope Gregory XII. His schooling with Vittorino da Feltre at Mantua inspired in him a lifelong love of classical culture. Eugenius IV, a relation on Correr's father's side, named him apostolic protonotary; he followed the Curia to Florence in 1434 where he was involved in the circle of humanists frequented by B. His career in the church was, however, characterized by disappointment, as he approached various positions but was denied one after another. In 1448, alienated from the papal Curia, he retired to the monastery of S. Zeno in Verona, and died just after finally being elected patriarch of Venice. Correr's literary productions in Latin included satires influenced by Horace and Juvenal; an eclogue *Lycidas*; a tragedy *Progne*; and a re-elaboration of Aesop. See P. Preto, "Correr, Gregorio," *DBI* 29 (1983): 497–500.

*Hermolaus Barbarus* Ermolao Barbaro (1410–1471). Nephew of Francesco Barbaro, he learned Latin and Greek at the school of Guarino at Verona. Eugenius IV named him (1436) apostolic protonotary; he was later named bishop of Treviso, then (1453) obtained the episcopal see of Verona. Throughout his busy ecclesiastic and political career Barbaro remained an impassioned participant in literature and culture, considering these pursuits an integral part of the *vita activa*. His many works included a defense of ancient poetry as pedagogically useful. See E. Bigi, "Barbaro, Ermolao," *DBI* 6 (1964): 95–96.

*Petrus Monteus Brixianus* Pietro da Monte, jurist and bishop of Brescia; became papal governor of Perugia in 1452.

*Iacobus Zenus Feltrensis et Belunensis* Jacopo Zeno, born c. 1418, died 1481. Bishop of Feltre and Belluno 1447–1460; in 1460 he became bishop of Padua, succeeding the deceased Fantino Dandolo. See King, *Venetian Humanism*, 447–449; Gams, *Series Episcoporum*, 776.

*Dominicus Torcellanus* Domenico Dominici (Domenico de' Domenichi), 1416–1478. Active in the Roman Curia under Calixtus III and Pius II, named bishop of Torcello in 1448 by Pope Nicholas V; in 1464 Pope Paul II named him bishop of Brescia. Rome was the focal point of Domenichi's work; an authority in the field of theology and a valued advisor to popes, he undertook commissions on reform and diplomatic missions, and wrote treatises on philosophical, theological, ecclesiological, and astronomical topics. H. Smolinsky, "Dominici, Domenico," *DBI* 40 (1991): 691–695, characterizes Dominici as a representative of the transitional phase between the late medieval and modern age: a man of letters whose library contained many classical works as well as contemporary humanist writings, in contact with many of the foremost humanists of his time, and favored by the humanist Pope Pius II, his theological thought was nevertheless closer to scholasticism. After B.'s death, Dominici would be an advocate of the publication of

*Italia illustrata*, to whom Gaspare Biondo would dedicate the *editio princeps* (1474).

*Petrus Thomasius* Pietro Tommasi. Born c. 1375–1380, d. 1458, Tommasi exemplies a type of erudite humanist physician often praised by B., and in his practice treated other eminent Venetians. Author of works on medicine and astrology, he collected manuscripts of classical works and corresponded, mostly on book collection and humanist ideas, with some of the foremost humanists of his time: e.g., Poggio Bracciolini, Francesco Filelfo, and Guarino Veronese. See King, *Venetian Humanism*, 434–436.

# Ninth Region, March of Treviso
# Commentary

The Augustan name Italia Transpadana is given the alternative of the March of Treviso, in Latin Marchia Tarvisina, a name for which B. apologizes as absurd. As Hay ("Italian View," 8) notes, B. gave to the regions of Italy names "derived ultimately from Pliny, [which] bore little relation to the political facts of his day," but these names were well-known to his contemporaries. His disparagement of the "absurd name" of Marchia Tarvisina accords with his condemnation of the Lombards on linguistic grounds.

The description of Padua is the third longest of a city. The extensive treatment of the latter is probably due in part to the model provided by Giovanni da Nono's *Visio Egidii Regis Patavii* (see Hyde, "Descriptions of Cities," 331); but surely in no small part also to Padua's prominence in the schooling of the Venetian aristocracy.

**[375B]** *Mincio* See above on **[360H]** where B. cites *Aen.* 10.205–206.

**[375C]** *Athesim propter amoenum* B. mistakenly, but understandably, attributes this pastoral-sounding phrase to the *Bucolics*, instead of the *Aeneid* (9.680). The context is the comparison of the Trojan heroes Pandarus and Bitias to oaks along a river bank; the Athesis provides an alternative example, after the Po, of an environment likely to include such oaks.

> quales aëriae liquentia flumina circum 679
> sive Padi ripis Athesim seu propter amoenum 680
> consurgunt geminae quercus intonsaque caelo. 681

> Such as tall twin oaks that rise with leafy tops
> High in the air near a flowing river,
> Either on the banks of the Po or beside the pleasant Adige.

**[375D]** *ut Plinium credamus. . . .* Although B. produces in *It. ill.* many astonishing readings of Pliny's *Naturalis Historia* because he had a very flawed manuscript of this work, this excerpt has the look of a paraphrase from memory, not an erroneous reading. The original is Pliny *NH* 19.141.4,

> Aricinum altitudine non excelsius, folio numerosius, quam tenuius. Hoc utilissimum existimatur, quae sub omnibus paene foliis fruticat cauliculis peculiaribus . . . Sabellico usque in admirationem crispa sunt folia. . . .
>
> The cabbage of Ariccia is not tall, and has leaves that are more abundant than tender. This variety is considered most useful, because it sprouts individual shoots under almost all its leaves. The leaves of the Sabine cabbage are marvelously curly. . . .

*L. Florus breviatoris verbis libuit apponere epitome* Although B. claims to give here Florus *verbis*, this is in fact a paraphrase of Florus 1.38.12 (H. Malcovati, ed., *Florus, Epitome de Tito Livio* [Rome 1938]).

**[376G]** *Libetque Cassiodori verba apponere . . . Variae* 12.4.4; for Cassiodorus, see above on **[345D]**.

**[376H]** **Famous men of Verona.** The description of Verona is the longest given any city in northern Italy, its length due perhaps to the existence of a medieval precursor, *Laudes Veronensis* (see Hyde, "Descriptions of Cities," cit. above on Milan, **[366G]**).

*Zeno* St. Zeno became almost a patron saint of Verona. He was eighth bishop of Verona; born in north Africa, he spread Christianity in Verona. He died around 380, after which legends of his miracle-working arose.

*Aemilius Macer Aemilius Macer Veronensis poeta in Asia moritur* appears for the year 17 B.C. (R. Helm, ed. *Die Chronik des Hieronymus* 2nd ed. [Berlin: Akademie Verlag, 1956], *Eusebius Werke*, 7:166).

*genuit Verona Rainaldum insignem sicut F. Petrarchae placet grammaticum.* Rinaldo da Villafranca, poet and grammarian.

*Ioannem Madium iureconsultum non incelebrem* Appears as Maggio de' Maggi, mentioned also by Guarino.

**[377A]** *Iacobum Lavagnolum . . . Iacobus equestris ordinis Lavagnolus* The grandfather, Iacopo Lavagnolo (Maior), was a famous physician praised by Guarino in a letter dedicating his translation of Plutarch's *Parallel Lives* to the younger Lavagnolo. The grandson, Jacopo Lavagnolo Minor, was a knight, a senator of Rome, a legal expert, and a student of Guarino. See Cosenza, 3:1954.

*Bernardus* Bernardus a Campanea de Verona wrote (by his own dating, in 1394) a ms. of Biagio Pelacani's *Quaestiones* on the eight books of Aristotle's *Physics*; see Cosenza, Mario, *Biographical and Bibliographical Dictionary of the Italian Humanists and of the World of Classical Scholarship in Italy 1300–1800*. 2nd ed. 5 vols. (Boston: G. K. Hall, 1962), 1:539.

*Ioannes . . . Salernus* Giovanni Salerno wrote a treatise on plants.

*Monticulenses & S. Bonifacii comites* The party of the Monticoli and the party of the Counts of Sambonifacio (the most powerful family around Verona) are the participants in the first documented factional strife at Verona. In spite of Shakespeare's inclusion of characters with this name, the Monticoli did not live at Verona, but were probably named for a *castello* in the territory of Vicenza. The expulsion of the counts of Sambonifacio resulted in a hundred years' exile.

[377A–B] *Azzo d'Este . . . Ezzelino da Romano* Supported by the emperor Frederick II, Ezzelino da Romano (1194–1259) built up a state comprising Verona and other cities of the March of Treviso, over which he ruled as a tyrant. See Giorgio Varanini, "Ezzelino da Romano," *Enciclopedia Dantesca* 2: 771–772; the ultimate source of this must be Rolandino di Padova (A. Bonardi, ed., *Cronica in factis et circa facta Marchie Trivixane*, in *RIS* v. 8, pt. 1, fasc. 1–2).

[377B] *della Scala Capitaneatus* is a vernacular title which Valla recommended using instead of the archaic *dux* with its anachronistic overtones; see Cochrane, *Historians and Historiography*, 149. The della Scala became tyrants when Ezzelino da Romano designated Mastino della Scala in 1259 as Podestà of Verona. Mastino was elected Captain of the People in 1262, a new office which prepared the way for the *signoria* of Verona. The title later evolved into the *Capitaneus Generalis Civitatis Veronae*. B. begins the tyranny of the della Scala with Cangrande, born probably 1291.

[377C] *Georgius Caballus* Giorgio Cavalli. Although the chronology corresponds to Biondo's description, the details of this individual's biography as represented by Biondo do not correspond to those described in L. Miglio, "Cavalli, Giorgio," *DBI* 22 (1979): 736–739.

**[377D]** *Alticherius* Altichierio, leading exponent of the Paduan School of painting; flourished in the last third of the fourteenth century. B. is the authority for his origins in Verona. See E. Arslan, "Altichiero," *DBI* 2 (1960): 557–558.

**[378H]** *Leonicum ... Omnibono cive ornatur* Nogara, *Scritti inediti*, xxxii, distinguishes between this Ognibene Leoniceno from Lonigo or Brendola, and the Paduan humanist Ognibene Scola (see above **[346F–G]**).

**[379A]** *Guilielmus, Ravennas archiepiscopus sedis apostolicae legatus* The sole Guilielmus listed (Gams, *Series Episcoporum*, 718) as bishop of Ravenna approaching the chronology of Ezzelino is Willielmus bishop of Ravenna, elected in 1190 and died 1201, before Ezzelino's period of activity.

**[379B]** *Palaemon* The grammarian Palaemon; died before A.D. 76. See Eusebius 262.19–23:

> Palaemon Vicentinus insignis grammaticus Romae habetur, qui quondam interrogatus, quid inter stillam et guttam interesset, gutta, inquit, stat, stilla cadit.
>
> Asked the difference between a solidified drop and a drop of liquid, the grammarian Palaemon, considered famous at Rome, said, "A solid drop stands still; a drop of liquid falls."

But see Suet. fr. 176, *gutta imbrium est, stilla olei vel aceti*; *TLL* 6.2.2370–2373; and Lewis and Short *s.v. stilla*, "a dense, viscous, gummy, fatty drop"; whereas *gutta* is a "natural, liquid drop."

*Antonius Luscus* Antonio Loschi, although a native of Vicenza, is associated with Pavia where, a fellow student of Gasparino Barzizza, he attended the University and entered service of the Visconti. B. must here refer to his *Inquisitio artis in orationibus Ciceronis*, composed around 1395, commentaries on individual orations of Cicero (cf. R. Sabbadini, *Le Scoperte dei Codici Latini e Greci nei Secoli XIV e XV*, 122). Witt, "*Footsteps*," 388–390, describes Loschi's importance in the first stage of Ciceronianism (as distinguished from the "mature Ciceronianism of the late fifteenth and early sixteenth centuries"). In the *Inquisitio*, Loschi attempted to apply Cicero's rhetorical theories to the ancient orator's speeches. "His detailed study of Cicero's construction of his orations rendered these masterpieces more accessible for those who aimed not merely ... to master the formal instructions for how to build an oration and organize its arguments but to re-create something approaching the style in which the orations had been composed" (Witt, "*Footsteps*," 390).

*Mathaeus Bissarius* Matteo Bissaro. Born in the last years of fourteenth century, he died in 1466. Native of Vicenza and its official orator; jurist, and poet, for which last occupation Leandro Alberti (*Descrittione di tutta Italia*, 473) is the authority. See E. Ragni, "Bissaro, Matteo," *DBI* 10 (1968): 690.

[379C] *unicum . . . facinus* Clavuot, 110, notes B.'s striking pro-Venetian attitude here. Glorifying this act of submission, as did many fifteenth-century writers, B. participates here in the myth of Vicenza as the first of Venice's mainland possessions; in fact Venice had ruled Treviso before Vicenza, on which see J. S. Grubb, *Firstborn of Venice* (Baltimore and London: Johns Hopkins University Press, 1988), 181. In 1404 Vicenza, her status precarious since the death of Giangaleazzo Visconti, was threatened by a siege by the forces of Francesco da Carrara of Padua. Faced with a restitution of the da Carrara tyranny, Vicenza chose the lesser evil and offered itself to Venice. In the next year (1405), Venice took over Verona and Padua; after 1426, Venice took from the Visconti control of Brescia, Bergamo, and Crema. Grubb, xvi n. 19, notes that in *De origine et gestis Venetorum* (1454) B. displays a somewhat different attitude.

[379D–380H]: **Rivers of Padua.**

*Fuisse etiam Bachilionem amnem Meduacum* . . . Clavuot (199) notes that B. bases his identification of the Meduacus (correctly, with the Bacchiglione) and the Timavus (erroneously, with the Brenta) almost exclusively on literary sources. Livy narrates, at 10.2.1–10, the expedition of Cleonymus between 304 and 293 B.C. Livy's description of the Meduacus is close enough to the location of the Bacchiglione for B. to think he recognizes the Bacchiglione; but he cannot have known that "At the end of the sixth century, disastrous flooding caused the Meduacus to form a new channel north of the city, while the Bacchiglione, flowing east from Vicenza, occupied the riverbed south of the city, eventually making early medieval Padua into an island" (Benjamin Kohl, *Padua under the Carrara, 1318–1405* [Baltimore and London: Johns Hopkins University Press, 1998], 3); this latter branch Clavuot terms the "Meduacus minor."

A note of explanation about my transcription here of B.'s long citation of Livy:

Modern texts, of course, present many divergences from B.'s text, different readings which are traceable to other mss. It is impossible to identify the ms. of Livy B. was using to cite in *It. ill.*; a text of Livy annotated by B. has yet to be found; and Clavuot, 213, suspects that in recording this passage from Livy (10.2.1–10), B. relied on his own notes in his own ms. of Livy rather than, as he does elsewhere, on a collection of topographically-oriented excerpts.

For purposes of comparison with B.'s citation, I have taken as a standard modern text of Livy the Oxford text of Walters and Conway (C. Walters and R. S. Conway, eds., *Titi Livi Ab Urbe Condita* [Oxford: Clarendon, 1919]). In transcribing B.'s long citation of Livy, I have noted with italics B.'s many differences (traceable to other mss.) to the Oxford Classical Text.

In explicating and interpreting this passage, however, B. reverts at **[380E]** to the reading *transgressa stagna* (which corresponds to the modern, orthodox reading), where he had in first citing the passage written *praetergressis stagna*. This suggests to me that he is here recalling from memory the text of Livy.

**[380F]** *Est enim Timavus* ... B. disastrously disagrees with unnamed contemporaries who, basing their opinion on Virgil, *Aen.* 1.242–246, concluded correctly that the Timavus was in Istria or Liburnia. B. bases his conclusions partly on Servius' commentary on *Aen.* 1.244–245, and thus identifies the seven mouths of the Timavus with Septem Maria. See McKay, *Vergil's Italy* 75–76, who cites Livy 1.1.3 on the foundation of Padua by the Veneti, a passage B. has omitted, if not to consult, at least to cite.

The ancient Timavus is identified by modern works as in "Istria between Aquileia and Trieste" (Lewis and Short, *s.v. Timavus*) or the modern Timavo which flows into the gulf of Trieste near S. Giovanni al Timavo (Oxford Latin Dictionary, *s.v. Timauus*). Both reference works base the identification on Mela (2.4.3; 2.61), Virgil, Vitruvius, Pliny *NH* 2.225; Martial 4.25.5, Statius *Silv.* 4.7.55, and inscriptions. Some of these are sources upon which B. bases his identification of the ancient Timavus with the Brenta. For analysis of B.'s method of reasoning here, see Clavuot 197–200; as Clavuot finds, 199, B. falls into error in misidentifying the Timavus because, as often, he privileges literary sources over other types of evidence (cf. Fubini, "Biondo Flavio," *DBI*, 547, on B.'s use of this method in *Roma instaurata*, where he neglects to fully credit archaeological and epigraphical data). The ancient sources B. cites are: Livy 10.2.1–10; Virgil *Aen.* 1.242–246, and Servius on *Aen.* 1.244–245; Antoninus Pius, *Itinerary* 270.3, 273.1; Lucan 7.194; and Martial 13.89. As Clavuot comments (199), B. here relies uncritically on topographical information derived from ancient literature. Although Clavuot claims that B. bases his argument here exclusively on literary sources, I would add that B. also employs, although in a minor role, direct observation. We know that B. was familiar with this territory, having lived at Ravenna and having served on various diplomatic initiatives in the service of Venice. At **[380F]** he appeals, in a general way, to direct observation, *sicut semper sonare videmus, eum litoris aut portus cuiuspiam fauces paulo violentior commotiorque ingreditur*; and at **[380H–381A]** he employs direct observation in a negative way, in an attempt to minimize the lack of hot springs opposite the island of Olivolo: *si vero calidi non apparent nunc fontes minime mirandum, nedum litoreis et maritimis locis in quae maris saepe desaevit violentia, sed in mediterraneis montanisque firmioribus multas aruisse fontes invenimus.*

B.'s familiarity with the area around Padua may, of course, have made him over-confident. Clavuot (200) notes B.'s citation exclusively of sources which support his thesis; his indifference to or re-interpretation of information contradicting his point; and his avoidance of testing a hypothesis while trying to prove his conviction by any means. A glaring example is B.'s seeming indifference to Pliny, *NH* 3.151 and 2.229. The first passage describes the islands off the Illyrian coast and identifies the hot springs opposite the mouth of the Timavus (*Clarae [sc. insulae] ante ostia Timavi calidorum fontium cum aestu maris crescentium*) with the famous islands near Istria of the Medea legend, which Zehnacker, 281, identifies with Lussin/ Losinj; Cherso; and the group of islands in the Gulf of Quarnaro.

*Superesse* Clearly the Basel edition's error, which I have corrected to *superasse* (the reading of the Venice 1482 edition).

**[380H]** *Et Martialis: Laneus* ... Martial 13.89. The adjective *Euganeus* describes a race, not a location; in ancient times, the Euganei inhabited the region of Venetia, which extended far enough north to cover the actual mouth of the Timavus in the Gulf of Trieste. Pliny *NH* 3.133 describes the home of the Euganei as *Verso deinde [in] Italiam pectore Alpium Latini iuris Euganeae gentes, quarum oppida XXXIIII enumerat Cato*. Zehnacker, *ad loc.*, cites Livy 1.1 and Cato *Orig.* fr. 41 P==II, 11 Chassignet with commentary p. 23. The passage from Livy locates the *Euganei* originally in the country between the Adriatic and the Alps; they were later forced to migrate towards the west by the Veneti and the Trojans. Intent on forcing the ancient literary evidence to support his identification of the Timavus, B. takes Martial's association of the epithet with the Timavus as locating the river near the Euganean Hills, whereas Martial may simply associate the river with this northern Italian race. The epigram in its entirety:

> Laneus Euganei lupus excipit ora Timavi,
> aequoreo dulces cum sale pastus aquas.

> The soft white flesh of a sea bass which swims against the tide in the mouths of the Euganean Timavus;
> a bass which has fed on the sweet freshwater along with the salt water.

Contrary to B.'s interpretation, Martial in 4.25.5 (one of Martial's frequent expressions of longing for northern Italy as preferable to the tedium of Rome) associates the Timavus correctly with the city of Aquileia and attributes to it seven mouths; the occurrence of *Euganeos* in the previous line identifies the Euganean lakes with Padua (*Antenoreo*), but this does not mean that the poet locates them near the Timavus.

> Aemula Baianis Altini litora villis
> et Phaethontei conscia silva rogi,
> quaeque Antenoreo Dryadum pulcherrima Fauno
> nupsit ad Euganeos Sola puella lacus,
> et tu Ledaeo felix Aquileia Timavo,
> hic ubi septenas Cyllarus hausit aquas:
> vos eritis nostrae requies portusque senectae,
> si iuris fuerint otia nostra sui.

> The shores of Altinum, rivaling the villas of Baiae, and the forest of Phaethon's funeral pyre, and young Sola, most beautiful of the Dryads, who married Paduan Faunus beside the Euganean lakes, and you, Aquileia, fortunate in the Timavus, birthplace of Leda's sons, where Cyllarus drank deeply from its sevenfold waters: you will be my place of rest and harbour of old age, if the place of my retirement can be of my choosing.

Fauno appended to his translation of *It. ill.* corrections of B.'s errors, including Sabellico's and Volterrano's identifications of the Meduacus with the Brenta, and the location of the Timavus. He transmits Sabellico's reasoning that the name of the harbor Malamocco is a corruption of "Meduaco"; and Sabellico's prescient correct description of the underground course of the Timavus.

Austin's commentary on *Aeneid* 1 (R. G. Austin, *P. Vergili Maronis Aeneidos Liber Primus* [Oxford: Clarendon 1971]), 94–95, gives an excellent and clear explanation of Virgil's description and the errors of later poets in locating the Timavus:

> The Timavus (Timavo) rises in the Julian Alps, and for just over half its course it flows underground; it emerges at San Giovanni di Tuba, and enters the sea a short distance away in the Gulf of Trieste. Scientific experiment has found that its waters reach the sea through a number of tunnels along a stretch of coast of about thirteen miles; the coastline has probably altered from ancient times by silting. Virgil's *fons*, which Antenor "sailed past," is the river itself in its final course, from the point of its emergence to its debouchment in the sea, so close to each other that "spring" and exit are poetically integrated . . . the *mons* is the massif from under which the Timavus emerges . . . the mountain booms . . . *mare* means the river, not the actual sea . . . Later poets were misled by *hic*.

**[381A] Padua.**

B.'s treatment of Padua is his third most extensive description of any city in northern Italy. He excuses his prolixity (**[381B]**) by the city's prestige; at **[381A]** he called Padua the most ancient and most famous city in Italy. Its early humanists' antiquarian interests (see below on **[382G]**, Mussato and Lovati) resulted in attribution of tombs to Antenor and Livy; and the perpetuation of false attribution of inscriptions. B. accepts here the ancient myth of the Trojan hero Antenor's founding of Padua and adduces Virgil and Livy as sources and credible proof of the truth of this foundation legend, although he makes no mention of the supposed "tomb of Antenor" (actually a Christian tomb). On the discovery of the inscription in the thirteenth century, and the discovery in 1413 of bones which were believed to be Livy's, see M. P. Billanovich, "Una miniera di epigrafi e di antichità: Il chiostro maggiore di S. Giustina," *IMU* 12 (1969): 197–293. The ultimate source for the discovery is found in the sequel to Rolandino's *Cronica* (see above on **[377A–B]**), *Annales Patavini* ed. A. Bonardi, in L. A. Muratori, *RIS* v. 8, pt. 1, 262: *inventa arca nobilis Antenoris, conditoris urbis Paduae,* *cum capitello, penes Sanctum Laurentium a porta Sancti Stephani*, cit. in G. Billanovich, *La Tradizione del Testo di Livio e le Origini dell'Umanesimo* (2 vols. [Padua: Editrice Antenore, 1981]) 1:3.

B. relies for the ancient history of Padua on sources for Rome's expansion into, and foundation of colonies in, northern Italy, and Rome's extension to Padua of favorable treatment. As G. Billanovich (*Tradizione*, 1:12) notes, Livy's account (at 10.2, cited by B.) of how the ancient Patavini repulsed the attack of King Cleonymus of Sparta and annihilated his army and fleet was for centuries the delight of Paduan antiquaries. After his summary of Padua's history, B. turns to praise of its public buildings (see Clavuot 144–115 for a summary and analysis). As he praised Bishop Guido Tarlati of Arezzo (**[308H–309A]**) and the Malatesta of Rimini and Cesena (**[344E]**), B. praises the Carrara as city-builders.

**[381A]** *Cicero . . . in Philippicis Phil.* 12.10.20–2; the context, which as often seems to mean little or nothing to B., is the preparation, in 43 B.C., of an embassy to Antony at Mutina, and Cicero's objection that various cities in Gaul would be disappointed to be offered peace instead of victory.

**[381D]** *praetorium* The Palazzo della Ragione; B. refers to the Venetians' rebuilding from 1420–1435 after the fire occurred.

**[381D–382E]** **The "tomb of Livy."** The existence at Padua of a cult of Livy created an atmosphere in which the discovery of an epitaph bearing the names of members of the family of T. Livius, and the discovery in 1413 of a casket containing bones near S. Giustina, coincided to inspire identification as the epitaph and tomb of the historian (as the chancellor of Padua Sicco Polenton wrote in 1414, "fama auget fidem"). Like most scholars until the 17th century, B. accepts the identification of the "tomb of Livy" on the basis of two inscriptions found at Padua: the first in B.'s text, *CIL* V, 2975; the second, *CIL* V, 2865, the stone inscribed with the epitaph of a freedman of the family of T. Livius. See R. Weiss, *Discovery*, 20–1:

> The fact that humanist Padua failed to note that the epitaph bore also the surname Halys and indicated that this Livius was a freedman, naturally shows the still primitive stage of antiquarian studies.

On this discovery see also B. L. Ullman, *Studies in the Italian Renaissance* (Rome 1955) 55–6; and M. P. Billanovich, "Falsi Epigrafici," *IMU* 10 (1967), 25–110, who notes, 27,

> . . . ci stupisce vedere come, già all'alba del XIV secolo, il circolo padavano onorava devotamente il presunto sarcofago di Antenore e la lapide, certo classica, ma attribuita a torto a Tito Livio. . . .

For the circumstances of the discovery and the sequence of assumptions leading to the identification by Lovati and his collaborators, who transmitted their interpretation to Petrarch and his immediate successors, see G. Billanovich, "La Cultura Veneta nel Medioevo," *IMU* 20 (1977) 1–18, 15–16. M. P. Billanovich, "Epigrafi e Antichità a S. Giustina di Padova," *IMU* 12 (1969), 197–293 traces in greater detail (282–287) B.'s role in perpetuating the erroneous identification of the two inscriptions with the historian Livy and with the tomb. The epithet *Concordialis* in the second inscription, which testifies to the existence of a cult of Concordia at Padua, B. imaginatively interprets as Livy's pride in his peacemaking among political factions.

**[382F]** *Lucius Magus* B.'s habit of wrenching citations from ancient authors from their context destroys the sense of Seneca's sentence. In the original, Seneca begins this address to his sons by referring to their wish to know what he thought was relevant to the topic at hand. He replies, on the subject of Lucius Magus, that he does not think his manner of speaking relevant to the discussion:

> Pertinere autem ad rem non puto, quomodo L. Magius, gener T. Livi, declamaverit (quamvis aliquo tempore suum populum habuerit, cum illum homines non in ipsius honorem laudarent sed in soceri ferrent), quomodo L. Asprenas aut Quintilianus senex declamaverit, transeo istos, quorum fama cum ipsis extincta est.

(L. Hakanson, ed., L. *Annaeus Seneca Maior Oratorum et Rhetorum Sententiae, Divisiones, Colores* [Leipzig: Teubner, 1989], Controversiarum 10, pref. 2).

*Paulus iurisconsultus* The jurist Julius Paulus, active in the time of Severus Alexander; see *SHA* 18.26.

*Martialis poeta* This is Martial 1.7 on Stella's poem *Columba*; cf., on Flaccus, Martial 1.76.

*Catullus vero Volusium poetam Patavinum. . . .* The identification of Volusius with Padua is at Catullus 95.7.

**[382G]** *Petrus de Abano* Peter of Abano (1250–1316) is sometimes called *conciliator* after the title of his most important work, *Conciliator differentiarum philosophorum et praecipue medicorum.* Between 1306 and 1315, Peter was one of the most famous professors of medicine and philosophy at the University of Padua, which thereby acquired a reputation as an Averroist institution. He believed that celestial influences determined events in the earthly/physical world, a natural determinism influential in medical theory of his times. In medicine a follower of Avicenna, he was condemned by the Inquisition for assertions contrary to the teachings of the Catholic church; his sentence (1316) to be burned was carried out in effigy as he had already died of natural causes. See Nancy G. Siraisi, *Arts and Sciences at Padua: The Studium Before 1350.* Studies and Texts, 25 (Toronto: Pontifical Institute of Medieval Studies, 1973), 50–51. Indispensable now for the prosopography and literary ambience of prehumanist Padua is Witt, "*Footsteps.*"

*Mussatumque et Lovattum* The greatest early humanists at Padua were notaries or legal experts as well as poets. Albertino Mussato (1261–1329) was a writer in the vernacular who treated patriotic and political affairs and was crowned in 1315 for his achievements in poetry and history. His best-known works are *Historia Augustua* and *Ecerinis* (on the tyrant Ezzelino da Romano), in which he imitated, respectively, Livy and Seneca; he was important in transmitting the tragedies of Seneca beyond the Veneto. Lovato Lovati, born 1240 or 1241, and died in 1309, became at the end of the 13th century leader of a small group of Paduans devoted to writing and studying poetry. He wrote a Latin epic on Tristan and Isolde. Mussato was his most brilliant pupil. Viti, "*Umanesimo letterario,*" 722, cites B.'s glancing treatment of them, even here when speaking of Padua, as an example of his indifference to the forerunners of the cultural renascence, an indifference rooted in his patriotic desire to confer cultural primacy on the Romagna. In addition to Witt, "*Footsteps*" 117–119, see M. Dazzi, *il Mussato preumanista (1261–1329)* (Vicenza: Neri Pozza, 1964); J. K. Hyde, *Padua in the Age of Dante* (New York: Barnes and Noble, 1966); and Siraisi, 44–49.

*Francis Zabarella* Francesco Zabarella, 1360–1417, early humanist, author of various orations, treatises, and letters, legal scholar, bishop of Florence and cardinal, friend of Pier Paolo Vergerio and other leading humanists. A professor of law at the University of Padua, Zabarella wrote treatises on various topics, not only in his specialty, canon law, but on metrics and philosophy. As usual, B. glosses over with a brief generality Zabarella's importance in the treatment of the legal problems of the Great Schism, in the Council of Constance, and in the dissemination of Petrarch's work and teaching.

*Pileus de Prata* Pileo da Prata, born probably 1329 or 1330, died 1400. From one of the most powerful families of the patriarchate of Aquileia and a protegé of the da Carrara, he was chancellor of the University of Padua, was then named archbishop of Ravenna (1370), but turned against Pope Urban V because of the latter's cruelty. Pileo da Prata then allied himself with the Avignonese antipope Clement and was excommunicated by Urban. See Gams, *Series Episcoporum*, 718.

**[382G]** *Marsilius quoque et....* In this context, Marsilius must be not the most famous Marsiglio of Padua, the author of *Defensor Pacis*, but rather Marsiglio di Santa Sofia, professor of medicine at Padua from the 1360s to the end of the century. He was the foremost member of a Paduan medical family. Giovanni Dondi dell'Orologio was a friend and correspondent of Petrarch and a physician and professor of medicine at the Studio padavano in the last half of the fourteenth century, but was most famous as an astronomer, and for his planetarium, which showed the courses of the sun, moon, and the five planets known at that time. His father Jacopo Dondi dell'Orologio's astronomical clock bestowed the *cognomen* dell'Orologio on him, and subsequently on his descendents. See T. Pesenti, "Dondi dall'Orologio, Giovanni," *DBI* 41 (1992): 96–104, and "Dondi dall'Orologio, Iacopo," *ibid.*, 104–111.

**[382H]** *Antonius Cermisonus* Antonio Cermisone, successful physician and professor of medicine at the universities of Pavia and Padua (at Padua 1414–1441). An important source of Cermisone's reputation was his compilation of medical case histories; see F. Di Trocchio, "Cermisone, Antonio," *DBI* 23 (1979): 773–4.

*Si prius Euganeas, Clemens, Helicaonis oras* Martial 10.93.1–2. But Biondo is reading Martial either from memory, or from a manuscript which does not have the modern reading *Helicaonis oras*; he cites this phrase as *Heliconis aras* and therefore believes this poem has to do with prophets and religion. It is actually a request to a friend to carry some poems to their intended recipient. Helicaon was the son of Antenor who founded Patavium (Padua).

*Lucanus* Lucan 7.192–5:

> Euganeo, si vera fides memorantibus, augur
> colle sedens, Aponus terris ubi fumifer exit
> atque Antenorei dispergitur unda Timavi, . . . .

See above on **[380F]** Austin's explanation of Lucan's, and others', misinterpretation of *hic* at *Aen.* 1.24 and consequent misplacement of the Timavus near Padua.

*Petrarch* Arquà Petrarca, where Petrarch had built a house on land given him by his patron Francesco il Vecchio da Carrara. The house and Petrarch's tomb can be visited today. The latter was built to echo the architectural elements of the "tomb of Antenor" at Padua; see G. Billanovich, "Cultura Veneta," 16 and plates III and IV.

**[383A]** *Martialis, nullae sic tibi blandientur undae, non fontes Aponi rudes puellis*: Martial 6.42.3–4; the modern Bagni d'Albano.

*Michael Savonarola* Michele Savonarola, 1385–1464, uncle of the famous fra Girolamo, was professor of medicine at the University of Padua, but dabbled also in writing ethical and historical works. He wrote *Libellus de Magnificiis Ornamentis Regie Civitatis Padue* probably in 1446. As court physician to Leonello and Borso d'Este, he was probably acquainted with B. The specificity of *in id* suggests that B. here refers to Michele Savonarola's treatise *De balneis et thermis naturalibus omnibus Italiae*.

**[383B]** *Aemula* Martial 4.25.1; see above on **[380H]**.

**[383D]** *Liquentia . . . amnis vetusti nominis* The modern river Livenza; cf. Pliny, *NH* 3.126:

> . . . flumen Liquentia ex montibus Opiterginis et portus eodem nomine, colonia Concordia, flumina et portus Reatinum, Tiliaventum Maius Minusque. . . .
>
> . . . the river Liquentia which comes down from the Opitergi mountains, and the harbor of the same name; the colony of Concordia, the river and the harbor of Reatinum, and the following rivers: the greater and the lesser Tiliaventum. . . .

See Zehnacker's comment, *ad NH* 3.126 on Servius' misinterpretation of Virgil's (*Aen.* 9.679) *liquentia flumina* as the name of a river: "ce contresens, en même temps qu'il confirme la localisation du cours d'eau, témoigne de la science géographique de Servius." There is no trace today of a greater and a lesser branch of the river Tagliamento, linguistically closest to Tiliaventum.

# Tenth Region, Forumiulium Commentary

This and the following chapter, "Histria," are the briefest in *It. ill.*, each comprising only two folio pages. Clavuot, 22 n. 4, surmises that this chapter's brevity indicates that Francesco Barbaro failed in obtaining of Guernerio d'Artegna information on the history of Friuli; and, 67, that the length of each chapter depends on the availability of literary sources (B. himself admitted **[328E]** that the length of the chapters in *It. ill.* depended to a certain extent on the number of references to the region's toponyms in ancient authors). Clavuot also, 67, notes that small mountainous areas such as Friuli, sparsely populated, were less familiar than urbanized parts of Italy to fifteenth-century cartographers, and B. probably had not directly observed such areas, and gave less attention to the more marginal border regions which were not prominent in early Roman history.

B.'s primary source for "Forumiulium" is the letter of Jacopo Simeoni da Udine, and almost half of it is thus dedicated to Aquileia (*Epistola Jacobi d Utino canonici Aquileiensis circa annum 1448 scripta ad Franciscum Barbarum locumtenentem Foriiulii*, in *Miscellanea di varie operette* [Venice 1750] 2.105–134). St. Jerome is also an important source for this chapter; the saint will provide the major focus of the next chapter, "Histria."

B.'s *Forumiulium* corresponds roughly to the region referred to by Pliny as *Carnorum regio*. For general geography and history of this region, with good bibliography and maps, see Harald Krahwinkler, *Friaul im Frühmittelalter: Geschichte einer Region vom Ende des fünften bis zum Ende des zehnten Jahrhundert* (Vienna, Cologne, and Weimar: Böhlau, 1992), 10–18.

**[384H]** *Taliaventum* Cf. Pliny, *NH* 3.126, *Tiliaventum Maius Minusque*. Zehnacker, *ad loc.*, guesses that this river corresponds to the modern Tagliamento, but comments that a greater and a lesser stream cannot today be distinguished.

**[385A]** *Aquileia* Clavuot, 242–244, compares B.'s summary of Simeoni's letter in this chapter with Simeoni's text, and concludes that B. followed Simeoni on the details of the foundation of Aquileia, but also integrates much of Simeoni's text into other passages in *It. ill.*

*Livius . . . in bello Macedonico* B. cites, with minor changes, 40.26.1–2, recounting events of 181 B.C.

**[385B]** *Iulius Capitolinus* B. cites almost *verbatim* these two excerpts (Hohl 2, 28–29 [29.33.1–2], 22–23 [25.1–2]), except that he calls *inferius* the selection which describes the announcement of the death of Maximinus senior, a passage which in our modern editions precedes that cited first by B., on the Aquileians' use of women's hair for bow-strings.

**[385D]** *Chromatius* Bishop of Aquileia 388–408, supporter of both Jerome and Rufinus, and John Chrysostom. See *Encyclopedia of Early Christianity* 2nd ed. 2 vols. (New York and London: Garland, 1997), 1,252; and R. Étaix and J. LeMarié, eds., *Corpus Christianorum Series Latina* v. 9A (Turnholt: Brepols, 1974). Correcting Simeoni, B. notes that Chromatius patronized Jerome, not the other way round.

**[386E]** . . . *Natisoni fluvio, cui nunc Lisontio est appellatio* As Zehnacker, *ad* Pliny *NH* 3.126, notes, the ancient Natiso corresponds only partially to the modern Natisone; its upper course was rather identifiable with that of the modern Isonzo ( *[Li]sontius*).

**[386F]** *Livius libro XXVIII* . . . B. is in error in his recollection of the place in Livy's history where this mention of Aquileia is found. It is actually Livy 39.22.6–7.

**[388G–H]** *clades illa fuit* . . . B.'s reference to Jerome's *De Viris illustribus* is the same passage that he cited earlier as proof that Jerome was born at Stridon **[388E]**.

# Eleventh Region, Histria Commentary

The chapter "Histria" is one of the two shortest in *It. ill.*, the other being the immediately preceding "Forumiulium." As Clavuot, 67, notes, the detailed treatment of St. Jerome and the justification of the Istrian peninsula's inclusion as part of Italy comprise its major part. The chapter contains nothing of the tracing of the hydrographic net and identification of towns and cities along the way that we find in B.'s treatment of regions in other chapters.

B.'s "Histria" is the Istrian peninsula which belonged to the province of Gallia Cisalpina, then was annexed to Italy, and belonged to the Augustan *X Regio*; when in 297 A.D. the reforms of Diocletian eliminated the Augustan regions, it became part of the province of Venetia et Histria.

[386H] *Eam Plinius ut in peninsulam excurrere* ... B. adopts Pliny's measurements for the the width and circumference of Istria, *NH* 3.129:

> Histria ut peninsula excurrit. Latitudinem eius XL, circuitum CXXV prodidere quidam, item adhaerentis Liburniae et Flanatici sinus, alii CCXXV, aliae Liburnae CLXXX.

> Istria juts out into the sea like a peninsula. Some have written that its width is 40 miles, and its circumference 125 miles, and that the same measurement holds good for the adjacent Liburnia and Gulf of Flanaticum; others say 225 (for Histria), 180 (for Liburnia).

[387A] *Plinius vero cum aliquorum confutasset errorem* ... B. reproduces in *oratio obliqua* Pliny, *NH* 3.22.128, who rejects the opinion of Cornelius Nepos and other "careless" writers that Histria was named for the river Hister which connected the Danube and the Adriatic, and debouched into the Adriatic. (Clearly the Basel edition's *Alpinos* should read *Alpis*.)

> Nullus enim ex Danuvio amnis in mare Hadriaticum effunditur. Deceptos credo, quoniam Argo navis flumine in mare Hadriaticum descendit non procul Tergeste, nec iam constat quo flumine. Umeris travectam Alpis diligentiores tradunt, subisse autem His-

tro, dein Savo, cui nomen ex ea causa est inter Emonam Alpisque exorienti.

There is no river which branches off from the Danube to debouche into the Adriatic Sea. They have been led astray as a result of the Argo's having traveled down a river to reach the Adriatic not far from Trieste, but it is unclear what river this was. More careful authors report that the Argo was carried on men's shoulders across the Alps, then proceeded up the Hister, then the Savio, then the Nauportus, which derives its name from this event, and has its source betwen Emona and the Alps.

Zehnacker, *ad loc.*, explains the ancient misconception that a subterranean branch of the Danube flowed into the Adriatic by the influence of the subterranean rivers under the karst (Carso) plateau; the Romans became acquainted with the course of the Danube at least in Octavian's, later Augustus's, campaigns in Illyria.

B. neglects to cite Martial here as an authority on toponyms, as he could have done, and does in other chapters. Relevant to the legend of the Argonauts' journey up the Danube and arrival at the Adriatic by way of the Timavus (a route differing to Pliny's description) are Martial 4.25.5–6 and 8.28.7–8 (reproduced below). The context of 4, unimportant here, as often, for B.'s purpose: Martial, as often, longs for retirement in northern Italy. In 8, Martial addresses a gift toga and interrogates it as to the origins of its wool. Cyllarus is the name of the horse of Castor and Pollux, sons of Leda and Argonauts.

et tu Ledaeo felix Aquileia Timavo,
    hic ubi septenas Cyllarus hausit aquas . . .

You, Aquileia, happy in the Timavus which carried Leda's sons,
here where Cyllarus drank the waters from its seven mouths . . .

an tua multifidum numeravit lana Timavum,
    quem pius astrifero Cyllarus ore bibit?

Or has your wool counted the mouths of the much-divided river Timavus, which loyal Cyllarus drank with his mouth, now a constellation?

**[387B]** *Petruspaulus Vergerius* (cf. above on **[346F]**). Witt, "*Footsteps*," 197 n. 84, identifies Vergerio as the "first to formulate a program of secondary education for the general student in his *De ingenuis moribus*." Fubini, "Biondo Flavio," *DBI* 537, notes the importance B. assigns to Vergerio throughout *It. ill.*, and terms this sentence "un elogio insolitamente enfatico." B.'s insistence on the Italian identity of Histria may be traced to his reliance on Vergerio, who considered Jerome a citizen of the world and the patron saint of humanism (see J. McManamon, *Pierpaolo Vergerio the Elder*, 122); a cosmopolitan perspective on Jerome and his native area is thus not surprising in B.'s work.

**[387C]** *F[l]anaticum ... Carnarium promontorium.* B. derives the name of this cape from the fierceness of storms around it. Clavuot, 98, adduces this explanation as an example of the medieval type of fanciful etymology of names from topographical characteristics. Pliny, *NH* 3.129, gives the correctly-spelled ancient name of Flanaticum.

**[388E]** *apud Sdrignam sive Stridonem* The ancient Stridon, location of the birthplace and tomb of St. Jerome (b. 331, d. 419 or 420), has never been definitely identified.

B. gives a fairly extensive treatment of Jerome as a famous man of Stridon. Jerome is, as is apparent in *It. ill. passim*, an important source for B. as well. Pierpaolo Vergerio's family observed a cult of St. Jerome, who was also patron saint of Capodistria (see McManamon, *Pierpaolo Vergerio the Elder*, 4–16, and 122, who notes that Vergerio disputed the identification of Jerome's birthplace, Stridon, with Sdregna). It may be that the convergence of the two figures from this area led B. especially to emphasize the saint's importance; and that this emphasis filled out what was one of the most meager chapters of *It. ill.* In addition, Jerome was B.'s patron saint (see his letter to Francesco Barbaro in Nogara, *Scritti Inediti*, 167, where B. credits the saint's intervention for his reinstatement in Nicholas V's Curia).

Jerome himself describes his native land in a way that is consonant with B.'s treatment of "barbarians," both in *It. ill.* and his earlier *Historiarum Decades*. The humanist then gives a second extensive digression, an argument for considering Histria a part of Italy, a passage whose length is motivated, as B. himself admits, by his desire to claim St. Jerome for Italy.

B.'s citation here tallies with Jerome, *de viris illustribus* 135.1–5:

> Hieronymus presbyter patre natus Eusebio, ex oppido Stridonis: quod a Gothis eversum Dalmatiae quondam Pannoniaeque confinium fuit, usque in praesentem annum id est Theodosii principis

> quartumdecimum haec scripsit: vitam Pauli Monachi, epistolarum ad diversos, librum unum, etc.
>
> Jerome, son of Eusebius, born in the town of Stridon which was destroyed by the Goths, and was on the border between Dalmatia and Pannonia, up to the present year, that is, the fourteenth year of the reign of Theodosius, has written the following: the Life of Paul the Monk; Letters to various men, one book. . . .

Simeoni had insisted on ancient Friuli's belonging to Italy (cf. Clavuot, 243). B.'s insistence upon Jerome's Italian identity is significant for two reasons. First, he bases the argument on linguistic facts, which connects this passage with his intense interest in linguistics. Second, this interest combines with an idea for which B. is noted: the first, albeit imperfect, vision of Italy as a unity. His claim for Jerome is *Italian* citizenship, not citizenship in a certain region or city-state. At the end of the *It. ill.*, then, B. leaves us with the suggestion, at least, of a claim to Italian unity founded on a linguistic argument.

# Northern Italy
# Bibliography

ABBREVIATIONS:

*CIL* = *Corpus Inscriptionum Latinarum*. Berlin: deGruyter, 1862 to date.
*DBI* = *Dizionario biografico degli italiani*. Rome: Istituto della Enciclopedia italiana, 1960 to date.
*ED* = *Enciclopedia Dantesca.* 5 vols. 2nd ed. rev. Rome: Istituto della Enciclopedia italiana, 1984.
*EncIt* = *Enciclopedia Italiana di Scienze, Lettere ed Arti.* Milan: Rizzoli, 1933 to date.
*IMU* = *Italia medioevale e umanistica.*
*RIS* = Ludovico Muratori, ed., *Rerum italicarum scriptores ab anno aerae christianae quingentesimo ad millesimum quingentesimum.* 25 vols. in 28. Milan, 1723–1751; G. Carducci and V. Fiorini, eds., *Rerum italicarum scriptores. Raccolta degli storici italiani dal cinquecento al millecinquecento.* New edition. Città di Castello, 1900– to date.

PRIMARY SOURCES

Alberti, Leandro. *Descrittione di tutta Italia.* Bologna: Giaccarelli, 1550.
Belgrano, Luigi T., ed. *Annales ianuenses* v. 1. Fonti per la storia d'Italia n. 11. Genoa, 1890. 1099–1173.
Biondo, Flavio. *De Roma triumphante libri decem; Romae instauratae libri iii; De origine et gestis Venetorum liber; Italia illustrata; Historiarum ab inclinato Romano imperio decades iii.* Basel: Froben, 1559.
———. *Decades, De origine et gestis Venetorum, Italia illustrata.* Verona: Boninus de Boninis, 1481–1482.
Boccaccio, G. *De montibus, sylvis, fontibus, lacubus, fluminibus, stagnis seu paludibus, de nominibus maris.* Edited and translated by Manlio Pastore Stocchi. Vol. 10. V. Branca, ed., *Boccaccio Tutte le opere.* Verona: Mondadori, 1998.

A. Bonardi, ed. *Cronica in factis et circa facta Marchie Trivixane*. *RIS* Vol. 8, pt. 1, fasc. 1–2. Città di Castello: S. Lapi, 1907.

———. *Rolandini Patavini Cronica Marchie Trivixane*. *RIS* Vol. 8, pt. 1. Città di Castello: S. Lapi, 1907.

Bracelli, Giacomo. *Iacopo Bracellii Genuensis De Bello Hispaniensi Libri Quinque. Eiusdem de Claris Genuensibus libellus. Orae Ligusticae descriptio*. Rome: apud Heredes Antonii Bladii Impressores Camerales, 1573.

Bruni, Leonardo. *Leonardo Bruni History of the Florentine People*. Edited and translated by James Hankins. I Tatti Renaissance Library. Cambridge, Mass. and London: Harvard University Press, 2001.

Catullus. *Catullus*. Edited by C. J. Fordyce. Oxford: Clarendon Press, 1961.

Cessi, R., ed. *Origo civitatum Italie seu Venetiarum [Chronicon Altinate et Chronicon Gradense]*. Rome, 1933

Cicero. *Cicero: Philippics*. Edited by D. R. Shackleton Bailey. Chapel Hill and London: University of North Carolina Press, 1986.

Chromatius. *Chromatii Aquileiensis Opera*. Edited by R. L'Étaix and J. LeMarié. Corpus Christianorum Series Latina. Vol. 9A. Turnholt: Brepols, 1974.

Cronaca di Genova. Fonti per la storia d'Italia. Vol. 85. Rome, 1941.

O. Cuntz, ed. *Itineraria Antonini Augusti et Burdigalense. Itineraria Romana I*. Leipzig: Teubner, 1929.

Fauno, Lucio. *Biondo da Forlì, Roma restaurata et Italia Illustrata tradotte in buona lingua volgare per Lucio Fauno*. Venice: appresso Domenico Gigli, 1558.

*Epistola Jacobi d'Utino canonici Aquileiensis circa annum 1448 scripta ad Franciscum Barbarum locumtenentem Foriiulii*. Venice, 1750.

St. Jerome. *Die Chronik des Hieronymus*. Edited by R. Helm. 2nd ed. Berlin: Akademie Verlag, 1956.

Livy. *Titi Livi Ab Urbe Condita*. 5 vols. Edited by C. Walters and R. S. Conway. Oxford: Clarendon Press, 1914. Reprint. Oxford: Clarendon Press, 1966.

Lucan. *M. Annaei Lucani Belli Civilis Libri Decem*. Edited by A. E. Housman. Oxford: Blackwell, 1927.

———. *Lucan De Bello Civili Book II*. Edited by E. Fantham. Cambridge: Cambridge University Press, 1992.

Martial. *M. Val. Martialis Epigrammata*. Edited by W. M. Lindsay. 2nd ed. Oxford: Clarendon Press, 1965.

*Annales mediolanenses. RIS* Vol. 16. Milan, 1730.

Nason, Vittore, ed. *Giovanni Conversini da Ravenna Rationarium Vite.* Accademia Toscana di Scienze e Lettere "La Colombaria" Studi LXXIX. Firenze: Olschki, 1986.

*Paul the Deacon History of the Longobards.* Edited with introduction by Edward Peters. Translated by William Dudley Foulke. Philadelphia: University of Pennsylvania Press, 1974.

Persius. *A. Persi Flacci Satirarum Liber.* Edited by W. V. Clausen. Oxford: Clarendon Press, 1956.

Petrarca, Francesco. *Petarch's Guide to the Holy Land: Itinerary to the Sepulcher of Our Lord Jesus Christ.* Edited and translated by Theodore J. Cachey, Jr. Notre Dame, Indiana: University of Notre Dame Press, 2002.

———. *Francis Petrarch Letters of Old Age: Rerum senilium libri I–XVIII.* Vol. 1, books 1–9. Translated by Aldo S. Bernardo, Saul Levin, and Reta A. Bernardo. Baltimore and London: Johns Hopkins University Press, 1992.

Pius II (Aeneas Sylvius Piccolomini). *Pii II Commentarii rerum memorabilium quae temporibus suis contigerunt.* Edited by Adrian van Heck. Studi e Testi 313–314. Vatican City [Biblioteca Apostolica Vaticana], 1984.

Pliny the Elder. *Pline l'Ancien Histoire Naturelle Livre III.* Edited and translated by Hubert Zehnacker. Paris: Société d'Édition «Les Belles Lettres», 1998.

Scriptores Historiae Augustae. *Scriptores Historiae Augustae.* Edited by E. Hohl. 2 vols. Leipzig: Teubner, 1927. Reprint with additions and corrections by C. Samberger and W. Seyfarth. Leipzig: Teubner, 1971.

Segarezzi, A., ed. *Libellus de Ornamentis Padue Michaelis Savonarole. RIS* v. 24 pt. 15. Città di Castello: Lapi, 1902.

Seneca the Elder. *L. Annaeus Seneca Maior Oratorum et Rhetorum Sententiae, Divisiones, Colores.* Edited by L. Hakanson. Leipzig: Teubner, 1989.

Virgil. *P. Vergili Maronis Opera Omnia.* Edited by R. A. B. Mynors. Oxford: Clarendon Press, 1969. Reprint 1972.

———. *P. Vergili Maronis Aeneidos Liber Primus.* Edited with commentary by R. G. Austin. Oxford: Clarendon Press, 1971.

## SECONDARY SOURCES

## BOOKS

Avellini, L. and L. Michelacci, eds., *La cultura umanistica a Forlì fra Biondo e Melozzo*. Atti del Convegno di Studi. Bologna: Il Nove, 1997.

Bertoni, Giulio. *Guarino da Verona, Fra Letterari e Cortigiani a Ferrara* (1429–1460). Geneva: Olschki, 1921.

Benario, H. A *Commentary on the Vita Hadriani in the Historia Augusta*. American Classical Studies 7. Atlanta: Scholars Press, 1979.

Bergonzoni, Franco and Giovanna Bonora, eds., *Bologna Romana*. Vol. 1, Fonti per la storia di Bologna. Testi 9. Bologna: Istituto per la Storia di Bologna, 1976.

Billanovich, G. *La Tradizione del Testo di Livio e le Origini dell' Umanesimo*. 2 vols. Padua: Editrice Antenore, 1981.

Clavuot, Ottavio. *Biondo's «Italia illustrata»: Summa oder Neuschöpfung? Über die Arbeitsmethoden eines Humanisten*. Bibliothek des Deutschen historischen Instituts in Rom 69. Tübingen: Max Niemeyer Verlag, 1990.

Cochrane, Eric. *Historians and Historiography in the Italian Renaissance*. Chicago: University of Chicago Press, 1981.

Cosenza, Mario. *Biographical and Bibliographical Dictionary of the Italian Humanists and of the World of Classical Scholarship in Italy 1300–1800*. 2nd ed. 5 vols. Boston: G. K. Hall, 1962.

DeNicolò, M. L. *Conca e Cattolica: La leggenda della città sommersa e le origini del nome*. Fano, 1993.

———. *La Strada e il Mare*. Villa Verucchio: La Pieve, 1993.

———. *Nuove ricerche su Conca città profundata*. Quaderni del museo di San Giovanni in Marignano I. San Giovanni in Marignano: Centro Culturale Polivalente, 1985.

Deschamps, Pierre C. E. *Dictionnaire de géographie ancienne et moderne*. Hildesheim: Georg Olms, 1965.

Epstein, Steven A. *Genoa and the Genoese, 958–1528*. Chapel Hill and London: University of North Carolina Press, 1996.

Ferguson, W. K. *The Renaissance in Historical Thought: Five Centuries of Interpretation*. Boston: Houghton Mifflin, 1948.

Franceschini, Adriano. *Artisti a Ferrara in età umanistica e rinascimentale: Testimonianze archivistiche*. 3 vols. Parte I dal 1341 al 1471. Ferrara: Gabriele Corvo Editore, 1993.

Gambi, L. *Cosa era la Padusa?* Faenza: Fratelli Lega, 1953.

Gams, Pius Bonifacius. *Series Episcoporum Ecclesiae Catholicae*. Regensburg: Josef Manz, 1873–1886. Reprint. Graz: Akademische Druck-u. Verlaganstalt, 1957.

Girgensohn, Dieter. *Kirche, Politik und adelige Regierung in der Republik Venedig zu Beginn des 15. Jahrhunderts*. 2 vols. Göttingen: Vandenhoeck and Ruprecht, 1996.

Gloria, A. *Monumenti della Università di Padova* (1318–1405). 2 vols. Padua, 1888.

Grafton, Anthony. *Commerce with the Classics: Ancient Books and Renaissance Readers*. Ann Arbor: University of Michigan Press, 1997.

Grubb, J. S. *Firstborn of Venice*. Baltimore and London: Johns Hopkins University Press, 1988.

Hall, W. H. *The Romans on the Riviera and the Rhone*. London 1898. Reprint. Chicago: Ares, 1974.

Hallenbeck, Jan. *Pavia and Rome: The Lombard Monarchy and the Papacy in the Eighth Century*. Transactions of the American Philosophical Society 72, pt. 4. Philadelphia: American Philosophical Society, 1982.

Harley, J. B. and David Woodward. *The History of Cartography*. Vol. 1, *Cartography in Prehistoric, Ancient, and Medieval Europe and the Mediterranean*. Chicago and London: University of Chicago Press, 1987.

Hay, Denis. *The Italian Renaissance in its Historical Background*. Cambridge: Cambridge University Press, 1977.

Hay, Denis, and J. Law. *Italy in the Age of the Renaissance*. London and New York: Longman, 1989.

Hyde, J. K. *Padua in the Age of Dante*. New York: Barnes and Noble, 1966.

———. *Society and Politics in Medieval Italy*. New York: St. Martin's, 1973.

Ianziti, Gary. *Humanist Historiography under the Sforzas: Politics and Propaganda in Fifteenth-Century Milan*. Oxford: Clarendon Press, 1988.

Jones, P. J. *The Malatesta of Rimini and the Papal State: A Political History*. Cambridge: Cambridge University Press, 1974.

King, M. L. *Venetian Humanists in an Age of Patrician Dominance*. Princeton: Princeton University Press, 1986.

Kohl, Benjamin. *Padua under the Carrara, 1318–1405*. Baltimore and London: Johns Hopkins University Press, 1998.

Kohl, Benjamin G., and Ronald G. Witt, eds. *The Earthly Republic: Italian Humanists on Government and Society*. Philadelphia: University of Pennsylvania Press, 1978.

Krahwinkler, Harald. *Friaul im Frühmittelalter: Geschichte einer Region vom Ende des fünften bis zum Ende des zehnten Jarhhundert*. Vienna, Cologne, and Weimar: Böhlau, 1992.

Larner, John. *The Lords of Romagna: Romagnol Society and the Origins of the Signorie*. Ithaca, NY: Cornell University Press, 1965.

Mallett, Michael. *Mercenaries and Their Masters: Warfare in Renaissance Italy*. London, Sydney, and Toronto: The Bodley Head, 1974.

Martindale, J. R. *The Prosopography of the Later Roman Empire*. 3 vols. Cambridge: Cambridge University Press, 1992.

Martines, Lauro. *The Social World of the Florentine Humanists 1390–1460*. Princeton: Princeton University Press, 1963.

Mazzocco, Angelo. *Linguistic Theories in the Humanists*. Leiden and New York: Brill, 1993.

McKay, Alexander G. *Vergil's Italy*. Greenwich, CT: Graphic Society, 1970.

McManamon, John M., S. J. *Pierpaolo Vergerio the Elder: The Humanist as Orator*. Medieval and Renaissance Texts and Studies 163. Tempe, Arizona, 1996.

Monfasani, John. *George of Trebizond: A Biography and a Study of His Rhetoric and Logic*. Columbia Studies in the Classical Tradition 1. Leiden: E. J. Brill, 1976.

Muir, Edward. *Civic Ritual in Renaissance Venice*. Princeton: Princeton University Press, 1981.

Muratori, L. *De corona ferrea*. 1698.

Nogara, B. *Scritti Inediti e Rari di Biondo Flavio*. Studi e Testi 48. Rome: Tipografia Poliglotta Vaticana, 1927.

Olivieri, Dante. *Toponomastica Veneta*. 2nd ed. Venice: Istituto per la Collaborazione Culturale, 1961.

Petracco Sicardi, G. and R. Caprini. *Toponomastica Storica della Liguria*. Genoa: Sagep Editrice, 1981.

Pizarro, Joaquín Martínez. *Writing Ravenna: The Liber Pontificalis of Andreas Agnellus*. Recentiores: Later Latin Texts and Contexts. Ann Arbor: University of Michigan Press, 1995.

Polloni, A. *Toponomastica romagnola*. Florence: Olschki, 1966.

Quirini, A. *Diatriba praeliminaris in duas partes divisa ad Francisci Barbari et aliorum ad ipsum epistolas*. Brescia, 1741.

Ravelli, Francesco. *Pagine Storiche di Ficarolo*. Bologna: Zanichelli, 1883.

Reynolds, L. D. and N. G. Wilson. *Scribes and Scholars*. 2nd ed. Oxford: Clarendon Press, 1974.

Sabbadini, Remigio. *Giovanni da Ravenna insigne figura d'umanista (1343–1408)* 2nd ed. Turin, 1961.

———. *Giovanni da Ravenna Insigne Figura d'Umanista*. Como: Ostinelli, 1924.

———. *Storia e critica dei testi latini*. 2nd ed. Padua, 1971.

Samaritani, A. *Regesta Pomposiae* I. Deputazione Provincia Ferrara di Storia Patria. Serie Monumenti 5 (1963).

Savini, G. *Le mura di Ravenna*. Ravenna, 1905.

Siraisi, Nancy G. *Arts and Sciences at Padua: The Studium Before 1350*. Toronto: Pontifical Institute of Mediaeval Studies, 1973.

Strauss, Gerald. *Sixteenth-Century Germany: Its Topography and Topographers*. Madison, Wisconsin: University of Wisconsin Press, 1959.

Sullivan, J. P. *Martial: The Unexpected Classic. A Literary and Historical Study*. Cambridge: Cambridge University Press, 1991.

Sumner, G. V. *The Orators in Cicero's Brutus: Prosopography and Chronology*. Toronto and Buffalo: University of Toronto Press, 1973.

Susini, Carlo, ed. *Storia di Forlì*. Vol. 1 *L'evo antico*. Bologna: Nova Alfa Editoriale, 1989.

Syme, Ronald. *Emperors and Biography: Studies in the Historia Augusta*. Oxford: Clarendon Press, 1971.

R. Thomsen. *The Italic Regions from Augustus to the Lombard Invasion*. Copenhagen: Gyldendalske, 1947.

Tiraboschi, Girolamo. *Dizionario Topografico Storico degli Stati Estensi*. 2 vols. Bologna: Forni, 1963.

Touring Club Italiano, *Emilia-Romagna*. Milan: Centro Grafico Linate, 1991.

———. *Friúli Venezia Giulia*. Milan: Vallardi,1963.

———. *Friuli Venezia Giulia*. 5th ed. Milan: Centro Grafico Linate, 1982.

———. *Liguria*. 4th ed. Milan: Vallardi, 1952.

———. *Lombardia*. 7th ed. Milan: Stucchi, 1954.
———. *Torino e Valle'd'Aosta*. 9th ed. Milan: Centro Grafico Linate, 1996.
———. *Venezia*. 3rd ed. Milan: Centro Grafico Linate, 1985.
———. *Veneto*. Milan: Centro Grafico Ambrosiano, 1969.
Uccellini, Primo. *Dizionario storico di Ravenna e di altri luoghi di Romagna*. Ravenna: Tipografia del Ven. Seminario Arcivescovile, 1855. Reprint. Bologna: Forni Editore, 1968.
Ullman, B. L. *Studies in the Italian Renaissance*. Rome, 1955.
Vinay, Gustavo. *L'Umanesimo subalpino nel secolo XV*. Turin: Gabetta, 1935.
Weiss, Roberto. *The Renaissance Discovery of Classical Antiquity*. Oxford: Blackwell, 1969.
Wickham, Chris. *Early Medieval Italy: Central Power and Local Society 400–1000*. 1981 Macmillan. Reprint. Ann Arbor: Ann Arbor Paperbacks, 1989.
Wilson, N. G. *From Byzantium to Italy: Greek Studies in the Italian Renaissance*. Baltimore: Johns Hopkins University Press, 1992.
Witt, Ronald G. *"In the Footsteps of the Ancients": The Origins of Humanism from Lovato to Bruni*. Studies in Medieval and Reformation Thought 74. Leiden, Boston, Köln: Brill, 2000.

## ARTICLES

Abbondanza, R. "Arsendi, Raniero." *DBI* 4 (1962): 333–339.
Amelotti, L. "Campofregoso, Tommaso." *DBI* 50 (1998): 448–451
Arnaldi, G. "Berengario I." *DBI* 9 (1967): 21–26.
Arslan, E. "Altichiero." *DBI* 2 (1960): 557–558.
Ashby, T. and R. Fell. "The Via Flaminia." *JRS* 11 (1921): 126–155.
Banti, O. "Bentivoglio, Antonio." *DBI* 8 (1966): 603–605.
Becker, H. J. "Calderini, Giovanni." *DBI* 16 (1973): 606–608.
Bernicoli, Silvio. "Flavio Biondi in Ravenna." *Il Ravennate Corriere di Romagna*. 4 December 1900: 68.
Besomi, O. and M. Regoliosi. "Valla e Tortelli." Pt. 1. *IMU* 9 (1966): 75–189.
Bigi, E. "Barbaro, Ermolao." *DBI* 6 (1964): 95–96.
Billanovich, G. "La Cultura Veneta nel Medioevo." *IMU* 20 (1977): 1–18.

Billanovich, M. P. "Falsi Epigrafici." *IMU* 10 (1967): 25–110.

———. "Una miniera di epigrafi e di antichità: Il chiostro maggiore di S. Giustina." *IMU* 12 (1969): 197–293.

Braggio, Carlo. "Giacomo Bracelli e l'Umanesimo dei Liguri al suo Tempi." *Atti della Società Ligure di Storia Patria* 23 (1890): 5–295.

Brunelli, G. "Este, Leonello (Lionello) d'." *DBI* 43 (1993): 374–380.

Calzolari, Mauro. "La Navigazione interna in Emilia Romagna tra l'VIIII e il XIII secolo." In *Vie del Commercio in Emilia Romagna Marche*, edited by Giuseppe Adani, 115–124. Cinisello Balsamo: Silvana, 1990.

Campana, A. "Biondo Flavio." *Enciclopedia Dantesca*. 1:634–635.

———. "Due note su Roberto Valturio." *Studi Riminesi e bibliografici in onore di Carlo Lucchesi*. Faenza: 1951:11–24.

———. "Passi inediti dell'«Italia illustrata» di Biondo Flavio." *La Rinascita* I (1938): 91–97.

———. "Poesie Umanistiche sul Castello di Gradara." *Studi Romagnoli* 20 (1969): 501–520.

Cappelletto, Rita. "Italia illustrata di Biondo Flavio." In *Letteratura italiana*, edited by Alberto Asor Rosa, vol. 1, 681–712. Torino: Einaudi, 1992.

Capitani, O. "Amidani, Niccolò." *DBI* 2 (1960): 792.

———. "Amidani, Vincenzo." *DBI* 2 (1960): 792.

Castner, C. J. "Direct Observation and Biondo Flavio's Additions to *Italia illustrata*: the case of Ocriculum." *Mediaevalia et Humanistica* N.S. 25 (1998): 93–113.

Chiappini, Alessandra. "Manfredo Maldenti forlivese tra Biondo Flavio, Civis Ravennae, Venetiae et Ferrariae e Ludovico Carbone." In *Ravenna in età Veneziana*, edited by Dante Bolognesi, 227–224. Ravenna: Longo Editore, 1986.

Conti, Giordano. "La ristrutturazione della cinta muraria di Cesena attorno alla metà del Quattrocento." *Studi Romagnoli* 31 (1963): 359–382.

Cracco, G. "Barbarigo, Francesco." *DBI* 6 (1964): 62–63.

———. "Barbarigo, Girolamo." *DBI* 6 (1964): 66–67.

Dall'Aglio, Pier Luigi. "*Fidentia*-Borgo San Donnino-Fidenza," *JAT* 7 (1997): 37–48.

DeNicolò, M. L. "I Caratteri della Storia di Cattolica; Miti, Leggende, Proverbi." *Studi Romagnoli* 45 (1994): 13–26.

DiTrocchio, F. "Cermisone, Antonio." *DBI* 23 (1979): 773–74.

Ermini, G. "Giovanni da Imola." *EncIt* 17 (1933): 243.

Esch, A. "Brandolini, Brandolino." *DBI* 14 (1972): 28–29.

Fabbri, Pier Giovanni. "Cesena e la signoria di Malatesta Novello." *Studi Romagnoli* 45 (1994): 233–257.

———. "Gli Inizi dell'Età di Malatesta Novello a Cesena." *Studi Romagnoli* 43 (1992): 281–306.

Fanelli, V. "Biondo, Gaspare." *DBI* 10 (1968): 559–560.

Franceschini, Adriano. "I Sostegni Rossettiani di Polesella." In *Uomini, Terre ed Acque: Politica e Cultura Idraulica nel Polesine tra '400 e '600*, edited by Franco Cazzola and Achille Olivieri, 55–89. Rovigo: Minelliana, 1990.

Fubini, Riccardo. "Biondo, Flavio." *DBI* 10 (1968): 536–559.

———. "Bracelli, Giacomo." *DBI* 13 (1971): 652–653.

———. "La geografia storica dell' 'Italia illustrata' di Biondo Flavio e le tradizioni dell'etnografia." In *La cultura Umanistica a Forlì fra Biondo e Melozzo*, edited by L. Avellini and L. Michelacci, 89–112. Atti del Convegno di Studi. Bologna: Il Nove, 1997.

Gaeta, F. "Barbo, Niccolò." *DBI* 6 (1964): 252–253.

Gambi, L. "Per una rilettura di Biondo e Alberti, geografi." In *Il rinascimento nelle corti padane*, 259–275. Bari: De Donato, 1977.

———. "Confini geografici e misurazione areale della regione romagnola." *Studi Romagnoli* 1 (1950): 191–196.

Gautier Dalché, Patrick. "Sur l' 'originalité' de la 'géographie' médiévale." In *Auctor et Auctoritas: invention et conformisme dans l'écriture médiévale*, edited by Michel Zimmermann, 131–143. Actes du colloque de Saint-Quentin-en-Yvelines (14–16 June 1999). Paris: École des Chartes, 2001.

Gilbert, Felix. "Biondo, Sabellico, and the Beginnings of Venetian Official Historiography." In *Florilegium Historiale: Studies in Honor of W. H. Ferguson*, edited by J. G. Rowe and W. H. Stockdale, 275–293. Toronto: University of Toronto Press, 1971.

Grafton, A. and L. Jardine. "Humanism and the School of Guarino: A Problem of Evaluation." *Past and Present* 92 (1982): 51–80.

Gualdo, G. "Barbaro, Francesco." *DBI* 6 (1964): 101–103.

Guillou, A. "Esarcato e Pentapoli, regione psicologica dell'Italia bizantina." *Studi Romagnoli* 18 (1967): 297–319.

Gullino, G. "Foscaro, Francesco." *DBI* 49 (1997): 306–314.

Hyde, J. K. "Medieval Descriptions of Cities." *Bulletin of the John Rylands Library* 48 (1968): 309–340.

Kohl, B. "Conversini, Giovanni." *DBI* 28 (1983): 574–578.
Mallett, M. E. "Dal Verme, Iacopo." *DBI* 32 (1986): 262–267.
———. "Dal Verme, Luchino." *DBI* 32 (1986): 267–270.
Martellotti, G. "Barzizza, Gasperino." *DBI* 7 (1965): 34–39.
Mazzocco, Angelo. "Decline and Rebirth in Bruni and Biondo." In *Umanesimo a Roma nel Quattrocento*, edited by P. Brezzi and M. dePanizza Lorch, 249–266. Rome and New York: Istituto di Studi Romani and Barnard College, 1984.
———. "Petrarca, Poggio, and Biondo: Humanism's Foremost Interpreters of Roman Ruins." In *Francis Petrarch, Six Centuries Later. A Symposium*, edited by Aldo Scaglione, 353–363. North Carolina Studies in the Romance Languages and Literatures Symposia 3. Chapel Hill, NC and Chicago: University of North Carolina and Newberry Library, 1975.
Miglio, L. "Cavalli, Giorgio." *DBI* 22 (1979): 736–739.
Moro, G. "Foscarini, Ludovico." *DBI* 49 (1997): 383–388.
Muccillo, M. "Fava, Niccolò." *DBI* 45 (1995): 420–422.
Palma, M. "Cebà (Grimaldi), Niccolò." *DBI* 23 (1979): 186–187.
———. "Castelli, Girolamo." *DBI* 21 (1978): 729–730.
Paoletti, L. "Benvenuto da Imola." *DBI* 8 (1966): 691–694.
Partner, P. "Brandolini, Tiberto." *DBI* 14 (1972): 43.
Pasztor, E. "Albergati, Niccolò." *DBI* 1 (1960): 619–621.
Petrucci, A. "Bracciolini, Poggio." *DBI* 13 (1971): 640–646.
Philipp, Hans. "Padus." *Paulys Realencyclopädie der Classischen Altertumswissenschaft*. Vol. 18 pt. 2: 2178–2202. Stuttgart: J. B. Metzlersche, 1942.
Pieri, P. "Alberico da Barbiano." *DBI* 1 (1960): 639–642.
Pillinini, G. "Bollani, Candiano." *DBI* 11 (1969): 287–289.
Pistilli, G. "Giustinian, Bernardo." *DBI* 57 (2001): 216–224.
Preto, P. "Correr, Gregorio." *DBI* 29 (1983): 497–500.
Ragni, E. "Bissaro, Matteo." *DBI* 10 (1968): 690.
Ravegnani, P. "Dandolo, Andrea." *DBI* 32 (1986): 342–440.
Ricci, G. "Il Peso del Passato: La Lenta Evoluzione del Quadro Urbanistico." In *Storia da Ravenna*. Vol. 4, *Dalla dominazione veneziana alla conquista francese*, edited by Lucio Gambi, 133–177. Ravenna: Marsilio, 1994.
Rutherford, D. "A Finding List of Antonio da Rho's Works and Related Primary Sources." *IMU* 33 (1990): 75–108.

Sabbadini, R. "Lettere e orazioni edite e inedite di Gasparino Barzizza." *Archivio storico lombardo* 13 (1886): 363–836.

Samaritani, Antonio. "Il 'Vicus Blasianus' tra Bessarione e Biondo Flavio." *Atti e Memorie della Deputazione Provinciale Ferrarese di Storia Patria*. Series 3, vol. 13 (1973): 157–172.

Smolinsky, H. "Dominici, Domenico." *DBI* 40 (1991): 691–695.

Torsiello, Mario. "Romagna." *EncIt* Supplement 2. Rome: Istituto della Enciclopedia Italiana, 1949: 740.

Tucci, Ugo. "Credenze geografiche e cartografia." *Storia d'Italia*. Torino: Einaudi, 1973. Vol. 5 pt. 1: 49–85.

Varanini, Giorgio. "Ezzelino da Romano." *ED* 2: 771–772.

Vasina, A. "del Cassero, Guido." *ED* 2: 345–6.

———. "Forlì." *ED* 2: 967–969.

Vasoli, C. "Bonatti, Guido." *DBI* 11 (1969): 603–608.

———. "Bruni, Leonardo." *DBI* 14 (1972): 618–633.

Ventura, A. "Canal, Niccolò." *DBI* 17 (1974): 662–668.

Viti, P. "Facio, Bartolomeo." *DBI* 44 (1994): 113–121.

———. "Filelfo, Francesco." *DBI* 47 (1997): 613–626.

———. "Umanesimo letterario e primato regionale nell' 'Italia illustrata' di F. Biondo." In *Studi filologici, letterari e storici in memoria di Guido Favati*, edited by G. Varanini and P. Pinagli, 2: 711–732. Medioevo e Umanesimo 29. Padua, 1977.

Weiss, Roberto. "Iacopo Angeli da Scarperia." In *Medioevo e Rinascimento. Studi in onore di Bruno Nardi*, 2: 803–817. Florence, 1955. Reprinted in *Medieval and Humanist Greek: Collected Essays by Roberto Weiss*, 255–277. Padua: Antenore, 1977.

White, Jeffrey A. "Towards a Critical Edition of Biondo Flavio's 'Italia Illustrata': A Survey and an Evaluation of the MSS." In *Umanesimo a Roma nel Quattrocento*, edited by P. Brezzi and M. DePanizza Lorch, 267–293. Rome and New York: Istituto di Studi Romani and Barnard College, 1984.

Witt, Ronald G. "Still the Matter of the Two Giovannis." *Rinascimento* 2nd ser. 35 (1995): 179–199.

# General Index

# Index of Places